ECONOMIC REFORMS AND TEXTILE INDUSTRY: PERFORMANCE AND PROSPECTS

Dedicated
to
My Parents

ECONOMIC REFORMS AND TEXTILE INDUSTRY : PERFORMANCE AND PROSPECTS

Jatinder S. Bedi

Commonwealth

Economic Reforms and Textile Industry : Performance and Prospects

Edition : 2027

ISBN : 81-7169-690-2

Published by :
COMMONWEALTH PUBLISHERS (P) LTD.
4831/24, Govind Lane,
Ansari Road, Darya Ganj,
New Delhi - 110002
Ph. : 23242541, 23272541
e-mail : commonwealthpublishers2016@gmail.com

Distributed by :
ARJUN PUBLISHING HOUSE
4831/24, Govind Lane,
Ansari Road, Darya Ganj,
New Delhi - 110002
Ph. : 23242541, 23272541
e-mail : arjunbooks2001@gmail.com
arjunpubhouse@gmail.com

Laser Typesetting by :
Dimple Computers
Delhi

Printed at :
Milan Enterprises
Delhi

Foreword

Despite significant industrial deepening over the last 50 years, Textile and Clothing continues to occupy the status of India's most important industry. This is so by almost all indicators, whether income generation, employment or exports, and several studies exist on it. But awkwardly, our knowledge about this important industry remains very incomplete. A large part of production remains in the unorganised sector, *i.e.* carried out by powerlooms, handlooms and in small scale garment manufacturing, data on which is still unreliable.

Production estimates for the sector continue to be based on yarn production in the organised sector, to which conversion rates of yarn to fabric are applied to work out overall production. However, many of the conversion ratios used are old and have little scientific basis. The consequence is the peculiar outcome that official estimates of consumption simply do not match the official data on supply. Absence of this basic balance between overall supply and demand, and even greater uncertainly regarding sub-sector breakdowns, plagues almost all existing discussion of structure and change in this industry. The present study, which is a revised version of the author's doctoral thesis at Jawaharlal Nehru University, is an exception. Although wide in its scope, the study begins by nothing the basic statistical infirmities regarding the sector and a serious attempt is made to resolve this problem.

Sector-wise estimates of production are worked out afresh using the latest available data on sector-wise count-specific conversion ratios from yarn to fabric and these are not only applied to count-specific yarn production but also checked against composition of fabric use. By comparing these estimates of fabric production with exports and domestic consumption, estimates of fabric production in piece-length, and of made-ups and garments is also worked out. The resulting estimates agree closely with data on apparent use but are quite different from official production estimates. One of the main findings of this study is that more than one third of hank yarn meant to be consumed in the handloom sector has in recent years been diverted to the powerloom sector, seriously affecting estimates of the size of these sectors. Further, based on these revised estimates of production, fresh estimates of employment and value added in textiles and clothing industry have also been derived.

This careful approach to consistency of data gives credibility to its larger purpose. This is to work out the state of textile and clothing industry during the year 1983, track its development till the present, and make projections to 2010-11. A basic premise that this study shares with many others is that policies pursued till the mid eighties, although designed to increase employment in textiles and clothing industry, posed a major hindrance in the path of modernisation and failed to achieve the objective of rapid growth in employment in the sector. In this context, it studies the impact of the National Textile Policy of 1985 and of the Economic Reforms introduced in 1991.

Apart from reconciling the data available, the study deals with three substantial issues: *(a)* the productivity of the spinning sector, in which the importance of disaggregation (by yarn count and vintage of spindles) is stressed; *(b)* the importance of structural shifts within the industry as also the links between cotton and synthetics, between spinning, weaving and finishing operations, and between the mill and decentralised sectors; and *(c)* the potentials from, and the nature of problems, that the industry is likely to face with economic liberalisation and the proposed dismantling of the Multi-Fibre Agreement following the W.T.O.

The analysis of productivity in the spinning sector uses a vintage approach, assuming count-wise constant returns to scale but allowing for changes in count-composition over time, and is perhaps more realistic than the usual production function approach. These estimates of productivity along with price and income elasticity analysis are used to assess competitiveness of the sector and also to discuss certain policy issues—*e.g.* the effects of excise concessions on hank and manual dying and reservation for the SSI sector especially in the garment segment. This is the basis for prediction of the demand and supply scenario of cotton and synthetic fibres, yarns, fabrics, made-ups, garments and spindles till year 2010-11 in the context of recent changes in Indian textile policy and the probable impact of the phase out of the Multi-Fibre Agreement.

On the whole, this is an extremely useful work in applied industrial economics which is distinguished by insights obtained from industrial experience and is crafted very competently on the basis of a thorough analysis of almost all available sources of relevant data.

Abhijit Sen

Acknowledgements

This book is based on my Ph.D thesis entitled submitted to Centre for Economic Studies and Planning Jawaharlal Nehru University. The present work was completed under the supervision of Professor Abhijit Sen. I wish to convey my gratitude to him for having devoted a great deal of time and effort in guiding this thesis.

I am indebted to Professor G.S. Bhalla for going through the thesis and giving valuable suggestions. I am also grateful to Professor Sheila Bhalla for her help and encouragement.

Professor C.P. Chandrasekhar went through some parts of my thesis. I am thankful. Thanks are also due to Dr. Subir Gokarn, who made useful comments for this book.

My stay at Vardhman Spinning and General Mills Limited as an Economist was useful in getting acquainted with the technical details of the textile and clothing industry. I gained immensely from my interaction with the Mr. S.P. Oswal, Chairman Vardhman Spinning and General Mills Limited. I wish to express my sincere gratefulness to him.

I would like to convey my gratefulness to my father-in-law Mr. A.N. Ahluwalia who went pains takingly through the draft.

And lastly, on a very personal note, I wish to thank my wife and my parents for bearing with me and providing unstinting support and encouragement to me for the entire period of my research.

Contents

	Foreword	*(vii)*
	Acknowledgements	*(xi)*
	List of Tables and Appendices	*(xiii)*
	List of Figures	*(xxvi)*
	List of Abbreviations	*(xxvii)*
Chapter		*Pages*
1.	Introduction	1
2.	Production, Productivity and Technological Changes in Indian Spinning Sector	37
3.	Structural Changes in the Indian Textile Industry	112
4.	Changes in Demand and Supply Pattern in Indian Textiles and Clothing Products	186
5.	Prospects for India's Textiles and Clothing Sector by the Years 2005-06 and 2010-11	334
6.	Summary and Conclusions	455
	Bibliography	490
	Index	500

List of Tables and Appendices

Table	Topic	Pages
2.1	Changes in Domestic Consumption Pattern for Cotton Hosiery Yarn	51
2.2	Estimates of Hosiery Yarn Production	52
2.3	Count Range-wise Production per Spindle for Hosiery Yarn	54
2.4	Carded and Combed Share in Count Range-wise Yarn Consumed within Mills and for Exports	55
2.5	Count Range-wise Production per Spindle of Woven Yarn	55
2.6	Changes in Count Range-wise Export Pattern	56
2.7	Changes in Count Range-wise Hosiery and Woven Yarn Exports	57
2.8	Changes in Mill Yarn Consumption Pattern	58
2.9	Changes in Mill Consumption and Woven Yarn Export Pattern	58
2.10	Changes in Hank Yarn Consumption Pattern	60
2.11	Combed and Carded Share in Cotton Hank Yarn	60
2.12	Count Range-wise Production of Cotton Hank Yarn	61
2.13	Count Range-wise Changes in Cotton Yarn Production	61
2.14	Carded and Combed Share in Cone and Other Yarn	62

Table	Topic	Pages
2.15	Count Range-wise Production per Spindle of Cone and Other Yarn	63
2.16	Combed Share in Cotton Yarn Consumed in Various Sectors over the Period	64
2.17	Count Range-wise Percentage Share of Combed Yarn in Production of Cotton Yarn	65
2.18	Weighted Average Production per Spindle for Cotton Yarn for Various Count Ranges	66
2.19	Weighted Production Per Spindle in Cotton Combed/Polyester Cotton Yarn for Various Count Ranges	68
2.20	Minimum Requirement of Modern Spindle over Time	69
2.21	Excess Capacity Installed than Minimum Required	71
2.22	Idle Spindles Expressed as Percentage of Installed Spindles	73
2.23	Year of Closure of Spindles Lying Closed on 31st March, 1997	74
2.24	Ownership-wise Productivity in Working Mills during 1996-97	76
2.25	Loss of Working Hours due to Under-utilisation of Spindles as Percentage of spindles Installed	78
2.26	Extra-working Spindles Required due to Technology Gap	80
2.27	Various Reasons for Operating below the Production Frontier	82
2.28	Age Composition of Installed Spindles	82
2.29	Productivity of Working Spindles	83
2.30	Comparison of Spindles Installed with Modern Equivalent	87

Table	Topic	Pages
2.31	Minimum Spindles Required for Cotton Yarn Production in SSI Sector during 1995-96	88
2.32	Productivity Analysis Extended for the Period 1996-97 to 1999-2000	90
App. 2.1	Economies of Scale in Case Time Variable is Replaced with Modernisation Variable	94
App. 2.2	Economies of Scale in Time Series Analysis (Mitra Study Results, 1999)	96
App. 2.3	Economies of Scale in Cross-Section Analysis	97
App. 2.4	Practical Relevance of assuming Count-wise Constant Returns to Scale Over Time but Allows for Changes in Count-composition	98
App. 2.5	Relevance of Methodology Used in this Study in Case of Hicks Non-neutral Technological Progress	99
App. 2.6	Age Composition of Spindles Installed	103
Appendix-Table		
*2.1	Spindles Availability during Various Years	104
*2.2	Replacement of Old Spindles as per cent of Installed	105
*2.3	Replacement Ratios as Percentage of Installed Spindles during Various Phases	107
*2.4	Expansion in India's Spinning Capacity	108
3.1	Production of Spun Yarn in the Small Scale Sector	117
3.2	Consumption of Fibres/Filaments	119
3.3	Production, Area and Yield of Cotton in India	120
3.4	Share of Different Staples of Cotton Consumption in Mills in India	121
3.5	Looms Activity	124
3.6	Shuttleless Looms in Selected Countries	125

Table	Topic	Pages
3.7	Official Conversion Rates for the Decentralised Sector	128
3.8	Cotton Yarn Consumption and Production of Cotton Fabrics in the Mill Sector	128
3.9	Civil Deliveries of Spun Yarn	134
3.10	Count Range-wise Weight of Fabrics and Conversion Rate in Various Sectors as Derived	142
3.11	Mill Sector Production of Cotton Fabrics in Various Count Ranges	143
3.12	Count Range-wise Fabrics Conversion Rate in the Mill Sector	144
3.13	Conversion Rates and Consumption of Yarn in the Mill Sector	145
3.14	Changes in Count Composition of Cotton Fabrics Produced in Powerloom and Handloom Sector	149
3.15	Parameters of Cotton Fabrics Produced in Various Sectors during 1996-97	150
3.16	Various Sectors Share and Weighted Conversion Rates	151
3.17	Production of Cotton Fabrics in Various Sectors Based on Delivery of Yarn	152
3.18	Official Data on Production of Cotton Fabrics in Various Sectors (Mn. Sq. Mts.)	153
3.19	Comparative Index for Fabrics Weight Produced from Various Fibres (Assuming Similar Count Composition of Yarn used and Similar Varieties of Fabrics Produced)	154
3.20	Conversion Rates for Various Blended Fabrics	156
3.21	Conversion Rates for 100% Non-cotton Spun Fabrics	158

Table	Topic	Pages
3.22	Conversion Rate for Various Filament Yarn	159
3.23	100% Non-Cotton Production of Fabric	160
3.24	Fiber-wise Production of Fabrics in the Country	161
3.25	Fibre-wise Fabric Production in the Country (as per Official Statistics)	162
3.26	Total Production of Fabrics in Various Sectors Based on Delivery of Yarn to Various Sectors	164
App. 3.1	Fibre-wise and Sector-wise Consumption of Yarn to Produce the Spun and Filament Fabrics	169
App. 3.2	Fibre-wise and Sector-wise Production of Fabrics Derived on the Basis of Delivery of Yarn	174
App. 3.3	Ratio of Various Blends Taken to Work out Conversion rates for Yarn and Fabrics	184
4.1	Exports of Cotton Fabrics from Various Sectors	189
4.2	Sector-wise Weights and Conversion Rates of Cotton Fabrics	191
4.3	Percentage Share of Various Sectors in Square Metres Equivalent of Fabrics Exports	192
4.4	Sector-wise Comparison of Fabrics Weight for Production and Exports	193
4.5	Exports of Cotton Woven Fabrics	195
4.6	Total Exports of Woven and Hosiery Fabrics	196
4.7	Exports of Cotton Made-Ups from Various Sectors	198
4.8	Exports of Cotton Made-ups from Various Sectors	199
4.9	Exports of Made-ups from Various Sectors	201
4.10	Exports of Garments	202

Table	Topic	Pages
4.11	Exports of Garments	203
4.12	Exports of Garments from Various Sectors	204
4.13	Exports of Cotton Fabrics in the Form of Fabrics, Made-ups and Garments	205
4.14	Percentage Share of Exports in the Form of Fabrics, Made-ups and Garments in Total Fabrics Equivalent Exports	207
4.15	Yarn Equivalent Exports in terms of Yarn, Fabrics, Made-ups and Garments	208
4.16	Percentage Share of Yarn Equivalent Exports in terms of Yarn Fabrics, Made-ups and Garments	209
4.17	Yarn Equivalent Exports from Various Sectors in the form of Yarn, Fabrics, Made-ups and Garments	210
4.18	Fibre Equivalent Exports in Cotton Textile and Clothing Products from Various Sectors	211
4.19	Total Exports of Cotton Equivalent Fibre in Cotton and Synthetic Textile and Clothing Products	213
4.20	Fibre/Filament-wise Production of Synthetic Fabrics during 1995-96	214
4.21	Fibre/Filament-wise Exports of Synthetic Fabrics during 1995-96	214
4.22	Fibre/Filament-wise Comparison of Synthetic Fabrics Weight for Export and Production	215
4.23	Fibre/Filament-wise Synthetic Made-ups Export during 1995-96	216
4.24	Fabrics, Yarn and Fibres/Filaments Equivalent Exports in Various Synthetic Textiles & Clothing Products during 1995-96	218
4.25	Fibre/Filament-wise Exports of Various	219

Table	*Topic*	*Pages*
	Synthetic Textiles and Clothing Products during 1995-96	
4.26	Fibre/Filament-wise Export of Cotton and Synthetic Textile and Clothing Products during 1995-96	220
4.27	Domestic Availability of Cotton and Synthetic Products during 1995-96	221
4.28	Per Capita Domestic Availability of Textiles and Clothing Products in the form of Fabrics and Fibre during 1995-96	221
4.29	Share of Various Fibres/Filament in Domestic Availability During 1995-96	222
4.30	Exports of Synthetic Fabrics during 1983 to 1999-2000	224
4.31	Exports of Synthetic Made-ups during 1983 to 1999-2000	225
4.32	Exports of Synthetic Garment in Pieces during 1990-91 to 1999-2000	226
4.33	Exports of Synthetic Garments during 1983 to 1999-2000	227
4.34	Fabrics, Yarn and Fibre Equivalent Exports in the form of Various Synthetic Textiles & Clothing Products during 1983 to 1999-2000	228
4.35	Yarn Equivalent Exports in Various Synthetic Textiles and Clothing Products during 1983 to 1999-2000	229
4.36	Synthetic Fabrics and Yarn Equivalent Exports and Domestic Availability during 1983 to 1997-98	230
4.37	Domestic Availability of Yarn in Synthetic Products	232
4.38	Estimates of Consumption of Man-made and	233

Table	*Topic*	*Pages*
	Cotton Fibre for Domestic Use in the form of Synthetic Products	
4.39	Exports of Cotton and Synthetic Fabrics in the form of Fabrics, Made-ups and Garments	236
4.40	Domestic Availability and Consumption of Cotton and Synthetic Products	237
4.41	Estimates of Domestic Availability and Consumption of Cotton Fabrics in Various Forms	240
4.42	Estimates of Domestic Availability and Consumption of Synthetic Fabrics in Various Forms	241
4.43	Yarn Equivalent Exports and Domestic Availability in Various Textiles and Clothing Items	243
4.44	Fibre/Filament Content in Textiles and Clothing Exports and Domestic Use	244
4.45	Cotton and Synthetic Fibre Content in Textiles and Clothing Products Available for Domestic Use	245
4.46	Per Capita Equivalent Import of Cotton and MMF in Textile and Clothing Products	247
4.47	Per Capita Availability of Cotton and MMF/ Filament Including Import Content	248
4.48	Consumption of Handloom Equivalent Cotton Fabrics in the Household, Non-household and Export Segments	252
4.49	Comparison of Production and Consumption Estimates for the Cotton Handloom Fabrics	253
4.50	Hank Yarn Delivery to the Decentralised Sector	254
4.51	Wholesale Prices Index of Cotton Hank and Cotton Cone Yarn	255

Table	Topic	Pages
4.52	Prices of Cotton Hank and Cotton Cone Yarn for 20s Carded	256
4.53	Prices of Cotton Hank and Cotton Cone Yarn for Finer Counts	257
4.54	Sector-wise Revised Estimates of Production of Cotton Fabrics	260
4.55	Diversion of Cotton and Synthetic Hank Yarn to Powerloom Sector	262
4.56	Production of Cotton and Synthetic Fabrics	264
4.57	Sector-wise Total Exports of Cotton Fabrics in the Form of Fabrics, Made-ups and Garments	268
4.58	Sector-wise Revised Availability of Cotton Fabrics for Domestic Consumption	272
4.59	Item-wise Share of Handloom Sector in Cotton Woven Fabrics Available for Domestic Consumption during 1983	277
4.60	Item-wise Share of Handloom Sector in Cotton Woven Fabrics Available for Domestic Consumption during 1992-93	277
4.61	Item-wise Share of Handloom Sector in Cotton Woven Fabrics Available for Domestic Consumption during 1998	278
4.62	Knitted and Woven Fabrics Equivalent Availability of Cotton and Synthetic Products for Domestic Use	288
4.63	Various Varieties Share in Domestic Consumption of Woven Fabric	290
4.64	Variety-wise Availability of Woven Fabrics for Domestic Use	291
4.65	Variety-wise Availability of Cotton Woven Fabrics for Domestic Use	293

Table	Topic	Pages
4.66	Percentage Share of Various Varieties in Cotton Woven Fabrics for Domestic Use	294
4.67	Variety-wise Availability of Synthetic Fabrics for Domestic Use	295
4.68	Total Production and Value Added in India's Cotton Textile Sector	302
4.69	Total Production and Value Added in India's Synthetic Textile Sector	303
4.70	Total Value of Cotton and Synthetic Textiles at 1993-94 Prices	305
4.71	Type of Fabrics Stitched in Domestic and Export Market	307
4.72	Main Varieties Consumed in Domestic Household Sector during 1998	308
4.73	Value Added in Tailoring Sector including for Ready-made Garments	309
4.74	Value Added in Textiles and Clothing Sector	311
4.75	Employment Estimates in Textile and Clothing Sector	321
App. 4.1	Various Countries/Regions Production of Cotton Fabrics	329
5.1	Product-wise Net Imports and Exports from Developed and Developing Countries during 1980-1995	352
5.2	World Gross Trade in Textile and Clothing Products during 1980-95	356
5.3	Fibre-wise Import of Various Products in World (1992)	357
5.4	Fibre-wise Import of Yarn by Selected Countries and Regions (1992)	358
5.5	Share of Cotton Fibre in USA's Import Over Time	359

Table	*Topic*	*Pages*
5.6	Revised Estimates of World Gross Trade during 1992	361
5.7	Revised Estimate of World Gross Trade during 1995 and 2005	362
5.8	Revised Gross World Trade Projection 2005	363
5.9	South Asia's Revised Estimate of Trade	365
5.10	South Asia's Share in World Trade Projections 2005	367
5.11	Fibre Consumption in Major Countries and Regions, 1980-95 and Projection for 2005	369
5.12	India's Item-wise Export Share in the World Import during 1994	370
5.13	India's Share in World Trade of Cotton Yarn and Cotton Fabrics	371
5.14	India's Share of Textiles and Clothing Exports to EEC and USA	374
5.15	India's Ranking Regarding Various Parameters during 1996	376
5.16(a)	Total Ring Yarn Costs in Various Countries: Spinning for Ne 30 Combed Cotton during 1997	377
5.16(b)	Total Ring Yarn Costs in Various Countries: Spinning for Ne 30 Combed Cotton during 1999	379
5.17(a)	1997 Total Fabric Costs in Various Countries: Weaving Grey 100 per cent Cotton 70/70, Ne 30 Warp & Weft, 66" Width	383
5.17(b)	1999 Total Fabric Costs in Various Countries: Weaving Grey 100 per cent Cotton 70/70, Ne 30 Warp & Weft, 66" Width	383
5.18	Country-wise Cost of Production per Shirt from Yarn	385

Table	*Topic*	*Pages*
5.19	Country-wise Comparison of per Shirt Domestic Sale Cost	387
5.20	Retailer Cost in USA of Shirt Produced in Various Countries	388
5.21	India's Share in World and South Asia's Gross Trade 1999-2000	393
5.22	India's Share in World and South Asia's Gross Trade by 2005-06	394
5.23	Item-wise India's Share in World Trade Over Time	395
5.24	Fibre-wise Gross World's Export in 1999-2000	395
5.25	India's Gross Export of Cotton Products : 1999-2000 to 2005-06 (Alt. I)	398
5.26	India's Gross Export of Synthetic Products : 1999-2000 to 2005-06 (Alt. I)	399
5.27	India's Net Trade by 2005-06	400
5.28	World Gross Trade in Yarn, Fabric, Clothing and Other Products: 1980-2005	402
5.29	India's Trade during 2005-06 (Alt. II)	403
5.30	India's Gross Export of Cotton Products: 1999-2000 to 2005-06 (Alt. II)	405
5.31	India's Gross Export of Synthetic Products: 1999-2000 to 2005-06 (Alt. II)	405
5.32	India's Fibre Wise Net Trade (IInd Alternative)	406
5.33	India's per Unit Export Realisation	408
5.34	India's Anticipated Export in Value Terms during 2005-06 (Alt. I)	408
5.35	India's Anticipated Export in Value terms during 2005-06 Alt. II	409
5.36	Per Capita Final Domestic Consumption (at 6% p.a. GDP growth) : Alt. I	416

Table	*Topic*	*Pages*
5.37	Per Capita Final Domestic Consumption (at 8% p.a. GDP growth) : Alt. II	419
5.38	Fabrics, Yarn and Fibre Equivalent Total Demand during 1999-2000	421
5.39	Fabrics Equivalent Demand in Various Forms during 1999-2000	421
5.40	Fabrics, Yarn and Fibre Equivalent Total Demand during 2005-06 (Alt. I)	422
5.41	Fabrics Equivalent Demand in Various Forms during 2005-06 (Alt. I)	423
5.42	Fabrics, Yarn and Fibre Equivalent Total Demand during 2005-06 (Alt. II)	424
5.43	Fabrics Equivalent Demand in Various forms during 2005-06 (Alt. II)	426
5.44	India's Trade	428
5.45	Fabrics, Yarn and Fibre Equivalent Total Demand during 2010-11	429
5.46	Fabrics Equivalent Demand in Various forms during 2010-2011	431
5.47	Mill, SSI and Ex-factory Requirements of Fibre/Filament Blends in India and World by 2005-06 and 2010-11	432
5.48	Requirement of Various Fibre/Filaments in India's and World by 2005-06	433
App. 5.1	Quota and Other Restrictions Used for Textile and Clothing Imports under the EU "Textiles Policy", 1996	451
App. 5.2	Impact of Quota Growth on Quantitative Restrictions under Article 2 of the Agreement on Textiles and Clothing	452

List of Figures

Figure	Topic	Pages
2.1	Isoquant	45
2.2	Production Possibility Frontier	45
2.3	Hicks Neutral Technical Progress Isoquants	46
2.4	Hicks Non-neutral Technical Progress Isoquants	100
3.1	Stages of Production of Fabrics	113
3.2(a)	Various Types of Yarn	114
3.2(b)	Various Types of Yarn Produced on the Cotton Spun System	116
4.1	Stages of Production of Textiles and Clothing Products and their Ultimate Uses	188

List of Abbreviations

AEPC	Apparel Export Promotion Council
AIFCOSPIN	All India Federation of Co-operative Spinning Mills
AIMA	Ahmedabad Institute of Management Association
APTMA	All Pakistan Textile Mills Association
ATIRA	Ahmedabad Textile Industry Research Association
CMIE	Centre for Monitoring Indian Economy Pvt. Ltd.
CSO	Central Statistical Organisation
DGCIS	Directorate General of Commercial Intelligence & Statistics
ESCAP	Economic and Social Commission for Asia and the Pacific
EU	European Union
Extra-EU trade	Trade from outside EU
FAO	Food and Agriculture Organization
GATT	General Agreement on Trade and Tariffs
GDP	Gross Domestic Product
Gms	Grams
GOI	Government of India
ICA	Indian Cotton Annual
ICAC	International Cotton Advisory Committee
ICICI	Industrial Credit and Investment Corporation of India

ICMF	Indian Cotton Mills Federation
ICRA	Investment Information and Credit Rating Agency of India Limited
IDBI	Industrial Development Bank of India
IFCI	Industrial Finance Corporation of India
IMF	International Monetary Fund
ITMF	International Textiles Manufacturing Federation
JTN	Japan Textile News
Kg	Kilogram
LDC	Less Developed Countries
Mn.	Million
NAS	National Accounts Statistics
NTC	National Textile Corporation
SA	South Asia
SIDBI	Small Industries Development Bank of India
SIMA	Southern India Mills' Association
SITRA	The South India Textile Research Association
Sq.mt	Square Metre
SRTEPC	Synthetic and Rayon Textile Exports Promotion Council
STC	State Textile Corporation
TEXPROCIL	The Cotton Textiles Export Promotion Council of India
TOI	Textile Outlook International
UN	United Nations
WTO	World Trade Organisation

1

Introduction

The Textile and Clothing is one of the most important industries in India. During 1997-98, it accounted for 4 per cent of GDP, 20 per cent of the manufacturing value added and one third of total export earnings. Further, it provides employment to millions of skilled and semi-skilled workers (Economic Survey, 1999). Since expenditure on clothing accounts for more than 10 per cent of total consumption expenditure, textile and clothing industry is important for consumers also.

There exist several studies on the changes in structure of textile and clothing industry in India. But the exact state of structure of this important industry in India is still very vague due to the non-availability of any reliable data on the unorganised sectors such as powerloom, handloom and garment industry. In fact several studies tried to work out the quantum of production in garment industry, but no firm data is available so far. The Textile Commissioner's estimates of production of fabrics in the handloom, powerloom and hosiery sector derived on the basis of delivery of yarn to various sectors do not add upto the Textile Committee data on domestic consumption (household and non-household sector) and TEXPROCIL data on exports.

The prime reason for the same is that the conversion rates of fabrics to yarn are not scientifically worked out. The difference in sector-wise production of fabrics is also caused by diversion of hank yarn to powerloom sector. The powerloom sector thus evades the excise benefit meant for the handloom sector in the form of excise concession on the hank yarn.

Thus once the reliable data on present state of textiles and clothing industry is not available, any estimates about the future projections is meaningless. This study thus makes an attempt to work out the state of textile and clothing industry during the period 1983 to 1999-2000 to capture the impact of New Textile Policy introduced during 1985 and comprehensive Economic Reforms introduced in 1991.

Textiles and clothing sector has undergone important structural changes during the last few decades. In particular, several structural changes at various stages such as yarn, fabrics, made-ups and garments have taken place during 80's and 90's in the background of new economic environment. Thus to understand these changes, it is important to understand the structure of Indian Textile and clothing industry, which is a bit complex. There exist several stages of value added namely spinning weaving and stitching. The production from fibre to spun yarn takes place through spinning process, but all the yarn need not go through spinning process. The fabrics from yarn are converted through weaving process and from fabrics to made-ups or garment is converted through stitching process. There is one additional value added at yarn or fabrics stage called dying processing.

The industry comprises the organised mill sector and the unorganised powerloom, handloom, khadi and garment sectors. The spinning process is dominantly taking place in organised mill sector, while the weaving, stitching and dying is manily taking place in unorganised sector. Weaving process takes place in mill sector and unorganised powerloom, handloom and khadi sectors. The dying processing is taking place after yarn or fabrics stage and is sometimes holds the integrated part of weaving unit or other sectors. The dying processing also takes place in independent processing units. The fabrics, produced in these forms are either exported or domestically consumed in the form of fabrics, made-ups and garments. The process of manufacturing made-ups and garments from fabrics is called stitching and is taking place in garment or tailoring units. Sometimes production of made-ups is taking place in integrated weaving units. The garments could be classified into tailor made garments and readymade garments, as final uses are the similar.

In the new liberalisation environment beginning from 1985, restrictions on exports of yarn, expansion norms for the mill sector and norms for use of fibre composition in the mill sector were relaxed. Further the custom duties on synthetic products and capital goods were lowered and process got accelerated after the new economic reforms introduced during 1991. Thus the import of capital goods and raw material became cheap. Despite the rise in domestic interest rates, the impact of lowering in custom duties were felt on the rise in capital-intensive technology in general. In the organised textiles sector also and particularly in the spinning sector, the capital labour ratio has increased. However, there exist several unanswered questions.

How it has happened that despite liberalisation policies pursued over a period of two decades, it failed to have any major impact on technology progress in weaving, dying and garment industry, though there has taken place a conisderable technology progress in spinning industry during the same period. What were the reasons for the failure of these policies in bringing the technology progress in these sectors? Further, it needs to be studied that what are chances of technology progess during the period 1999-2000 to 2010-11 in weaving, dying and garment sector, keeping in view the expected changes in policies to be pursued.

The cheap capital availability should lead to high capital investment especially when it was supported by rise in demand by opening export window. That is what exactly seems to have happened in the spinning industry. However, the cheap capital availability in spinning industry led to excess capacity as replacement of old machinery was slow, and even the replaced spindles from the organised sector was finding their way into the SSI spinning units.

Thus the prospects of Indian textiles and clothing industry are studied in detail keeping in view the MFA phase out and its impact on World, South Asia and India's trade. This has been studied in the context of expected changes in domestic environment and their impact on exports and domestic demand.

Thus, in brief the main objective of this study is to analyse the impact of economic reforms of mid eighties and comprehensive economic liberalisation policies introduced in 1991 on the structure of the Indian textile and clothing industry and changes there in. For analysis, the period of this study is divided into two phases *i.e.* 1983 to 1990-91 and 1990-91 to 1999-2000. An attempt is made to study the impact of liberalisation policies on spinning industry and on weaving sectors, namely, mill, powerloom and handloom. The changes in the pattern of export and domestic pattern of consumption in the form of fabrics, made-ups and garments are worked out. These changes are studied along with the supply constraints in the country. After working out the structure of industry and changes therein over the period of time, an attempt is made to project the alternative possible future scenarios of the textiles and clothing industry by the year 2005-06 and 2010-11 (after the MFA phase out).

However, to study these structural changes in the industry, it is important to know the various ups and down the industry has undergone through in the past and the factors responsible for the state of affairs of industry during mid-eighties. Thus the following section is devoted to brief background of textile industry.

Background

Textile industry in India had a long but chequered history. Nehru rightly said that the history of cotton and textiles is not only the history of the growth of modern industry in India, but in a sense, it might be considered the history of India during the past one hundred years. When I think of textiles, my mind goes back some thousands of years to the period when India perhaps was the only country producing these textiles and exporting them to distant lands. The early beginnings of civilisation are tied up with the manufacture of textiles and history might well be written with this as the leading motif (Nehru, 1948). India was no doubted a leading producer and exporter of textiles during the mercantilist period. The birth of the industrial revolution combined with the increasing political dominance of India by Britain resulted in the reduction of India exports to Britain and slowly reversed the process (Sreenivasan, 1984).

With the consolidation of the British power in India, once the products of the industrial revolution were introduced into India, it was inevitable that the revolution itself should follow. The first cotton mill to be started in India was Bowreah Cotton Mill Company in Calcutta during 1818. The first cotton-spinning mill in Bombay was established in 1851 and in Ahmedabad in 1859. The industry started growing rapidly except for a few temporary set backs.

The 19th and the first three decades of the 20th century also saw a tug of war between Lancashire and Indian mills. At the end of 1933, custom duties on yarn imported from Britain were lowered. In return Indian exports were allowed to share the British quotas of exports to other countries. India was not having independent quota at that time. The impact of import substitution measures taken during 1930s led to the growth of textile industry in India. The powerloom sector also grew during this period, although it was first introduced as early as 1904 in Ichalkaranji. The growth of powerloom sector was mainly based on the purchase of second hand machinery from the mills. By the end of 1930s, more than 6000 such looms were known to exist (Mehta, 1954).

At the time of the Second World War, textile industry was passing through a difficult phase. With Japan entering the war the prospects for Indian industry improved significantly. In fact, the Indian industry was unable to cope with increased demand and the nation was facing shortage of cloth with demands pouring from various government departments. The export of yarn increased from 37 million lbs in 1939 to 93 million lbs in 1941 and that of cloth from 195 million yard to 936 million yard during the same period. There was a drop in production and exports during 1942 due to disruption caused by the "Quit India" movement (Sreenivasan, 1984). The export of yarn fell to 15 million lbs and of cloth to 427 million yards in 1945.

At the time of independence, there were, 1,030 thousand spindles and 202 thousand looms installed in Indian mills. There were also an estimated two and half million handloom weavers in the country. The mills were producing nearly 4000 million metres of cloth and the handlooms accounted for approximately 1300 million metres. The mill sector employed nearly 0.7 million workers and thus was the largest organised sector in the country.

1950-85 period

After independence the national government formulated a policy with the aim of promoting the growth of industry, providing adequate clothing at reasonable price to consumers, particularly to the weaker section of the society, and earning the much needed foreign exchange through exports.

The dependence of the decentralised sector on the mill sector for yarn and the advantages of existing economies of scale in the mills' sector made government intervention a necessity to enable the decentralised sector to co-exist in the same product market as the mill sector.

The import substitution policies were further intensified after independence, which reduced any danger of competition to the domestic producers. However, import of cotton increased from 7 lakh bales to 11 lakh bales during 1956-1960 as a substantial share of cotton growing areas went to Pakistan at the time of partition. An important technological development at the international level during the early fifties, was the beginning of the production of synthetic fibres. The substitution of cotton with synthetics became quite popular in the sixties. The government however imposed restrictions on the development of synthetic products in India. The use of any other yarn by the composite mills in the warp of any cloth than yarn spun by themselves was prohibited up to 1985 (Uchikawa, 1998).

The cotton mills industry, weaving in particular, remained stagnant since 1950 because of the official patronage granted to khadi and handloom in pursuance of the Swadeshi movement and Gandhian philosophy. This patronage had the backing of the argument that techniques of production, which required maximum number of labour, should be encouraged to achieve the twin objectives of economising on scarce capital and employing abundant labour available in the country. Several types of protections were given to the decentralised sector at various times. Restrictions on the additional installation of looms in the mills sector were among the first of these. The requirement that mills produce adequate yarn in hanks suitable for handlooms and subsidy to handloom fabrics were others incentives given to the decentralised sector. The government policy of discouraging adoption of techniques, which could lead to curtailment of labour, proved a damper to the growth of organised textile weaving industry.

It was realised at that stage itself that gradual change in the pattern of production of handlooms was in the best interest of mass consumers and the industry itself. Thus a committee appointed in 1952 under the chairmanship of Kanungo recommended that over a period of time and in a phased manner, handloom should be gradually converted to powerlooms in the decentralised sector. But, due to strong opposition from the handloom sector, the recommendations of the committee could not be implemented.

Several committees including the Karve (1955) and Ashok Mehta (1964) committee were appointed from time to time to examine the whole question of rationalisation of weaving industry. Karve committee opposed the recommendations made by the Kanungo committee. It recommended the ambar charkha as efficient mode of production and suggested that there should be no expansion of spinning and weaving capacity except in the handloom sector. Ashok Mehta Committee recommends the adoption of powerloom by the handloom co-operatives to increase the production and earnings of handloom weavers. This committee also suggested the freeze in mill capacity expansion.

The first textile policy to suggest growth of all sectors in a harmonised way was announced in 1978. Another policy was announced on 9th March 1981, which suggested as follows:

1. The spinning capacity to be developed mainly in the co-operative sector.
2. Expansion of mill sector to be allowed for exports only.
3. Un-authorised powerloom sector to be recognised and marginal expansion in capacity allowed.
4. The cloth requirements to be met mainly through development of hanloom sector.

It was suggested that the aforesaid objectives be realised through the combination of fiscal, licensing, reservations and other interventions. The 1981 policy laid stress on more exports, expansion of powerlooms and development of machinery sector through technology imports. These were not taken care of in the 1978 policy.

The result was the existence of wide range of techniques co-existing in the cotton textile industry. Spindle capacity was more than doubled from about 11.00 million in 1951 to 24.42 million in 1985. The spun production increased from 602 million kilograms in 1951 to 1309 million kilograms in 1983. The share of cotton yarn in spun yarn declined from 98.20 per cent in 1951 to 83.42 per cent in 1983. The production of spun yarn grew to 1454 million kilograms during 1985-86.

On the other hand, weaving capacity has remained stagnant after independence at around 0.20 million looms. Mill cloth production was 3727 million metres in 1951 and reached a new high of 4852 million metres in 1956. Since then there has been either stagnation or a gradual reduction in mill cloth production. In 1980, the cloth production was 4176 million metres. The eighties show a further decline in mill cloth production. Production was 3528 million metres in 1983, which further declined to 3411 million metres in 1985.

The phenomenon of stagnation of looms in mill sector is partly due to the government's policy of freezing mill cloth output in order to encourage handlooms and powerlooms, and partly due to basic economic factors. These factors contributed to the trend of continuous shift of emphasis from the weaving to the spinning in mills sector after independence. The average numbers of spindles per loom rose from 56 in 1951 to 86 in 1971. The figure futher rose to 116 spindles per loom in 1985. On the other hand, stagnation in the production of fabrics in the organised sector is compensated by the growth of the decentralised sector. The production of cotton woven fabrics in the decentralised sector increased from a mere 1013 million metres in 1951 to 4686 million metres in 1970. The rise in production of decentralised sector was much steep after the seventies. The production increased to 8006 million metres in 1983. The share of decentralised sector in total production of woven fabrics increased from a mere 21 per cent in 1951 to as high as 69 per cent in 1983. The production of fabrics in the decentralised sector further increased to 9016 million metres in 1985. The powerloom sector is mainly responsible for the observed growth in the decentralised sector. It is encroaching upon the share previously produced by the mills and hanloom sectors (Singh, 1989).

The major defect of textile policy up to 1985 under the policy regime was its insulation from foreign competition and its consequent failure to keep pace with the rapidly changing technological development in the sector. Indian policies during this time restricted competition. Within the consumer goods sector, in particular in textile industry, a major emphasis was given to maximising of employment through encouragement of handloom sector. It was in this context that textile industry failed to keep pace with the rapidly changing technological development in this sector. The most serious effect of lack of technological development was on reducing the competitiveness of the Indian textile industry. India's exports of cotton fabrics decreased from US $ 245.12 million in 1950 to US $121.11 million in 1960. Further, synthetic fibres have been the most dynamic sector in the world textile market since the early 1960s. The discouragement of this important product innovation in India had profound consequences not only for technological progress in the synthetic sector, but also that in the cotton sector. The performance of textile industry was affected by indifferent weather cycles, which affected the raw material supply, as the industry was dominantly cotton based. This eroded the health of the industry. The slow growth of economy in general and of agriculture, in particular, added to the problem. The income factor slowed the pace of growth in domestic demand. Further, the elimination of competitiveness among various sectors affected the quality of Indian textiles and clothing products. The net result was that India gradually lost its dominant position in the world textile exports.

India's share in world textile and clothing exports declined steeply from more than 5.0 per cent during the early 60s to around 2.9 per cent in the 70s. With the oil crisis during 1973, it became imperative for India to increase its exports. The industry started restructuring itself during mid seventies. However, textile industry found itself unable to compete in world economy primarily because of technological backwardness. India's share in world textile and clothing further declined to 2.14 per cent during 1980. India's share in world trade remained at around the same level throughout the eighties (Uchikawa, 1998).

The restriction on capacity expansion as well as flexibility in fibre use composition in the mill sector along with the imposition of heavy excise duties, control on import of polyester fibre and technology for modernisation in the organised sector are cited as some of the main reasons for decline in the mill fabrics production and the rising share of powerloom sector in total production of fabrics.

To sum up, the textile policy in India till 1985 was driven by the objective to maximising employment through labour intensive handloom sector. The handloom sector was to be safeguarded against competition from modern textile industry through a whole set of measures. The most significant of these included reservation of articles for exclusive production in the handloom sector, imposition of quota and product restrictions on mill sector and discouragement of powerloom expansion through stringent regulations regarding their registration and granting of excise benefits to handloom products. In addition, several restrictions were imposed on the mill sector such as control on imports of polyester fibre and technology for modernisation.

By and large, the industry in the early 1980s was characterised by poor capability and quality by global standards. That there was technology stagnation in textile industry was also brought out by a survey undertaken in 1979, which found that 62 per cent of the stock of weaving machinery in the mills was more than 30 years old (India 1979). The net result of the aforesaid policies was lack of modernisation, decay of mill sector and a rapid decline in the competitiveness of textile industry.

Before we review the New Textile Policy (NTP, 1985) and New Economic Reforms introduced during 1991, it is important to review the literature on the subject related with the structural changes in Indian textile Industry and Impact of MFA phase out.

Review of Literature

Review of literature till 1985

Several studies have been carried out on cotton mill industry. Those prior to 1950 mainly concentrated on historical and institutional aspects and studies basically location, size and integration of units in the industry (Loknathan 1935, Gandhi 1940, Sastry 1943, M.M. Mehta 1949 and S.D. Metha 1953-54). It was only in the fifties that aspects like employment, technology, capital output and capital labour co-efficient (Rosen 1959) was studied. A number of qualitative studies on the question of choice of techniques were made during this period and the cotton textile industry was used frequently to vividly describe and classify the nature of the problem and the issues involved (Raj 1956, Sen 1960, Bhalla 1964). The export pessimism of the fifties and the sixties promoted studies on export trends in textiles. A number of problems and hypotheses were examined to explain the declining trend in term of stagnating world demand, widening cost differentials due to increasing domestic raw cotton prices and wage rates (Singh 1964, Nayyer 1973), domestic demand pressure (Paul and Mote 1970) and changes in labour productivity (Rao 1980). Other aspects such as import substitution of raw cotton to cellulosic fibres, capacity utilisation and hedging activity in raw cotton (Dharma Kumar *et. al.* 1965), emergence of industrial labour fora in Bombay Cotton Mills (Morris 1965), wage determination (Papola 1968) was also examined. The determinants of investment, both fixed and inventory, dividend behaviour and profitability of textile companies have been studied at length (V.K. Sastry 1966, Purananda and Hanumantha Rao 1966, Krishnamurthy and D.U. Sastry 1970 and 1975, Barthwall 1977).The impact of growth on the balance of payments (Kumarasundram 1962) and the impact of government regulations on technology and market structure (Desai 1983) have also been discussed. The market structure of the industry in relation to growth and technical change has also been investigated (Chandrasekhar 1981). Sastry (1984) studied stagnation in demand and productivity performance in textile industry.

A lot of literature exists on the consumer behaviour in India. The estimates on expenditure elasticities for clothing reveal most of these are above unity (Bhattacharya, 1964). Moreover, expenditure elasticities for clothing has increased over the period of time (Iyengar and Jain 1974). Textile Committee (1977) has estimated income and price elasticities on the basis of consumer panel data for various fabrics at different prices and income levels for 1974 and 1975. Radhakrishna and Murthy have estimated expenditure and price elasticities for several commodities including clothing in the framework of Linear Expenditure System (LES). These estimates are made for rural and urban areas for lower, middle and upper income groups. The most elaborate complete demand system has been estimated by Sukumari Murthy in 1983 in his optimisation exercise carried out in a LES framework. Ahmedabad Textile Industry Research Association

(ATIRA) 1985) has also attempted to estimate demand parameters through LES. Sastry (1984), questioned the demand function with standard static variety and tried Houthakkar-Taylor dynamic formulation without success. The vast majority of Indian population is very poor, it would be unrealistic to expect the poor to have stocks of clothing. Their cloth purchases are generally limited to the barest minimum and are made on festive or special occasions. It is therefore reasonable to argue that the concept of stock of clothing has little relevance for the bulk of the population, which is poor. In the estimation of demand functions for cotton mill cloth, he used two alternative functional forms, linear and log-linear. Both aggregate and per capita formulations of the demand function are estimated in the double log functional form. Omkar Goswami (1985), using Linear Expenditure System (LES) model for the period 1974 to 1983 concluded that food prices did not matter. Thus in this study the estimates of future domestic demand are worked on the basis of price and income last cities. Most of the methodological issues elaborated by various scholars are discussed in different chapters of this study while examining the related questions, while few of important have been discussed in detail in the following sections one by one.

The Official Estimates of Production of Fabrics Literature

The existing literature has wide coverage of structural changes in Indian textiles and clothing industry, but all these studies are based on official statistics of production of fabrics, which are misleading. As put by Misra (1993), official statistics on the production of fabrics hide as much as they reveal. Unfortunately not only the conversion rates on which the official estimates on fabrics production are based, have not been scientifically derived, but have also remained unchanged for about three decades. What is even more important is that no distinction has been made in the application of these conversion factors between the powerloom and the handloom sectors depite significant dissimilarities in the yarn consumed as well as in the fabrics woven in these two sectors.

Various studies by the Investment Information and Credit

Rating Agency of India Limited (ICRA) and the South India Textile Research Association (SITRA) were also ciritical about the conversion rates adopted by official agencies on an arbitrary basis. Misra (1993) and ICRA (1996) tried to rework the conversion rates for various sectors in their studies. But there was also a major snag in these studies. Though these studies clearly pointed out that count of yarn and ply were important to work out the fabrics weight, no attempt was made by them to scientifically develop the count-range wise conversion rates.

The problem in official estimates of production of fabrics is clear when one compares the estimates of production of fabrics with consumption estimates. However, the analysis of consumption of fabrics requires conversion norms to work out the common unit, which are not readily available. For example it gives total fabrics exports in million square metres (mn. sq. mt.), total made-ups exports in million rupees (mn. Rs.) and garments exports in million pieces (mn. pcs) but no scientific attempt was made to derive the fabrics equivalent direct and indirect exports in terms of fabrics, made-ups and garments. Similarly no scientific attempt was made to derive the yarn equivalent or fibre equivalent direct or indirect yarn exports in terms of yarn, fabrics, made-ups and garments. ATIRA (1987) did attempt to work out direct and indirect yarn equivalent for textile and clothing exports but conversion rates taken are based on official assumptions, which are arbitarary and not scientifically drawn.

Similar problem is faced to convert the Textile Committee household and non-household data, which is available in sq. mt. equivalent by working out some scientific conversion rates. This study made a detailed attempt to work out conversion rates of fabrics from yarn for each count range and then are used to work out the total production of fabrics. These estimates of production of fabrics are then compared with the fabrics equivalent consumption worked out in square metres (exports plus domestic) by adopting some scientific method.

Diversion of Hank Yarn to Powerloom Sector Literature

To work out the relative performance of various sectors, the share of each sector in production and exports are to be worked out. However, due to expected diversion of hank yarn to powerloom sector, there is an inherent snag in the estimates of production of sectorwise woven fabrics derived in this study on the basis of yarn delivery to various sectors, though overall production of fabrics in the country are expected to be approximately the same.

There exist various studies, which agree that there is a diversion of hank yarn to the powerloom sector. According to Jain, the evidence to substantiate the assumption that there is large-scale overestimation of handloom output can be had from the following facts:

1. In 1975, the survey on Household purchases of cotton textiles revealed that the share of handloom and Khadi cloth in total household purchases was only 16 per cent whereas the official estimates of cloth production placed the share of handloom at nearly 30 per cent for this year. Based on this, a study done by the Planning Commission in 1978-79 came to the conclusion that handloom production was overestimated (and correspondingly powerloom production under estimated) by around 500 million metres in 1975.
2. Some survey have reported use of yarn by powerlooms for the manufacture of dyed saris.
3. The powerloom sector has grown at much faster pace than the official statistics on cone yarn deliveries would warrant. This indirectly confirms the suspicion that a substantial proportion of the yarn shown as being consumed in the handloom sector is in fact consumed in the powerlooms.

Thus the estimates of sector-wise production of fabrics should be corrected for these distortions, which could be worked out on the basis of demand (domestic plus exports) analysis. Some studies have expressed that similar distortions are possible in export analysis as well in order to get advantage of handloom quota. According to Sheela Thakar Bhide (1996), several exporters and importers confirmed during interviews that certain quantity of powerloom fabrics is being exported as handloom fabrics. The analysis in this study regarding the sector-wise and item-wise exports worked out in square metre equivalent indicate that the extent of such diversion is not expected to be large and it is mainly a propaganda. Had there been a large extent of export diversion of powerloom fabrics as handloom fabrics, it would have been difficult to explain the decline in exports of cotton handloom fabrics after 1994-95 as the exports and quota utilisation increased from the powerloom sector during the same period. It is difficult to sell powerloom fabrics as handloom fabrics as it is easily distinguishable. Otherwise also, the powerloom sector has very limited scope to pass off its production as handloom sector in domestic and exports market. This, for example, is relevant in those cases where the categories of products are exclusively reserved for the handloom sector and several institutions purchasing fabrics have been asked to buy only handloom production. It is not easy to sell fabrics through duplications to these institutions. Moreover, non-household purchases constitutes small share of total domestic consumption.

Thus the data provided by the Handloom Export Promotion Council on handloom exports and that of the Textile Committee on consumer purchases could be considered reliable for the handloom sector, as these fabrics are easily distinguishable from the fabrics produced by the other sectors.

The Competitiveness of Powerloom Sector Literature

Several views have been expressed regarding the continued growth of the powerloom sector both before and after economic liberalisation in 1991. One argument that was advanced before liberalisation was that powerlooms were expanded because of restrictions put on the mills for the expansion of looms and production of artificial fibre fabrics. But despite the removal of restriction consequent to the new economic policy, the powerloom sector has continued to flourish. This has naturally raised doubts on the credibility of the arguments that restrictions on the expansion in mill sector are the major reason for the growth in the powerloom sector. It was in this context that controversy regarding excise and wage biases in favour of powerloom sector becomes more relevant. Thus the argument such that low wage rates in the powerloom sector compared to mill sector, advantages of prevalent malpractice in avoiding excise duty, diversion of hank yarn to powerloom sector are forwarded.

Mazumdar (1984) suggests that at identical wages, mills are more efficient than powerlooms. Misra (1993) uses somewhat different data set from that of other studies to argue that, in fact, the difference between mill and powerloom favours the mills at pre-tax prices. But when the excise on cloth is added to mills, the balance tilts in favour of powerlooms becuase of the alleged tax evasion by them. But this view has also been disputed. The arguments advanced by Misra and Mazumdar are based on several cost studies of mill and powerloom sectors. It is, however, argued that these databases are not reliable. This is because these studies have taken data from best practice mills and compared it with the data for average powerlooms. It was further argued that though it is true that powerlooms sometimes evaded excise duties but mills were also doing the same. The other argument was that though the wages in powerloom sector were nominally lower but considering the difference in the cost of living between various cities, difference in real wages may not be very high. It is further argued that in actual practice the main benefit like concessional loans and modernisation subsidies were also taken by the mill sector as against powerloom sector who have to borrow money from the money lenders at very high rate in the absence of getting it from financial institutions. Further, the policy package of discouraging small powerlooms from growing beyond a certain size has put major constraint on improvement in technology. Hence, the ability of the powerloom sector to expand rapidly cannot be credited to the policy biases alone in favour of the powerloom sector (T.

Roy 1998b)[1]. It is argued that the rapid growth of powerloom sector and pattern of industrialisation is founded on (1) unlimited supply of low-quality labour, (2) developing system of inter-firm co-ordination, (3) agglomeration based on such systems, and (4) continuous accumulation of capital 'from below", in artisan activities in the past, and in modern small-scale industry and agriculture more recently (Roy, 1998b).

Considering these factors, the success of powerloom sector cannot be linked to policy biases in mill and powerloom weaving sector. But the above scenario is likely to undergo a change, as there is a possibility that the future reforms in garments sectors may encourage the largescale investment in this segment. This may encourage the demand of fabrics in larger lots and hence help in utilising economies of scale for various varieties. In certain segments, where economies of scale are not large enough, demand for smaller lots may continue and hence powerloom sector may remain relatively more competitive in those segments.

These kinds of developments would encourage the competition in mill and powerloom sectors. Therefore, it is important that policy biases against powerloom sector are also removed and it is given similar credit facilities and other concession as available to the mill sector. One of the recent examples of policy biases towards the mill sector is disbursement of Technological Upgradation Fund (TUF). As per policy TUF worth Rs. 25000 crore is to be disbursed in the textile sector in the next five years at an interest rate subsidy of 5 per cent. Whereas financial Institutions like the Industrial Development Bank of India (IDBI), Industrial Finance Corporation of India (IFCI) and Industrial Credit and Investment Corporation of India (ICICI) will be lending about Rs. 17500 crore to medium and large companies, Small

1. However, the fact remains that the rapid expansion of powerloom sector is ascribed to its efficiency in delivering fabrics in small lots to garment producers. The mills on the other hand are unable to enjoy the usual economies of scale because the market demands small lots of differentiated products.

Industries Development Bank of India (SIDBI) the nodal agency for distributing loans to the small scale industries would be lending only Rs. 8000 crore. This is despite the fact that the decentralised sector is the largest producer in the fabrics segments where modernisation is required. It is therefore, necessary that new textile policy should address to these issues.

An attempt has been made in this study to study the sector-wise competitiveness by analysing the performance of various sectors. This is done on the basis of relative and absolute performance of these sectors in domestic and exports markets and considering various constraints under which these sectors have to operate. The ultimate impact of this on scales of economies and technological progress has been discussed in this study. In the weaving sector adequate technological progress could not take place due to lack of competitive environment and irrational excise duty structure. In addition social goals also could not be met to the desired level as fabrics production in handloom sector started declining. This is partially because benefits meant for this sector were actually enjoyed by the powerloom sector.

Impact of MFA literature

The MFA has hindered the exports from developing countries in several ways. Ricardo Faini and Alberto Heimler, have opined that Multi Fibre Arrangement (MFA), has only succeeded in slowing down rather than halting or even reversing the process of shifting comparative advantage in Textiles & Clothing (T&C) towards developing countries. Several other scholars have also tried to evaluate the welfare cost of restrictions by using advanced econometric techniques. Prominent among them were Cline (1987), Goto (1990), and Hertal (1996).

Various studies analysed the impact of restriction on quantity, price as well as choice of quality. These studies were unable to arrive at a clear link between restrictions and lack of quality improvement in textiles when the products were not homogenous. However, it is widely believed that in the case of clothing, restrictions have caused quality improvement in general. In addition it was argued that quota alone does not ensure the automatic flow of exports for the quota holder. There are enough cases of over utilisation and under utilisation of quotas.

Regarding the impact of quota restrictions on qualitative changes, Bedi (2000) found that India's experience is not different from other countries. An attempt is made in this study to analyse India's cost competitiveness vis-a-vis other competitors. The other competitive parameters of textiles and clothing industry *vis-a-vis* other competitors are also analysed. In this regard, India's share of export in major importers of textile and clothing items in the world is worked out. India's comparative position with respect to various parameters such as installed spindles, rotors, shuttles and shuttles looms, raw materials consumption etc. have been analysed.

This study is primarily concerned with analysing the impact of liberalisation policies on the changes in the structure of textile industry. The following sections are devoted to a discussion of New Textile Policies (1985) and their impact on the textile and clothing industry.

New Textile Policy (1985)

The marked decline in the fortunes of textile industry in both modern and handloom sectors till mid eighties forced the policy makers to initiate a new policy frame known as the New Textile Policy (NTP). The policy makers realised that the multiplicity of objectives had inhibited the achievement of the main task of textile industry that is to increase the production of cloth of acceptable quality at reasonable prices to meet the clothing requirement of a growing population. Henceforth, the approach to the textile industry was sought to be guided by this main objective (GOI, 1985). Recognising these problems the new textile policy introduced in 1985 marked a major departure from its earlier policy by emphasising production rather than employment as its main objective.

The NTP (1985) was introduced in the background of following policy environment.

- Inflexibility in fibre use for mill sector. Mills were allowed to use cotton-dominated fibre and prohibited from using synthetic fibre.
- Restrictions to expand capacity in weaving segment for mills.
- Heavy excise and custom duties on synthetic products.
- Restrictions on free import and export of cotton and cotton yarn.

With the introduction of NTP (1985), several of above restrictions were removed. NTP (1985) included several measures to preserve the handloom sector. These included modernisation measures for handlooms, increase in spinning in khadi sector, ensuring yarn availability at reasonable prices, encouraging production of mixed and blended fabrics in handloom sector, promoting marketing facilities and finally introduction of contributory thrift fund for the workers. Another important component of NTP was opening of export windows for cotton yarn and other manufacturing. The proposed restructuring of the textile industry in the NTP included measures to provide fuller flexibility in the fibre-use and pragmatic policies to increase competition and promote healthy growth in the industry. These were undoubtedly meant for the growth in mill sector. Thus, a Textile Modernisation Fund, soft loan scheme of the Industrial Development Bank of India (IDBI) and Rehabilitation Fund for workers (*i.e.* to facilitate easing out of the workers by mills) was envisaged.

The NTP was criticised on the ground that it failed to meet the social objectives. It was felt that the policy would prove detrimental to the interests of vulnerable and disadvantaged social groups involved in handloom weaving. It was further argued that the policy failed to take into account the specific problems faced by different sectors like the mill, powerloom and handloom sectors. Some scholars argued that it was only a sectoral understanding that could enable one to appreciate the relevant advantages or disadvantages individual sectors have in textile production and marketing. Any attempt to view the textile industry in terms of the process, it was argued, would not only overlook or ignore the specificities of each of the sectors determined by the requirement of raw materials and capital, employment structure, labour conditions, production and marketing structure and consumer demand pattern, but would in fact tend to treat all the sectors to be equal in their ability to compete in the market at various stages of production (T. Roy, 1996).

The NTP introduced in 1985 had a far-reaching effect on export competitiveness and growth of domestic demand, especially on synthetic products and employment in hanloom sector. The immediate effect was modernisation of spinning industry. The result was that an industry notorious for inefficiency was allowed to re-equip itself to sustain and enhance competitiveness and began to play a key role in exports and export-led industrial growth.

Thus, increasingly from the late 1980s, new capacity was coming up in units that were quite different from their predecessors. In 1987, most units, even the larger ones, had only plain looms. In 1990, Abid Hussain Committee observed that a good number of automatic looms, like the Laxmi-Ruti, had become increasingly popular in the Indian market. Powerlooms and smaller composite mills were the main users of the Ruti looms (India, 1990).

The policies introduced as a consequence of NTP resulted in large increases in exports. The major consequence of opening export window for yarn was rise in yarn price with large fluctuations. Contrary to the promise of NTP to provide yarn to handlooms at reasonable prices, the effect was just the opposite. The Abid Hussain Committee found out that one of the major reasons for decline of handloom sector lay in the failure of government to enforce hank yarn obligations on the spinning mills. The NTP was responsible for an unprecedented crisis in the handloom sector. There was a sharp decline in handloom fabrics and large-scale displacements of weavers driving many of them to the brink of starvation. Central to the handloom crises was the scarcity and steep rise in market prices for cotton yarn. The mills failed to honour the commitment of providing fifty per cent of their total marketable yarn or forty per cent of their total production to handloom sector. In fact, the availability of handloom sector had not been 40 per cent of the total spun yarn as suggested by Abid Hussain Committee but only about 22 to 24 per cent (India, 1990). To add to the scarcity of yarn availability, exports rose rapidly from 40 million kilograms in 1987-88 to 94 million kilograms in 1990-91. Secondly, a substantial quantity of hank yarn was diverted to the powerloom sector. Thirdly, handloom sector was not provided yarn of specific count needed by them. This mismatch left both of them dissatisfied. To add to the problem the main export was in 20 to 40 counts needed for the handloom sector.

As stated earlier, the main benefits, of NTP were increase in exports, especially of cotton yarn, modernisation of spinning industry and increase in the share of synthetic fibres both in the domestic market and in exports. By 1990, the industry had regained its pre-eminence in India's exports. Despite that growth, India's share in world textile and clothing was very small at the end of 1999-2000.

Economic Reforms 1991

India undertook a package of structural reforms and enconomic liberalisation in 1991. The main aim of these policy changes was to integrate the Indian economy with world economy. With the macro economic reforms, many of the controls were lifted; tariffs were drastically reduced particularly on capital goods. Although the protection to consumer goods industry continued, the level of protection significantly reduced and most of the items were freed from quantitative restrictions. Further, even though export subsidies were withdrawn, the steep devaluation of the rupee made exports of manufactured goods highly competitive and profitable. In textile industry, rapid restructuring started even before 90's *i.e.* during 1985 with the introduction of new textile policy.

The reduction of custom duties on synthetic intermediate products and capital goods, and liberalisation of trade during the nineties, led to increase in imports and rise of production of synthetic products and modernisation of sectors especially spinning. India's textiles and clothing share in world textiles and clothing trade was low at 2.23 per cent during 1990. It picked up somewhat during the nineties. The exports of Textiles/Clothing during 1997-98 aggregated to 10.37 billion (excluding exorts of Jute, Coir Handicrafts items), which constitute 31.07 per cent of country's exports. India's share in world exports was 3.09 per cent during 1997-98 in value terms. (World Trade Organisation, 1996).

The textile sector witnessed maximum growth in yarn exports. Yarn exports rose sharply from 95 million kilograms in 1991 to 555 million kilograms in 1999-2000. Since, the yarn of less than 40 count constitutes a major portion of exports, this resulted in very high domestic prices for the handloom weavers. This is turn has resulted in a major set back and crisis for the handloom industry. Further, weaving in modern textile industry is still being discriminated through various means. This has hampered the modernisation of weaving units despite lowering of custom duties. Irrational excise duty structure further reduced incentives for modernisation. The social cost of transition is being paid by millions of poor weavers in the handloom industry, while the powerloom sector is growing. The benefits of excise relief on the hank yarn are ultimately enjoyed by the powerloom sector. It is being argued that a major share of hank yarn is ultimately being consumed in the powerloom sector.

To sum up, the new textile policy initiated in 1985 and the policy of economic liberalisation initiated in 1991 have had a profound affect on the textile industry in India. On the one hand the result is rapid modernisation of spinning industry and on the other hand it stepped up a serious process of rationalisation in the entire sector. In the organised textile sector, the process of restructuring initiated during the eighties resulted in large-scale redundancy in the textile sector and un-employment of lakhs of workers in textile industry of Ahmedabad, Kanpur and other textile centres.

Scope of the Study and Methodology

This study makes an attempt to work out the state of textile and clothing industry during the period 1983 and 1988-89 to 1999-2000. The main objective of this study is to find the impact of liberalisation policies on the changes in structure of textiles and clothing industry during the two phases of liberation and prospects of textiles and clothing industry by 2005-06 and 2010-11.

- First Phase of Liberalisation 1983 to 1990-91, to capture the impact of New Textile Policy (NTP, 1985) introduced during 1985. The data for most of variables for the period 1984 to 1987-88 is not available, the year 1983 is taken as first year of the study.
- Second Phase of Liberalisation 1990-91 to 1999-2000, to capture the impact of Economic Reforms introduced during 1991.
- To project the alternative possible future scenarios of the Textiles and Clothing industry by the year 2005-06 and 2010-11 (after the MFA phase out).

The methodology adopted in this study is discussed in the following sections.

Spinning Sector

In spinning sector, to work out production, productivity and technology changes, the methodology used is different than the traditional production function approach. The prime reason for not pursuing traditional production function approach is the lack of required detailed data on spinning sector for all India, practical difficulties in measurement of various variables specially fixed capital and econometric problem and conflicting results obtained from cross and time series analysis. Thus a methodology is used in this study, which effectively, assumes count-wise constant returns to scale overtime but allows for changes in count-composition, seems to be more realistic than a simple production function approach. To work out the productivity by this method, it was important to work out the change in count composition in various varieties such as hank, cone, hosiery, carded and combed. This is worked out with the help of particular region data on count composition for various varieties such as hank, cone and hosiery and adjusted it wherever necessary with all India data on fibre-wise count range-wise composition.

The method used here takes into consideration various kinds of actual product mix and count combination, which could be produced in the given technology. The alternative productions for various count combinations are derived from ATIRA technical data. By using this technique, one could find out the minimum number of spindles required at modern technology to produce the required yarn for various count ranges. An attempt has been made to work out the number of spindles actually used at full capacity utilisation and how many extra spindles are used compared to minimum required at the latest technology. This is required due to technology gap and difference in age composition of existing spindles.

An attempt is made in this study to estimate the difference between actual production and what is achievable at latest available technology. Four main causes are generally responsible for low productivity. These are (1) Closure (2) Idle but not declared closed (3) Under-utilisation of working spindles and (4) Age composition. The method used is to first work out production frontier for the total installed spindles in the industry assuming their productivity at the latest available technology and 100 per cent capacity utilisation.

Weaving Sector

There exist several studies on the changes in structure of textile and clothing industry in India. But the exact state of structure of this important industry in India is still very vague due to the non-availability of any reliable data on the unorganised sectors such as powerloom, handloom and garment industry.

In fact several studies tried to work out the quantum of production in garment industry, but no firm data is available so far. The Textile Commissioner's estimates of production of fabrics in the handloom, powerloom and hosiery sector derived on the basis of delivery of yarn to various sectors do not add up to their consumption estimates. The Textile Committee data on domestic consumption (household and non-household sector) and TEXPROCIL data on exports do no add up to official estimates on production of fabrics. The simple economic logic suggests that demand and supply should broadly match in the long run. Stocks cannot just go on accumulating. Why should one go on producing a product, which has no demand in the market?

Thus unless the data on present state of textiles and clothing industry is not reliable, any estimates about the future projections is meaningless. This study thus makes an attempt to work out the state of textile and clothing industry during the period 1983 and 1988-89 to 1999-2000. For working out the variety-wise production of fabrics in various sectors, the count composition data in various varieties is used using SITRA data. In this study, an attempt has been made to develop the conversion rates for various count ranges based on various variety-wise parameters of fabrics available from the ATIRA (1984). The data in ATIRA report is collected through questionnaire. The ATIRA has published details about various parameters (like reeds, picks and ply) for various varieties of fabrics produced in 33 mills. Based on these parameters, the wight of fabrics for each variety could be worked out. To work out the conversion rate for various count ranges for the mill sector, the wightage to each variety is given according to count composition of yarn consumed in the country in the mill sector. The conversion rates for other sectors in various count ranges are worked out on the basis of conversion rates derived in the mill sector. The wighted average conversion rates for total fabrics for various years differ in our analysis depending upon the share of various sectors as well as count range-wise proportion in each sector. The count range-wise proportion of yarn consumed in different sectors is worked on the basis of variety-wise total consumption and their count range-wise production.

These conversion rates are used to work out the production of fabrics in the country in various varieties. The changes in production of fabrics in various varieties and count composition are discussed in detail. The count composition-wise data on production of fabrics was only available for the mill sector so far. Thus this study has significant contribution in working out the changes in quality of fabrics in various sectors.

Comparison of Estimates of Consumption & Production of Fabrics

Having derived the production estimates of cotton, blended and synthetic fibres, it is important to analysis the changes in consumption pattern for Indian textiles and clothing products. The fabric produced in the country has to be ultimately used in some final forms such as fabrics, made-ups and garments. The fabric produced is either exported or consumed domestically or kept in stock to be sold during the next period.

The estimates of fabrics equivalent exports are worked out by adding exports in the form of fabrics, made-ups and garments both for cotton and synthetic products. The exports in these products are added by first converting to a common units say square metre from pieces, rupees etc. by applying conversion rates. As it is important to link up the requirements at various production stages and to make projections, the yarn and fibre equivalent exports is worked out in terms of textiles and clothing products. By subtracting the fabrics, yarn and fibre equivalent exports of textiles and clothing products from production plus imports, the fabrics, yarn and fibre equivalent domestic availability is worked out both for cotton and synthetic products separately. The fact that the estimates of domestic availability of cotton and synthetic fabrics derived by us are not much different than the estimates of household and non-household consumption given by the Textile

Commissioner, these should give credence to the methodology used in this study.

Hank Yarn Diversion to Powerloom Sector

The similarities at aggregate level hides wide discrepancies at sectoral and fibre level. Some inherent draw-backs in the survey, like short memory of consumers, communication and other errors, wrong identification of fabrics are expected. However, as handloom fabrics are easily distinguishable, the consumers should not find many problems in identifying handloom sector fabrics. The mismatch between demand (exports plus households and non-household consumption) and production of cotton handloom fabrics derived on the basis of delivery of hank yarn to decentralised sector could be mainly attributed to diversion of hank yarn to the powerloom sector. The hank yarn is meant to be consumed in the handloom sector. Based on this analysis and conversion rate of handloom fabrics from yarn, an attempt has been made in this study to work out the extent of diversion of cotton hank yarn to the powerloom sector. On the basis of these demand estimates, the sector-wise revised estimates of production of fabrics are re-worked from the earlier estimates of sector-wise production of fabrics derived in this study on the basis of delivery of yarn to various sectors.

The obligations on the mills to produce a certain minimum percentage of their production (including exports) in hank form and shortage of domestic availability of spun yarn (especially cotton yarn) could be mainly attributed to the rise in diversion of hank yarn to powerloom sector. The modernisation of spinning industry has resulted in large increases in the exports of yarn (specially of cotton yarn) and low of domestic availability. This led to overall rise in cotton prices and large-scale diversion of hank yarn to powerloom sector during 1990's. Under these circumstances, it becomes very difficult for the handloom sector to co-exist along with the powerloom and the mill sectors. The cost of production is high in handloom sector, the advantage of handloom is linked to certain type of yarn or certain type of loom-woven design. Thus the survival of handlooms depends upon the segmented market in these varieties as well as ensured supply of related inputs.

Estimates of Value Added & Employment in Textiles & Clothing Sector

An attempt has been made in this study to rework the total value added in textiles and clothing sector and employment in various sectors on the basis of these revised estimates of sector-wise production of fabrics. The technical detail regarding workers employed per loom in various sectors per unit of production of fabrics are available from existing literature. Similarly, the data related to ex-factory prices for various sectors and share of value added in output of various sectors is available from existing literature.

Latest Developments in Textile Policy

The New Textile Policy (hereafter NTP 2000) was announced on November 2, 2000. The most significant feature of the policy is that garments have been dereserved from the small-scale sector. The persistence of reservation of garments for the small-scale sector was one of the main reasons for the failure of a generally favourable policy environment to induce modernisation in not just the garment segment, but also in weaving. In the domestic market, fabric is mainly demanded in smaller lots by small garment units spread all over the country. The production of fabric in smaller lots is not very efficient for the mill sector, especially for units operating with modern technology such as air jet or shuttle less looms, both of which operate at very high speeds. As was expected as a follow-up step after dereservation, the finance bill 2001 introduced MODVAT from the fibre to the garment stage with a 16 per cent excise duty. However, certain exemptions in the form of excise concession for hank yarn and for manual dyeing break the chain in MODVAT process. Similarly, the duty at the processing stage by independent processing houses for the small units is shifted away from ad valorem to specific duties. Thus the purpose of introducing MODVAT has been diluted.

The Finance Bill 2001 reduces the gap between excise duty

on grey and dyed fabrics. The escalating duty on additional value added at dyed stage discourage investment in large dyeing units. Another problem area, which was not addressed in the finance bill, is the relatively high excise and custom duty on synthetic yarn compared to cotton yarn.

The industry is set to face a dramatically new environment in coming years after the MFA phase out. The government has postponed the lifting of import restrictions to buy time for the industry. This should be used to push through a very quick process of restructuring for improved efficiency for improved performance latter.

Projections Regarding World, South Asia and India's Trade

The analysis regarding India's future export potential is based on Textiles Outlook International (Economic Intelligence Unit) analysis regarding expected trade of World and South Asia. This is based on the expected supply of raw material, shipment of different type of machinery in recent past, and expected demand pattern in different countries/regions. The recent changes in pattern are also taken into account. However, certain modifications including data updating have been made. Textile Outlook International (TOI) predictions for textiles and clothing scenario by 2005 are based on Food and Agriculture Organization (1992) data. The data modifications in TOI analysis are based on the following facts. The ICAC data showed higher cotton yarn exports compared to Food and Agriculture Organization (FAO) data, while the cotton fabrics exports are lower in case of ICAC. We have made the adjustment in FAO cotton trade statistics, as data published by Export Promotion Councils and various countries match with ICAC statistics. The other modifications such as changes in composition of items have been made on the basis of latest pattern and expected trend in new economic environment. The base year for making projections have been shifted to 1999-2000 instead of 1995 (as in case of TOI analysis) on the basis of latest available information at the time of projections. this was important as export of cotton yarn from India increased at a very fast rate during 1996-97.

While Textiles Outlook International (TOI) makes estimates for South Asia as a whole, we have tried to disaggregate these for India by using derived data from the FAO. The projections in this study are not only for net imports and exports from various countries/regions, but for gross imports and exports as well. In this study, two alternatives are predicted regarding future trade for two periods 1999-2000 to 2005-06 and 1999-2000 to 2010-11. The second alternative is based on the assumption that slow down in growth of per capita consumption of various developed and other countries may not take place as assumed in TOI analysis despite high-rise in demand from Eastern European Countries. The export potential in quantity and value terms for cotton and synthetic items is worked out by 2005-06 and 2010-11.

Projections Regarding Domestic Consumption of Textiles and Clothing Products in India

The projections regarding future domestic demand for India in this study are based on fitting of two equations for the period 1975 to 1998-99. The dependant variables taken in these equations are per capita domestic availability of cotton and per capita synthetic fabrics domestic availability. The data for domestic availability of fabrics is worked out for the year 1983 and period 1988-89 to 1998-99. For other years, the estimates about domestic availability of fabrics are worked out by using conversion rate of yarn for fabrics derived in this study for the nearest period to the year for which approximations are to be made. These conversion rates are used to update the available data regarding domestic availability from other sources. The independent variables taken were wholesale prices index of the product, wholesale price index of substitute prices, relative quality of cotton and synthetic products and per capita income. Based on these parameters, the total domestic demand of fabrics is worked out for two periods 1999-2000 to 2005-06 and 1999-2000 to 2010-11 on the basis of expected increase in GDP and relative prices of cotton and synthetic products. The two alternatives are worked out on the basis of growth in GDP in the range of 6 to 8 per cent per annum.

Total Demand of Fibre, Yarn, Additional Spindles, Fabrics, Made-ups, and Garments by year 2010-11

Thus by adding exports and domestic demand, the demand of fabrics is worked out, which is segregated into demand of fabrics, made-up and garments. The demand for yarn and fibre could also be worked out from it by using the conversion rates. In our projection regarding India, we have also projected the requirement of cotton, other fibres/filaments, yarn, spun yarn, fabrics, made-ups, garment and additional spindles required.

We have also analysed the constraints from supply angle as well. The main weaknesses in India's textiles and clothing related with Operation, Structure and Guidelines are listed, which need to be addressed to meet the possible challenges, in the new economic environment. The study analyses the requirement of the spindles and various fibres by year 2005-06 and 2010-11 to meet the demand. The future requirement of looms is not predicted due to numerous complexities depending upon the future policies regarding handloom, powerloom and mill sectors. Moreover, the base line estimates about looms and their age composition are not available.

Chapter Scheme

This study is divided into six chapters. Chapter one, after a brief introduction, gives detail of methodology. One of the major areas of restructuring is modernisation of spinning industry. The second chapter deals with the spinning industry with a view to working out the productivity in spindles, which could be used for estimating future requirement of spindles. The chapter goes into the various detail of spinning industry in order to work out productivity. The method used is not the conventional one of production function approach, but the optimal productivity based on the latest available technology during 1996-97. An attempt has been made to analyse the various causes that constrain the industry to operate below the production frontier. The age composition of spindles is worked out by adding the gross spindles installed each year. The numbers of replaced spindles for various years are worked out by subtracting yearly gross installed spindles from the addition in spinning capacity over the period of time. The replacement ratio over time is then worked out by dividing the replaced spindles with the total number of gross added spindles. An attempt is then made to find the productivity of working spindles. The causes of low productivity are then identified in terms of closure and under utilisation of installed spindles and age composition of working spindles.

In addition to spinning, the other part of textile industry is weaving. The third chapter deals with the structural changes that have taken place in fabrics. There seems to be a serious problem with available official data on production of fabrics since availability of fabrics (production minus exports) does not match with the consumption data compiled by the Textile Commissioner. Hence, there is a need to rework the estimates about production of fabrics by taking appropriate yarn to fabric conversion rates. An attempt is then made in chapter 3 to rework the production figures for sector and fibre-wise production of fabrics.

The fabric produced is either exported in the form of fabrics, made-ups and garments or consumed domestically. In fourth chapter, an attempt is made to work out the domestic availability of fabrics after taking out direct and indirect net exports of fabrics. It is significant to note that the estimates of domestic availability derived in this way are consistent with the estimates of domestic consumption in household and non-household sectors. A general perception is that a great deal of hank yarn is actually being diverted to the powerloom sector. An attempt has also been made to quantify the extent of this diversion. On the basis of gap between demand and supply figures of fabrics and conversion rates of yarn to fabrics, diversion of hank yarn to powerloom sector is worked out. The revised sector-wise estimates of production of fabric are worked out on the basis of diversion of hank yarn. The fibre-wise and item-wise composition in domestic and export market is analysed for the year 1983 and for periods 1988-89 to 1999-2000. The competitiveness of various sectors on the basis of their export and domestic share are worked out considering various sectors constraints under which these sectors are operating. Similarly, an attempt has been made to find out the total employment and value added on the basis of sector-wise revised estimates of fabric production.

In Chapter 5, the impact of trade restrictions on qualitative changes in the exports of developing countries to developed countries was worked out. It has been found that the impact of restrictions on textiles exports from developing countries are not clear, while the quality of product in general improved in the case of clothing. The results are not different in the case of India's exports of textiles and clothing products. An attempt is made to work out the projection of demand and supply of various textile and clothing items by year 2005-06 and year 2010-11. The projection about India's textile and clothing products cannot be made in isolation from the world market. India's export can only increase if, there is demand in world market and India is competitive.

It is in this context that India's present position in textile industry relative to major importing and exporting countries in the world is analysed. An attmept has been made to find out how the present Multi Fibre Agreement (MFA) system is hindering India's export potential. The preferential treatment given by developed countries to several of its regional and other allies along with high trade barriers on import from developing countries are affecting the growth in exports from developing countries. The impact of preferential treatment would automatically diminish, as the barriers of trade on the developing countries will be lowered with the MFA phase out. In that case, the competitiveness of various stages of production such as yarn, fabrics and garment has been analysed. An attempt has also been made to identify some of the other constraints to rapid growth of textile and clothing exports. The future growth rate in textile and clothing industry would depend on its capacity to modernise and withstand external competition.

Domestic demands for India have been projected till 2005-06 and 2010-11 by working out price and income elasticities for fabrics consumption. From the total domestic estimates (exports and domestic demand), the requirements for fibre, yarn, spun yarn, fabrics, made-ups, garments and spindles have been worked out. These have been compared with the possible supply constraints. The main gaps between demand and supply would appear in the availability of raw material. But in the matter of spindles and weaving, there is clear need for appropriate restructuring. Having identified the gaps in capacity availability in raw materials and to some extent in spindles, the sixth chapter contains a brief summary of the main findings and policy measures needed for bringing about restructuring of India's cotton textile industry.

2

Production, Productivity and Technological Changes in Indian Spinning Sector

This chapter deals with structural changes in production of spun yarn, age composition of installed spindles and its impact on productivity that has taken place after the introduction of New Textile Policy (NTP) 1985. The objective is to find the impact of change in technology (age composition of spindles) on the growth in productivity of working spindles so that the future requirement of spindles could be worked out in the country.

Review of the Literature on Measurement of Productivity

Most of existing literature works out the productivity of spindles by simple division of production in quantity terms with the number of spindles required. This method ignores the fact that productivity of spindles for various counts of yarn differ widely. The other methods commonly used to work out Total Factor Productivity (TFP) are to see the impact of change in bundle of inputs on production. It is very difficult to add up heterogeneous kinds of inputs by assuming aggregate production function. Thus for calculation purpose the constant returns to scale and perfect competition is assumed so that the total production gets exhausted and failure of any of these assumption lead to biased estimates. Thus, TFPG is the difference between the growth of output and the growth of inputs (suitably weighted). The increase in productivity in the short run can be achieved by improving managerial and organisational competence and in the long run through technical progress (modernisation).

$$TFPG = Gq - (S1 \times G1 + Sk \times Gk + Sm \times Gm)$$

$$S1 + Sk + Sm = 1$$

TFPG is the growth rate of TFP, Gq, Gl, Gk and Gm is the growth rate of output, labour, capital and inputs respectively and Sq, Sl and Sm are the income shares of three inputs in gross output. The share of labour for each year is calculated by dividing total emolument by gross value added/ output (both at current prices) and then period average is taken.

The other method commonly used to measure productivity is production function approach using Cobb Douglas, CES or Translog production functions. The production function approach could capture five parameters of technological change such as output elasticities of labour and capital, exogenous variable, economies of scale and modernisation. In this method, the dependent variable taken is value of output or value added and independent variables taken are fixed capital cost, labour and other inputs. The Cobb-Douglas production function assumes unitary elasticity of substitution, while CES production function assumes constant elasticity of substitution. Translog production function is least restrictive. All parameters of technology could be worked out by using Translog function and it even take care of varying elasticity of substitution, which changes proportionally to the capital intensity. Thus the method seems to be theoretically very sound.

$$F(q) = aL + bK + cM + dL^2 + eK^2 + fM^2 + gLK + hKM + iML$$
$$+ jt + kt^2 + lLt + mKt + nMt$$

The productivity growth is worked out by t coefficient. However, there are lots of problems involved in measuring technology progress. The correlation between the various variables and whether the variable can be treated as exogenous or pre-determined are the few among these. Various measures could be taken to deal with these problems, but the solution is easier said than done. The other major problem involved is of measuring one or more variable. Despite considerable research to measure capital stock, there exist the major lacuna in measuring the extent of depreciation in each year and base year capital stock. The choice of deflator and base year price is another major problem, which can cause the overestimation or underestimation of results to a considerable extent.[1]

The other problems involved in these methodologies include decision regarding dropping or/and adding of one or more variables. Any wrong decision in this regard could led to the biased in estimates of other parameters and it is

---

1. There are several examples in this regard. Various examples could be cited in this regard. Goldar (2000), points out that a shift in the base year of price indices of output and materials say from 1970-71 to 1981-82, may lead to a substantial change in the estimated growth rate of productivity. This point comes out clearly from a comparison of the TFP indices presented in their 1994 and 1995 papers. For the period 1980-81 to 1988-89, one set of estimates (which use price indices with 1970-71 base) give a growth rate of TFP of —0.11 per cent per annum, while the other set of estimates (which use price indices with 1981-82 base) give a growth rate of 3.91 per cent per annum. This means, while in one case the growth rate of TFP is found to have declined sharply in the 1980s, in other case there is an increase. Since the construction of intermediate input price index requires taking a weighted average of price indices of different input-output sectors, the choice of base year of the price indices affects also the results of productivity estimates based on three-input model. So many questions could be raised about the use of appropriate price index for various variables and about the base level. No price index or base level is perfectly capturing the appropriate weight of various inputs. Goldar (2000) say, this probably explains why the estimates of productivity growth obtained in the study of Trivedi, Prakash and Sinate differ so much from the estimates reported in the studies of Rao, and Pradhan and Barik. These are not the only cases in sight. The whole lot of literature is available on the difference in productivity estimates and each author claims its results and methodology to be more practical and better than the other ones under existing constraints.

difficult to say which is appropriate fit to measure productivity.[2]

Moreover, the data availability is another problem. In the absence of data on the capacity utilization (even in Annual Survey of Industries, which is the major source for detailed register sector data on various variables for Indian Industry), one is not sure what one is trying to measure in the name of productivity from data on material, labour and capital. The problem get aggravated due to measurement problem of capital stock at constant prices even by using perpetually inventory method after appropriately adjusting for accumulation and depreciation of capital over the period of time. In the stock of capital, even those firms data is included, which are mostly or completely lying closed since past thirty or even more years. These mills are not contributing at all or much in the production process.

The objective in this study is to work out the productivity growth in spinning industry caused by change in technology change so that future requirement of spindles could be worked

2. Srivastava (2001) used various possible alternatives to measure productivity, which are based on different methodologies and assumptions. The results derived regarding productivity growth from each method were very different, as is obvious with different assumption regarding scale economies, neutral or non-neutral technology progress or dropping time variable or without any major restrictions. The conclusion drawn regarding technical parameters for each industry were based on the robust results drawn from all the methods. Thus, the exact number regarding growth in productivity over the period of time could not be confirmed, despite using very sophisticated production functions and spending considerable time on the exercise. The only conclusion the various studies including of Srivastva could made with some approximation was the decline in growth of productivity in various manufacturing sectors during nineties compared to eighties. About the textile sector, there were mixed evidence in this regard. The conflicting results obtained from various sophisticated econometric approaches and lack of confirmation regarding best method in existing circumstances is the reason that various studies preferred to adopt the traditional method of Growth Accounting to measure productivity.

out from the demand estimates of spun yarn. The data on Indian spinning sector is not available separately and the results derived by various scholars using ASI data on factory sector cover the entire organised textile sector. In addition to above limitations, another lacuna in deriving results based on ASI (a major source of industrial sector-wise data on all India basis) are that the productions of various non-textile goods are also included in textile industry, while production of various textile goods is excluded from the textile sector. This is because a firm may be producing various products but is placed in a industry based on its dominant product with highest share in production value.

In this kind of situation, the productivity analysis derived in various studies based on the entire organised textile sector gives picture of some complex structure and hence cannot be compared with the results derived in this study in strict sense. In textile sector, the spinning sector is modernising at a very rapid rate, while the modernisation in weaving segment is yet to take place at a desired level. Moreover, the structure of textile sector is very heterogeneous and include cotton, non-cotton spun, blended or filament products.

Initially, an attempt is also made in this study to work out parameters of technological change in spinning sector by fitting a Cobb-Douglas production function for time series (See Appendix 2.1). The results thus obtained in this study are similar to the one obtained in other studies, where generally economics of scale are one Mitra (1999) (Appendix 2.2). It has been worked out that economics of scale are close to one (0.96) in case the regression is run along with the time variable and varies from 0.90 to 0.92 in the case time variable is replaced with the modernisation variable.

An attempt is then made to fit the Cobb-Douglas production function for cross section data using count-wise data. Count of yarn tells us the length of yarn per kilogram of yarn. Thinner the yarn, finer it is and longer the length per kilogram of yarn. Thicker the yarn, coarser it is and shorter the length per kilogram of yarn. By fitting a production function on cross section data, it has been observed that the constant returns to scale are not applicable. There exists high economic of scale (1.36 to 1.41) for the cross section data, in case constant returns to scale assumption is relaxed. The scale economies explain the increasingly shift in production towards coarser counts as capital and labour requirements per unit of output are low for coarser counts (Appendix 2.3).

Thus the results obtained by using cross section and time series data are different, which raises doubt about the derived estimates based on the production function approach. Thus an attempt is made in this study to find the production, technological change and its impact on productivity in spinning industry by using count-composition wise analysis. The prime reason for not pursuing traditional production function approach is the lack of required detailed data on spinning sector for all India, practical difficulties in measurement of various variables and econometric problem and conflicting results obtained from cross and time series data. Thus a methodology is evolved which could be useful to work out the impact of technology change on productivity. It is hoped that the methodology used in this study, which effectively, assumes count-wise constant returns to scale over time but allows for changes in count-composition, is more realistic than a simple production function approach.

Methodology Used

Thus an attempt is made in this study to find the production, technological change and its impact on productivity in spinning industry by using count-composition wise analysis. The change in ratio of production per spindle from one count composition to another is available from SITRA norms. The SITRA norms at various count composition have been evolved by it on the basis of sample survey of various mills over the time and remained more are less similar. These norms are available for each variety and fibre of yarn and the past experience shows the proportions (norms available for earlier years) are not changing over time at various count compositions. Moreover, to produce the spun yarn per spindle at various count/count composition of specific variety a fixed amount of labour[3] and raw material is required[4] for a given technology, which remains same over time. Hence technology progress takes place of Hicks-neutral in spinning industry over the period of time.[5]

The methodology used here is to first estimate the minimum number of homogenous spindles required of latest available technology during the last year for which data is available to produce the various counts of fibre yarns of different varieties such as carded, combed, hank and cone. The production per spindles (for a count say 30s of cotton hosiery yarn) of latest available technology spindle is used to work out production per spindle at various counts/count compositions.[6] Similar procedure could be followed for the labour and input used. This could be expressed in mathematical terms, as given here.

Actual production at Count S_i could be produced with factors of production and inputs

---

3. In actual practice, the labour used may not be exactly same as minimum required in several mills due to inefficiencies or labour laws. However, to produce a given count composition of spun yarn per spindle, a fixed amount of labour (skilled and unskilled) is required and cannot be substituted with any other factors of production. Thus the increasing use of labour than minimum don't have any impact on capital productivity.
4. This does not mean that the given count composition of cotton or other spun yarn can only be produced by given variety of cotton or fibre. However, the fact remains that most of mills do not deviate from using the fixed staple length fibre to produce the given count composition of yarn, unless the given variety of fibre is not available. If it all this takes place it is not common and is short-term phenomena. This is because it is not economical to under spun yarn from given variety of fibre.
5. There were certain other technical changes such as use of rotors for spun yarn production below 20s (20 count). The production per rotor is equivalent to production by 5 spindles at any count of spun yarn produced.
6. Productivity of 30s cotton hosiery yarn is 160 Gm/Spinde/Shift as per experts opinion at latest available technology during 1996-97.

= Total Actual Production at

$$f(K_i L_i M_i) = a_i K_i + b^i L_i + c_i M_i \qquad \text{—(i)}$$

$$\sum_{i=1}^{n} S_i = \sum_{i=1}^{n} a_i K^i i + \sum_{i=1}^{n} b L_i + \sum_{i=1}^{n} c_i M_i \qquad \text{—(ii)}$$

For total production at various count composition, this could be written as given in equation (ii)

Here $a_i + b_i + c_i = 1$. But values of a_i, b_i, and c_i can be different for each i.

By using the above formula, one could work out the total number of spindles, labour and inputs required to produce the spun yarn at various counts of different verities. The final sum of spindles, labour and inputs required would be the sum of spindles, labour and inputs required at various counts of yarn. An attempt is then made to find out how far below the industry is operating by comparing the number of minimum spindles equivalent required with the total number of spindles installed or actually working spindles or spindles working at full capacity. This comparison has been made over the period of time to look at the changes in gap. An attempt has been then made to work out the causes of working below the maximum production potential (the production frontier at the known modern technology) such as age of machinery or under-utilisation of capacity etc.

As already discussed, a given count/count composition of specific variety yarn could only be produced with the given amount of fixed capital (say spindles), labour and inputs and may be represented by a specific point of production function. This does not mean that the substitution between various factors of production is not taking place, it is very much taking place but not at a specific count but to move from one count/count composition to another. The decision about the count composition of various verities of spun yarn to be produced is taken by the firm management on the basis of cost of factors of production, inputs and prices of various products. Thus the impact of managerial efficiency in managing to procure input at low prices or selling at attractive rate or procuring fund at low cost is not captured in this methodology, as the objective is to deal with physical quantity and avoid any biases caused in values due to distortions in prices. This methodology along with traditional production function approach may be helpful in separating out the impact of technical co-efficient from managerial efficiency. In the traditional production function approach, the mixing of issues (measurement of Managerial and Technical Efficiency) is leading to errors in measuring both technical productivity and managerial efficiency.

The methodology used in this study make it convenient to sum up the various counts of yarn, which are based on technical coefficients and hence the biasedness caused due prices not representing true value are avoided. Thus the adding problem of various heterogeneous factors of production has been solved, without bringing in any price factors or deflator, which could cause error in estimations.[7]

The methodology used in this study could also be explained by the drawing a figure. The formula *(ii)* could represent the specific count composition or a point on a given Isoquant or Production Possibility Frontier (PPF) (Figures 2.1 and 2.2). This is represented in following figures.

The spindles required at technology t to produce the given count composition and variety and fibre of yarn are then compared with actual spindles installed. This approach is similar to the Malmquist Approach Codli (1999). In the formula this could be expressed as

$$D_0^t (X, Y) = 1/Di^t (X, Y) = \text{minimum } \{\lambda : (Y/\lambda, X) \in P^t (X)\}$$

7. Moreover, this methodology does not take any assumption regarding elasticity of labour or capital output, as in the case of production function or Translog methods. This method takes into account the actual elasticity at various counts of yarn. The elasticity of substitution of labour and capital could be different at various points of capital intensity and need not necessarily change proportional to capital intensity as in the case of Translog production function. This is another advantage of using this methodology as against the production function approach.

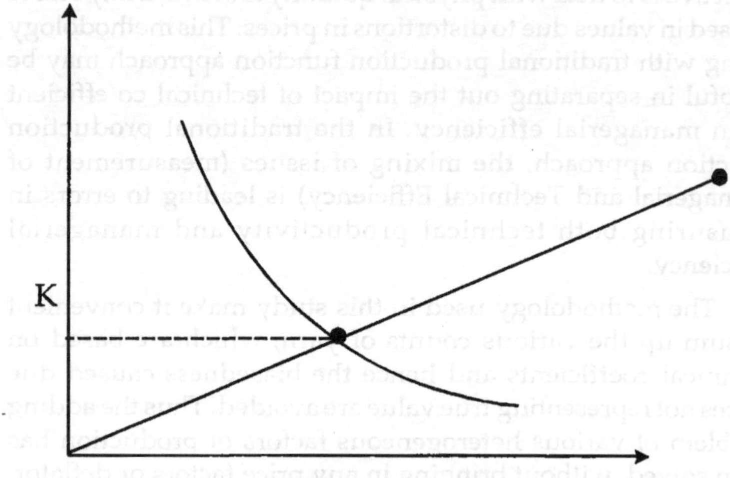

Figure 2.1. Isoquant.

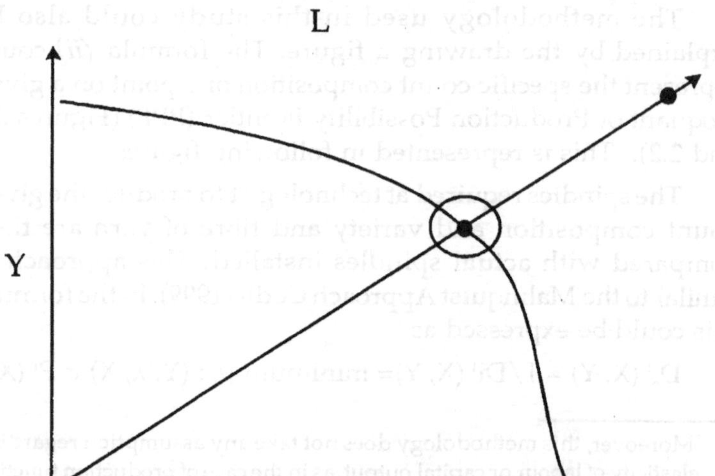

Figure 2.2. Production Possibility Frontier.

Output distance function for given output vector, Y, and input vector X → K

$$\frac{1}{\lambda} = \frac{\text{Actual Production at given resources or working}}{\text{Production with similar resources at technology t.}}$$

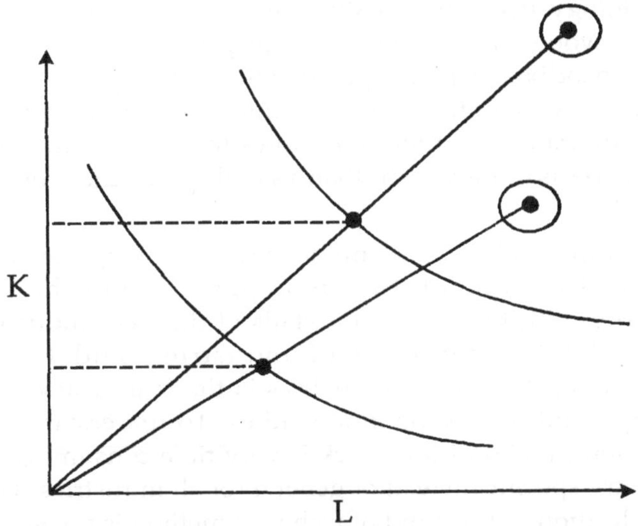

Figure 2.3. Hicks Attential Technical Progress Isoquants.

The same procedure is repeated for over time. Thus the gaps between the working or actual spindles installed of actual technology used are compared with the latest available technology during 1996 for each year (Figure 2.3). The gap could be due to low utilisation of working or installed spindles or technology gap between installed spindles and spindles of latest available technology. To work out the gap due to technology difference, the working spindles at 100 per cent capacity utilisation are worked out.

For working out the age composition of installed spindles, gross capacity expansions are worked out over the period of time. The replacement rate of old machinery has also been worked out by subtracting the net addition in installed capacity from the gross installed spindles.

Attempt is made to see the practical relevance of assumption in the methodology used in this study, which assumes count-wise constant returns to scale over time but allows for changes in count-composition in Appendix 2.4. Similarly an attempt is made to find the usefulness of methodology used in this study in the case of technology progress would not have been taken place of Hicks neutral type (Appendix 2.5). It is hoped that the methodology used in this study, which effectively, assumes count-wise constant returns to scale over time but allows for changes in count-composition, is more realistic than a simple production function approach.

This methodology seems to have advantage over the traditional production function approach, but the non-familiarity with the technical details of different industries, non-availability for most of industries, and lack of generalisation for all the industries is the main cause of its non-applicability in economic studies. To understand it in production function framework is very time consuming and is industry specific instead of general for all industries. Thus, the application of this kind of technical method is not sighted in economic studies.

The following database is used for the analysis.

Data Sources and Approach

The data on count range-wise and fibre-wise yarn production and spindles installed are available from various issues of the Compendium of Textile Statistics issued by the Office of the Office of the Textile Commissioner, GOI, Mumbai and Annual Report of the Ministry of Textiles, The Indian Cotton Mills Federation (ICMF) *Handbook of Statistics on Cotton Textile Industry* and its *Annual Report.*

The statistics on gross new spindles added (expansion plus replacement) and working capacity and average hours worked per year are obtained from International Textiles Manufacturing Federation (ITMF), Zurich. Production norms for different counts and various fibres are obtained from publication of South Indian Textile Research Association (SITRA). Data to work out count composition within count ranges is used from SIMA reports.

Spun yarn is produced after spinning the raw fibre, filament yarn excepted. Filament yarn is not spun and is directly used or used after some twists as input for weaving fabrics or other textile goods. There are various systems on which spun yarn could be produced. One is cotton spinning system and other is worsted spinning system. Silk yarn is spun on a different kind of spinning system. The wool yarn and wool/acrylic blends are generally spun on worsted system. However, the dominating system of spinning in India and in most parts of the world is the cotton spinning system. This study deals with production, productivity and technology changes in cotton spinning system. Thus the spun yarn produced on the cotton-spun system is hereafter referred as spun yarn.

The detailed analysis deals with the organised sector till the period 1996-97 as detailed data for the small scale sector on variables such as working spindles and hours worked are not available. The organised sector is the dominating sector in the spinning industry. The production by small-scale sector would be discussed later to have an overall view. The total spun yarn produced in the organised mill sector amounted to 2688 million kilograms during 1996-97. The detailed analysis is taken upto the period 1996-97 as official procedure to report the data has been changed after that year. The official data now are not reporting spun yarn production data separately for the organised and SSI spinning units separately for various count ranges. As discussed above, the dropping of SSI sector from detailed analysis was essential as detailed data for the small scale sector on variables such as working spindles and hours worked are not available. Thus it is making the combined analysis for both the sectors jointly difficult. Thus the analysis for the period 1997-98 to 1999-2000 is dealt separately at the end of the chapter.

The spun yarn (cotton spinning system) can be classified into three broad groups *viz.* cotton yarn, blended yarn and 100% non-cotton yarn. The production per spindles depends upon several factors such as fibre composition, share of various counts in production, and carded to combed share in yarn, the ratio of hosiery yarn to woven yarn etc., age of the machinery and capacity utilisation.

The production per spindle depends upon the count of yarn produced as well as variety of yarn produced in a given technology. This is expressed in the following formula developed by SITRA experts.

Production per Spindle = ((Spindle speed x 1000 x Efficiency)/((Count$^{1.5}$) x (44.4) x (3.14) X Tm))

Efficiency depends upon the time required to change sliber. Efficiency varies from 82 per cent to 95 per cent. Higher the count better the efficiency is.

Here Tm = TPI x (Count)$^{-0.5}$. TPI stands for twist per inch. Thus, Tm depends upon the variety of yarn and count of yarn.[8] The variety of yarn depends upon several parameters such as carded and combed ratio, which itself depends upon hosiery and woven yarn ratio in the total cotton yarn production. The woven yarn combed and carded ratio also differ depending upon whether yarn is meant to be used for exports or in the form of hank or cones or in the mill sector. The self-consumption of yarn in mill sector for fabrics production has higher combed ratio as quality products are mainly produced in the mill sector. In this study, we have taken into account all parameters, which could affect production per spindle.

So, other things remaining the same, production per spindle is higher for hosiery yarn compared to woven yarn

8. Tm varies between 3.4 to 3.5 for cotton hosiery combed, 3.8 to 3.85 for cotton hosiery carded, 3.9 to 3.95 for cotton weaving combed, and 4.10 to 4.15 for cotton weaving carded depending upon the count of yarn being spun. Tm is higher for coarser counts.

Spindle speed is higher for finer counts. The speed varies between around 9000 rpm and 17000 rpm depending upon the count.

So, other things remaining the same, productivity is higher for hosiery yarn compared to woven yarn and is higher for combed yarn compared to carded yarn. The productivity also depends upon the type of fibre used in spinning.

and is higher for combed yarn compared to carded yarn. The production per spindle also depends upon the type of fibre used in spinning. The above formula is only used for those counts of yarn for which the information was not available from the SITRA norms for productivity. The norms for relative productivity of various counts of yarn produced from various fibres are available from the SITRA publications on *Norms for Spinning Mills* and *Norms for productivity*. One could find out the productivity of modern spindles for various counts on the basis of these norms and specific counts productivity at latest technology.

One of the limitations of data is that individual count-wise production figures are not available at the all India level, although production figures are available for various count-ranges. But even then the production for each variety like hosiery, cone, carded and combed, etc. are not available separately. However, in the absence of published data on all India level for several variables such as carded and combed ratios, count-wise production within count range for various varieties and several other parameters, reliance has to be put on regional reports prepared by SIMA and All India Federation of Co-operative Spinning Mills (AIFCOSPIN).

The production combination widely differs across several regions, but in the absence of any reliable information on all India basis, we are left with no other option but to use disaggregated regional data for each variety and for various count ranges. These estimates of share of various varieties within each count range are then applied on the count range-wise aggregate data available for all India. As there are only a few main counts produced in each count range for each variety, this kind of categorisation could be of great help in reducing the margin of error.

The analysis is undertaken for each variety separately.

Cotton Yarn

Hosiery Yarn

To work out the count range-wise analysis for the hosiery sector, the problem is that no estimates are available even for the total production of hosiery yarn. Only estimates about the total delivery of hosiery yarn to decentralised sector are available for each year, which do not include exports of hosiery yarn. The count range-wise data for delivery of hosiery yarn to decentralised sector is available only for the year 1983. Therefore, it is important to first capture the changes in the count composition of yarn delivered to hosiery sector. It can only be derived indirectly by using the changes in count composition in total production of cotton yarn, which is available for each year. The method used is to take 1983 ratios between the proportion of each count range delivered to hosiery sector and total production of cotton yarn respectively and using these as weights for each count range. In the first instance, these ratios are then used for making count range-wise yearly estimates for hosiery by multiplying these weights with yearly count range-wise production of cotton yarn. The second step is to readjust these count range-wise figures arrived at proportionally for distributing the given total hosiery yarn delivery for each year. Table 2.1 gives the estimates of count range-wise delivery of hosiery yarn for years 1983 and 1996-97. The year-wise data is given in the Appendix 3.1.

Table 2.1
Changes in Domestic Consumption Pattern for Cotton Hosiery Yarn

Count	*Delivery of Cotton Hosiery Yarn to Decentralised Sector*			
	1983 %Share	*1996-97 % Share*	*1983 Mn. Kgs*	*1996-97 Mn. Kgs*
0-10s	0.61	1.41	0.56	5.60
11-20s	18.67	18.66	17.10	74.28
21-30s	13.89	12.33	12.72	49.09
31-40s	58.45	60.12	53.52	239.29
41-60s	6.20	5.72	5.68	22.77
61-80s	1.95	1.50	1.79	5.97
>80s	0.22	0.25	0.20	1.00
Total	100.00	100.00	91.57	398

Source: Derived from *Compendium of Textile Statistics* issued by the Office of the Textile Commissioner, GOI, Mumbai.

Once the count range-wise deliveries of hosiery yarn are worked out for each year, the next problem is to estimate the hosiery yarn production. The data regarding exports of hosiery yarn is not separately available. The year-wise share of cotton hosiery yarn in total export of cotton yarn was taken same as its share in total consumption of cotton yarn for the decentralised sector in each year. It is also assumed that count composition for the exports of hosiery yarn is same as that of delivery of hosiery yarn to the decentralised sector. Despite several limitations this was the best available solution to work out estimates of total hosiery yarn production (Table 2.2).[9]

Table 2.2
Estimates of Hosiery Yarn Production

(Mn. Kgs)

Count	*Hosiery 1996-97*		
	Total	*Combed*	*Carded*
0-10s	7.15	0.00	7.15
11-20s	94.78	18.21	76.58
21-30s	62.64	24.22	38.42
31-40s	305.34	203.45	101.89
41-60s	29.06	9.55	19.50
61-80s	7.62	7.62	—
>80s	1.28	1.28	—
Total	507.86	264.33	243.54

Source: Derived from *Compendium of Textile Statistics* issued by the Office of the Textile Commissioner GOI, Mumbai, TEXPROCIL and SIMA statistics.

9. An attempt was also made to find the total hosiery yarn production in the country by using SIMA statistics for the period April-December'96. The SIMA statistics are based on the data from over 200 reporting mills. The share of hosiery yarn in each count-range of total cotton yarn production is derived from the count-wise statistics available from SIMA data for the period April-December'96. These shares are then applied for determining count range-wise total hosiery production by applying it on the count range-wise total cotton yarn production in the country. The export of hosiery yarn is calculated by subtracting delivery of hosiery yarn from the derived estimates on production. The share of hosiery yarn export in total export of cotton yarn derived

(Contd.....)

The total production of hosiery yarn in the country is derived from these ratios worked out to be 507.86 million kilograms during 1996-97, which accounted for 24.79 per cent of the total production of cotton yarn in the organised sector during that year. However, the delivery of hosiery yarn to decentralised sector was reported at 398 million kilograms and exports of hosiery yarn are estimated at 109.86 million kilograms.

The carded and combed shares in each count ranges are derived by using the count-wise hosiery yarn data available from SIMA reports. By applying the count range-wise combed share, one could find out that combed share in hosiery yarn is estimated at 52.05 per cent for the year 1996-97.

Productivity Norms for Hosiery Yarn

Using the SITRA norms regarding the count-wise production per spindle and the count-wise delivery of hosiery yarn, one could work out the count range-wise production per spindle at the latest available technology during 1996 separately for carded and combed hosiery yarn (Table 2.3). The weighted average production for each count-range can be worked out by using the following formula.

Production per spindle per shift per day =
(Total Production per shift)/
((Combed Production per shift/
Production per spindle per shift for Combed Yarn) +
(Carded Production per shift)/Production per spindle per shift for Carded Yarn))

(Contd....)

this way is almost same as that of share of hosiery yarn in total cotton yarn consumption available for the production of fabrics. The count composition derived this way however differs than derived by the above method. This method is not used for this study as the regional data is used only within count ranges for specific varieties to arrive at all India results. The variations within count-range for specific varieties across regions are not much.

Table 2.3
Count Range-wise Production per Spindle for Hosiery Yarn (gms/spindle/shift at Modern Spindles Available During 1996-97)

Count	*Hosiery Productivity*		
	Combed	*Carded*	*Total*
0-10s	—	530.30	530.30
11-20s	249.73	239.80	241.65
21-30s	167.23	153.38	158.45
31-40s	115.77	105.60	112.17
41-60s	80.50	92.38	88.10
61-80s	57.22	—	57.22
>80s	22.39	—	22.39

Source: Derived from SIMA data and South India Textile Research Association (SITRA) norms.

These count range-wise productivity could be used over time as count composition within count ranges do not change much.

Woven Cotton Yarn

Woven cotton yarn can be further classified into three categories namely (1) cotton yarn exported and consumed in composite mills, (2) cotton hank yarn and (3) the other cotton yarn including that consumed in the powerloom sector. In all these sectors, the carded and combed ratios differ quite substantially.

Exports and Consumption of Woven Cotton Yarn in Mill Sector

In the case of the mill sector, it could be assumed that mills use almost similar quality of yarn to produce fabrics as is used for export purposes. Thus, the carded and combed share in various count ranges of yarn consumed in composite mills could be taken as same as in the case of exports (Table 2.4).

Using the SITRA productivity norms on the data available on the count-wise delivery of woven yarn from SIMA for the year 1996, the productivity norms for the mill and export of woven cotton yarn for each count-range are worked out separately for combed and carded yarn (Table 2.5).

Table 2.4
Carded and Combed Share in Count Range-wise Yarn Consumed within Mills and for Exports

Count	*Mill & Exports Sector*	
	Combed Share	*Carded Share*
0-10s	26.76	73.24
11-20s	33.65	66.35
21-30s	54.81	45.19
31-40s	74.61	25.39
41-60s	88.40	11.60
61-80s	91.96	8.04
>80s	92.95	7.05

Source: Derived from TEXPROCIL.

Table 2.5
Count Range-wise Production per Spindle of Woven Yarn (gms/spindle/shift at Modern Spindles Available During 1996-97)

Count	*Mills & Exports Woven Yarn Sectors Productivity*		
	Combed	*Carded*	*Total*
0-10s	559.65	534.32	540.87
11-20s	275.00	250.11	257.97
21-30s	165.25	144.23	155.04
31-40s	112.12	99.28	108.56
41-60s	69.32	61.91	68.37
61-80s	45.60	40.28	45.12
>80s	32.31	28.05	31.97

Source: Derived from TEXPROCIL.

However, the question is how to find out share of various count ranges in mill and woven yarn exports. To find out the changes among various count ranges over the period of time, the count range-wise consumption of woven yarn in the mill and exports sectors are derived separately.

The data for the required count ranges were available for the year 1983. The published data of cotton yarn export for the period 1988 to 1996 is available for the count ranges 0-40s, 41-60s, and >60s. We also got data from Texprocil for the count wise export detail from 1991 to 1996 for calendar years. We derived data for financial years by using count range-wise ratios of the relevant calendar year and aggregate exports of yarn during the financial year. For the 1988 and 1989 calendar years, the count wise detail was not available. The required count ranges for year 1988-89, 1989-90 and 1990-91 are worked out by using the derived count ranges ratios for the year 1991-92 and adjusting proportionally for the aggregates at various levels for which data was available.

In Table 2.6, the changes in count range-wise composition of cotton yarn exports have been given over the period of time. The year-wise data is given in Appendix 3.1.

Table 2.6
Changes in Count Range-wise Export Pattern

	Exports Share among various count ranges		*Exports*	
	1983	*1996-97*	*1983*	*1996-97*
Count	*% Share*	*% Share*	*Mn. Kgs*	*Mn. Kg*
0-10s	11.19	9.88	0.77	53.00
11-20s	29.22	18.85	2.01	101.10
21-30s	17.15	36.65	1.18	170.30
31-40s	26.45	18.04	1.82	83.81
41-60s	12.94	6.71	0.89	31.18
61-80s	0.73	3.82	0.05	17.73
>80s	2.62	1.62	0.18	7.55
Total	100.00	100.00	6.88	464.67

Source: Derived from TEXPROCIL.

The share of hosiery yarn in export over the period of time is worked out in our earlier analysis. The export of yarn is divided into woven and hosiery cotton yarn in Table 2.7 on the basis of information from Tables 2.1, 2.2 and 2.6.

In order to work out the count range-wise consumption of cotton yarn to produce fabrics in the mill sector, the count range-wise data on production of cotton fabrics in the mill sector is used. The mill sector in the weaving segment in this study meant only composite mills[10]. The count-range wise weights of cotton fabrics are applied on data on production of fabrics to arrive at count range-wise consumption of cotton yarn. The detail of this method is explained in chapter 3. The results thus derived are given in Table 2.8. The year-wise data is given in Appendix 3.1.

Table 2.7

Changes in Count Range-wise Hosiery and Woven Yarn Exports

(Mn. Kgs)

	Hosiery		*Woven*	
Count	*1983*	*1996-97*	*1983*	*1996-97*
0-10s	0.00	1.55	0.77	51.45
11-20s	0.11	20.05	1.90	81.05
21-30s	0.08	13.64	1.13	156.66
31-40s	0.34	66.05	1.48	17.76
41-60s	0.04	6.29	0.85	24.89
61-80s	0.01	1.65	0.04	16.08
>80s	0.00	0.28	0.18	7.27
Total	0.58	109.86	90.50	354.81

Source: Derived from Compendium of Textile Statistics issued by the Office of the Textile Commissioner, GOI, Mumbai and TEXPROCIL.

10. The cotton yarn delivered to non-SSI woven mills would also be of good quality. But the exclusion or inclusion of non-SSI weaving mills would not make much difference as cotton fabrics in this sector amounts for only 29.33 million square metres and yarn consumption in this sector is estimated at 4.07 million kilograms during 1996-97. The production of 100% cotton fabrics in the composite mills was 1180 million square metres and yarn consumed for the purpose is estimated at 167 million kilograms in Chapter 3. However, non-SSI weaving sector is growing and may become a significant force in the years to come.

Table 2.8
Changes in Mill Yarn Consumption Pattern

	Percentage Share of Various Count Ranges		*Consumption of Yarn Among Various Count Range*	
	1983	*1996-97*	*1983*	*1996-97*
Count Ranges	*% Share*	*% Share*	*Mn. Kgs*	*Mn. Kgs*
0-10s	5.19	9.42	19.06	15.77
11-20s	31.33	44.53	115.01	74.51
21-30s	38.80	28.61	142.45	47.88
31-40s	21.39	12.46	78.33	20.85
41-60s	1.42	1.67	5.21	2.80
61-80s	0.77	1.32	2.83	2.21
>80s	1.15	1.98	4.24	3.32
Total	100.00	100.00	367.12	167.34

Source: Derived from Compendium of Textile Statistics issued by the Office of the Textile Commissioner, GOI, Mumbai.

From the results worked out above, one could find out the count range-wise exports and consumption in mill sector of woven cotton yarn. This is given in the Table 2.9.

Table 2.9
Changes in Mill Consumption and Woven Yarn Export Pattern

Count Range s	*Mill and Woven Exports Share Among Various Count Ranges*		*Total Mill and Woven Exports Among Various Count Ranges*	
	1983	*1996-97*	*1983*	*1996-97*
	% Share	*% Share*	*Mn. Kgs*	*Mn. Kgs*
0-10s	5.31	12.80	19.82	64.59
11-20s	31.31	30.23	116.91	152.57
21-30s	38.44	35.50	143.55	179.19
31-40s	21.37	10.18	79.81	51.39
41-60s	1.62	5.35	6.06	27.01
61-80s	0.77	3.79	2.87	19.12
>80s	1.18	2.15	4.42	10.87
Total	100.00	100.00	373.43	504.74

Source: Derived from Compendium of Textile Statistics issued by the Office of the Textile Commissioner, GOI, Mumbai and TEXPROCIL.

The above analysis shows that over the period of time the ratios of various count ranges within and among the sectors have changed.

The share of cotton yarn consumption in the mill sector declined significantly over a period of time. It has declined from 33.81 per cent in 1983 to 21.21 per cent in 1988-89 to 8.85 per cent in 1995-96 and 8.17 per cent in 1996-97. On the other hand share of cotton yarn export has increased rapidly over a period of time. This has happened because numerous Export Oriented Units (EOU) have come up during the period. Export of cotton yarn out of total production of cotton yarn has increased from 0.63 per cent in 1983 to 3.08 per cent in 1991-92 and then to 14.63 per cent in 1995-96 and further to 22.68 per cent in 1996-97. The mill consumption as well as exports of woven cotton yarn in total production of cotton yarn declined from 34.39 per cent in 1983-84 to 23.90 per cent in 1989-90 and then to 19.91 per cent in 1995-96 and later increased to 24.75 per cent in 1996-97. This would definitely affect the share of combed yarn in total production of yarn to a certain extent.

Hank Yarn

The data for count range-wise delivery of hank yarn is available for years 1983 and 1996-97 and is given in Table 2.10. It is clear from the data that the delivery of hank yarn has increased mainly in the 0-10s and 31-40s count ranges. We do not have count range-wise continuous data for all the periods in between for most of sectors other than exports and mill consumption.

The count range-wise changes in hank yarn for other years could be worked out by sum two point data using two-step method as count range-wise changes for cotton yarn are smooth. Firstly, the data for intervening years calculated by simply assuming constant annual compound growth rate. Secondly, these have then been adjusted proportionally for each count range to match with available aggregate data for each year (Appendix 3.1).

Table 2.10

Changes in Hank Yarn Consumption Pattern

Count	*Hank Yarn Share Among Various Count Ranges*		*Total Hank Delivery Among Various Count Ranges*	
	1983	*1996-97*	*1983*	*1996-97*
	% Share	*% Share*	*Mn. Kgs*	*Mn. Kgs*
0-10s	20.54	49.89	59	234
11-20s	33.96	18.55	97	87
21-30s	13.35	5.76	38	27
31-40s	17.23	17.91	49	84
41-60s	9.65	4.05	28	19
61-80s	4.15	1.92	12	9
>80s	1.11	1.92	3	9
Total	100.00	100.00	286	469

Source: Derived from data of Compendium of Textile Statistics issued by the Office of the Textile Commissioner, GOI, Mumbai & Development Commissioner for Handloom, GOI, New Delhi.

Regarding other information such as carded and combed share within each count range, SIMA data on hank yarn delivery is used (Table 2.11).

Table 2.11

Combed and Carded Share in Cotton Hank Yarn

Count	*Hank Cotton Yarn*	
	Combed Share	*Carded Share*
0-10s	0.00	100.00
11-20s	0.00	100.00
21-30s	0.00	100.00
31-40s	0.00	100.00
41-60s	23.83	76.17
61-80s	41.32	58.68
>80s	88.93	11.07

Source: Derived from SIMA data.

One could work out the overall combed share in hank yarn by applying it on the count range-wise delivery of hank yarn. This is the sector where the combed share is lowest. In 1983, the combed share is estimated at 5.0 per cent, which get further reduced to 3.5 per cent in 1996-97.

The count range-wise productions per spindle used for hank yarn are the same as for woven yarn. By applying the carded and combed ratios of hank yarn, one could arrive at following count range-wise weighted productivity (Table 2.12).

Table 2.12
Count Range-wise Production of Cotton Hank Yarn (gms/spindle/shift at Modern Spindles Available During 1996-97)

Count	*Productivity for Cotton Hank Yarn*
0-10s	534.32
11-20s	250.11
21-30s	144.23
31-40s	99.28
41-60s	63.53
61-80s	42.32
>80s	31.78

Source: Derived from SITRA productivity norms and SIMA data on count-wise combed and carded production within the count-ranges.

Other Cotton Yarn Production

The count range-wise data on total production of cotton yarn is available for the period 1983 to 1996-97. The data for the first and last year of the study is given in the following Table 2.13.

Table 2.13
Count Range-wise Changes in Cotton Yarn Production

Count	*Total Cotton Yarn Production*			
	Mn. Kgs		*Percentage share*	
	1983	*1996-97*	*1983*	*1996-97*
0-10s	118	441	10.81	21.52
11-20s	288	489	26.37	23.87
21-30s	257	397	23.53	19.38
31-40s	282	489	25.82	23.87
41-60s	83	132	7.60	6.44
61-80s	44	59	4.30	2.88
>80s	20	42	1.83	1.95
Total	1092	2049	100.00	100.00

Source: Derived from data of Compendium of Textile Statistics issued by the Office of the Textile Commissioner, GOI, Mumbai and Development Commissioner for Handloom, GOI, New Delhi.

The data regarding count range-wise production for other cone yarn is derived by subtracting the count range-wise production of hank yarn, hosiery yarn, mill yarn consumption and woven yarn exports from count range-wise production of cotton yarn in the organised sector. This means cotton yarn left over after being exported and consumed in the hosiery sector, mill sector and hank, are included in these estimates.

This left over yarn is mainly consumed in the powerloom sector in the form of other cones, beams and pirms. In addition to the yarn consumed in the powerloom sector these estimates also include cotton yarn consumed in the other forms and also include stock depletion/addition in each year. The count range-wise delivery of cotton yarn to powerloom sector over the period of time is given in Appendix 3.1. The production per spindle in each count range for carded and combed yarn in this segment is taken same as that of count-range wise production per spindle of woven yarn. However, the carded and combed ratios taken are different. The carded and combed share in other cone yarn is derived by using count range-wise SIMA data for the same variety *i.e.* from delivery of cone yarn for the period Jan-March'96. The results thus arrived are given in Table 2.14.

Table 2.14
Carded and Combed Share in Cone and Other Yarn

Count	*Powerloom and Other Sectors*	
	Combed Share	*Carded share*
0-10s	0.00	100.00
11-20s	2.43	97.53
21-30s	20.49	79.51
31-40s	5.06	94.94
41-60s	36.58	63.42
61-80s	39.51	60.49
>80s	99.56	0.44

Source: Derived from SIMA data.

By applying the productivity of woven yarn, one could calculate the weighted productivity for each count range (Table 2.15).

Table 2.15
Count Range-wise Production per Spindle of Cone and Other Yarn (gms/spindle/shift at Modern Spindles Available During 1996-97)

	Powerloom Sector Productivity		
Count	*Combed*	*Carded*	*Total*
0-10s	559.65	534.32	534.32
11-20s	275.00	250.11	250.66
21-30s	165.25	144.23	148.09
31-40s	112.12	99.28	99.86
41-60s	69.32	61.91	64.43
61-80s	45.60	40.28	42.23
>80s	32.31	28.05	32.29

Source: Derived SITRA productivity norms and SIMA data on count-wise combed and carded production within the count-ranges.

Carded and Combed Share in Production of Cotton Yarn

The year-wise carded and combed share in each variety are worked out on the basis of count-wise analysis undertaken above and are given in Table 2.16. The analysis shows that cotton-combed share varies from 26 per cent to 30 per cent of the total production of cotton yarn. These estimates of combed share are used to work out the total requirement of fibre by applying the conversion rates of yarn from fibre. The conversion rate of yarn from various fibre is taken as inverse of the amount of fibre required on an average to produce one unit of yarn. The experts opinion is that the wastage in case of cotton combed yarn varies around 29 to 31 per cent on an average compared with 12 to 14 per cent in case of carded yarn.

From these approximations, it could be worked out that wastage in the organised sector would be in the range of 17.75 to 18.25 per cent over time to produce one kg of cotton yarn. This means approximately 1.1775 to 1.1825 kg of cotton is required to produce one kg of cotton yarn in the organised sector. However, the data regarding consumption of raw cotton is not separately available for the cotton yarn. It is available for the cotton and cotton blended spun yarn.

Table 2.19
Weighted Production per Spindle in Cotton Combed/Polyester Cotton Yarn for Various Count Ranges
(gms/spindle/shift at Modern Spindles Available During 1996-97)

Year	*1983*	*1988-89*	*1992-93*	*1994-95*	*1995-96*	*1996-97*
0-10	559.65	559.65	559.65	559.65	559.65	559.65
11-20	272.93	267.46	263.71	262.42	259.92	259.15
21-30	165.35	165.67	165.85	165.96	166.17	166.21
31-40	113.40	114.56	114.80	114.94	115.10	115.18
41-60	69.93	71.59	72.52	73.29	74.09	74.51
61-80	46.44	48.40	49.08	49.63	51.00	51.42
>80	32.16	31.66	31.36	31.07	30.58	30.11
Weighted for Cotton combed	101.77	98.49	104.67	104.52	104.72	110.63

Source: Derived SITRA and SIMA data.

The above analysis shows that although the combed productivity is higher than carded productivity for various count ranges, but the weighted average productivity is lower. This is because of much higher percentage share of higher counts in combed yarn for which the productivity is relatively lower. In the ninth plan documents; the weighted productivity of combed cotton yarn is taken higher.

The productivity of combed yarn within a count range is not change much and hence could be standardised. Here also we have chosen the year 1994-95 for the reasons explained earlier for cotton yarn. The weighted productivity would depend upon count composition.

So, count range-wise production per spindle for the modern spindles of 1996-97 technology have been standardised for the polyester cotton yarn on the basis of 1994-95 results. Using this as an index, we develop relative indices for other spun yarns, by using SITRA data.

From SITRA data, it is observed that if the Index of polyester cotton (PC) is 100, then the index of polyester viscose (PV) is approximately 120, viscose (V) 93.5, polyester (P) 120 and acrylic (A) 126. These were the main fibres in spun yarn. For all other fibres we used productivity norms of PC.

These indices have been used to standardise the count range-wise production per spindle for various spun yarns from the count range-wise productivity of polyester cotton blended yarn. By using count range-wise data on yarn production of different fibres/blends from Compendium of Textile Statistics and standardised productivity norms, one could work out minimum spindle required over time at latest available technology during 1996-97.

These productivity targets are the optimum level with the latest available technology at 100 per cent utilisation. This means that the spindles are working for 365 working days and 24 hours. However, these norms provide the margin for stoppages due to change of sliver and other unavoidable requirements in the working process. This could be considered as the optimum productivity per spindle per shift at the latest available technology.

Table 2.20
Minimum Requirement of Modern Spindle over Time

	Total Spun Yarn Mn. Kgs.	*Optimum Achievable Productivity per spindle per shift (gms)*	*Modern spindle Required at 100 per cent Capacity Utilisation Mn.*
1983	1309.00	121.17	9.87
1988-89	1587.58	115.03	12.60
1989-90	1652.30	118.76	12.71
1990-91	1823.88	121.79	13.68
1991-92	1805.33	123.57	13.34
1992-93	1895.30	126.01	13.74
1993-94	2066.78	126.90	14.87
1994-95	2083.96	129.21	14.73
1995-96	2378.85	127.20	17.08
1996-97	2694.25	139.77	17.60

Source: Derived from Compendium of Textile Statistics issued by The Office of the Textile Commissioner, GOI, Mumbai and ITMF data.

Once, the minimum number of spindles required for the production of various fibres spun yarn are derived, the total modern spindles required to produce the total spun yarn can be calculated. These are then compared with actual number of spindles installed. The purpose is to make a comparison to know how much we are operating below the optimal level at latest available technology during 1996-97. The gap between the two turns out to be quite wide. We have basically identified four reasons for operating below the production frontier. These include (1) many of the existing spindles are declared closed (non-operational), (2) the mills which although are not registered as closed but remained closed partially and/or for the most part of year on the basis of daily working averages, (3) the low productivity caused by under-utilisation of working spindles capacity, and (4) the low productivity caused due to age composition of machinery. Here, we have tried to quantify the effect of each of these in causing the comparative low productivity compared to what it could have been at the level of modern technology. The analysis has been done over a period of time to find how much improvement has taken place in the level of productivity and to what an extent it has been triggered by the liberalisation policies. An attempt has also been made to go into the age composition of spindles installed and their capacity utilisation as it is important to determine the investment requirement for future growth in production. All these issues are discussed in detail in the following section.

Comparison of Spindles Required with Spindles Installed

An attempt is made to compare the installed capacity with the minimum spindle required. The ITMF data provides us the information on year-wise working spindles and rotors and number of working hours in Indian textile industry for the calendar years over the period of time. As the comparison would have been more meaningful in the case of availability of average spindles installed during the financial years. In the absence of availability of data on average spindles installed during financial year over a longer period, the calendar year data on installed spindles is used. This will make some but not significant differences. The estimates of spindles equivalent installed are worked out by applying for each rotor equivalent to 5 spindles criterion. The spindles equivalent installed are then compared with the minimum spindles required at the latest available technology. The results are given in Table 2.21.

This means, that we are using around double the number of spindles required. However, this excess capacity is based on the assumption that spindles installed are modern and are fully utilised. The excess capacity as a percentage of installed capacity declined after the introduction of New Textile Policy, 1985 (NTP). However, in the second phase of reforms, the excess capacity as a percentage of installed capacity remained almost at the same level as in the base year (1990) with marginal decline during the years 1995 and 1996.

The objective here is to find out the details of main causes for this excess capacity. These include closures, idle capacity, low capacity utilisation and old machinery. These four reasons could be broadly clarified into two categories : Idle spindles status and working spindles status.

Table 2.21
Excess Capacity Installed than Minimum Required

Year	*Spindles Installed Mn.*	*Rotors Installed 000*	*Spindles Equivalent Installed Mn.*	*Minimum Spindles Required Mn.*	*Percentage Excess of Installed Spindles*
1983	23.41	5.5	23.44	9.87	57.89
1988	26.41	40.00	26.61	12.60	52.65
1989	26.55	47.70	26.79	12.71	52.56
1990	26.65	66.90	26.98	13.68	49.30
1991	27.41	69.90	27.76	13.34	51.95
1992	28.13	115.00	28.70	13.74	52.13
1993	28.32	129.90	28.97	14.87	48.67
1994	29.39	155.70	30.17	14.73	51.18
1995	31.23	194.50	32.20	17.08	46.96
1996	31.83	230.00	32.98	17.60	46.64

Note: Spindles installed are considered at the end of year means 31st December.

Source: Derived from ITMF data.

Idle Spindles Status

The idle spindles could be classified into two categories *(i)* closed spindles falling under mills declared closed and *(ii)* closed spindles falling under mills not reported closed, but part of its unit is not working on daily average working basis. Textile Commissioner reports the data for non-operational spindles falling under closed mills, while the data for the working spindles are given by the ITMF. Both these sets of data are used to estimate the number of spindles, which are closed but not falling under mills declared closed (Table 2.22).

The idle capacity explains more than around half of the excess capacity. The idle spindles as percentage of installed declined steeply in the first phase of reforms. However, in the second phase of reforms, it returned to pre-reforms level by the end of year 1996. The cause of it could be found out in the opening up of yarn export, which led to excess demand in the initial phase of reforms and better utilisation of existing spindles. However, the increased demand also resulted in installation of more modern spindles. The investment rates increased substantially after the second phase of liberalisation. This may be because of substantial reduction in tariffs on capital imports. The further increase in new capacity during the second phase of reforms caused excess installed capacity and hence more and more old spindles became obsolete.

The status of idles spindles is discussed in two sections.

(i) Year-Wise Status of Closed Spindles

The status of closed spindles as on 31st March, 1997 is as follows. There were total 5.47 million spindles lying closed as per the report by mills. If we include those spindles also which were closed before 31st March 1997, but information about these closures was delivered later, then revised estimates of closed spindles could be placed at 5.54 million. Official statistics take it 5.47 million, as they do not include those reported late.[11]

The estimates about year-wise close down position of spindles and rotors as on 31st March 1997 is given in Table 2.23. The statistics point to the fact that there are mills, which

11. In this study, Textile Commissioner's data is often referred as Official data.

Table 2.22
Idle Spindles Expressed as Percentage of Installed Spindles

Year	*Spindles Active Mn*	*Rotors Active 000*	*Spindles Equivalent Active Mn.*	*Spindles Equivalent Installed Mn.*	*Spindles Equivalent Idle Mn.*			*Idle % of Installed*
					Closed	*Not Closed*	*Total*	
1983	16.70	5	16.72	23.44	-	-	6.72	28.68
1988	20.89	36	21.07	26.61	3.40	2.14	5.54	20.82
1989	20.71	43	20.92	26.79	3.63	2.24	5.87	21.91
1990	21.75	60	22.05	26.98	3.24	1.24	4.48	16.60
1991	21.90	63	22.21	27.76	3.19	2.36	5.55	19.99
1992	20.62	103	21.13	28.70	3.84	3.73	7.57	26.37
1993	21.22	128	21.86	28.97	3.57	3.54	7.11	24.54
1994	20.92	151	21.68	30.17	3.59	4.90	8.49	28.14
1995	22.05	189	22.99	32.20	4.05	5.15	9.20	28.59
1996	22.475	223	23.59	32.98	4.85	4.54	9.39	28.48

Note: ITMF statistics use the definition of active spindles as average number of active during the year for the period 1986 to 1996. However, definition of active spindles was different for the period 1971 to 1985. According to this definition active spindle were considered as were maximum number active. The present criterion used is better than earlier one for calculating productivity.

Source: Derived from Office of the Textile Commissioner and ITMF data.

remain closed for 30 years even. How relevant is it to include these spindles into the installed capacity.

From the Textile Commissioner data on closure, it is found that there are also a few mills, which re-open after a few days of closure. There are instances when a mill has re-opened after 12 years. Vasanta Mills (Pvt.) Ltd., with installed capacity of 44696 spindles and 266 looms, is one such example. This mill closed on 13th November, 1984 due to financial difficulties and shortage of raw materials. Bankers froze their accounts. It registered itself reopened on 19th August 1996. Prabhu Spinning Mills (Pvt.) Ltd. closed on 25th June, 1987 and re-opened on 31st December, 1992. U.P. Sahakari Katai Mills (Co-operative) closed on 3rd October, 1991 and reopened on 23rd July, 1996.

Table 2.23
Year of Closure of Spindles Lying Closed on 31st March, 1997

Period	*Spindles Closed Number*	*Year-wise share of spindles closed*	*Rotors Closed Number*	*Year-wise share of Rotors Closed*
1967	7,960	0.14		
1970	9,000	0.16		
1976	22,380	0.40		
1982	133,812	2.41		
1983	168,457	3.04		
1984	345,860	6.24		
1985	129,424	2.34		
1986	469,039	8.46		
1987	391,728	7.07		
1988	130,846	2.36		
1989	93,072	1.68		
1990	89,963	1.62		
1991	528,854	9.54	336	2.72
1992	332,528	5.60	368	2.98
1993	296,840	5.36	320	2.59
1994	581,536	10.49	576	4.66
1995	559,285	10.09	1,152	9.31
1996	1,054,826	19.03	9,449	76.39
1997 (March)	197,282	3.56	168	1.36
Total	5,542,692	100.00	12,369	100.00

Source: Derived from Office of the Textile Commissioner data.

The management wise closed spindles and rotors as percentage of installed spindles is given in Table 2.24 and Table 2.25. In circumstances when the mills can reopen after remaining closed for a long duration, we have to make some kind of assessment of those spindles which have been working on date, but go out of operation for most part of year due to frequent closure of mills. An assessment of the mills repeatedly closed and reopened since 30th December 1992 to March 1997 and are open on 31st March 1997 is required. We made assessment that around 0.5 million spindles fall into this category, which are dominantly falling under private spinning units (78% of total). This means in addition to 5.54 million closed spindles, there are 0.5 million spindles which were prone to frequent closures.

On the other hand, the equal number of spindles (0.5 million) might have gone out of operation temporarily for reasons such as power shortage and stoppages. This means we could safely assume that approximately 5.5 million spindles out of these 6 million spindles are expected to be not in good health (including closed as well as those, which close frequently).

(ii) Idle Spindles (Mills Not Reported Closed) Status

These spindles are remaining idle for most of the year but are not registered as closed, as their units are not reported as closed to Textile Commissioner. The total number of such spindles is 4.54 million (Table 4.22). These spindles are spread over all the organisations. However, a large portion of the installed spindles in National Textiles Corporation (NTC) working mills seems to remain idle as could be gauged from the very low productivity of these spindles (Table 2.24).

The productivity of spindles in NTC working mills is worked out to be only 30.92 kgs per spindle per year during 1996-97, which is very low compared to average production of 93.50 kgs per spindle in the country during the same period. One of the reasons for it is low utilisation of spindles at 58.2 per cent for the NTC working mills.[12] Thus it seems that around

12. The capacity utilisation is even poor for weaving segment of NTC mills not declared closed and is only 17.3 per cent.

41 per cent of 4.55 million spindles, which remain closed but are not falling under units reported closed, belong to NTC units. Approximately 2.71 million spindles belong to other organisations.

The other reasons for the low productivity of NTC spindles include below capacity use of working spindles due to frequent closures and outdated technology. NTC spinning mills are operating under financial constraints and most of their resources are utilised in paying wages and salaries, purchasing the raw material. There is hardly any amount left for modernisation. Most of spindles installed in NTC mills are outdated.

One of the limitations of the above exercise is that the estimates are based on crude approximations as productivity is worked out without considering the count or fibre composition of spun yarn. However, the count or fibre compositions are not expected to be much different among various organisations.

Having reviewed the idle spindles and their status, we are discussing the state of working spindles such as their working hours, productivity etc. in detail in the following section.

Working Spindles Status

The state of working spindles state of could be analysed under two broad heads *(i)* average working hours of average working spindles and *(ii)* age composition of spindles installed.

(i) Average Working Hours of Average Working Spindles

The working hours of spindles during the year at full capacity utilisation on three shifts should be 8*3*365=8760 hours except in leap year when it should be 8784 hours. This is considered as 100 per cent capacity utilisation. The utilisation of working spindles is compared with the maximum utilisation (at 100 per cent level) in column II of Table 2.25.

The under utilisation due to low working hours seems to be 14.1 per cent of the active spindles and 10.1 per cent of the active spindles during 1996. The utilisation of working spindles is continuously increasing. This may be due to the fact that as

Table 2.24

Ownership-wise Productivity in Working Mills during 1996-97

Organisation	*Spindle Equivalent Installed Mn.*	*Spindle Equivalent in Working Mills Mn.*	*Spun Yarn Production including in fabrics (Mn. Kgs)*	*Productivity in Working Mills Kgs/ Spindle/year*
Co-operative Spinning	3.51	3.00	260.86	86.98
NTC Total	3.70	3.16	39.194+35.588+(72.827 +72.682)*(1.11* 0.14185)+=97.69	30.92
Private Total	17.50	17.44	2341.86	134.28
STC Total	1.40	0.79	191.17-97.69=93.478	118.93
Total	34.53	28.98	2694.25	92.97

Note: *(i)* Closed spindles are worked out in above analysis

(ii) One of the limitations of this exercise is that the estimates are based on crude approximations as productivity are worked out without considering the count or fibre composition of spun yarn. Moreover, the capacity utilisation is not taken into account. Hence, the above exercise is very crude and gives only broad indication of efficiency in various organisations.

(iii) Productivity are worked on spindles working as on 31st March 1997 and not on the basis of average spindles working during the year due to lack of data on management wise working status. This is another limitation of the above exercise.

(iv) In the case of NTC mills, the production of spun yarn is 39.194 million kg, job work done is for 35.588 million kg spun yarn, cloth production is 72.827 million metres and fabrics produced for job work is 72.682 million metres. The weight of fabrics produced in NTC mills is taken as 141.85 gm/m^2.

(v) 1 Rotor is taken equivalent to 5 spindles.

Source: Derived from Office of the Textile Commissioner.

Table 2.25

Loss of Working Hours due to Under-utilisation of Spindles as Percentage of Spindles Installed

Year	*Spindle Equivalent Active Mn.*	*Active Spindles Percentage Utilisation*	*Spindle Equivalent Working at 100% Utilisation Mn.*	*Spindles Equivalent Loss due to low Utilisation Mn.*	*Installed Spindles Equivalent Mn.*	*Loss due to Utilisation as Percentage of Installed Spindles*
1983	16.72	79.69	13.32	3.40	23.44	14.51
1988	21.07	81.97	17.27	3.80	26.61	14.28
1989	20.92	82.33	17.22	3.70	26.79	13.81
1990	22.50	82.38	18.54	3.96	26.98	14.68
1991	22.21	82.38	18.30	3.91	27.76	14.09
1992	21.13	83.40	17.63	3.51	28.70	12.23
1993	21.86	83.43	18.24	3.62	28.97	12.50
1994	21.68	84.87	18.40	3.28	30.17	10.87
1995	22.99	86.04	19.78	3.21	32.20	9.97
1996	23.59	85.87	20.26	3.33	32.98	10.10

Note: ITMF statistics use the definition of active as average number of active during the year for the period 1986 to 1996. However, for the period 1971 to 1985, active was considered as maximum number active during the year. The present criterion used is better than the earlier one, as it is more useful to calculate productivity.

Source: Derived form ITMF data.

new technology spindles got installed, old spindles become absolete Under idle working conditions, 90 per cent capacity utilisation should be considered as the achievable target. This is based on the fact that the average working days should be taken as 350 in a year and not 365. Similarly, approximately another 5 per cent under-utilisation of capacity could be considered as normal in addition to 350 working days. This means one should aim for reducing excess than that 10 per cent under-utilisation of capacity. There was only 4 per cent extra under-utilisation of working spindles than the desired level during 1996.

(ii) Age of Installed Spindles

The analysis so far reveal that 28.48 per cent of excess capacity is explained for the year 1996 due to idle spindles and 10.10 per cent due to low average working hours. This explains (28.48+10.10=38.58) 38.58 per cent of the excess spindles required during the year 1996 out of total 46.37 per cent excess installed capacity than minimum required at latest available technology during 1996-97. The 8.06 (46.64-38.58=8.06) per cent remaining gap could be attributed to the difference in technology. The minimum spindles of latest technology required for the production of the required spun yarn are 17.60 million as against 20.31 million equivalent working at 100 per cent capacity utilisation. This means (20.26-17.60=2.66) 2.66 million extra spindles in the total installed capacity of 32.98 million equivalent. This comes to 8.06 per cent of the total installed spindles (Table 2.26).

The technology gap between the working spindles and latest technology has significantly reduced since 1991 (during the second phase of reforms), while it increased during the first phase of reforms especially during the period 1983 to 1988. The age composition of installed spindles and rotors could provide the answers for the excess working capacity at 100 per cent utilisation than minimum required (See Appendix 2.6).

One could question the increase in the excess spindles used due to technological gap during the first phase of

Table 2.26

Extra-working Spindles Required due to Technology Gap

Year	*Spindles Worked Mn. Equivalent 100% Utilisation*	*Spindle Equivalent Required at latest technology Mn.*	*Extra Spindle Used due to technology Gap Mn.*	*Installed Spindles Equivalent Mn.*	*Excess Spindles as % of minimum required at latest technology*	*Excess Spindles due to old technology as % of installed Spindles*
1983	13.32	9.87	3.45	23.44	35.06	14.72
1988	17.27	12.60	4.67	26.61	37.62	17.55
1989	17.23	12.71	4.51	26.79	35.56	16.83
1990	18.54	13.68	4.86	26.98	32.75	18.01
1991	18.30	13.34	4.96	27.76	37.18	17.87
1992	17.63	13.74	3.89	28.70	28.68	13.55
1993	18.24	14.87	3.37	28.97	22.66	11.63
1994	18.40	14.73	3.67	30.17	24.92	12.16
1995	19.79	17.08	2.71	32.20	15.87	8.42
1996	20.26	17.60	2.66	32.98	15.40	8.06

Source: Derived from ITMF data.

liberalisation, especially during the period 1983 to 1988, despite the installation of new spindles. The excess spindles due to technology gap as a percentage of installed spindles increased from 14.72 per cent in 1983 to 17.55 per cent in 1988. As argued earlier, demand increased at faster rate than the capacity expansion, which brought in the use of old spindles. The active spindles increased by 4.35 million from 16.72 million to 21.07 million during this period, while the new spindles installed were only 2.18 million. (Appendix 2.6) The decline in technology gap latter during ninties could be attributed to rise in investment and under utilisation of old machinery. The excess spindles as per cent of installed spindles due to technology gap reduced to 8.06 per cent during 1996-97. The share of idle spindles in total installed spindles increased sum 16.60 to 28.48 per cent during 1990 to 1996. The share of idle spindles as percentage of installed spindles declined from 28.68 per cent during 1983 to 16.60 per cent during 1990. This explains the rise in technology gap of installed spindles during the period 1983 to 1988.

The various reasons analysed above for the excess spindles installed than required at latest available technology to produce the yarn are summed up in Table 2.27. It is observed that the excess installed spindles than minimum required as per cent of installed spindles is not declining despite the fact that new spindles are being increasingly installed. This is basically due to excess capacity and non-dilution of old technology. Should we follow the example of China, where they actually want to reduce the spindles by 10 million by the turn of century? All these questions are related with policy matters such as whether we are in a position to dispose off the old technology. For this we should study the age composition of spindles installed in detail from Appendix 2.6.

Obviously, the productivity of the existing spindles within a composition where old ones dominant cannot be equal to the productivity of modern spindles. The spindles with the latest technology can produce 160 gms/spindle/shift cotton yarn of 30s hosiery combed. This productivity refers to spindles at latest technology available during 1996-97.

Table 2.27
Various Reasons for Operating below the Production Frontier

Year	*Closed spindle as per cent in Installed*	*Idle not closed as % Installed*	*Loss due to low utilisation of working spindles as % of Installed*	*Excess Spindle due to old technology as % of Installed*	*Total*
1983	28.68	—	14.51	14.72	57.89
1988	12.78	8.04	14.28	17.55	52.65
1989	13.55	8.36	13.81	16.83	52.56
1990	12.00	4.60	14.68	18.01	49.30
1991	11.49	8.50	14.09	17.87	51.95
1992	13.38	12.99	12.23	13.55	52.13
1993	12.32	12.22	12.50	11.63	48.67
1994	11.92	16.22	10.87	12.16	51.18
1995	12.58	16.01	9.97	8.42	46.96
1996	14.70	13.78	10.11	8.06	46.64

Note: Spindles installed are considered at the end of the year *i.e.* 31st March.
Source: Derived from above analysis.

Age Composition of Installed Spindles and Productivity Growth

The year-wise investment data derived in Appendix 2.6 show that over the period of time 11.80 million spindles equivalent are less than ten years old, 18.82 million less than twenty years old, 21.62 million less than 30 years old, 26.59 million less than 41 years old, and 27.76 million less than 46 years old. There are 5.84 million spindles even older than 46 years (Table 2.28). With such an age composition of spindles, frequent closure of spindles cannot be avoided.

As the productivity of spindles available at latest technology during 1996-97 could be taken as constant, the productivity due to change in age composition over the period of time has caused 2.38 per cent per annum change in per spindle productivity during the period 1988 to 1996. The productivity index improved from 72.66 in 1988 to 86.66 in 1996. This is worked out by assuming productivity index of spindles of latest available technology during 1996-97 as 100.

The increase in productivity is even higher for the period 1990-96 at 2.85 per cent per annum.

Table 2.28
Age Composition of Installed Spindles

Age of Spindles	*Spindles Shipped Mn.*	*Rotors Shipped (in 000)*	*Spindles Equivalent Shipped Mn.*	*Total Mn.*
0-10 years	10.52	256.72	11.80	11.80
11-20 years	6.92	19.28	7.016	18.82
21-30 years	2.80	—	2.80	21.62
31-41 years	4.97	—	4.97	26.59
41-46 years	1.17	—	1.17	27.76
>46 years	5.84	—	5.84	33.60

Source: As derived by the author.

Another way of putting this argument is that whereas in 1988, 37.62 per cent extra spindles were required compared to latest technology in 1988 and in the year 1996 the extra spindles required as compared with the norms of latest technology was 15.40 per cent (Table 2.29).

It is generally believed that for five years new machinery continues to have almost the same productivity. After five years, however productivity starts to decline at 0.5 per cent per annum due to depreciation. Similarly, the experience shows that technology progress takes place after around five years, which causes a rise in productivity by about 1 per cent per annum. This means that spindles are likely to have less productivity of 1.50 per cent, on an average, each year compared with modern spindles. However, the technology progress of 1 per cent per annum differs from the derived figure of 1.88 (2.38-0.5) during 1988 to 1996 because the replaced spindles are likely to be very old with very low productivity.[13]

13. The productivity index of replaced spindles is worked out. There were 23.59 million working spindles during 1996. From the analysis in Table 2.28, some of these working spindles could be approximately 40 years old, which may be first to be replaced. Hence the productivity index of replaced spindles could be taken as $1/((1.015)^{35})$=59 as compared to 100 for modern spindles.

(Contd....)

Table 2.29
Productivity of Working Spindles

Year	*Spindle Equivalent Worked Mn. (100% Ut)*	*Modern Spindle Equivalent Required Mn.*	*Productivity of Spindles Working Compared to modern (in %)*	*Productivity of modern spindles at 1996-97 technology compared to the working (in %)*
1983	13.33	9.87	74.04	135.06
1988	17.34	12.60	72.66	137.62
1989	17.23	12.71	73.77	135.56
1990	18.16	13.68	75.33	132.75
1991	18.30	13.34	72.90	137.18
1992	17.68	13.74	77.71	128.68
1993	18.24	14.87	81.52	122.66
1994	18.40	14.73	80.05	124.92
1995	19.79	17.08	86.31	115.87
1996	20.31	17.60	86.66	115.40
Point to point/p.a. Growth Rate 1983-91			0.25	
Trend Growth Rate 1988-96			2.38 (7.11)	
Trend Growth Rate 1990-96			2.85 (5.67)	

Note : (i) Figures in bracket shows T-statistics for compound growth rate based on semi-log trend.
Source: Derived by the author.

From the above analysis, it becomes clear that 17.60 million modern spindles are required at full capacity utilisation to produce the spun yarn production during 1996-97 at given count composition. However, under ideal working conditions of 90 per cent utilisation, we would need 19.56 million modern spindles.

During the year 1996-97, the age composition of working spindles seems to be fairly modern. This could be gauged from the fact that total working spindles at present are 23.59 million and are operating at 85.87 per cent capacity utilisation. The age composition of installed spindles show that 21.62 million spindles are less than 30 years old. These less than 30 years old working spindles constitutes around 91.65 per cent of the total working spindles during 1996-97. However, these spindles with less than 30 years age composition are not able to be utilised ideally as most of the installed spindles seems to be joining the fray when things are relatively better, while old spindles go out of operation and put their shutters down during the tough times. As worked out in Table 2.40, the actual production of spun yarn during 1996 could have been produced with the existing capacity of 21.62 million spindles less than 30 years old at 90 per cent level of utilisation. This means the existences of excess spindles of old technology are

---

This means the spindles, which are being replaced in 1996, are having productivity of 30s combed hosiery cotton yarn =160x.59=94.4 gm/S/S and are around 40 years old at the time of replacement. On the other hand, the productivity of modern spindles at count composition during 1996-97 was 139.77 gm/spindle/shift (Table 2.20). Thus the productivity of replaced spindles at the count composition of 1996-97 would be 82.46 gm/spindle/shift at 100 per cent capacity utilisation. The productivity index of working spindles over the period of time could also be worked out as

Productivity index = ((Productivity Index during 1988-89) x (Spindles Worked)-(Productivity Index of Spindles Replaced) x (No. of Spindles Replaced)+(Productivity Index of Gross Spindles Added x (Gross No. of Spindles added at around 90 per cent utilisation))/(Total No. of Spindles Working)

This equation approximately gives similar result as of Index of productivity derived in Table 2.29.

affecting the viability of comparatively new spindles to some extent. This is hindering the modernisation process. Imposing a uniform tax on per spindle installed may be helpful in further accelerating the modernisation process by creating disincentives for old spindles of outdated technology.

Considering the present age composition of working spindles, the speed at which modernisation of spindles is taking place and the impact of MFA phase out on technological progress, it is expected that the age of most of working spindles in the organised sector may be less than 30 years by 2010-11.

In other words, this means that the spindles older than 15 years during 1996-97 may not remain in operation by year 2010-11. The 2.04 million (19.56-11.59-5.95) equivalent additional spindles of 1996-97 technology were required to produce the composition of spun during 1996-97 in the organised sector with a age composition of less than twenty years (90 percentage utilisation).

For the targets till year 2010-11, it is possible that, the spindles older than 1981-82 may go out of operation, which means additional 3.14 million equivalent at 1996-97 technology spindles may go out of operation (Table 2.30 and Appendix 2.6). Hence the 2.04+3.14 =5.18 million spindles are required to produce the spun yarn during 1996-97 with spindles less than technology older than 1981-82.

This would mean that roughly 17.92 million installed spindles in the organised sector during 1996-97, which are installed after 1981-82 are expected to go out of operation by year 2010-11. The number may increase further in case the age composition may decline less than 30 years old spindles by the year 2005-06. This means there is need of large scale restructuring.[14]

In fact, out of these 17.92 million spindles 14.78 million are installed after 1976-77. Most of these 14.78 million spindles are already out of operation in practice. Out of these 14.78

14. China is planning to dispose off 10 million spindles by the turn of century.

Table 2.30
Comparison of Spindles Installed with Modern Equivalent

Age of Spindles Equivalent Installed Mn.	*Average Weighted Productivity Index (Modern spindles Productivity=100)*	*Equivalent Spindles to Latest Technology available during 1996-97 Mn.*	*Installed Spindles Technology Year Range*	*Equivalent Spindles to Latest Technology Available during 1996-97 Mn.*
0-10 years old 11.804	98.17	11.59	1991-92 to 1996-97	7.39
			1986-87 to 1991-92	4.20
11-20 years old 7.016	84.59	5.93	1981-82 to 1986-87	2.79
			1976 to 1981-82	3.14
21-30 years old 2.80	72.89	2.04	1971 to 1976	0.79
			1966 to 1971	1.25
31-41 years old 4.97	62.34	3.10	1961 to 1966	1.89
			1955 to 1961	1.21
41-46 years old 1.17	57.87	0.68	1950-51 to 1955	0.68
>46 years old 5.84			Older than 1950-51	
Spindle Required	17.60 Mn. at 100 per cent utilisation. 19.56 Mn. at 90 per cent utilization			

Source: As derived by the author.

million spindles, 37.5 per cent were already closed, and another 26 per cent remained out of operation for most part of the year. Of the remaining 5.38 million spindles, falling under the category of working spindles, 3 million were in the age group 31-40 years, 1.17 million in the age group 41-46 and the remaining 1.21 million more than 46 years old during 1996. The viability of these spindles, which will add nine years to their age by year 2005-06, could be well imagined in an environment of rapid technological progress. Thus, the above assumption seems relevant.

SSI Spinning Units

However, the problem in restructuring is that older spindle, when even disposed off, are not wiped off the production process and find place in small spinning units. In the case SSI sector spun yarn production of 106 million kilograms during 1995-96 is also taken into account, the additional spindles worked out on the basis of count composition of SSI sector (derived on the basis of cotton yarn given in Table 2.31) are =106x1000/(183.39x3x365)=0.5279 million at 100 per cent capacity utilisation.

or at 90 per cent capacity utilisation =.5279/.9=0.59 million.

Table 2.31
Minimum Spindles Required for Cotton Yarn Production in SSI Sector during 1995-96

Count	*Production (mn. Kgs)*	*Productivity (gms/s/s)*	*Spindles Required (mn.)*
0-10s	38	535.10	0.065
11-20s	22	250.22	0.08
21-30s	8	153.21	0.048
31-40s	26	105.22	0.226
41-60s	4	67.66	0.054
61-80s	1	42.99	0.02
>80	0	31.24	
Total Cotton	99	183.39	0.493
Total spun	106	183.39	0.528

Note : (i) At 90% utilisation, spindles required are 0.59.

Source: Derived from Office of the Textile Commissioner data.

Hence, on the whole 2.63 (2.04+0.59) million equivalent additional spindles of modern technology during 1996-97 are required at 90 per cent capacity utilisation to produce the actual production of spun yarn in the organised and SSI sector during 1996-97 by spindles less than 20 years old. However, the age composition criterion for SSI sector could not be similar to the organised sector. The SSI would be able to use the relatively better technology disposed off from the large units. The spindles equivalent installed in SSI sector were 1.56 million (1.44 mn. spindles and 24050 rotors) during 1996-97, the age composition of which is not available, but is believed to be of old technology. Thus SSI spinning units analysis is dealt separately.

Changes in the Structure of Industry during the Period 1996-97 to 1999-2000

The above analysis clearly brings out that the economic reforms introduced after 1985 have brought several structural changes in the spinning industry. In fact, during the last one decade, India witnessed one of the highest investments in the world in new spindles installed due to availability of machinery at competitive prices. The trend continued for the period 1996-97 to 1999-2000 as well. The total number of short spindles shipped in India during 1990-99 was 11.53 million spindles, which accounts for 36 per cent of the total spindles shipped in the world.

This has resulted in improved productivity of the spinning sector. Presently, the productivity of working spindles is very close to the optimal level. The capacity utilisation of working spindles has also improved, as old spindles were gradually becoming obsolete.

The analysis undertaken above could be extended till year 1999-2000 from the count-wise total production of spun yarn in the organised sector and unorganised sector. The analysis for the period 1996-97 to 1999-2000 is taken separately as the basic data available from official sources changed after that year. The data till year 1996-97 was available separately for the organised and unorganised sector. The official sources since then has changed the procedure and started giving count-range-wise combined data for the organised and unorganised sector. In this section an attempt is made to extend the above detailed analysis till year 1999-2000 under the given data limitations.

Table 2.32
Productivity Analysis Extended for the Period 1996-97 to 1999-2000

Year	*Spun Yarn Production Mn. Kgs.*	*Average count calculated*	*Productivity/ Spindle/ Year at 100% Ut (kg)*	*Minimum Modern Spindle Required Million*	*Installed Spindles Equivalent Mn.*
1983	1309.00		121.17	9.87	23.44
1988-89	1587.58		115.03	12.60	26.61
1989-90	1652.30	32.71	118.76	12.71	26.79
1990-91	1823.88	32.08	121.79	13.68	26.98
1991-92	1805.33	31.96	123.57	13.34	27.76
1992-93	1895.30	31.56	126.01	13.74	28.705
1993-94	2066.78	31.47	126.90	14.87	28.97
1994-95	2083.96	31.22	129.21	14.73	30.17
1995-96	2378.85	31.34	127.20	17.08	32.20
1996-97	2694.25	29.27	139.77	17.60	32.985
1996-97*	2793.87	—	140.76	18.13	—
1997-98*	2973.12	29.37	143.73	18.89	—
1998-99*	2807.71	29.50	143.83	17.83	—
1999-2000*	3045.45	29.47	147.62	18.84	—

* Includes Spun Yarn Production of SSI units.

Note: To work out the average count the methodology is given in Bedi (2000).

Source: As Derived by the Author.

To meet the additional requirement of spun yarn production during the period 1996-1997 to 1999-2000, the additional spindles required are 1.24 million (18.84-18.13) at 100 per cent utilisation or 0.71 million at 0.79 per cent utilisation. The investment in new spindles equivalent taken place during 1996-97 to 1999-2000 is 4.22 as derived from ITMF data. The technology of these spindles installed after 1996-97 is likely to be better compared to 1996-97 technology. These spindles are equivalent to 4.32 million spindles of 1996-97 technology.

Thus, it appears that the most of spun yarn requirements during 1999-2000 was met with spindles installed after 1981-82. There was shortage of only 0.86 (5.18-4.32) million spindles of 1996-97 technology to operate with technology installed after 1981-82. The present crisis in spinning industry is felt as not only replacement of old spindles is taking place at slow pace, but even the replaced spindles from mill sector are not discarded, but are being installed in the SSI spinning units.

Summing Up

- The productivity in spinning sector is worked out by first working out count-composition, share of carded and combed and various varieties of yarns such as hank cone and hosiery produced in each count range. The methodology used is based on SITRA norms of production per spindle for each count and variety of spun yarn produced. The prime reason for not pursuing traditional production function approach is the lack of required detailed data on spinning sector for all India, practical difficulties in measurement of various variables and econometric problem and conflicting results obtained from cross and time series data. Thus a methodology is evolved which could be useful to work out the impact of technology change on productivity. It is hoped that the methodology used in this study, which effectively, assumes count-wise constant returns to scale over time but allows for changes in count-composition, is more realistic than a simple production function approach.
- The liberalisation policy has affected the working environment in the spinning industry in various ways. The total number of idle spindles as a percentage of installed spindles declined from 28.68 per cent to 16.60 per cent to meet the increase in demand during 1985 to 1990, the first phase of liberalisation.
- The investment in modern spindles increased at a higher rate during 1990 to 1996, the second phase of liberalisation. The gross installed spindles per year on

average increased at 1.32 million per year during 1990-91 to 1996-97 compared to 0.74 million during 1983 to 1990-91. As the modern spindles increased, the old spindles became obsolete and the share of idle spindles in total installed spindles increased from 16.60 to 28.48 per cent during 1990 to 1996. The excess spindles required due to the technology gap between working spindles and spindles of latest available technology level during 1996-97 as a percentage of installed spindles thus increased from 14.72 per cent in 1983 to 18.01 per cent in 1990, which declined to 8.06 per cent in 1996. This process of modernisation continued even during 1997-98 to 1999-2000. However, unfortunately, the continuity in the data break as the data for the official data on count-wise production for the organised and unorganised sector is not separately available and is aggregated for both sectors after year 1996-97.

➡ The number of excess spindles being used can be determined by the difference between the working spindles and the minimum number of spindles required of latest technology (1996-97). This excess, expressed as a proportion of the minimum number required, may be a better measure of the technology gap. The excess spindles required as per cent of working spindles at 100% utilisation due to technology gap declined from 35.06 in 1983 to 32.75 in 1990 and further to 15.40 per cent in 1996.

➡ The analysis undertaken above could be extended till year 1999-2000 from the count-wise total production of spun yarn in the organised sector and unorganised sector. The analysis for the period 1996-97 to 1999-2000 is taken separately as the count range-wise data is not separately available after 1996-97. The investment in new spindles equivalent taken place during 1996-97 to 1999-2000 is 4.22 as derived from ITMF data and technology of these spindles is likely to have better productivity compared to 1996-97 technology. It is worked out that the most of present (1999-2000) spun yarn requirement is produced with spindles installed after year 1981-82. There is need of 0.86 million additional spindles at 1996-97 technology to produce the spun yarn production during 1999-2000 with spindle installed after year 1981-82.

➡ It is expected that around 19.68 million spindles of relatively old technology presently installed in the organised sector may go out of operation by the year 2010-11 either due to closure or would remain out of operation for most part of the year or may be wound up. In fact most of these units are already not working. The present crisis in spinning industry is felt as not only replacement of old spindles is taking place at slow pace, but even the replaced spindles from mill sector are not discarded, but are being installed in the SSI spinning units.

APPENDIX 2.1

Economies of Scale in Case Time Variable is Replaced with Modernisation Variable

In the time series data an attempt has been made to find technological parameters by fitting a Cobb-Douglas production function. For the time series data, the capital is taken as number of working spindles in India during the period 1977 to 1996-97 available from Compendium of Textile Statistics, Office of the Textile Commissioner. The labour data used is available from Annual Survey of Industry and data used is of man hours worked. The men hours worked are added up for cotton, spinning, weaving and processing in mills and spinning, weaving and processing of manmade textile fibre. The NIC code for these industries presently are 235 and 247. The NIC code for cotton spinning, weaving and processing before 1990-91 was 231. The man-hours used for weaving fabric are taken out by using SITRA norms to work out the man-hours worked for spinning yarn. The value added is worked out by multiplying the count range-wise production of spun yarn with average value added for each count range. The value added for various count ranges is estimated by using SITRA norms.

The modernisation variable is prepared by first working out the share of less than 10 years old spindles in total installed spindles during the base year *i.e.* 1977. For the next years, the modernisation ratio is worked out by using following formula.

Modernisation ratio at time t = (Modern spindles of less than 10 years old during base year + ((Additional installed spindles each year after the base year) (1+pt))) / (Total installed spindles during base year + ((Additional Installed spindles each year after the base year) (1+pt)))

Here t is time and p varies from 0.005 to 3. This means it is assumed that the productivity of new spindles is higher than old spindles varying from 0.5 per cent to 3 per cent each year respectively in the following three separate regressions.

Productivity of new spindles is taken at 0.5 per cent higher each year

Log V = a_0 + a_1 Log K + a_2 Log L + Modernisation ratio (M)

a_1 = 0.63 (0.16), a_2 = 0.27 (0.13), M = 0.019 (0.003)

Number of observation = 20, Degree of freedom 16, R square 0.987.

Note: Figures in brackets show standard error.

The economies of scale in this equation are thus worked out to be 0.90 and technological progress grew at 1.9 per cent per annum.

Productivity of new spindles is taken at 1.0 per cent higher each year

Log V = a_0 + a_1 Log K + a_2 Log L + Modernisation ratio (M)

a_1 = 0.62 (0.16), a_2 = 0.28 (0.13), M = 0.018 (0.003)

Number of observation = 20, Degree of freedom 16, R square 0.987.

Note: Figures in brackets show standard error.

The economies of scale in this equation are thus worked out to be 0.90 and technological progress grew at 1.8 per cent per annum.

Productivity of new spindles is taken at 2.0 per cent higher each year

Log V = a_0 + a_1 Log K + a_2 Log L + Modernisation ratio (M)

a_1 = 0.63 (0.16), a_2 = 0.28 (0.13), M = 0.017 (0.003)

Number of observation = 20, Degree of freedom 16, R square 0.986.

Note: Figures in brackets show standard error.

The economies of scale in this equation are thus worked out to be 0.91 and technological progress grew at 1.7 per cent per annum.

Productivity of new spindles is taken at 3.0 per cent higher each year

$\text{Log } V = a_0 + a_1 \text{ Log } K + a_2 \text{ Log } L + \text{Modernisation ratio } (M)$

$a_1 = 0.63\ (0.16)$, $a_2 = 0.29\ (0.13)$, $M = 0.016\ (0.003)$

Number of observation = 20, Degree of freedom 16, R square 0.987.

Note: Figures in brackets show standard error.

The economies of scale in this equation are thus worked out to be 0.92and technological progress grew at 1.6 per cent per annum.

The economies of scale in the above four equations vary from 0.90 to 0.92. The four modernisation ratio are worked out by assuming growth in productivity of modern spindle installed each year varying from 0.5 per cent to 3 per cent per annum as compared to modern installed spindles precious year. The results thus obtained in this study are similar to the one obtained in other studies. Mitra (1999) worked out economies of scale as one.

APPENDIX 2.2

Economies of Scale in Time Series Analysis (Mitra Study Results, 1999)

Mitra (1999) worked out economies of scale and technological progress for various industries at two digit level by using Cobb-Douglas production function in the double log form for the period 1976-77 to 1992-93.

$\text{Log } V = a_0 + t + a_1 \text{ Log } L + a_2 \text{ Log } K + rt + E\ (t)$

$E(t) = V\ (t) + U\ (t)$

Where a_1 and a_2 are potential elasticities of value added with respect to the inputs (Capital and Labour), a_0 is the intercept, r is the rate of Hicks-neutral technological progress, V is value added and K and L are the capital and labour variables, and E(t) is error term at time t respectively.

The results obtained for industry 23 (Cotton Textiles), 24

(Wool, Silk and Synthetic Fibre Textiles) and 26 (Textiles Products) are given below—

For Cotton Textile Industry (23)

a_1 = 0.248 (4.58)*, a_2 = 0.776 (12.536) *, r = 0.0012 (0.234)
R^2 = 0.92

Note: Figures in bracket show t statistics.

The economies of scale thus worked out are 1.024 (0.248 + 0.776) and technological progress grew at a rate of 0.12 per cent per annum in cotton textile industry.

For Wool, Silk and Synthetic Fibre Textiles (24)

a_1 = 0.317 (5.79)*, a_2 = 0.617 (5.016) *, r = 0.011 (1.19)
R^2 = 0.91

Note: Figures in bracket show t statistics.

The economies of scale thus worked out are 0.96 (0.31+0.653) and technological progress grew at a rate of 1.1 per cent per annum in wool, silk and synthetic fibre textiles industry.

For Textile Products (26)

a_1 = 0.245 (3.38)*, a_2 = 0.652 (8.02)*, r = 0.006 (0.638)
R^2 = 0.95

Note: Figures in bracket show t statistics.

The economies of scale thus worked out are 0.897 (0.245+0.652) and technological progress grew at a rate of 0.6 per cent per annum in textile products.

APPENDIX 2.3

Economies of Scale in Cross-section Analysis

An attempt is made to fit the Cob-Douglas production function for cross section data. The variables used in this regression are labour and capital as independent variables and value added as dependent variables. The capital represents the various kind of other machines required to balance the production of 1000 spindles at various counts of yarn. Information about machines required to balance 1000 spindles to produce various counts of spun yarn is provided by SITRA. These machines are speed frames, draw frames, cards, blow rooms and auto- coners which are required in different numbers. By using various machinery per unit costs, we have calculated the total fixed capital cost including of spindles required to produce spun yarn at each count. The labour required to balance production of 1000 spindles for various counts is also given in SITRA studies as HOK (Hours per 100 kilograms of yarn) and OHS (Operatives per 1000 spindles). Using the SITRA norms about values of various counts of spun yarn, and applying it on quantity of yarn produced at each count to balance 1000 spindles the possible values of production are worked out at each count with given machinery and labour.

Thus a production function could be used with the value added as dependent variable and labour and capital as dependent variable for cross section data for various count of yarn. A Cobb-Douglas production function then fitted on cross-section data, gives high economic of scale (1.36 to 1.41). The scale economies explain the increasingly shift in production towards coarser counts as capital and labour requirements per unit of output are low for coarser counts.

APPENDIX 2.4

Practical Relevance of assuming Count-wise Constant Returns to Scale Over Time but Allows for Changes in Count-composition

An attempt is made to see the practical relevance of assuming count-wise constant returns to scale over time but allows for changes in count-composition. To run a unit at reasonable capacity, it is important to produce various count combinations for which a minimum amount of raw material, labour, capital and managerial staff is required. The economic minimum size for the mill to satisfy these criteria is 25000 spindles. Thus in spinning sector, any firm operating below that size is not using its resources economically. In spinning sector, almost all the mills are operating above that size and hence are using resources economically.

Now once that minimum size is achieved, and the capacity is expanded further, the production for each count is obviously going to expand proportionally to the capacity expansion, as per technical sense. Thus the scale economies are unitary in technical sense. There is possibility that the demand for products is increased in such a proportion that all factors of production are not optimally used due to division factor. As the methodology used in this study is to compare the minimum spindles required with actual used at 100 per cent capacity utilisation, this aspect is taken care of. The point which is not taken into account in this method is the fact that the larger firms are capable of procuring inputs (cotton, fuel, electricity etc.), financial and other clearances from the government at lower cost due to its managerial efficiency or its economic size. In this study, impact of managerial efficiency is not looked into and only technical efficiency is studied.[15]

APPENDIX 2.5

Relevance of Methodology Used in this Study in Case of Hicks Non-neutral Technological Progress

The production per spindle depends upon the count of yarn produced as well as variety of yarn produced in a given technology. This is expressed in the following formula developed by SITRA experts.

Production per Spindle = ((Spindle speedx1000x Efficiency) / (((Count)$^{1.5}$)x(44.4)x(3.14)xTm))

Efficiency depends upon the time required to change sliber. Efficiency varies from 82 per cent to 95 per cent. Higher the count better the efficiency is.

Here Tm = TPIx(Count)$^{(-0.5)}$. TPI stands for twist per inch. Thus, Tm depends upon the variety of yarn and count of yarn. Spindle speed is higher for finer counts. The speed varies between around 9000 rpm and 17000 rpm depending upon the count for the latest technology. However, the technology

15. Traditional production function approach and approach adopted in this study. The data could be used to separate out the managerial and technical efficiencies.

progress in the past so far had caused increase in speed proportionally for all the count yarn produced and hence assumption of Hicks neutral technological progress at each count yarn is practically relevant.

An attempt is made in this Appendix to find the relevance of this methodology in case the technology progress would not have been of Hicks neutral type over the period of time. By using the formula *(ii)*, one could work out the total number of spindles and/or labour required at the best available technology during the last year. For total production at various count compositions, this could be written as

Total Actual Production at

$$\sum_{i=1}^{n} S_i = \sum_{i=1}^{n} a_i K^t i + \sum_{i=1}^{n} b_i L_i \qquad \text{—(ii)}$$

The formula *(ii)* could represent the specific count composition or a point on a given Isoquant or Production Possibility Frontier (PPF). The point is a summation of several type of count composition of spun yarn, which could be produced with different combinations of capital and labours.

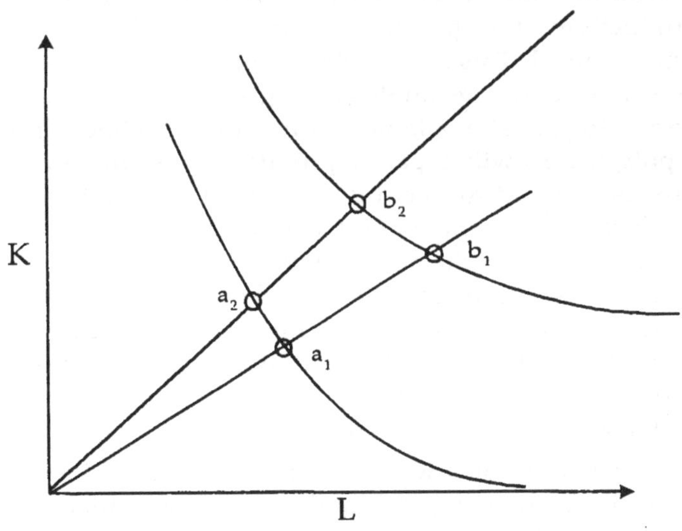

Figure 2.4. Hicks Non-neutral Technical Progress Isoqouant.

The spindles required at technology t to produce the given count composition and variety and fibre of yarn are then compared with actual spindles installed, which may not necessarily be on parallel isoquant to the current isoquant (Figure 2.4). This is a point of deviation from earlier assumptions, in which it was assumed that the technology progress at each count of spun yarn was hicks neutral.

Now the gap between two set of technology would have been larger in the case the production composition would have taken place at point a compared to point b. This means any shift in production composition over time may be misunderstood as technology progress. In case of Hicks neutral technology progress the gap would have been same at all points of productions on the isoquant.

The measurement of productivity in this case require three types of productivities namely capital, labour and inputs. Firstly, the percentage share of the minimum number of spindles required at latest available technology are compared with the actual used (working or/and installed) over the period of time. This tells not the growth in total factor productivity, but growth in partial productivity of spindles actually used. This is the point of difference in Hicks neutral and non-neutral technology progress. Similarly, using the norms for latest available technology for labour and other inputs, the growth in partial productivity of labour and other inputs is used at second and third stage. These three productivities are very important technical parameter to explain that how much is the potential of new technology to displace each of these inputs over the period of time, which the simple partial productivities cannot. Thus these technical ratios can be used to find out the future requirements of spindles, labour and raw cotton to produce the expected count composition with the change in technology.

One could also work out the Total Factor Productivity (TFP) by comparing the total production which could be produced with the quantum of inputs used at various periods of time at latest available technology with the actual production during each period. To add up the inputs at latest available technology, the weights for various inputs are required.

$$TFP = (Slt \times L + Skt \times K + Smt \times M) / (Sl \times L + Sk \times K + Sm \times M) = (Q) / (Sl \times Ll + Sk \times Kl + Sm \times Ml)$$

Here, Q, L, K and M are the output, labour, capital and inputs actually used for various years to produce the given count composition of yarn. Sl, Sk, and Sm are the weights for inputs labour, capital and input respectively at 't' technology.

As discussed in review of literature earlier, it is very difficult to add up heterogeneous kinds of inputs by assuming aggregate production function. One alternative is to study the firm level data of those units operating with latest available technology to work out the share of various inputs. SITRA is doing this kind of analysis.

Another alternative is to identify few firms operating with latest available technology at full capacity utilisation in a competitive environment. Thus the share of various inputs say for example labour is worked out by dividing total emolument by gross output (both at current prices) for all these firms. Thus the perfect competition is assumed in addition to assumption of count-wise constant returns to scale over time but which allows for changes in count-composition. Thus the total production gets exhausted and failure of any of these assumption leads to biased estimates.

Thus an attempt is made in this Appendix to make adjustments in case technology progress takes place of hicks non-neutral type. Despite limitations, the methodology seems to be better than the traditional method of working productivity by production function approach, even in the case of hicks non-neutral technology progress. This is because in this approach, the elasticity of substitution could vary across various counts and it could also change without any restriction over time. Similarly, studying the firm level data could modify the industry in which the unitary returns to scale for the count-wise is not applicable. These flexibilities in this methodology make this methodology considerably better than the traditional method of production functions.

APPENDIX 2.6

Age Composition of Spindles Installed

The official data on spindles given by the Textile Commissioner gives the total number of installed spindles at the end of each year for each state and the country as a whole. It is not possible to calculate the age of spindles installed since the data has no information of additional spindles installed each year.

In this study two methods have been used for calculating the age of spindles in India. In the first method, data used is available from various issues of ITMF, Zurich. These reports refer to spindles shipped by the participant manufacturer as sale for both domestic market and export market, which were shipped during the year under review. The shipment means total number of spindles sold by the manufacturers on shipper in each country, whether manufactured or imported (net). The ITMF obtains this data from textile manufacturers all over the world. During 1997, ITMF compiled data with the co-operation of 80 textile machinery manufacturers. The data for 1997 covers for various textile segments, namely, spinning, draw texturing, weaving and knitting machinery. It covers all the countries with the exception of Mainland Chinese manufacturers of spinning machines. The age of spindles is worked out by building a perpetual year-wise inventory of spindles added in the country.

The results derived above are cross-checked for India with the availability of spindles in the country derived by second method. In the second method, estimates regarding availability of spindles are calculated by adding production plus net imports of ring frames by using Federation of Indian Textile Engineering Industry statistics (FITE).[16] These are then converted into spindles equivalent by multiplying by 440. This is because the numbers of spindles per standard ring frame are equal to 440 and long ring frames are of almost double the capacity than the standard ring frames. However, the data given in the Federation of Indian Textile Engineering Industry

16. Standing Committee of the Federation of Indian Textile Engineering.

statistics adjusts the long ring frames for standard ring frames.

We compare the data for last ten years by these two methods.

Appendix—Table 2.1
Spindles Availability during Various Years

Period	*Shipment Production (C.Y.)*	*Ring Frames Exports (Cotton Spinning) F.Y.*	*Ring Frames Imports (Cotton Spinning) F.Y.*	*Spindle Equivalent Availability*
(1)	*(2)*	*(3)*	*(4)*	*(5)=((2)-(3)+(4))*440*
1987-88	476,684	1,830	3,473	653,840
1988-89	623,855	1,986	492	657,360
1989-90	433,662	2,841	6,565	963,600
1990-91	1,059,665	3,993	656	1,468,280
1991-92	1,228,615	3,495	265	1,421,200
1992-93	864,140	2,960	309	1,166,440
1993-94	1,026,896	3,092	18,126	1,292,280
1994-95	1,272,536	3,855	3,501	1,542,640
1995-96	2,020,240	4,317	3,555	1,745,480
1996-97	1,516,763	2,725	6,451	915,640
Period				
1990-96	8,988,855	24,437	276,133	9,551,960
1987-96	10,523,056	31,094	425,641	11,826,760

Note: C.Y. refers to Calendar Year and F.Y. to Financial Year.
Source: Derived from various issues of ITMF and FITE

There is year-to-year difference in two data source mainly because of following reasons. The data coverage in the ITMF and FITE may be different because the period considered is calendar year in ITMF reports and financial year in FITE reports. However, one of the important reason for the difference seems to be the fact that the ITMF data basically relate to the spindles physically taken out of the manufacturing units and are likely to be in the process of installation. The data takes into consideration the production and stock depletion in the machinery of the manufacturing units. This data is definitely more useful in the study where we are considering the addition in new installed spindles to start the working process. However, the estimates of availability of spindles include besides investment by the spinner changes in the stock of spindles manufacturers. The machinery once produced has to be absorbed in the long run for working and hence the long run data for the period 1987-96 and 1990-96 from two sources are close to each other.

For analysis in this study, the ITMF statistics have been used for studying the number and age of spindles. This is because of two reasons. First ITMF data closely represent the addition to spinning capacity each year. Secondly, the continuous data are available on shipment since 1974.

By using ITMF data on spindles shipped and Textile Commissioner data on the number installed at the end of the year over the period of time, it is possible to assess what percentage of the installed spindles are being replaced.

Appendix—Table 2.2
Replacement of Old Spindles as per cent of Installed

Period	*Shipment (Calendar Year)*	*Installed Spindles Mn.*	*Addition in Installed capacity*	*Replacement as % of Inst. Spin.*
(1)	(2)	(3)	(4)	(5)
1973		18.14		
1974	45,000	18.50	360,000	-1.74
1975	336,048	19.36	860,000	-2.83
1976	545,832	19.89	530,000	0.08
1977	438,176	19.70	-190,000	3.16
1978-79	561,320	20.08	380,000	0.92
1979-80	832,048	20.74	660,000	0.86
1980-81	826,950	21.23	490,000	1.62
1981-82	465,668	21.93	700,000	-1.10
1982-83	547,920	22.91	980,000	-1.97
1983-84	638,171	24.28	1,370,000	-3.19
1984-85	977,062	25.57	1,290,000	-1.29
1985-86	968,524	26.02	450,000	2.03
1986-87	664,490	26.12	100,000	2.17
1987-88	476,684	26.25	130,000	1.33

(Contd....)

(Contd...)

(1)	*(2)*	*(3)*	*(4)*	*(5)*
1988-89	623,855	26.46	210,000	1.58
1989-90	433,662	26.59	130,000	1.15
1990-91	1,059,665	26.67	80,000	3.68
1991-92	1,228,615	27.82	1,150,000	0.29
1992-93	864,140	28.09	270,000	2.14
1993-94	1,026,896	28.60	510,000	1.84
1994-95	1,272,536	30.70	2,100,000	-2.89
1995-96	2,020,240	31.75	1,050,000	3.16
1996-97	1,516,763	32.22	470,000	3.30

Note: Installed spindles are considered at the end of year *i.e.* 31st march. Data for some of the years given for the spindles shipment in the ITMF volumes do not tally with the corresponding figures for the ten years period when added up, and hence require adjustment in few figures. Some changes were made after consulting several volumes of ITMF and data from other sources.

Source: Derived from ITMF and Office of the Textile Commissioner data.

From the derived replacement ratios as the percentage of installed spindles (given above), it can be concluded that over the period of time, industries have started spending increasingly towards replacement. Replacement ratio for the period 1990-96 comes to 1.68, against 0.36 during 1974-80. This indicates that old machinery is being increasingly displaced by new machinery. Nevertheless since the stock of old spindle is very large they continued to be more dominant in the production process (Table 2.3 of Appendix).

Keeping the above facts and the last period's available ratio of 0.36 in mind, we expected that the replacement ratio as percentage of installed spindle could be taken as equal to 0.36 for the period 1971-73, 0.30 for the period 1966-70, 0.25 for the period 1961-65 and 0.20 for the period 1950-60.

Given this ratio, it comes out that there has been an addition of 8.01 million spindles in gross installed spindles over a period of 23 years between 1950 and 1973. This is derived from the available data on net installed spindles from Textile Commissioner by using above replacement ratios. In 1950, the number of spindles was 11 million, which increased to 18.14

million in 1973. Whereas the net additional shipment was 7.14, the spindles written off numbered 0.87 million.

Appendix—Table 2.3
Replacement Ratios as Percentage of Installed Spindles during Various Phases

Period	*Average Installed Spindles (Mn.) =((n-1)+n/2)*	*Increase in Installed Capacity*	*Replacement as per cent of Install Spindles*	*Cumulative Spindles Shipment (Mn)*
1990-96	28.60	5,630,000	1.68	8.99
1987-96	27.91	6,100,000	1.59	10.52
1981-96	26.31	10,990,000	0.90	14.78
1974-96	24.23	14,080,000	0.77	18.37
1974-80	19.49	3,090,000	0.36	3.59
1950-73	15.58	7,140,000	—	8.01
1950-96	—	—	—	26.38

Source: Derived from ITMF and Office of the Textile Commissioner data.

From the above-derived data for the period 1950-73, the year-wise series of spindles shipped since 1951 till 1996-97 has been estimated in Table 2.4 of Appendix.

Table 2.4 of Appendix shows that the 1974-80 period has shown a slow down in investment, which picked up later. The ten-year-old spindles ratio in the total installed spindles slided down during the same period. It was 26 per cent in first half of seventies, which slided down to 14 per cent level in the second half of the seventies before going up to more than 32 per cent in 1996.

Another interesting finding is that around 82 per cent of the spindles installed are less than 46 years old *i.e.* installed after the year 1950. This means the remaining 18 per cent are even older than 46 years.

Appendix—Table 2.4
Expansion in India's Spinning Capacity

Year	Installed Spindles in Mn. (At Year end)	Comulative spindles shipment since 1951 in Mn.	Age of Spindles as on 31st March, 1997		Spindles shipment since 1951 as Percentage of Installed spindles	Cumulative shipment for last ten years in Mn.	Spindles shipped in last 10 years as a % of installed spindles
			Less than (Years)	No. of Spindles in Mn.			
(1)	(2)	(3)	(4)	(5)	(6)	(7)	(8)
1950	11.00	—			—		
1955	12.05	1.17	45	26.38	9.67		
1960	13.66	2.90	40	25.21	21.26	2.90	21.26
1961	13.83	3.11	35	23.48	22.47		
1962	14.11	3.42	34	23.27	24.26		
1963	14.66	4.01	33	22.96	27.34		
1964	15.43	4.81	32	22.37	31.20		
1965	16.12	5.54	31	21.57	34.39	4.38	27.16
1966	16.67	6.14	30	20.84	36.84		
1967	17.09	6.61	29	20.24	38.69		
1968	17.43	7.00	28	19.77	40.18		
1969	17.67	7.29	27	19.38	41.28		
1970	17.88	7.56	26	19.09	42.27	4.65	26.03
1971	18.11	7.85	25	18.82	43.36	4.74	26.20

(Contd....)

(Contd....)

(1)	(2)	(3)	(4)	(5)	(6)	(7)	(8)
1972	17.98	7.79	24	18.53	43.31	4.37	24.28
1973	18.14	8.01	23	18.59	44.17	4.00	22.08
1974	18.50	8.06	22	18.37	43.55	3.24	17.53
1975	19.36	8.39	21	18.32	43.35	2.85	14.72
1976	19.89	8.94	20	17.99	44.94	2.80	14.07
1977	19.70	9.38	19	17.44	47.60	2.77	14.04
1978-79	20.08	9.94	18	17	49.50	2.94	14.62
1979-80	20.74	10.77	17	16.44	51.93	3.48	16.76
1980-81	21.23	11.60	16	15.61	54.63	4.04	19.03
1981-82	22.91	12.61	15	14.78	55.05	4.82	21.05
1983-84	24.28	13.25	14	13.77	54.57	5.24	21.57
1984-85	25.57	14.23	13	13.13	55.64	6.17	24.13
1985-86	26.02	15.19	12	12.15	58.40	6.80	26.14
1986-87	26.12	15.86	11	11.19	60.72	6.92	26.49
1987-88	26.25	16.34	10	10.52	62.23	6.96	26.51
1988-89	26.46	16.96	9	10.04	64.10	7.02	26.54
1989-90	26.59	17.39	8	9.42	65.41	6.62	24.91
1990-91	26.67	18.45	7	8.99	69.19	6.86	25.71
1991-92	27.82	19.68	6	7.93	70.75	7.62	27.39
1992-93	28.09	20.55	5	6.7	73.14	7.93	28.25
1993-94	28.60	21.57	4	5.83	75.43	8.32	29.10
1994-95	30.70	22.85	3	4.81	74.42	8.62	28.08

(Contd....)

(Contd...)

(1)	(2)	(3)	(4)	(5)	(6)	(7)	(8)
1995-96	31.75	24.87	2	3.53	78.32	9.67	30.46
1996-97	32.22	26.38	1	1.51	81.88	10.52	32.66

Note: Installed spindles are considered at the end of year *i.e.* 31st march. We have deliberately taken installed spindles for the financial year though shipment period is calendar year, as the spindles shipped take some time to get installed. Weighted Age of expected working spindles of around 23.48 million is around 13.17 years and weighted age of working spindles around 25.21 million is around 14.70 years.

Source: As derived by theAuthor.

3

Structural Changes in the Indian Textile Industry

The textile industry has a complex structure. There exist several stages of value added namely spinning weaving and stitching. The production from fibre to yarn takes place through spinning process. The fabrics from yarn are converted through weaving process and from fabrics to made-ups or garment is converted through stitching process. There is one additional value added at yarn or fabrics stage called dying processing.

The industry comprises the organised mill sector and the unorganised powerloom, handloom, khadi and garment sectors. The spinning process is dominantly taking place in organised mill sector, while the weaving, stitching and dying is mainly taking place in unorganised sector. Weaving process takes place in mill sector and unorganised powerloom, handloom and khadi sectors. The organised industry is barely over 175 years old, while the handloom industry is the oldest in the country. The dying takes place after yarn or fabrics stage either in integrated units along with weaving or other activities. However, the dying processing mainly takes place in independent processing units.

The fabrics produced in various sectors are either exported or domestically consumed in the form of fabrics, made-ups and garments. The process of manufacturing made-ups and garments from fabrics is called stitching and is taking place in garment or tailoring units. Sometimes production of made-ups is taking place in integrated weaving units. The garments could be classified into tailor made garments and readymade garments, as final uses are the similar. This is a deviation from the traditional definition of garments, where only readymade garments are generally taken as garments.

Yarn, fabrics and made-ups segment are part of the textiles products in the International Trade Classifications, while garments fall within the clothing products. In this chapter, we will be basically dealing with the textiles sector and estimates about production of garments will be dealt in Chapter 4.

Having discussed the method for estimating the requirement of spindles for complete modernisation of spinning industry in the previous chapter, this chapter is devoted to working out conversion rates from yarn to fabrics stage of production to work out the estimates of production of fabrics. The inter-linkages of various stages of productions or conversion rates are important to work out the requirements from one stage to another. Thus the conversion rates from fibre to yarn and yarn to fabrics are worked out for each fibre or blend of yarn.

The careful working out of conversion rates is important, to know the state of industry and to facilitate the future projection. The variations among the composition of count ranges, affects the weighted conversion rates from yarn to fabrics. An attempt is thus made to work out count range-wise conversion rate to work out accurate estimates of production of fabrics.

Stages of Production from Fibre to Fabrics

The production of fabric process passes through various stages such as fibre cleaning, spinning, processing, and dying and weaving etc. In the case of filament yarn the spinning stage is not required and filament yarn is directly woven. Therefore, filament yarn is considered as raw material for weaving production. The fabrics is produced from fibre by going through processing stages as shown in Figure 3.1.

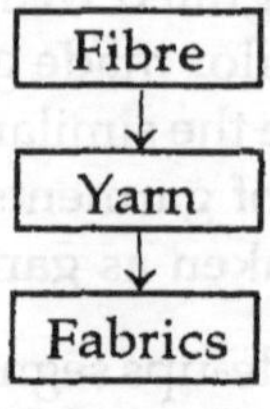

Figure 3.1. Stages of Production of Fabrics.

All the yarns are not produced through spinning, filament yarn is an example. As filament yarn does not require spinning process, for the estimation of spindles requirement, its share was excluded in working out the production, productivity and technological change in spinning sector in Chapter 2. However, filament yarn has to be covered while dealing with fabrics related input and output items.

The variety and composition of fibre is important to study as it has ultimate impact on the variety of final output. Spinning is the process in which yarn is produced from fibre.

The fibre used could be natural or man-made fibre (MMF). Natural fibres are cotton, wool and silk, i.e. those fibres, which are naturally available. Polyester, viscose, acrylics and other miscellaneous fibres are produced through chemical processing. Yarn production from these fibres could be classified into three groups namely spun yarn, filament yarn (and its further classifications) and the tyre yarns (and its further classification) as shown in Figure 3.2(a).

Total yarn production in the country in all the above three forms is estimated at 4041 million kilograms during 1999-2000. The production of yarn was 2232 million kgs during 1990-91. Yarn production showed approximately 6.82 per cent per annum growth rate during the period 1990-91 to 1999-2000. The high growth at the base level must have similar impact at the value-added stages unless there were leakages in the form of exports. The imports at different intermediary stages of production have an opposite impact.

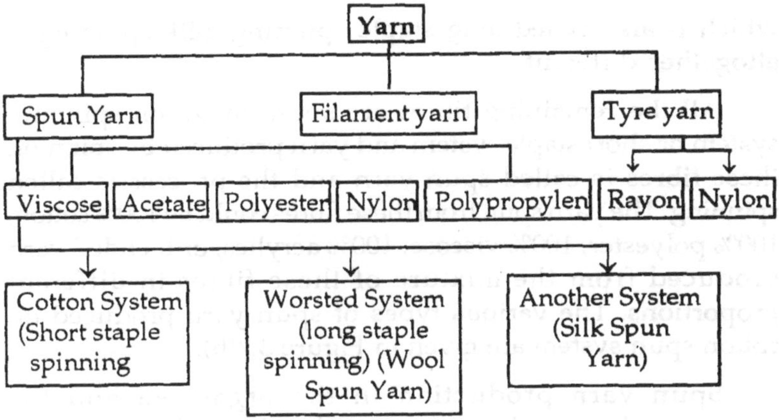

Figure 3.2(a). Various Types of Yarn.

The major share of yarn available in the country (except tyre yarn and small proportion for some other miscellaneous uses) is consumed for production of fabrics. Yarn is also used to produce thread, which is further used for stitching made-ups and garments. This study deals with fabrics and related products and the tyre yarn production is excluded in this analysis.

The total spun yarn and filament yarn (excluding tyre yarn) production is estimated at 3940 million kilograms during 1999-2000. The production was 2051.5 million kilograms during 1990-91. It grew by 7.52 per cent per annum during the period 1990-91 to 1999-2000.

Spun Yarn

Spun yarn production (including silk and wool yarn production) in the organised and the unorganised sectors amounted to 3147 million kilograms during 1999-2000 as against 1908 million kgs in 1990-91, there by recording growth rate of 5.72 per cent per annum during the period 1990-91 to 1999-2000. There are various types of systems on which spun yarns are manufactured.

Wool is generally spun on worsted spinning system,

which is also called long staple spinning. Silk spinning is altogether different.

All the remaining fibres are spun on cotton spinning system or short staple system and yarn produced by spinning these fibres is called spun yarn and the process is called spinning. The yarn spun from these fibres could be 100% cotton, 100% polyester, 100% viscose, 100% acrylics, or blended yarn produced from the mixture of these fibres in different proportions. The various types of spun yarn produced on cotton spun system are given in Figure 3.2(b).

Spun yarn production in the organised and the unorganised sectors is predominantly taking place on cotton spun system (short staple). The short staple spun yarn is still the most important segment and data on this segment could be relied upon due to its dominance in the organised sector. Filament yarn is emerging as another important input in fabric production. The analysis in this study is going to be focussed on production of fabrics, made-ups and garments from spun and filament yarn.

Short Staple Spinning

The spun yarn (cotton spun system) is produced on short staple spinning. The spun yarn production in the organised and SSI Spinning units increased from 602 million kilograms during 1950-51 to 2794 million kilograms during 1996-97 and further to 3046 million kgs in 1999-2000. The share of SSI sector in it was 5.09 per cent during 1999-2000. As for this study, the other spun yarns except cotton system spun yarn are not studied, cotton system spun yarn would thereafter be referred as the spun yarn.

Spindles is the machinery used to spun yarn. However, rotors are used for the production of coarser counts. Spun yarn below count 10 (10s) is mainly produced on rotors. Significant percentage of spun yarn in count range 11-20s is also produced on rotors. Productivity per rotors for particular count is equivalent to around 5 times the production per spindle for same count. Count (s) of yarn tells the fineness of yarn. Finer (higher) the count better is its quality and thinner is the yarn. On the other hand, coarser the count thicker is the yarn.

The Indian spinning sector has witnessed a phenomenal growth during the last four decades. The spindles increased from 11 million in 1951 to 34.59 million (including SSI sectors spindles) by the end of March 97. The spindles installed further increased to 37.08 million (including SSI sectors spindles) by the end of March 2000. The rotors increased from 45 thousand in 1989 to 300.34 thousand in March 1997, and to 444.80 thousand in March 2000. The main growth in the spindle sector has taken place in the spinning sector, while the number of spindles has declined in the composite mills.

The maximum numbers of spindles are installed in state of Tamilnadu accounting for 32.88% of total spindles in the country. Tamilnadu, Maharashtra and Karnataka are the major yarn producing states.

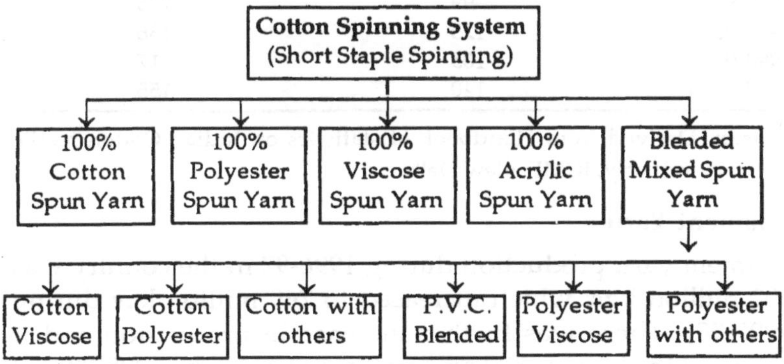

Figure 3.2(b). Various Types of Yarn Produced on the Cotton Spun System.

Short staple spinning is dominantly taking place in the organised sector. In the recent years there has been considerable growth in the production of yarn by small scale spinning units (SSI). The SSI spinning units are mostly concentrated in the state of Tamil-Nadu. There are, however, quite a few units in other states as well. The production of spun yarn in SSI was 46 million kgs during 1992-93, 106 million kg during 1996-97, 135 million kgs during 1997-98, and 155 million kilograms during 1999-2000, there by showing a high growth rate of 19 per cent per annum from 1992-93 to 1999-2000 (Table 3.1). The production of cotton yarn by SSI sector is estimated at 99 million kilograms during 1996-97, which increased to 140 million during 1999-2000. The cotton yarn share in total SSI spun yarn production was 90 per cent during 1999-2000.

Table 3.1
Production of Spun Yarn in the Small Scale Sector

(Mn kgs)

Year	*Cotton*	*Total Spun Yarn*
1992-93	46	46
1993-94	75	75
1994-95	110	110
1995-96	106	106
1996-97	99	106
1997-98	125	136
1998-99	105	117
1999-2000	140	155

Source: Derived from Handbook of statistics on Indian Cotton textile industry, ICMF, New Delhi.

Filament Yarn

Filament yarn production during 1996-97 in the country was 602 million kgs, which increased to 769 million kgs during 1997-98. There was further increase in production and it achieved the level of 850 million kgs latter during 1998-99 and 894 million kgs during 1999-2000.

Spun Yarn (Cotton System) and Filament Yarn

Spun and filament yarn grew by 8.53 per cent per annum from the period 1990-91 to 1997-98. There was decline in spun and filament yarn production to 3658 million kgs during 1998-99 due to slow down, but it increased to 3940 million kgs during 1999-2000. In case, tyre yarn is excluded, the total spun and filament yarn production in the organised and small-scale sector (excluding silk and wool yarn and tyre yarn) increased from 3395 million kgs in 1996-97 to 3729 million kgs in 1997-98 and further to 3890 million kilograms during 1999-2000. Since spun yarn (cotton system) and filament yarn account for 97.5 per cent of total yarn including silk, wool and tyre yarn during 1999-2000, the present study is mainly confined to this segment.

The high growth of spun and filament yarn production is due to very high growth rate of filament yarn. The spun yarn share in total spun and filament yarn is on the decline. It declined from 86.8 per cent in 1990-91 to 79.8 per cent in 1997-98 and decline continued further to 78.3 per cent during 1999-2000. However, in this spun yarn production, the production of yarn at Charkhas, which is consumed in the handloom sector for fabrics production has not been taken into account. The handloom sector, which consumes yarn from charkhas is called the khadi sector. Thus, the data for Khadi (Charkha) sector is also not taken into account for this study.[1]

Fibre/Filaments Consumption

The raw material required to produce yarn is called fibre. The total fibre/filament yarn consumption was 3326 million kgs during 1995-96. It grew to 3720 million kgs during 1996-97 and to 4215 million kgs during 1997-98. There was decline in its consumption to 4088 million kg during 1998-99, but increased to 4433 million kilograms during 1999-2000.

The analysis of consumption of fibres/filament reveals that cotton and polyester are two important fibres consumed (Table 3.2). The cotton fibre has shown a steep fall in total fibre/filament consumption over eighties and nineties. The share of cotton in total fibre/filament consumption was 82.11 per cent in 1983. It declined to 73.00 per cent in 1991-92. The share of cotton was 64.51 per cent during 1997-98. There was further decline to 60.79 per cent during 1998-99 and to 59.82

1. Estimates about the production of fabrics in the Khadi sector are 105 million Sq. Mt during 1995-96, which comes to around 0.1 Sq. Mt. per capita availability.

per cent during 1999-2000. It is expected that the cotton fibre share is going to decline further in future. Despite that the cotton fibre growth is going to play an important role in the future growth of industry. This is because there is a limit to which cotton could be substituted for synthetic. So cotton fibre availability is important.

Table 3.2
Consumption of Fibres/Filaments

(Mn Kgs)

Fibre/ Filament	*1995-96*	*1996-97*	*1997-98*	*1998-99*	*1999-2000(p)*
		Fibre			
Cotton	2308	2565	2719	2485	2652
PSF	256	303	458	501	572
VSF	200	173	198	183	207
ASF	72	78	111	94	94
Other Fibre	10	10	02	02	875
Total Fibre	2846	3129	3488	3265	3527
		Filament			
PFY	371	491	630	727	802
NFY	42	37	30	29	29
Cellulosic FY	54	51	54	51	48
Polypropylene	13	12	13	15	17
Total Filament	480	591	727	822	896
		Total Fibre/Filament			
Fibre/Filament	3326	3720	4215	4087	4423

Source: Annual Report, ICMF 1997-98.

The current cotton yield level in India is almost half compared with world average yield and hence there is a possibility to increase further cotton production by increasing cotton yield. The area, production and yield of cotton in India is given in Table 3.3.

Variety Perspective of Cotton Fibre

The varitial perspective of cotton is important, as it will affect the type of product to be produced from it. The share of major varieties in total production of cotton in India is given in Table 3.4.

Table 3.3
Production, Area and Yield of Cotton in India

Cotton Year	*Area Mn. Hectare*	*Productin Mn. Nales*	*Yield Kg/Hectare*
1961-62	8.0	5.3	112
1971-72	7.8	7.4	162
1981-82	8.1	8.4	177
1985-86	7.5	11.5	261
1990-91	7.4	11.7	267
1991-92	7.7	11.9	268
1992-93	7.5	13.8	316
1993-94	7.3	12.2	286
1994-95	7.9	13.9	300
1995-96	9.1	16.9	316
1995-96*	9.1	17.0	320
1996-97 *	9.1	17.8	332
1997-98*	8.9	15.8	302
1998-99*	9.3	16.5	302
1999-2000*	8.6	15.6	307
Gr. Rt. 1990-91 To 1999-2000	2.4	3.7	1.3
t-Stat istics	4.2	4.0	2.3

Note: 1. Cotton year September to August.
2. Gr. Rt. = Compound growth rate based on semi-log trend for the period 1990-91 to 1999-2000.
3. * Cotton year = October to September.

Source: Indian Cotton Annual, various issues.

Ginning and Pressing

The kapas has to go through ginning and pressing stages before being used as input for the textile sector. The essential function of ginning is to separate the lint from the seed fragments, pods, leafy matter and other trash. In India most of ginning units are small. A number of gins are serviced by the pressing units, where the fluffy lint is squeezed into bales of 170+-5 kgs using steam presses. Each pressing factory has a distinct pressmark, which identifies the bale (ICRA, 1996).[2]

2. *(i)* The tolerance of +-5 kgs was introduced in the 1985 Cotton Control Order. Prior to that the specified tolerance was +-10 kgs.

(Contd...)

Table 3.4
Share of Different Staples of Cotton Consumption in Mills in India

(per cent)

Year	*Short Staples*	*Medium Staples*	*Superior Medium*	*Long Staples*	*Extra Long Staples*	*Total (in Million Bales)*
1992-93	3.23	44.10	16.16	26.86	8.22	100.00
1993-94	3.69	41.74	20.30	26.56	6.89	100.00
1994-95	5.40	36.25	18.90	29.43	5.91	100.00
1995-96	7.07	36.67	18.87	30.02	5.40	100.00
1996-97	7.51	35.76	19.69	31.67	4.82	100.00
1997-98	5.72	31.44	19.30	37.48	4.24	100.00
1998-99	4.21	28.99	17.71	39.98	3.97	100.00
1999-2000	4.74	32.74	16.54	32.31	2.92	100.00

Source: Compendium of Textile Statistics, Office of the Textile Commissioner, Ministry of Textiles (GOI) and Handbook of Statistics, ICMF.

Data in this sector is hard to come by. This is notwithstanding the expressed objectives of superior statistical coverage embodied in both the Ginning Act of 1925 and the Cotton Control Order of 1955. The last comprehensive data on the number of gins pertains to 1962.

The state of data is evident from the fact that the 1985 Expert Committee on Textiles which devoted four whole paragraphs on the need to modernise the ginning mills, while cautioning against the "labour displacing" content of superior saw gins, did not see it fit to present or discuss any statistics.

(Contd...)

(ii) "The existing gins in the country are generally very old and belong to the category known as roller gins.... the Committee would urge provision of concessional finance (from financial institutions) for replacement of the existing gins..... Saw ginning of cotton improves the quality of lint... replacement of existing roller gins... (Implies) displacement of labour.... (therefore) saw ginning can be advocated mainly in areas of irrigated cotton."

Source: ICRA Limited (1996), Paras 8.3, 8.4, 8.5 and 8.6 page 31, New Delhi.

Conversion Rate of Fiber to Yarn

The raw material required to produce yarn is fibre. The conversion rate for yarn varies for various fibres. Conversion rate for yarn means the fibre required per unit of yarn production. The conversion rate for yarn mainly depends upon the compositions of various blends of spun yarns as well as carded and combed ratios in total yarn. It also depends to some extent on the quality of fibre used and technology of spinning. The weighted conversion rate for fibre to yarn could be arrived at by dividing total consumption of fibre with total production of yarn. The consumption of fibre is not separately available for the production of various kinds of blended yarn. The experts' opinion has been used to take average share of various blends in the different blended yarns (Appendix 3.3). Regarding the carded and combed share in cotton blended yarn, various experts were of the opinion that it is safe to take approximately 75 per cent yarn as combed yarn and the remaining 25 per cent as carded.

After making these assumptions, an attempt is then made to arrive at the conversion rate for various fibre yarns by applying hit and trial method.[3] The conversion rates for fibre to yarn is estimated for 100% cotton yarn as 1.17, Polyester and Acrylic 1.025 and Viscose 1.09 (it is high due to high moisture in viscous fibre), Grey wool 1.087, dyed wool 1.1364. The filament yarn is already yarn and so conversion rate is taken as 1.

Weaving Process

Weaving is the process through which yarn is converted into the fabrics stage. The various sectors in which fabrics is produced are composite mills and decentralised sector.

3. However, here lies another problem as the estimates of fibre consumption to produce yarn differ as per various official sources. We have basically relied for this on the data published in the Compendium of textile statistics, Textile Commissioner as well as on Handbook of cotton textile industry, ICMF. The difference in these two sources was for a few years and was marginal.

Mill Sector

Mills having both spinning and weaving capacity are called composite mills. As the spinning sector is discussed in detail in Chapter 2, this chapter concentrate on weaving segment. The composite mills mainly consume their own yarn for production of fabrics. Weaving capacity in the composite mills is declining for a number of years. The situation has not even changed with the removal of restriction in the creation of capacity in the textile sector as permitted by the textile policy 1985.

The non-SSI weaving units are also falling in the organised sector, as is the case for mill sector. They are not composite units in the sense that weaving and spinning is not done in the same unit. Some of these weaving units are set up independently by the same group having independent spinning units, but for all practical purposes they are treated as separate units. The concept of independent profit centre has resulted in this sector gaining importance recently. In fact, some of the units with latest available technology are set up under the non-SSI-weaving sector. The total number of installed looms in non-SSI weaving units was 122,668 as on 31st March 1997, fifty six per cent of it was in private sector.

However, Textile Ministry is lately combining the data of composite and non-SSI units under the head of mill sector (composite mills). Earlier non-SSI unit data were put under the powerloom sector. The capacity expansion in the composite mills was not very encouraging. During 1956, there were 291 mills, 10.61 million spindles and 203 thousand shuttle looms in the composite sector. The number of weaving mills (including non-SSI weaving units) declined to 281, spindles to 9.96 million, shuttle loom to 118 thousands and shuttleless looms 7.95 thousands in the composite sector during 1996-97. The number of mills increased marginally to 285, spindles to 9.62 million, shuttle loom to 120 thousands and shuttleless looms to 7.95 thousands during 1999-2000.

The capacity utilisation in weaving segment is very poor. In 1998-99 the average utilisation of looms was only 29.17 per cent of the total installed looms, which further declined in subsequent years. Clearly a large proportion of looms remained closed for most part of the year. The capacity utilisation of looms in the organised sector is given in Table 3.5.

Table 3.5
Looms Activity

Year	*Average Installed Looms ('000)*	*Average Working Looms ('000)*	*Working Looms as % of Installed*	*Daily Average Working Looms ('000)*	*Average Utilisation of Installed Looms*
1995-96	135.82	94.83	69.82	56.00	41.23
1996-97	132.36	81.66	61.70	55.36	41.82
1997-98	123.58	68.80	55.67	40.93	33.12
1998-99	123.94	65.51	52.86	36.15	29.17
1999-2000*	122.67	55.79	45.48	—	—

* Data is as on March 2000 for the year 1999-2000.

Source: Annual Report, ICMF.

This reflects the poor condition of the weaving mills in the country. Indian weaving mills are working in poor conditions and are not adequately modernised is also brought out by the low number of shuttleless looms installed in India (Table 3.6). Shuttleless looms are a new development in weaving segment since eighties and could be considered as index of modernisation.

It is clear that countries competing with India have much larger number of shuttleless looms than India. In fact modernization of weaving capacity is mainly taking place in other Asia and Oceania countries except India. The pattern was similar in the subsequent two years after 1997 as well. The number of shuttle-less looms shipped in India during 1999 was 341 (1.6 per cent) as against 21,319 in Asia and Oceania countries. Asia and Oceania countries constitute around 67.00 per cent of the total shipment in World of shuttle-less looms during 1999. The share of these Asia and Oceania countries was 62.00 per cent of the shipment during the whole period 1990-99.

Table 3.6
Shuttleless Looms in Selected Countries

Country	*Shuttleless Looms till 1997*
China	66,086
Republic of Korea	29,806
Indonesia	29,156
Taiwan	27,212
India	7,160

Source: International Textile Manufacturing Federation (ITMF), Zurich.

The ownership-wise distribution of the total 122.67 thousand looms installed (shuttle and shuttleless) on 31st March, 2000 indicates that per cent share of private sector was 55.55, public 44.21 (30.07 in National Textile Corporation (NTC) and 14.14 in State Textile Corporation (STC)) and Co-operatives 0.24 of the total weaving capacity installed in the country. However, the production of fabrics was much more concentrated in private mills as share of public sector was only 8.07 per cent. Out of the total installed looms, 70.84 thousand looms were closed, which accounts for 55.00 per cent of the total installed looms. Around 70.00 per cent of the looms falling under closed mills belong to private sector, 12.30 per cent to NTC and 17.70 per cent to STC during 1997-98.

The number of workers employed in textiles mills (both in spinning and composite) was 1,027,393. The private sector employs the maximum 69.80 per cent share of the total workers employed in textiles mills. The per cent share of NTC, STC and Co-operative mills is 11.27, 8.49 and 10.44 per cent in the total workers employed in textiles mills. The number of workers employed in total closed mills (both spinning and weaving) accounted for 253,773, out of which 76.68 per cent are lying in private mills. The per cent share of workers employed in closed mills of NTC, STC and Co-operative were 8.75, 10.05 and 4.52 per cent respectively of the total workers employed in closed mills.

Decentralised Sector

Despite the fact that it plays a pivotal role in meeting the clothing needs of the country, the data regarding unorganised weaving sector are very unreliable. In the unorganised segment of weaving, there are four sectors namely the powerloom sector, the hosiery sector, the handloom sector and the Khadi sector. In this study, Khadi sector is not taken into account as it uses yarn made on charkha, which is not taken into account for the spinning sector discussed in Chapter 2 of this study. On the other hand, yarn used by powerloom, hosiery and handloom sector is made in the organised and SSI spinning units. The unorganised weaving sector in this study thus refers to powerloom, hosiery and handloom sectors.

The data for the hosiery sector was in fact not separately available in official statistics till recently. The data on cloth production by the non-SSI weaving units and SSI hosiery units were being shown as cloth produced by the powerloom sector. The Sub-Group on "Overview of the Textile Industry" (one of the sub-groups formed by the main working group for the Ninth Five Year Plan on textile and jute industry), recommended that hosiery/knitting sector should be considered as a separate sector and need not be clubbed under the powerloom sector. As a result, the official estimates regarding production of hosiery fabric have been worked out separately since 1985. Likewise, the sub-group also recommended that cloth production by the non-SSI weaving units should be included under the production of cloth by the organised mill sector. Subsequently, the official data of cloth production for the year 1994-95 and after have been realigned in accordance with the views of the Sub-Group on "Overview of Textile Industry" for the Ninth five-year Plan. The idea of keeping hosiery-knitting sector as separate was desirable due to its different nature than powerloom sector. However, inclusion of non-SSI weaving units with the composite mills was not essential. It should have been made a separate sector. Therefore in this study, we have maintained earlier definition and considered mill sector as composite mills. This was important to maintain *(i)* consistency with old data required for the period of the study *(ii)* delivery of yarn by mill sector included yarn consumed by the non-SSI sector.

Per Capita Availability of Fabrics

The per capita availability of fabrics for home consumption has increased at a rate of 3.6 per cent per annum from 1990-91 to 1997-98 and reached the level of 30.92 sq. mts during 1997-98 as per official statistics. There was decline in availability during 1998-99 and 1999-2000 compared to year 1997-98 to 28.19 and 30.55 metres respectively. This is officially derived by dividing the difference in official production and direct and indirect fabrics exports in the form of fabrics, made-ups and garment calculated by official agencies by the mid year population.[4]

The comparison of availability of fabrics with the aggregate household purchases published by the Market Research Wing, Textiles Committee reveals that there is too much difference in these two statistics. This difference is too high to be explained by the consumer non-household purchases or carry over stocks (as will be discussed in detail later). Moreover, this difference is widening over the period of time. This clearly brings out that something is wrong with either the fabric's production statistics or consumption statistics. The official estimates of consumption are based on regular consumer survey. Clearly, the suspicion arises on the estimates of fabrics production in the decentralised sector as the estimates of fabrics production are based on arbitrary conversion rate fixed at one point of time. This calls for a total review of the estimates of production of fabrics.

Estimates of Fabrics Production in the Decentralised Sector

The production of cloth in the unorganised sector (powerloom, hosiery and handloom) is calculated on the basis of delivery of various types of yarn to the decentralised sectors and their conversion rates (Table 3.7). Conversion rate of fabrics from yarn is the number of square metres of cloth produced per kilogram of yarn.[5]

4. Compendium of Textile Statistics, Textile Commisoner.
5. Khadi sector consumes self made yarn on khadi. Hence, estimates of fabrics production are separately given for this sector later on for comparison.

Table 3.7
Official Conversion Rates for the Decentralised Sector

Type of Yarn	*Conversion Rates*			
	Mts/Kg	*Mts/Kg*	*Sq. Mts./Kg*	*Gms/Sq. Mts.*
	Old	*Revised*	*Revised*	*Revised*
1. Cotton Yarn	10.00	10.75	12.40	80.645
2. Blended Yarn	8.00	11.10	12.90	77.52
(i) 100% Non Cotton Yarn	9.06	11.10	12.90	77.52
(ii) Filament Yarn				
(a) Celluosic (viscose)	9.06	13	16.00	62.52
(b) Synthetic	14.00			
Nylon		25	31.00	32.26
Polyester		13	14.50	68.966

Source: 1. Report of the Working Group on Textile Industry for the Eighth Five Year Plan, Ministry of Textile (GOI, 1989).
2. Compendium of Textile Statistics, Office of the Textile Commissioner, Ministry of Textiles, G.O.I. (1996), p. 44.

It appears that while deriving production estimates the weight of fabric per square metres in the decentralised sector seems to be taken too low by any standard. This becomes clear if these figures are compared with the average weight of cotton fabric in mill sector as derived from the ICMF data.

Table 3.8
Cotton Yarn Consumption and Production of Cotton Fabrics in the Mill Sector

Mill Sector	*1983*	*88-89*	*89-90*	*90-91*	*91-92*	*92-93*	*93-94*	*94-95*
Yarn Mn. Kgs	364	280	260	248	220	188	175	150
Fabrics Mn. Sq. Mts.	2785*	2100	1957	1859	1651	1407	1356	1247
Gms/ sq. mt	130.70	133.33	132.86	133.41	133.25	133.62	129.06	120.29

*Converted to sq. mts.

Source: Derived from *Handbook of Statistics on Indian Cotton Textile Industry*, ICMF, New Delhi.

It is obvious from data in Table 3.8 that the difference was quite substantial for example in 1995-98. The conversion rate of fabrics taken was about 50% in the mill sector compared with the decentralised sector.

There exist several studies, which criticised the method adopted in official statistics to obtain the decentralised sector production of fabrics. Misra (1993) argued that official statistics on the production of woven cloth hide as much as they reveal. This is because of the basic asymmetry in the method of estimation of cloth in the organised and the decentralised sectors. Since the variety of these estimates are crucially contingent on the methodology adopted, it seems worthwhile to explore this issue in some detail.

The asymmetry arises from the fact that while the production figures for the composite mill sector are based on the returns filed by the individual mills, there are no firm statistics on the actual production of cloth in the decentralised sector. Production of cloth in the latter is indirectly estimated from the statistics of yarn delivered for civil consumption as opposed to the yarn consumed by the mills. It would be immediately obvious that the accuracy of the production based on yarn delivery statistics would depend crucially on the accuracy of the conversion rates that are postulated in terms of metres of cloth output per kilogram of yarn consumed. Unfortunately, despite the vital importance of this issue for purpose of planning and policy, neither it has not received much official attention, nor has sufficient research been done in this regard. This has seriously vitiated the veracity of these estimates (Misra, 1993).

According to it, what is even more important is that no distinction has been made in the application of these conversion factors between the powerloom and handloom sectors despite significant dissimilarities in the yarn consumed as well as in the cloth woven in each sector (Misra, 1993).

Conversion rates between yarn and cloth are mainly a factor of the following parameters.

(a) the nature of the yarn, namely; its fibre composition

(cotton, blended or man-made) and mode of production (spun or filament) etc.;

(b) The count of yarn indicating its fineness or coarseness;

(c) Reed and pick of cloth indicating the closeness of the weave.

As regards the type of yarn, other specifications being the same, man-made filament yarn weaves more cloth than spun yarn per kilogram of weight. Further, the metreage of cloth woven varies directly with the fineness of the yarn, *i.e.* a greater area of cloth can be woven per kilogram of finer (higher count) yarn than coarser (lower count) yarn. Finally, the closer the weave (higher the reed/pick count) of the cloth the lower the metres of cloth for the same weight of the yarn.

It will be evident that the calculation of conversion factors cannot be a one-time exercise but has to be continuously updated to take into account the changing composition and construction of the cloth woven (Misra, 1993).

ICRA (1996) draft study on cotton sector was also critical of the official conversion rates. Despite, the fact that these studies stressed the need to develop conversion rates scientfically, no attempt was made in this direction.

Therefore, it is important to make an attempt to scientifically derive conversion rate for each sector and fibre independently in a detailed analytical manner and then apply that on the consumption of yarn in different sectors. However, the method to work out the production of fabrics in each sector on the basis of delivery of yarn to various sectors has a flaw. One school of thought says that estimates of handloom production of fabrics based on hank yarn deliveries are gross over estimates and that handloom production probably does not account for more than a small percentage of total cloth output. The most articulate advocate of this point of view is Jain (1983). Since this issue has important policy implications and is frequently raised in academic as well as official discussions, it is necessary to examine Jain's arguments. Jain's main thesis is that a large proportion of what is officially shown, as handloom production is infact produced on powerlooms. As there is no census on production and employment in the decentralised sector (except an unreliable one in 1987 regarding handloom sector, all estimates of handloom production have to be derived necessarily from the quantum of hank yarn deliveries to this sector.[6] The hank yarn is meant to be consumed in the handloom sector. This method is extremely unreliable because of the following factors.

It has been suggested that evidence to substantiate the assertion that there is large-scale overestimation of handloom output can be had from the following facts.

1. In 1975, the survey of household purchase of cotton textiles revealed that the share of handloom and khadi cloth in total household purchases was only around 16 per cent whereas the official estimates of cloth production placed the share of handloom at nearly 30 per cent for this year. Based on this, a study done by the Planning Commission in 1978-79 came to the conclusion that handloom production was overestimated (and correspondingly powerloom production underestimated) by around 500 million metres in 1975.
2. Some surveys have reported the use of hank yarn by powerlooms for the manufacture of dyed sarees.
3. The powerloom sector has grown at a much faster pace than the official statistics of cone yarn deliveries would warrant. Thus it is suspected that a substantial proportion of the yarn shown as being consumed in the handloom sector is in fact consumed by the powerlooms.

Misra argued that it is obvious that hank yarn will be diverted for use on powerlooms on a significant scale only if

6. Presently National Council of Applied Economic Research (NCAER) is conducting a detailed census on handloom and powerloom sector, the results of which are awaited.

it is profitable to do so *i.e.* if it works out cheaper than using regular cone yarn. It is true that the reeling of yarn into hanks involves an additional cost as a result of which, despite the fact that hank yarn is exempt from excise duty, there is little difference between the market prices of hank and cone yarn in counts below 40s. There is also cost involvement in converting hanks into cones, which is proportional to the count of the yarn—the finer the yarn, the greater the cost. This conversion from hank to cone yarn is required to use hank yarn into the powerloom sector. The statutory stipulation on marketing of hank yarn is that 85 per cent of it must be of counts 40s or below. Thus, it will be quite evident that there is essentially, no compelling economic incentive for converting hanks into cones for use by the powerloom sector in view of the additional costs involved. It is nevertheless true that powerlooms do use some hank yarn for the production of coloured saris primarily because it is easier to dye the yarn in this form of packing. On the other hand, some yarn is also consumed in the handloom sector as sized beams.

Misra (1993) concluded that in the absence of hard evidence, it is extremely difficult to establish the hypothesis of decimation of handloom on the basis of the alleged diversion of hank yarn for powerloom production. Keeping the above in mind, an attempt has been made in this chapter, to estimate the production of fabrics in each sector on the basis of delivery or availability of yarn to various sectors. However, in the next chapter an attempt has been made to estimate the extent of hank yarn diversion by using demand and supply analysis for cotton handloom fabric. Satyam Committee on Report of the Expert Committee on Textile Policy, submitted to parliament after I submitted my thesis. This report has mentioned on the basis of a survey undertaken by the office of Textile Commissioner that about 39 per cent of the hank yarn delivered is consumed by the powerloom sector, while only 0.44 per cent of the cone yarn delivered is consumed by the handloom sector. It is understood that the office of the textile Commissioner is in the process of revising the method of estimation of cloth production in the decentralised sector.

A committee has also been constituted to revise the conversion rates.

Availability of Spun Yarn for Production of Fabrics in the Decentralised Sector

Total spun yarn production in the country increased from 1102 million kgs in 1975-76 to 2794 million kgs during 1996-97 and further to 3046 during 1999-2000. The spun yarn production after 1992-93 is available for organised and SSI sector separately. Export of cotton yarn increased from 4.69 million kgs. to 464.9 million kgs and further to 555 million kgs during the same periods, while export of man made spun yarn increased from 10.3 million kgs to 78.27 million kgs from 1989-90 to 1995-96 and further to 129.55 million kgs during 1999-2000. The remaining spun yarn is available for domestic consumption. Some of it is consumed in mill sector and remaining is delivered to decentralised sector. The yarn delivered to decentralised sector is mainly meant for fabrics production after adjusting for stock addition/depletion, and consumption for thread production. The sector-wise delivery of spun yarn produced in spinning mills as well as spinning mills and SSI spinning units is given in Table 3.9.

As discussed above, the count range-wise data on delivery of yarn is important to workout meaningful conversion rate of fabrics from yarn. From the variety-wise delivery of spun yarn produced in the spinning mills, the count range-wise delivery of spun yarn by the mills to various decentralised sector was worked out in Chapter 2. However, in this chapter the production of spun yarn in the SSI spinning units are also to be included as same are also used in production of fabrics. The count range composition of delivery of spun yarn of hosiery, hank, cone and beams and pirms by SSI spinning units is taken as same as those of count composition of delivery of these verities of spun yarn delivered by the mill sector. The estimates of spun yarn delivery by the SSI spinning units for production of fabrics is 111 million kg during 1995-96, which is only 3.31 percentage of total yarn consumption in mill and decentralised sector to produce fabrics (Appendix 3.1).

Table 3.9
Civil Deliveries of Spun Yarn

(Mn. kgs.)

Year	*Hanks*		*Hosiery Cones*		*Other Cones*		*Beams & Pirns*	
	Cotton Yarn	*Blended & 100% Non-Cotton Yarn*	*Cotton Yarn*	*Blended & 100% Non-Cotton Yarn*	*Cotton Yarn*	*Blended & 100% Non-Cotton Yarn*	*Cotton Yarn*	*Blended & 100% Non-Cotton yarn*
(1)	*(2)*	*(3)*	*(4)*	*(5)*	*(6)*	*(7)*	*(8)*	*(9)*
1983-84	289	53	95	10	290	73	25	2
1984-85	302	52	98	10	303	71	26	2
1985-86	315	62	103	12	316	84	27	2
1986-87	338	56	111	12	339	78	29	2
1987-88	343	58	113	12	344	81	29	2
1988-89	315	39	157	16	434	142	26	3
1989-90	310	38	176	15	459	153	22	4
1990-91	342	33	197	20	530	171	26	4
1991-92	328	36	205	22	496	204	18	6
1992-93	348	38	236	17	551	216	19	7
1993-94	376	42	271	22	586	244	17	8
1994-95	370	52	267	34	514	268	11	6
1995-96	435	67	362	40	559	263	21	5
1996-97	469	67	398	46	530	314	20	8
1992-93*	377	38	236	17	568	216	19	7

(Contd.....)

(Contd....)

(1)	(2)	(3)	(4)	(5)	(6)	(7)	(8)	(9)
1993-94*	422	42	271	22	615	244	17	8
1994-95*	438	52	267	34	556	268	11	6
1995-96*	504	67	362	40	596	263	21	5
1996-97*	519	71	398	46	564	347	20	8
1997-98*	540	58	436	78	522	342	17	9
1998-99*	473	56	413	90	458	385	16	10
1999-2000*	514	60	421	89	494	427	16	10

* Includes spun yarn production in small spinning units from 1992-93 onwards.

Source: Compendium of Textile Statistics, Office of the Textile Commissioner, Ministry of Textiles (GOI).

The analysis undertaken in Chapter 2 to work out count range-wise delivery to various sectors is explained here briefly for easy reference. Count range-wise yarn delivered to handloom sector is worked out from the two years data for the period 1983 and 1996. The count range-wise delivery of cotton yarn to various sectors for the year 1983 is available from handbook of Statistics, Indian Cotton Mills Federation (ICMF). The unpublished data for year 1996 is obtained from Development Commissioner for Handloom, GOI, New Delhi. The data for intervening years is obtained by assuming two ways adjustment. In the first stage, the constant growth rate is assumed for all the years. In the second stage, adjustment has been made proportionately among all the count-ranges to make the total equivalent to total delivery of cotton hank yarn. For the powerloom and hosiery sector, the procedure to work out count range-wise delivery to various sectors is bit different. The data for count range-wise delivery to powerloom and hosiery sector is available for year 1983. The data for other years for each sectors *i.e.* powerloom and hosiery sector are derived by making two ways adjustments. Firstly the share of various count ranges in these varieties changes in accordance with the change in count ranges in total cotton yarn production. Secondly, after making first adjustment, the relative share of each count range is thus further adjusted proportionately to balance the total with cotton yarn delivery to powerloom and hosiery sector separately for each year (Appendix 3.1).

There was some difficulty in extending the analysis for the period 1997-98 to 1999-2000 have taken place some changes in data procedure in Official Statistics after 1996-97. The change in procedure include non-reporting of yarn consumed in composite mill sector, non-availability of count range-wise yarn produced in the organised sector separately etc. The analysis is thus extended for the years 1997-98, 1998-99 and 1999-2000 assuming the proportionate change in count-range composition in all the decentralised sectors as that of production of yarn. The values thus arrived for each count ranges are then adjusted proportionately for arriving at aggregate delivery of yarn to each sector for the period 1997-

98 to 1999-2000. This exercise is similar for all sectors after year 1997-98. For the mill sector, the consumption of yarn to produce fabrics in the mill sector for the year 1997-98 to 1999-2000 is taken as same as that of the year 1996-97.

These count range-wise consumption of cotton yarn in various sector is then multiplied by the count-range-wise conversion rates to arrive at sector-wise estimates of count range-wise production of fabrics in quantity terms.

Conversion Rate of Fabrics from Yarn

Once, the count range-wise delivery to powerloom, hosiery and handloom sectors is worked out, the next step is to work out conversion rate of yarn for fabric. The conversion rate of yarn for fabric is the number of square meters of fabrics, which can be produced, with one kilogram of yarn. The conversion rate of fabrics from yarn is the inverse of weight of fabrics. The conversion rate for fabrics depends upon the (1) fibre, (2) count of yarn[7] and (3) reed and picks.

Weight of woven fabric in gms/sq. mt. =

$$\frac{(\text{Reeds} \times 39.37 \times 1.06 \times 1000)}{(1690 \times \text{S2/Ply})} + \frac{(\text{Picks} \times 39.37 \times 1.09 \times 1000)}{(1690 \times \text{S1/Ply})}$$

S1 and S2, are count of yarn used for fabric products, S1 is warp count. S2 weft counts. Warps are put first and are kept lose in length. Wefts are put later in width wise, number of ends per inch of weft length are called reeds. Numbers of warp ends per inch of weft length are called picks. The wefts require more yarn per sq. mt. (1.09 sq. mt.) than warp (1.06 sq. mt.).[8]

---

7. Count of yarn tells us how many ('000) metres length of yarn is equals 1 kg. Lighter (thinner) the yarn more metres in one kilogram and hence finer (higher) will be the count (S). Heavier the yarn less metres in one kilogram and coarser (lower) will be the count.
8. The conversion of yarn into fabrics leads to further loss of around 0.5 per cent of yarn as wastage, which is more or less equal to the thread consumed in stitching fabric into garments and is thus not taken into account.

The share of various varieties in each count range as well as share of each count in the total count range yarn are important to find out the weighted average conversion rates in each count range. The average count of yarn could not be taken as substitute for count range-wise detailed analysis.

For the purpose of calculating conversion rate for woven fabrics in various count ranges, one of the requisite is to know the varieties of fabrics produced from various counts, their construction in terms of reeds and picks and ply used. We got details of various (varieties produced and there parameters such as reeds, picks counts, fabrics used etc) sponsored by ATIRA, 1984 (Ahmedabad Textile Industry Research Association) and AIMA (Ahmedabad Institute of Management Association) on Inter Firm Comparison of Costs, Productivity and Damage Reports. This second report is based on internal data of the mills for the period July to September 1983. By using these Parameters in above formula, conversion rates for each variety were obtained.

Once the conversion rate for each variety is worked out, it is important to find the share of various varieties produced. The share of various varieties should be considered in accordance with the number of varieties produced from a particular count, percentage of that count of yarn consumed for weaving, and the share of that count of yarn in total yarn used for weaving in its count-range. This means each count used for weaving is distributed among major varieties produced from that count.

However, the problem is that the data on count-wise yarn production in India is not available. The all India production of spun yarn is available in various count ranges. We have to rely on three different sources for working out count and variety-wise composition within various count ranges. These include SIMA (South Indian Mills Association); AIFCOSPIN and TEXPROCIL. SIMA data for year 1996 is most detailed one and the latest hence our analysis mainly depends upon that data. However, some adjustment has been made in SIMA data to incorporate few important counts of yarn which were not reported to be produced during 1996 by the SIMA mills. For these counts the share within the count-range is applied from other reports. As, there are only a few counts, which are dominantly produced within the count range irrespective of whether it is domestically used or exported or based on various regions, the results derived on the basis of regional report may not cause too much deviation of results from actual ones. This is also confirmed later from the fact that the results derived by using TEXPROCIL and AIFCOSPIN data do not differ much.

We have arrived at the following conversion rate within various count ranges.

0-10s: The cloths which are being produced in this count range are mainly denim, Do-suit, Khadi, towel, sheeting, and canvas. The main woven counts within this category are 6, 7 and 10s. The main count used in the double[9] and multiple form are 6s, 7s and 10s. The weight of main varieties of fabrics in this count range varies from as high as 560 gms/sq.mt to 153 gms/sq.mt. The average weight works out is 244.94 gms/sq.mt in the mill sector for the count range 0-10s.

11-20s: The main varieties produced in the 11-20s are sheeting, drill, dedh suti, towel, do suit, coating, khadi, umbrella, and long cloth. The reed and picks vary quite a lot among various counts. In the count range 11-20s, the main counts from which the fabrics are produced are 12s, 14s, 16s, 18s, 19s and 20s. The weight of fabrics varies from 307.57 gms to 99 gms/sq.mt. The average weight works out is 160.53 gms/sq.mt average

21-30s: The main varieties produced in this range are sheeting, sarees, poplin, dhoti, long cloth, coating, casement, bed sheets, patto, chintz, umbrella, twill, satin, checks, crepe, suci, towel and trouser. The reed and picks for various varieties vary quite a lot. In the count range

9. The double or multiply fabrics has better finish.

21-30s, the main counts used for fabric production are 21s, 22s, 23s, 24s, 26s, 28s, and 30s. The double ply count used is mainly of 24s, and 30s. The weight of fabrics varies from 195 gms/sq.mt to 65 gms/sq.mt in this count range.

31-40s: The main varieties of fabrics produced are poplin, shirting, patto, long cloth, suci-cotton, cambric, lungi, sheeting, and coating. The range of reeds and picks for various varieties vary quite a lot. In the count range 31-40, the main counts used for woven fabrics are 32s, 33s, 34s, 35s, 36s, 38s, 39s, and 40s. The main double counts used were 36s, 38s, and 40s. The weight in this count range varies from 194 gms/sq.mt to 52 gms/sq.mt.

41-60s: The main varieties produced are cambric, butta, voile, and coating. In the count range 41-60s, the main count from which fabrics are produced are 42s, 44s, 50s, 55s, 56s, 60s. The double ply count used is mainly of 42s. The weight for various varieties varies from 182 gms/sq.mt to 58 gms/sq.mt.

61-80s: The main varieties produced are cambric, voile, saris, handkerchiefs, khadi, lawn, and rubia. The main counts used for fabrics production are 62s, 63s, 64s, 65s, 68s, 70s, and 80s. The weight of these varieties varies from 94 gms to 40 gms/sq.mt. The double ply counts used are 70s and 80s and that too having only 0.33 per cent and 3.78 per cent share in count range.

>80s: The main varieties produced are cambric, butta, dhoti, khadi, and rubia. The main counts used in this range for woven fabrics production is 84s, 90s, 100s and 110s. The fabrics produced are mainly from double ply and hence heavier compared to average fabrics in the count range 60-80s. The reeds and picks for various varieties are generally high and range between 52 and 82. The weight of fabrics varies from 93 gms to 69 gms/sq.mt for the mill sector.

The average weight for various count ranges in the mill sector has been calculated by using the proportion of yarn consumed for weaving in each count-range. The mill sector fabrics weight and conversion rates thus derived for various count-ranges are given in Table 3.10. These results are comparable with the results derived by undertaking similar exercise from TEXPROCIL and AIFCOSPIN data.

The conversion rates derived this way for the mill sector, are used to derive weights for the powerloom and handloom sector. For the comparison of relative weight of fabrics in mill and powerloom sector, the difference between reeds and picks is important, which in turn depends upon the technology used. As some of the mills use superior kind of machines, these are able to produce dense cloths. On the other hand a lot of NTC and other old composite mills are sick. On the whole technology used in mill sector is superior compared to the powerloom sector. In fact, a high percentage of looms installed in powerloom sector as discards of mill sector. But in this study, the fabrics produced by small weaving mills are considered as part of powerloom sector fabrics. These independent weaving units use superior technology. However, the share of small weaving mills in total production of fabrics in powerloom sector is very small. In the case of handloom sector, the construction of fabrics is even less dense than the powerloom sector.

By consulting several experts regarding the difference between reeds and picks in various sectors for various count-ranges, the results derived are given in Table 3.10. The weighted average conversion rates depend upon the share of various sectors as well as count range-wise proportion in each sector.

These conversion rates are applied on the count range wise yarn consumption in various sectors. The data for count range-wise production of cotton fabrics thus derived for the powerloom, handloom and hosiery sectors are given in Appendix 3.2. The data for fabrics produced in mill sector for various count ranges of fabrics is available in official statistics and is given in Table 3.11.

Table 3.10
Count Range-wise Weight of Fabrics and Conversion Rate in Various Sectors as Derived

Count Range	*Mill Sector*		*Powerloom Sector*		*Handloom Sector*	
	Gms/Sq. Mt.	*Conversi on Rate*	*Gms/Sq. Mt.*	*Conversi on Rate*	*Gms/Sq. Mt.*	*Conversi on Rate*
0-10s	244.94	4.08	222.68	4.49	213.00	4.69
11-20s	176.00	5.68	149.33	6.70	142.69	7.01
21-30s	120.50	8.30	119.79	9.48	114.09	9.93
31-40s	110.00	9.09	109.52	9.78	104.31	10.24
41-60s	73.75	13.56	69.75	14.34	66.58	15.02
61-80s	51.94	19.25	49.47	20.21	47.22	21.18
>80s	78.44	12.75	78.44	12.75	74.87	13.36

Source: Derived by the author.

The official data for production of fabrics in mill sector is available for count-ranges different than derived for other sectors.[10] In order to make the comparison among various sectors more meaningful, it is important to have data for similar count ranges for all the sectors. Thus the production of fabrics in mill sector is worked out/or similar in count ranges as derived for other sectors.

This is worked out in various stages. Firstly, an attempt is made to find the conversion rate of fabrics in mill sector for count ranges for which the production of fabrics data in mill sector is available. This is worked by applying the same method as was used for count ranges for which production of spun yarn is available (Table 3.12).

10. This is because the count ranges for yarn are given according to speed of spindles, while the count-ranges for fabrics are given according to the varieties of fabrics. The count ranges in this study for fabrics are also taken as that of count ranges for yarn such as 0-10s,11-20s, and so on. This is mainly because of availability of yarn data for these count ranges from which figures for fabrics are derived. Moreover, for the count ranges specified for yarn, the share of various counts do not change much over the period of time and hence the same conversion rates could be applied for a specific count range. This is not relevant in the case of count ranges specified for fabrics.

Table 3.11

Mill Sector Production of Cotton Fabrics in Various Count Ranges

(Mn. Sq. Mts.)

Count	*Variety*	*1983**	*1988-89*	*1990-91*	*1991-92*	*1993-94*	*1994-95*	*1995-96*
0 < 17	Coarse	295	241	244	225	226	233	233
17 < 26	Medium B	693	568	549	498	428	380	369
26 < 41	Medium A	1619	1119	890	773	581	494	412
41 < 61	Fine	70	79	77	59	31	42	36
>60	Super Fine	108	93	99	96	90	98	81
Total	All	2785	2100	1859	1651	1356	1247	1131

***1983 figures are available in terms of linear metres and are converted into sq. mts.**

Source: **Derived from Handbook of Statistics on Cotton Textile Industry, ICMF, New Delhi.**

Table 3.12
Count Range-wise Fabrics Conversion Rate in the Mill Sector

Count Range	*Fabrics Variety*	*Weight Gms/Sq.Mt*	*Conversion Rate*
0-<17s	Coarse	194.42	5.14
17-<26s	Medium B	158.23	6.32
26-<41s	Medium A	114.22	8.76
41-<61s	Fine	73.75	13.56
≥61	Super Fine	64.79	15.43

Note: 2ply 36s fabrics fall in 26-40s and not in 10-20s count range.
Source: Derived by the author.

Secondly, these conversion rates are then applied on the count range-wise production of fabrics in mill sector to work out the consumption of yarn in the mill sector for these count ranges. As specified above these count ranges as specified for the production of fabrics are different than count ranges specified for the production of yarn.

Thirdly, the count range-wise consumption thus derived are converted to count ranges specified for yarn by applying appropriate weights to various counts within these count ranges. The weights for within the count ranges are obtained by analysing SITRA data on count-wise proportion within count ranges from the study on Norms for Spinning.

Fourthly, the total consumption of cotton yarn derived by the above method is then compared with the actual consumption of yarn in the mill sector. As the data for these count range-wise consumption of cotton yarn in the mill sector is available for the year 1983, some adjustments are made to arrive at appropriate weights within the count ranges. The results for consumption of cotton yarn as derived by this method are comparable with actual consumption of yarn in mill sector till year 1993-94 (Table 3.13). However, after the year 1993-94, the percentage difference increases and is quite high for the year 1995-96.

The reason for rise in difference since year 1995-96 seems to be change in official definition of mill sector. The figures for mill sector after the year 1993-94 are inclusive of production of cloth by the non-SSI weaving units, which earlier used to be included in the decentralised sector. With this change in definition, the earlier concept of self-consumption of yarn in the mill sector lost relevance and ICMF handbook is no more providing the detail about the same. According to the new definition of mill sector, the yarn could be purchased from the open market for producing the fabrics. This has become increasingly relevant, as quality of yarn in the open market has improved with the technology progress in the spinning units.

Table 3.13
Conversion Rates and Consumption of Yarn in the Mill Sector

Parameter	1983-84	1988-89	1989-90	1990-91	1991-92
Derived Conversion Rate	7.63	7.60	7.49	7.49	7.46
Derived Consumption of Yarn (Mn. kgs)	364	276	261	248	221
Actual Consumption of Yarn (Mn. kgs)	364	280	260	248	220
Year	**1992-93**	**1993-94**	**1994-95**	**1995-96**	**1996-97**
Derived Conversion Rate	7.48	7.28	7.28	7.13	7.13
Derived consumption of Yarn (Mn. kgs)	188	186	171	159	167
Actual Consumption of Yarn (Mn. kgs)	188	175	150	134	—

Source: Derived by the author.

These count range-wise consumption of yarn in the mill sector derived this way are used to find the count range-wise production of fabrics in mill sector by applying the conversion rates for count ranges 0-10s, etc. derived earlier (Table 3.10). The count range-wise production of fabrics in different sectors is given in (Appendix 3.2). The total estimates of fabrics production thus worked out are 31127 million square metre during 1999-2000, which are much lower than official estimates of 38627 million square metre during the same period. The growth in estimates of production of fabrics grew at 5.59 per cent per annum during the period 1990-91 to 1999-2000 as against growth rate of 6.41 per cent per annum in official estimates.

The count range-wise production of fabrics is worked out from this exercise. This is amajor contribution as the Textile Commissioner data on production of fabrics lack any measurement regarding quality of fabrics.

Production of Cotton Fabrics

The share of cotton fabrics in total fabrics production has declined from 58.0 per cent to 42.5 per cent during 1991-92 to 1999-2000. The decline in share of cotton fabrics in total production of fabrics taken place in all the count ranges, but the decline in percentage points was nominal in the count range 41-60s.

Mill Sector

The share of mill production in total production of cotton fabrics declined from 25.8 per cent in 1983 to 12.7 per cent in 1990-91, 6.0 per cent in 1996-97 and further to 4.7 per cent in 1999-2000. The production of cotton fabrics by the mill sector declined in all the count ranges except for 0-10s during 1991-92 to 1999-2000, though the decline was steep in the medium count ranges. This indicates that although mill sector is losing its share of production in all kinds of fabrics due to certain comparative disadvantages such as high excise duties and wages, etc. compared to the decentralised sectors, it is still struggling to maintain its capacity utilisation in the coarser varieties. The content of yarn is more in coarser varieties and mills have advantage of relatively cheap yarn availability from its own manufacturing units. On the other hand, the comparatively low decline in fabrics produced from superfine counts could be explained from the fact that a few mills are using advanced technology. Thus despite several liberalisation policies pursued during one and half decades of period, mill sector continued to loose it's share in total production of fabrics.

Production of Woven Fabrics in the Decentralised Sector

The productions of fabrics in the powerloom and handloom

sector have been worked out separately from the delivery of yarn to these sectors (Appendix 3.2). However, the results presented in Table 3.14 are given for combined powerloom and handloom sector, as separate data could be misleading due to diversion of hank yarn to powerloom sector. The share of these two sectors in total production of cotton fabrics accounts for 61.8 per cent. The conversion rate derived is much lower than the official conversion rate of 12.40.

On the other hand, production of the powerloom and handloom sectors has decreased in all count ranges during 1990-91 to 1999-2000, except in the count range 0-10s and 20-30s. The major cause of it is the decline in overall share of cotton fabrics in total production of fabrics.

Hosiery Sector

The production process in the hosiery sector is entirely different. However, due to lack of data on the variety-wise parameters, we used the same weights as in powerloom sector for each count range. The experts are of the view that the results derived this way may not be much off the mark. In the case of cotton hosiery fabrics, the shares of all count ranges increased during 1990-91 to 1999-2000.

The production of hosiery fabric has increased from 881 million square metres to 3986 million square metres from 1983 to 1999-2000. The hosiery sector share in total production of cotton fabrics has increased from 9.44 per cent in 1983 to 15.48 per cent in 1990-91 and further to 30.13 per cent in 1999-2000. The average weight for hosiery fabric varies from 101.60 gms/sq.mt to 105.62 gms/sq.mt during the period 1983 to 1999-2000 (Appendix 3.2) depending upon the count composition. The hosiery sector has shown maximum growth rate of 9.54 per cent per annum during the period 1990-91 to 1999-2000. The hosiery varieties are substituting in certain varieties of the woven fabrics.

Count Range-wise Production of Cotton Fabrics

After reviewing the count range-wise changes in production of fabrics in different sectors, a similar attempt is made for the total production of cotton fabrics. The production of fabrics has not grown at the same rate across several count ranges. The share of 0–10s (0-10 count) and 31-40s has increased from 7.4 and 33.8 per cent to 14.6 and 36.3 per cent respectively in the total production of cotton fabrics during the period 1991-92 to 1999-2000. The share of other count ranges in total production of cotton fabrics has declined in all the remaining count compositions. The production of cotton fabrics has basically moved towards coarser varieties over the period of time. This explains the comparatively lower growth rates for the production of fabrics compared with consumption of cotton yarn in the sector. In these circumstances, any attempt to assume constant conversion rates over the period as is being done in official statistics is misleading.

Comparison of Different Sectors Producing Cotton Fabrics

An attempt is made to make a comparison among the kind of fabrics produced and yarn consumed in various sectors. From the derived data in Appendix 3.1 and Appendix 3.2. The sector-wise results derived for year 1996-97 are given in Table 3.15.

The average count of yarn used is highest for the hosiery sector and lowest for the mill sector. This partially explains the high weight of fabrics in the mill sector and low weight of fabrics in the hosiery sector. The weight of fabrics in mill sector is also high due to dense construction compared with other sectors. The average count of yarn is different than the average count of fabrics as derived from data in Appendix 3.1 and Appendix 3.2.

A similar comparison is undertaken in Table 3.16 over a period of time. It is clear from the data that production of woven cotton fabrics has slowed down considerably. The substitution of cotton woven fabrics with fabrics made from other fibres is one possible reason. On the other hand, the demand has shifted in favour of hosiery products, which were earlier used in the form of woven fabrics. The detailed analysis about the changes in demand pattern in domestic and export segment is undertaken in Chapter 4.

Table 3.14

Changes in Count Composition of Cotton Fabrics Produced in Powerloom and Handloom Sector

Count Range	*Production of Cotton Fabrics in Powerloom and Handloom Sectors (Mn. Sq. Mts.)*					*Count range-wise Share in Total Production of Powerloom and Handloom Sectors*				
Year	*1983*	*1990-91*	*1991-92*	*1996-97*	*1999-2000*	*1983*	*1990-91*	*1991-92*	*1996-97*	*1999-2000*
0—10	438	756	790	1868	1840	7.74	8.78	10.04	20.56	22.50
11—20	1041	1289	1215	1298	1170	18.38	14.96	15.44	14.29	14.31
21—30	916	1108	991	1129	1126	16.17	12.86	12.60	12.43	13.78
31—40	1338	2392	2243	2407	2207	23.62	27.77	28.49	26.48	26.99
41—60	953	1497	1275	1104	947	16.82	17.38	16.20	12.15	11.58
61—80	802	1240	1016	885	574	14.15	14.40	12.91	9.74	7.03
>80	177	331	341	396	313	3.12	3.85	4.33	4.36	3.82
Total	5665	8613	7872	9088	8176	100.00	100.00	100.00	100.000	100.00
Share	60.72	69.51	68.41	64.6	61.8					
Fabrics Weight Mn/sq.mt.	104.72	104.26	106.97	121.37	125.24					
Conversion Rate	9.55	9.59	9.35	8.24	7.98					

Source: Derived by the author.

Table 3.15
Parameters of Cotton Fabrics Produced in Various Sectors during 1996-97

	Mill	*Handloom & Powerloom*	*Hosiery*	*Decentralised*	*Total*
Average count of Yarn Consumed (S)	25.82	27.05	34.57	29.04	28.72
Average Weight of Fabrics gms\sq. mt	141.85	121.37	105.08	116.58	118.70
Conversion Rate (Fabrics Produced per kg of Yarn)	7.05	8.24	9.52	8.58	8.42
Fabrics Production (Mn. Sq. Mts.)	1193	9088	3788	12875	14068
Yarn Consumption Mn kgs.	167.35	1103	398	1501	1668.35
Sector-wise Yarn Consumption Share %	10.03	66.11	23.86	89.97	100.00
Sector Wise Fabrics Production Share %	8.39	64.60	26.92	91.52	100.00

Source: Derived by the author.

The estimates about the production of cotton fabrics in the handloom and powerloom sector derived in this chapter are revised in Chapter 4 on the basis of estimates of diversion of hank yarn to powerloom sector. But the combined estimates of production of fabrics in the handloom and powerloom sector remains unchanged. Thus the comparison here with official statistics is mainly restricted to woven and hosiery fabrics in the decentralised sector.

The official figures of production of fabrics in different sectors are given in the Table 3.18. Textile Commissioner's estimates of production of cotton fabrics are 5772 million square metres higher compared with estimates derived in this study during 1996-97, which increased to 5760 million square metre during 1999-2000. The official estimates of cotton hosiery

Table 3.16
Various Sectors Share and Weighted Conversion Rates

Sectors	Conversion Rate (Sq.Mts/Kg)					Share of Various Sectors in Total Production of Cotton Fabrics				
	1983	1990-91	1991-92	1996-97	1999-2000	1983	1990-91	1991-92	1996-97	1999-2000
Mill	7.64	7.50	7.47	7.05	7.05	29.80	15.02	14.37	8.39	8.07
Powerloom and Handloom	9.55	9.59	9.35	8.24	7.98	60.72	69.51	68.41	64.6	61.81
Hosiery	9.62	9.74	9.68	9.52	9.47	9.44	15.48	17.24	26.92	30.13
Decentralised sector	9.56	9.62	9.41	8.58	8.42	70.16	85.00	85.65	91.52	91.94
Total	8.89	9.23	9.07	8.42	8.29	100.00	100.00	100.00	100.00	100.00
Official rate for decentralised sector	10.00*	12.40	12.40	12.40	12.40					

*Linear metres per.
Source: As derived by the author.

Table 3.17
Production of Cotton Fabrics in Various Sectors Based on Delivery of Yarn

(Mn. Sq. Mts.)

	Mill	*Powerloom*	*Handloom*	*Powerloom & Handloom*	*Hosiery*	*Total*
1983	2785	3119	2546	5665	881	9331
1988-89	2100	4760	2890	7650	1545	11295
1989-90	1957	4926	2790	7716	1721	11394
1990-91	1859	5601	3012	8613	1918	12390
1991-92	1651	5059	2813	7872	1984	11507
1992-93	1407	5674	3206	8880	2288	12575
1993-94	1356	6041	3535	9576	2618	13550
1994-95	1247	5429	3664	9093	2579	12918
1995-96	1131	6191	4342	10533	3539	15203
1996-97	1193	5289	3799	9088	3788	14069
1997-98	1196	4822	3921	8743	4150	14089
1998-99	1173	4253	3443	7696	3918	12688
1999-2000	1067	4488	3688	8176	3986	13229
Point to point % p.a. Gr. Rt. for 1983 to 1990-91	-5.61	8.72	2.43	6.17	11.76	4.13
Gr. Rt. 1990-91 to 1999-2000	-5.26	-2.60	2.81	-0.43	9.54	1.28
t-statistics	-6.10	-2.36	2.49	-0.40	9.19	1.60

Note: *(i)* Gr. Rt. = compound growth rate based on semi-log trind 1990-91 to 1999 2000.
(ii) The separate estimates about the handloom and powerloom sectors are revised later in Chapter 4 and are different than estimates given above. However, the combined production in powerloom and handloom sector remains to be same.

Source: As derived by the author.

Table 3.18

Official Data on Production of Cotton Fabrics in Various Sectors

(Mn. Sq. Mts.)

Year	*Mill*	*Powerloom*	*Handloom*	*Powerloom & Handloom*	*Hosiery*	*Total*
1985-86	2716	4391	4035	8426	1325	12467
1986-87	2594	4563	4193	8756	1377	12727
1987-88	2346	4629	4254	8883	1397	12626
1988-89	2100	5702	3911	9613	1945	13658
1989-90	1957	5965	3837	9802	2177	13936
1990-91	1859	6887	4237	11124	2448	15431
1991-92	1651	6383	4065	10448	2548	14647
1992-93	1407	7306	4686	11992	2944	16343
1993-94	1356	7836	5241	13077	3357	17790
1994-95	1247	7036	5429	12450	3307	17019
1995-96	1131	7042	6239	13253	4488	18900
1996-97	1193	7267	6441	13679	4940	19841
1997-98	1196	6694	6699	13826	5403	19992
1998-99	1173	5917	5861	12525	5121	17948
1999-2000	1067	6329	6376	12705	5217	18989
Gr. Rt.	-5.26	-1.18	5.32	2.05	9.82	2.87
t-statistics	-6.10	-1.38	5.65	2.73	9.69	4.13

Note: *(i)* Figures for mill sector are exclusive of production of fabrics in the non-SSI weaving units and figures for powerloom sector are inclusive of non-SSI weaving units.

(ii) Gr. Rt. = Compound growth rate based on semi-log trend for the period 1990-91 to 1999-2000.

Source: Compendium of textile statistics, 2000, Office of the textile Commissioner, G.O.I., Mumbai and Annual Report, Ministry of Textiles, 1999-2000.

fabrics are 1231 million square metre and of cotton woven fabric 4529 million square metre higher compared to derived in this study during 1999-2000. After analysing the estimates of production of cotton fabrics, similar attempt is made for other fabrics in the following section.

Conversion Rate of Fabrics Produced from Various Synthetic Yarns

It is possible to work out the relative weight of fabrics made from various fibres in case the count used and variety of fabrics produced are of similar type. Assuming the index for weight of cotton fabrics as 100. Then the index for weight of fabrics produced from other fibres assuming similar count composition and similar variety as in case of cotton fabrics is given in Table 3.19. This has been derived by using SITRA norms available from various studies and opinion of experts.

Table 3.19
Comparative Index for Fabrics Weight Produced from Various Fibres (Assuming Similar Count Composition of Yarn used and Similar Varieties of Fabrics Produced)

Fibre	Nylon	Cotton	Viscose	Polyester	Wool	Acrylic	Polyproline
Index	89	100	100	96	95	91	80

Source: Derived from SITRA studies on norms and experts opinion.

Therefore, to calculate the conversion rate of fabrics from yarn for each of these fibres/filaments, adjustments in conversion rate of cotton fabrics for each count range have been made proportional to the ratios given in Table 3. However, in the case of blended yarn, another requisite to find the conversion rate is to find the blend ratio. The assumed blend rates as derived using experts opinion are as given in Appendix 3.3.

In case of filament yarn, conversion rates of fabrics from yarn for various count ranges is calculated by using count-wise (denier-wise[12]) available data and various varieties produced (reeds *picks) from each count. Keeping in mind the wide-fluctuations within the count-ranges over time for filament

12. Count = 5715/Denier.

yarn (unlike spun yarn), the conversion rates are revised in this study on regular basis depending upon the availability of data and the extent of fluctuations in count compositions within the count-range. The conversion rates of fabrics from filament yarn are higher compared to other fibres mainly in the count ranges above 60s because of very high-count composition.

Availability of Synthetic Yarn

The count range-wise production of synthetic yarn is available for various fibres/filaments. The yarn availability for each fibre/filament is worked out by adjusting import, exports and other uses. In some fibres, the data regarding the import, export, and changes in stock is available at aggregate level such as total blended yarn, or 100 per cent spun yarn or total spun yarn (excluding cotton yarn). The adjustment thus are made at each possible disaggregated stage regarding the changes in stocks, net exports etc. depending upon the availability of data.

As the fibre and filament-wise delivery to various sectors is not available, the count range-wise conversion rates of powerloom sector are applied to work out count range-wise estimates of synthetic fibre/filament-wise production of fabrics. The estimates of production of synthetic fabrics at various aggregate blends are discussed in the following section.

The weighted conversion rate of blended fabrics varies from 10.04 to 11.97 for various years (Table 3.20). This means difference is as wide as 19 per cent over a period of time. In these circumstances, how could one justify constant conversion rate over a period of time. This clearly points out that the conversion rate should not only be worked out scientifically but revised on year to year basis in consonance with changes in count range and fibre composition. The official estimate about blended fabric conversion rate is 12.90 for the unorganised sector, which is much higher than estimates derived in this study over time.

The count range-wise changes are also worked from Appendix 3.2. The share has been calculated for two periods

Table 3.20
Conversion Rates for Various Blended Fabrics

Year	Cotton Viscose	Cotton Polyester	Cotton & Other	Polyester Viscose	PVC Total	Others	Blended	Productin of Fabrics Mn. Sq. Mt	
	Conversion Rate (Sq. Mt./kg)							Derived	Official
1983	13.56	13.74	11.55	10.51	11.51	10.06	11.97	1683	1265
1988-89	13.56	13.74	11.55	10.51	11.51	10.06	11.88	2168	2321
1989-90	13.16	13.26	11.44	10.48	13.72	10.01	11.57	1942	2118
1990-91	13.03	13.07	11.96	10.51	12.48	10.12	11.51	2312	2371
1991-92	12.34	13.44	10.90	10.79	12.82	9.94	11.74	2614	2712
1992-93	11.34	12.93	9.88	10.89	11.43	10.11	11.57	2649	2684
1993-94	10.21	13.42	8.45	10.71	17.44	10.23	11.58	3328	3155
1994-95	9.73	12.80	8.16	10.29	9.44	9.78	11.00	3446	3661
1995-96	9.16	12.81	8.63	10.08	9.97	9.39	10.81	3759	4025
1996-97	9.25	12.69	8.63	9.90	9.97	9.39	10.59	4658	4888
1997-98	9.15	12.30	8.36	9.63	12.93	9.10	10.30	6073	5751
1998-99	9.29	12.04	8.37	9.51	10.83	9.91	10.22	6146	5700
1999-2000	9.36	11.41	8.41	9.48	10.36	10.31	10.04	6292	5913
Official	12.90	12.90	12.90	12.90	12.90	12.90	12.90	—	—

Note: Conversion rate for different fibres is derived from the count range-wise production of these fibres yarn. As data for opening and closing stocks and exports is not available for count range-wise, it does not cover that. Hence, the final conversion rate derived by making adjustment at various stages differ than mentioned in above table. The total production of fabrics are derived by making adjustment at various stages.

Source: As derived by the author.

1991-92 and 1996-97 as data for count range production of several fibres/filaments were not available before 1991-92. The blended fabrics share of all count ranges in the count range wise total production of fabric has gone up except for the count range 41-60s and >80s. The share of production of blended fabric has increased from 13.2 per cent in 1991-92 to 16.8 per cent in 1996-97 and further to 20.21 during 1999-2000. The fibre wise changes in count composition for various blended fabrics have also been worked out in Appendix 3.2.

100% Non-Cotton Spun Fabric Production

The conversion rate for the 100 per cent spun fabrics production are derived in the same way as in the case of blended fabrics production.

The conversion rates derived by us vary in the range of 9.40 to 12.96 over time (Table 3.21). This means the difference of 38 per cent over time in the highest and lowest conversion rates as derived on the basis of count range-wise composition. The official conversion rate used for 100% non-cotton spun fabrics is fixed at 12.90.

The share of 100% spun fabric in production of total fabrics has increased from 5.5 to 5.7 per cent between 1991-92 and 1996-97 and then jumped to 9.3 per cent during 1999-2000. The share of 100% spun fabric in various count ranges has increased during this period except for the count ranges 31-40s and >80s.

The official figures are not separately available for the production of 100% non-cotton spun fabrics. The data are available in official statistics for 100% non-cotton fabrics, which include 100% non-cotton spun fabrics as well as fabrics produced from filament fabrics.

Production of Filament Fabrics

The filament conversion rates of fabrics from yarn for various count ranges is calculated by using count-wise (denier-wise[13]) available data and various varieties produced (reeds *picks)

13. Count = 5715/Denier.

from each count. Keeping in mind the wide-fluctuations within the count-ranges specially for count above 60s for filament fabrics (unlike spun yarn), the conversion rates are revised in this study over time depending upon the availability of data and the extent of fluctuations in count compositions within the count-range. The conversion rates of fabrics from yarn for filament fabrics are higher compared to other fibres mainly in the count ranges above 60s.

Table 3.21
Conversion Rates for 100% Non-cotton Spun Fabrics

Year	*Viscose Fabrics*	*Polyester Fabrics*	*Acrylic Fabrics*	*Other Fabrics*	*100% Spun*	*Production of Fabrics*
			SqMts/Kg			*Mn.Sq. Mts*
1983	8.89	21.54	9.93	9.62	9.40	709
1988-89	8.89	21.54	9.93	9.62	9.63	851
1989-90	8.82	22.06	9.87	9.85	9.58	980
1990-91	8.78	21.45	10.36	9.38	9.76	1007
1991-92	8.88	20.51	10.31	9.62	10.14	1095
1992-93	8.82	19.85	10.37	10.23	10.25	1118
1993-94	9.01	20.37	10.37	9.66	10.61	1299
1994-95	8.95	19.78	10.20	9.62	10.90	1476
1995-96	8.88	19.25	10.33	9.53	11.09	1855
1996-97	8.79	19.86	10.12	9.53	11.73	1586
1997-98	8.83	18.41	9.92	9.59	12.01	2169
1998-99	8.87	17.62	9.82	9.78	12.56	2431
1999-2000	8.73	17.58	9.51	9.68	12.96	2894
Official	12.90	12.90	12.90	12.90	12.90	—

Note: Conversion rate for different fibres is derived from the count range-wise production of these fibres yarn. As data for opening and closing stocks and exports are not available count range-wise, it does not cover that. Hence, the final conversion rate derived by making these adjustments at various aggregate levels of blends differ than mentioned in table above. The total production of fabrics is derived by making adjustment at various stages.

Source: As derived by the author.

The conversion rate derived in this study for Nylon is higher than official estimates, while for viscose filament yarn is lower (Table 3.22). On the other hand, the derived conversion rate for polyester filament yarn was high for most of years, but it declined recently due to use of coarser count composition. The comparison for overall conversion rate for filament fabrics is not possible, as official data is not available for the same.

Table 3.22
Conversion Rate for Various Filament Yarn

(Sq.Mts/Kg)

Year	*Nylon*	*Polyester*	*Viscose*	*Total*
1991-92	34.54	14.05	11.65	15.79
1992-93	32.69	14.01	11.94	15.56
1993-94	33.81	14.05	11.60	15.66
1994-95	32.98	14.15	11.83	15.68
1995-96	35.29	13.58	11.54	15.21
1996-97	33.47	11.80	11.43	13.16
1997-98	33.73	12.71	11.42	13.44
1998-99	36.88	12.15	11.27	12.91
1999-2000	38.63	12.02	11.09	12.90
Official	31.00	14.50	16.00	

Note: Conversion rate for different fibres is derived from the count range-wise production of these fibres yarn. As data for opening and closing stocks and exports are not available count range-wise, it does not cover that. Hence, the final conversion rate derived by making adjustments at various stages differ than mentioned in table above. The total production of fabrics is derived by making adjustments at various stages.

Source: As derived by the author.

The share of filament fabrics in total production of fabric has increased from 23.6 per cent to 28.0 per cent between 1991-92 and 1996-97 and then steeply increased to 36.44 per cent during 1999-2000. The share of count range-wise production of filament fabric in the count range-wise total production has increased except for the count range 11-20s and 61-80s.

100% Non-Cotton Fabrics Total Production

The official statistics for production of fabrics are inclusive of filament and 100% non cotton spun fabric production, the similar data is worked in the Table 3.23 from the results derived above. The results derived for 100% non-cotton fabrics in this study are close to the official estimates despite difference in filament and fibre wise conversion rates. The 100% non-cotton fabric production has shown maximum increase compared with other fibres.

Table 3.23
100% Non-Cotton Production of Fabric

(Mn. Sq. Mts)

Year	*100% Spun*	*Filament*	*Total*	*Total Official Estimates*
1983	709	2266	2975	—
1988-89	851	3928	4779	4039
1989-90	980	4176	5156	4544
1990-91	1007	4802	5809	5126
1991-92	1095	4675	5770	5229
1992-93	1118	4942	6060	6018
1993-94	1299	6110	7409	6527
1994-95	1476	6758	8234	7495
1995-96	1855	7364	9219	8535
1996-97	1586	7787	9373	9569
1997-98	2169	10456	12625	11153
1998-99	2431	10866	13297	11895
1999-2000	2894	11342	14236	13725

Source: As derived by the author.

Total Production of Fabrics

The total production of fabrics in the country from various fibres is worked out in Table 3.24. The comparison of these estimates with official estimates given in Table 3.25 shows that the major difference lies in estimates of cotton fabrics.

The count range-wise analysis from data in Appendix 3.2 shows that share of 0-10, 21-30 and 41-60 increased in total production of fabrics, while share of other count ranges increased in total production of fabrics during the period 1991-92 to 1999-2000.

Sector-wise Total Production of Fabrics

To work out the production of fabrics in powerloom, handloom and hosiery sectors for synthetic fabrics, one requires delivery of synthetic yarn to these sectors as well as conversion rates for these sectors. The data regarding fibre/

Table 3.24
Fibre-wise Production of Fabrics in the Country

Year	*Cotton*		*Blended*		*100% Non-Cotton (Spun)*	*Filament*	*100% Non-Cotton*		*Adjustments*		*Total*
	Mn.Sq. Mts.	*Share*	*Mn.Sq. Mts*	*Share*	*Mn.Sq. Mts.*	*Mn.Sq. Mts.*	*Mn.Sq. Mts.*	*Share*	*Mn.Sq. Mts.*	*Share*	*Mn.Sq Mts.*
1983	9331	66.7	1683	12.0	709	2266	2975	21.3	0	0.0	13989
1988-89	11296	62.3	2168	12.0	851	3928	4779	26.4	-111	-0.6	18131
1989-90	11394	61.9	1942	10.6	980	4176	5156	28.0	-97	-0.5	18395
1990-91	12390	60.7	2312	11.3	1007	4802	5809	28.5	-98	-0.5	20412
1991-92	11507	58.0	2614	13.2	1095	4675	5770	29.1	-67	-0.3	19824
1992-93	12575	59.4	2649	12.5	1118	4942	6060	28.6	-122	-0.6	21162
1993-94	13551	56.4	3328	13.9	1299	6110	7409	30.9	-282	-1.2	24006
1994-95	12918	53.0	3446	14.1	1476	6758	8234	33.8	-230	-0.9	24369
1995-96	15203	54.5	3759	13.5	1855	7364	9219	33.0	-262	-0.9	27919
1996-97	14068	50.6	4658	16.8	1586	7787	9373	33.7	-305	-1.1	27794
1997-98	14089	44.8	6073	19.3	2169	10456	12625	40.1	-1306	-4.1	31481
1998-99	12688	42.5	6146	20.6	2431	10866	13297	44.6	-2284	-7.7	29847
1999-2000	13229	42.5	6292	20.2	2894	11342	14236	45.7	-2630	-8.5	31127
Gr. Rt.	1.28	—	12.27	—	11.65	11.03	11.15	—	—	—	5.59
t-statistics	1.60	—	14.63	—	12.51	14.15	15.22	—	—	—	10.12

Note : (i) Gr. Rt. = Compound growth rate based on semi-log trend for the period 1990-91 to 1999-2000.
Source: As derived by the author.

filament-wise synthetic yarn delivery to various sectors are not available as discussed earlier, but combined data for synthetic yarn are available. Moreover the count range-wise data is not available even for the total synthetic yarn delivery to various sectors.

Table 3.25

Fibre-wise Fabric Production in the Country (as per Official Statistics)

Year	*Cotton*		*Blended*		*100% Non-Cotton*		*Total*
	Mn.Sq. Mts	*Share*	*Mn.Sq. Mts*	*Share*	*Mn. Sq. Mts*	*Share*	*Mn. Sq. Mts*
1983	10130	77.1	1372	10.4	1635	12.4	13137
1988-89	13658	68.2	2321	11.6	4039	20.2	20018
1989-90	13936	67.7	2118	10.3	4544	22.1	20598
1990-91	15431	67.3	2376	10.4	5126	22.4	22933
1991-92	14647	64.8	2712	12.0	5229	23.1	22588
1992-93	16343	65.3	2684	10.7	6018	24.0	25045
1993-94	17790	64.8	3155	11.5	6527	23.8	27472
1994-95	17019	60.4	3661	13.0	7495	26.6	28175
1995-96	18900	60.1	4025	12.8	8535	27.1	31460
1996-97	19841	57.8	4888	14.3	9569	27.9	34298
1997-98	19992	54.2	5751	15.6	11153	30.2	36896
1998-99	17948	50.5	5700	16.0	11895	33.5	35543
1999-2000	18989	49.2	5913	15.3	13725	35.5	38627
Gr. Rt.	2.87		11.29		11.50		6.41
t-statistics	4.13		15.56		31.82		14.49

Note: *(i)* Non SSI weaving units data not included in Mill sector.
(ii) Gr. Rt. = Compound growth rate is % p.a. based on semi-log trend method during 1990-91 to 1999-2000.

Source: Data taken from Handbook of Statistics on Cotton Textile Industry, ICMF.

Thus two-step method is used to derive the conversion rates for various decentralised sectors. Firstly, the ratio of conversion rates for synthetic and cotton fabrics for the decentralised sector is worked out. In the second stage, this ratio is used to find the conversion rate for each sector separately from the conversion rate of cotton fabrics for each sector. The sector-wise production of fabrics then worked out is adjusted proportionally to arrive at overall production of synthetic fabrics derived earlier. The sector-wise production of fabrics thus arrived are combined with the production of cotton fabrics in various sectors to find the total production of cotton and synthetic fabrics in various sectors. The total production of cotton and synthetic fabrics for various sectors derived in this study and official estimates are given in Table 3.26.

The comparisons show that the main difference lies in the production estimates of handloom and powerloom sectors. The official estimates are 6201 million square metres higher for powerloom and handloom sectors compared with the estimates derived in this study during the year 1999-2000. The official estimates are 1289 million square metres higher for production of hosiery fabrics. Thus the total production of fabrics derived in this study is 7500 million metres lower compared with the official estimates. This means the official estimates are 24.1 per cent higher compared with estimates derived in this study during the year 1999-2000.

Summing Up

- The conversion rate of fabrics from yarn is worked out in this study, which comes out to be different than the conversion rate assumed/derived by the Textile Commissioner. The conversion rate in this study is worked out count range-wise for various fibres/filaments and blends. In the case of cotton fibre, conversion rates are worked out for each of the sectors. The weighted conversion rate worked out in this study changes over time depending upon composition of counts, fibres and sectors of production. The total estimate of fabrics production thus worked out in this study is 31127 million square metres during 1999-2000, which is much lower than the Textile Commissioner estimate of 38627 million square metres during the same period. The major difference lies in the estimates of cotton fabrics. The estimate of 14236 million square metres of production of cotton fabrics derived in this study is 4753 million square metres lower than the Textile Commissioner's estimates.
- The sector-wise comparison of production estimates of fabrics reveals that the main difference compared to official statistics is due to production estimates of the powerloom and handloom sectors. The official estimates of fabric production in the

Table 3.26
Total Production of Fabrics in Various Sectors

Year	Estimates Derived in this study						
	Mill		*Hosiery*		*Handloom and Powerloom*		*Total*
	Mn.Sq. Mts	*Share*	*Mn.Sq. Mts*	*Share*	*Mn.Sq. Mts*	*Share*	*Mn.Sq. Mts*
(1)	*(2)*	*(3)*	*(4)*	*(5)*	*(6)*	*(7)*	*(8)*
1983	3604	25.8	1001	7.2	9385	67.1	13989
1988-89	2902	16.0	1733	9.6	13496	74.4	18131
1989-90	2667	14.5	1892	10.3	13837	75.2	18395
1990-91	2589	12.7	2148	10.5	15674	76.8	20412
1991-92	2376	12.0	2247	11.3	15201	76.7	19824
1992-93	2000	9.5	2490	11.8	16672	78.8	21162
1993-94	1990	8.3	2885	12.0	19130	79.7	24006
1994-95	1987	8.4	2981	12.2	19401	79.4	24369
1995-96	1726	6.2	3999	14.3	22194	79.5	27919
1996-97	1666	6.0	4353	15.7	21776	78.3	27794
1997-98	1658	5.3	5100	16.2	24723	78.5	31481
1998-99	1517	5.1	5016	16.8	23314	78.1	29847
1999-2000	1457	4.7	5085	16.3	24585	79.0	31127
Gr. Rt.	-6.02	—	11.21	—	5.78	—	5.59
t-statistics	-11-88	—	12.72	—	9.56	—	10.12

(Contd....)

(Contd....)

(1)	(2)	(3)	(4)	(5)	(6)	(7)	(8)
			Official Estimates				
1983	3604						13137
1988-89	2902	14.5	2149	10.7	14967	74.8	20018
1989-90	2667	13.0	2375	11.5	15556	75.5	20598
1990-91	2589	11.3	2696	11.8	17643	77.0	22928
1991-92	2376	10.5	2827	12.5	17385	77.0	22588
1992-93	2000	8.0	3182	12.7	19863	79.3	25045
1993-94	1990	7.2	3637	13.2	21845	79.5	27472
1994-95	1987	7.1	3748	13.3	22440	79.6	28175
1995-96	1726	5.5	5038	16.0	24696	78.5	31460
1996-97	1666	4.9	5533	16.1	27099	79.0	34298
1997-98	1658	4.5	6394	17.3	28844	78.2	36896
1998-99	1517	4.3	6277	17.7	27749	78.1	35543
1999-2000	1457	3.8	6374	16.5	30786	79.7	38627
Gr. Rt.	-6.02	—	11.13	—	6.60	—	6.41
t-statistics	0.94	—	0.95	—	0.96	—	0.96

Note: (i) Gr. Rt. = Compound growth rate based on semi-log trend for the period 1990-91 to 1999-2000.

Source: Official data from *Handbook of Statistics on Cotton Textile Industry*, ICMF & others as derived by the author.

powerloom and handloom sectors are 24585 million square metres during 1999-2000. The official estimates derived are 6201 million square metres higher compared with the estimates derived in this study for the same period. On the other hand, the official estimate of hosiery fabrics are 1289 million square metres higher than the estimate derived in this study during 1999-2000.

➡ The share of mill production in total production of fabrics declined from 25.8 per cent in 1983 to 12.7 per cent in 1990-91, 6.0 per cent in 1996-97 and further to 4.7 per cent in 1999-2000. On the other hand, the share of handloom and powerloom sectors increased from 67.1 per cent 1983 to 78.3 percent in 1990-91, 78.3 per cent in 1996-97 and further to 79.7 per cent during 1999-2000. The maximum increase in share has taken place in the production of hosiery fabrics in total production of fabrics. The share of hosiery fabrics in the production of total fabrics increased from 7.2 per cent to 16.3 per cent during the period 1983 to 1999-2000.

➡ The shares of powerloom and handloom sectors worked out separately in this chapter on the basis of delivery of yarn are not accurate as a lots of hank yarn is being diverted to the powerloom sector. The revised estimates of fabrics production in these two sectors are worked out in Chapter 4. However, the total production of powerloom and handloom sector remains same. As count range-wise diversion of hank yarn to the powerloom sector could not be worked out, the count range-wise analysis for production of fabrics in the powerloom and handloom sectors is undertaken jointly in this Chapter.

➡ The production of fabrics has not grown at the same rate across several count ranges. The share of 0–10s (0-10 count) and 31-40s has increased from 7.4 and 33.8 per cent to 14.6 and 36.3 per cent respectively in the total production of cotton fabrics during the period 1991-92 to 1999-2000. The analysis for count range-wise changes are observed for the period 1991-92 to 1999-2000 as data for filament fabrics before 1991-92 is not available for various count-ranges. In the case of blended fabrics, the shares of count-ranges 0-30s and 61-80s in total production of blended fabrics have increased from 28.8 per cent to 59.6 per cent and 11.7 to 12.0 per cent, respectively, during the period 1991-92 to 1999-2000. In the case of 100 per cent non-cotton spun fabrics the share of 0-10s, 21-30s and above than 40s have increased. In the case of filament fabrics, the main increase has taken place in the count composition of 41-60s from 35.4 to 56.1 per cent. The shares of 11-20s, 31-40s and >60s have declined in total production of filament fabrics, while that of other count ranges have increased in total production of filament fabrics. The analysis for filament fabrics takes into consideration changes in each count composition during each year, as count-wise (denier-wise) production data for each year is available.

- ➡ The count range-wise analysis shows that share of 0-10, 21-30 and 41-60 increased in total production of fabrics from 4.8 per cent to 8.5 per cent, 15.9 per cent to 22.0 per cent and 21.5 per cent to 27.3 per cent respectively. The share of other count ranges decreased in total production of fabrics.

- ➡ The share of cotton fabrics in total fabrics production has declined from 58.0 per cent to 42.5 per cent during 1991-92 to 1999-2000. The decline in share of cotton fabrics in total production of fabrics has taken place in all the count ranges, but the decline in percentage points was nominal in the count range 41-60s.

- ➡ The sector-wise analysis for count range-wise production of fabrics could only be undertaken for the cotton segment, as data related to count range-wise delivery of various synthetic fibre yarns to various decentralised sectors are not available. The production of cotton fabrics by the mill sector declined in all the count ranges except for 0-10s during 1991-92 to 1999-2000, though the decline was steep in the medium count ranges. On the other hand, production of the powerloom and handloom sectors has decreased in all count ranges during 1991-92 to 1999-2000, except in the count range 0-10s and 20-30s. On the other hand, in the case of hosiery fabrics the shares of all count ranges increased during 1991-92 to 1999-2000.

APPENDIX 3.1

Fibre-wise and Sector-wise Consumption of Yarn to Produce the Spun and Filament Fabrics

Mn.kgs.

Year	1983	1988-89	1989-90	1990-91	1991-92	1992-93	1993-94	1994-95	1995-96	1996-97	1999-98	1998-99	1999-2000
Count						**Consumption of Cotton Yarn in Mill Sector**							
0-10	18.89	15.46	16.68	15.65	14.44	12.32	14.50	14.95	14.95	15.77	17.92	16.08	15.99
11-20	114.02	93.41	93.26	91.72	83.68	69.34	76.17	71.84	70.64	74.51	77.46	69.52	69.12
21-30	141.25	101.99	92.40	85.89	75.64	65.10	59.48	51.37	45.39	47.88	50.69	45.49	45.24
31-40	77.67	53.68	47.59	42.70	37.08	32.72	27.87	23.70	19.76	20.85	15.09	13.55	13.47
41-60	5.16	5.83	6.27	5.68	4.35	3.02	2.29	3.10	2.66	2.80	2.84	2.55	2.53
61-80	2.80	2.41	1.97	2.57	2.49	2.23	2.33	2.54	2.10	2.21	2.24	2.01	2.00
<80	4.20	3.62	2.95	3.85	3.73	3.34	3.50	3.81	3.15	3.32	3.37	3.02	3.00
Total	363.99	276.39	261.13	248.06	221.41	188.06	186.14	171.30	158.65	167.35	169.61	152.22	151.36
Mill Share	34.71	23.10	21.19	18.47	17.36	13.54	11.67	11.87	9.66	10.03	10.07	10.07	9.48
Count						**Consumption of Cotton Yarn in Powerloom Sector**							
0-10	36.24	54.30	60.71	79.11	81.91	99.08	114.19	103.83	109.40	145.30	137.15	118.49	133.03
11-20	53.97	62.75	71.35	85.40	79.76	85.46	95.01	86.04	87.99	93.12	83.21	77.35	79.14
21-30	56.71	66.87	67.02	79.54	70.79	83.49	92.23	84.51	98.68	87.85	83.26	74.56	85.04
31-40	85.25	150.45	157.53	174.36	162.64	190.65	193.22	164.77	164.66	148.75	140.72	117.34	130.41
41-60	37.58	66.85	61.70	69.05	58.47	74.53	78.85	71.16	71.97	54.99	52.34	45.98	45.64
61-80	27.24	37.99	42.39	47.07	38.40	33.13	33.86	31.02	61.41	33.34	25.97	23.63	21.06
<80	10.55	20.78	20.30	21.48	22.03	20.66	24.64	25.67	22.88	20.65	16.35	16.65	15.68
Total	307.53	460.00	481.00	556.00	514.00	587.00	632.00	567.00	617.00	584.00	539.00	474.00	510.00
Powerloom Share	29.32	37.95	39.20	41.40	40.57	42.29	42.13	39.28	37.58	35.00	32.00	31.34	31.95
Count						**Consumption of Cotton Yarn in Hosiery Sector**							
0-11	0.56	0.89	1.07	1.38	1.62	1.94	2.47	2.53	3.50	5.60	6.20	5.87	6.18
11-20	17.10	21.41	26.07	30.91	32.60	34.74	42.57	43.51	58.23	74.28	77.87	79.45	76.16

(Contd....)

(Contd....)

Year	1983	1988-89	1989-90	1990-91	1991-92	1992-93	1993-94	1994-95	1995-96	1996-97	1997-98	1998-99	1999-2000
21-30	12.72	15.98	17.15	20.17	20.26	23.77	28.95	29.93	45.74	49.09	54.57	53.64	57.32
31-40	53.52	103.53	116.08	127.27	134.05	156.28	174.60	168.03	219.76	239.29	265.56	243.04	253.08
41-60	5.68	11.84	11.70	12.97	12.40	15.73	18.34	18.68	22.77	24.72	25.42	24.51	22.80
61-80	1.79	2.91	3.48	3.82	3.52	3.02	3.41	3.52	9.12	5.97	5.45	5.45	4.55
<80	0.20	0.43	0.45	0.47	0.55	0.51	0.67	0.79	0.92	1.00	0.93	1.04	0.92
Total	91.57	157.00	176.00	197.00	205.00	236.00	271.00	267.00	362.00	398.00	436.00	413.00	421.00
Hosiery Share	8.73	12.95	14.34	14.67	16.18	17.00	18.07	18.50	22.05	23.86	25.88	27.31	26.37
Count						**Cotton Yarn Consumption in Handloom Sector**							
0-10	58.69	68.48	70.46	85.32	89.91	108.85	128.05	134.31	153.08	258.95	273.63	236.41	264.56
11-20	97.03	87.86	91.94	102.26	97.21	104.23	118.28	123.57	136.69	96.28	96.31	89.53	91.30
21-30	38.15	35.04	32.32	35.64	32.28	38.11	42.97	45.42	57.36	29.88	31.70	28.39	32.27
31-40	49.23	67.66	65.21	67.07	63.67	74.70	77.27	76.02	82.17	92.96	98.44	82.09	90.94
41-60	27.58	38.21	32.46	33.76	29.09	37.11	40.07	41.72	45.65	21.03	22.40	19.68	19.47
61-80	11.85	12.87	13.22	13.64	11.33	9.78	10.20	10.78	23.09	9.96	8.69	7.90	7.02
<80	3.18	4.88	4.39	4.31	4.50	4.23	5.14	6.18	5.96	9.96	8.83	8.99	8.44
Total	285.71	315.00	310.00	342.00	328.00	377.00	422.00	438.00	504.00	519.00	540.00	473.00	514.00
Handloom Share	27.24	25.99	25.26	25.47	25.89	27.16	28.13	30.35	30.70	31.11	32.05	31.28	32.20
Count						**Total Consumption in Mill, Powerloom, Hosiery and Hondloom Sector**							
0-10	114.39	139.13	148.93	181.46	187.88	222.19	259.22	255.62	280.93	425.61	434.89	376.86	419.77
11-20	282.12	265.43	282.62	310.29	293.24	293.76	332.03	324.96	353.54	338.19	334.85	315.85	315.72
21-30	248.83	219.89	208.89	221.24	198.97	210.47	223.63	211.23	247.17	214.70	220.22	202.09	219.87
31-40	265.67	375.32	386.40	411.39	397.45	454.34	472.96	432.52	486.52	501.85	519.81	456.01	487.89
41-60	75.99	122.73	112.14	121.45	104.32	130.39	139.55	134.66	145.00	101.58	103.00	92.72	90.44
61.80	43.67	56.18	61.06	67.10	55.73	48.17	49.80	47.86	95.72	51.48	42.35	38.99	34.63
<80	18.12	29.71	28.09	30.12	30.81	28.74	33.95	36.45	32.92	34.94	29.48	29.70	28.03
Total	1048.80	1208.39	1228.13	1343.06	1268.41	1388.06	1511.14	1443.30	1641.65	1668.35	1684.61	1512.22	1596.36

(Contd.....)

(Contd....)

Year	1983	1988-89	1989-90	1990-91	1991-92	1992-93	1993-94	1994-95	1995-96	1996-97	1997-98	1998-99	1999-2000
Adjustment	1048.81	1212.00	1227.00	1343.00	1267.00	1388.00	1500.00	1443.30	1641.65	1668.35	1684.61	1512.22	1596.36
Cotton Share	75.41	71.07	70.69	69.56	67.07	68.21	65.91	62.61	62.72	59.33	54.15	51.50	51.65
Count						**Total Cotton Yarn Production**							
0-11	118	144	160	197	211	241	278	282	310	479	503	450	509
11-20	288	277	313	354	342	346	385	389	415	511	508	489	504
21-30	257	248	247	277	255	284	314	321	391	405	427	396	455
31-40	282	419	436	456	440	487	494	470	490	515	542	468	524
41-60	83	133	122	129	113	136	144	145	153	136	144	131	131
61-80	44	55	61	64	54	44	45	46	95	60	52	49	44
<80	20	34	33	33	35	31	37	43	40	42	37	39	37
Total	1092	1310	1372	1510	1450	1569	1697	1696	1894	2148	2213	2022	2204
Count						**Exports of Cotton Yarn**							
0-10	0.77	3.67	5.54	10.68	20.85	13.41	17.02	21.54	26.27	53.00	53.11	36.99	31.94
11-20	2.01	7.70	11..61	22.40	29.81	21.41	30.36	42.92	44.89	101.10	101.30	131.97	133.37
21-30	1.18	8.43	12.70	24.50	35.07	46.29	79.84	92.47	103.88	170.30	170.64	166.94	211.6
31-40	1.82	6.54	9.85	19.01	23.40	29.15	31.43	42.70	43.08	83.81	84.00	97.77	127.12
41-60	0.89	5.36	9.30	7.52	8.70	7.95	8.66	12.11	22.41	31.18	31.63	30.43	29.33
61-80	0.05	4.24	6.42	2.94	5.51	8.15	8.70	11.70	15.27	17.73	17.75	15.12	13.81
<80	0.18	4.43	6.70	3.07	2.61	2.27	2.83	5.10	5.70	7.55	7.57	7.38	7.67
Total	6.88	40.38	62.12	90.11	125.95	128.63	178.83	228.53	261.50	464.67	466	486.6	554.74
Count						**Total Blended Yarn Consumption**							
1-10	—	0.85	0.52	0.99	0.85	2.25	2.02	3.68	4.43	5.93	13.62	16.89	18.99
11-20	—	22.57	23.22	23.06	21.20	26.30	36.02	50.43	67.71	90.32	132.36	142.84	155.89
21-30	—	18.29	27.32	47.29	66.18	72.93	98.27	133.11	167.03	210.97	239.24	243.05	264.22
31-40	—	67.34	58.01	62.41	57.56	57.22	64.39	68.74	63.20	76.05	87.46	82.25	78.18
41-60	—	57.21	51.37	59.15	70.50	69.74	75.88	62.89	61.39	66.58	71.2	69.27	66.23

(Contd....)

(Contd...)

Year	1983	1988-89	1989-90	1990-91	1991-92	1992-93	1993-94	1994-95	1995-96	1996-97	1997-98	1998-99	1999-2000
61-80	-	14.43	10.63	11.84	15.56	16.42	25.96	25.33	30.44	32.84	37.74	38.76	36.02
>80	-	4.62	1.96	1.95	1.98	2.31	1.98	1.52	1.06	1.13	0.95	1.86	1.29
Total	141.00	185.31	173.03	206.69	233.86	247.17	304.52	345.70	395.26	483.82	582.57	594.92	620.82
Adjustment*	141.00	185.31	167.88	201.14	223.48	233.92	291.13	323.70	358.36	440.72	582.57	594.92	620.82
Adjustment**	140.63	182.56	167.64	200.62	222.36	228.97	287.58	314.00	349.43	442.73	582.57	594.92	620.82
Blend Share	10.11	10.71	9.66	10.39	11.77	11.25	12.64	13.62	13.35	15.75	18.73	20.26	20.09
Count						**100% Spun Yarn Consumption**							
1-10		0.66	1.12	0.40	0.46	0.61	0.79	1.39	1.64	3.49	9.27	13.43	18.44
11-20		22.55	27.14	25.54	28.41	25.84	24.42	28.80	34.64	26.89	30.6	30.7	35.7
21-30		25.70	30.45	28.35	35.32	41.70	47.82	53.41	75.26	58.64	59.99	73.63	88.94
31-40		40.31	44.95	48.81	49.56	50.20	57.82	62.89	68.67	55.70	56.52	49.34	48.37
41-60		2.68	2.49	3.07	7.40	6.47	8.76	11.32	14.52	14.89	16.46	17.8	23.47
61-80		0.37	0.41	0.28	0.28	0.28	0.64	0.45	0.86	1.13	1.61	2.42	3.09
>80		0.00	0.71	0.74	0.04	0.03	0.01	0.00	0.00	1.40	3.1	3.47	2.62
Total	76.00	92.27	107.27	107.19	121.47	125.13	140.26	158.26	195.59	162.13	177.55	190.79	220.63
Adjustment*	76.00	92.27	102.36	103.31	110.62	112.47	127.43	138.31	172.20	131.54	177.55	190.79	220.63
Adjustment**	75.47	88.36	102.36	103.31	110.62	112.50	125.45	136.85	169.52	137.36	177.55	190.79	220.63
100% Spun Share	5.43	5.18	5.90	5.35	5.86	5.53	5.51	5.94	6.48	4.89	5.71	6.50	7.14
Count						**Total Spun Yarn Consumption**							
1-10		140.64	150.57	182.85	189.19	225.05	262.03	260.69	287.00	435.02	457.78	407.18	457.20
11-20		310.55	332.98	358.89	342.85	345.90	392.47	404.19	455.89	455.40	497.81	489.39	507.31
21-30		263.88	266.66	296.88	300.47	325.10	369.72	397.75	489.46	484.31	519.45	518.77	573.03
31-40		482.97	489.36	522.61	504.57	561.76	595.17	564.15	618.23	633.60	663.79	587.60	614.44
41-60		182.62	166.00	183.67	182.22	206.60	224.19	208.87	220.91	183.05	190.66	179.79	180.14
61-80		70.98	72.10	79.22	71.60	64.87	76.40	73.64	127.02	85.45	81.70	80.17	73.74
>80		34.33	30.76	32.81	32.83	31.08	35.94	37.97	33.98	37.47	33.53	35.03	31.94
Total	1265.80	1485.97	1508.43	1656.94	1623.74	1760.36	1955.92	1947.26	2232.50	2314.30	2444.73	2297.93	2437.81

(Contd....)

(Contd....)

Year	1983	1988-89	1989-90	1990-91	1991-92	1992-93	1993-94	1994-95	1995-96	1996-97	1997-98	1998-99	1999-2000
Adjustment*	1264.91	1482.92	1497.00	1646.93	1599.98	1729.47	1913.03	1894.15	2160.60	2248.44	—	—	—
Other Use (Non-Cot)		10.00	9.00	9.00	6.00	11.00	25.00	21.00	24.00	28.00	—	—	—
Adjustment**	1264.91	1472.92	1488.00	1637.93	1593.98	1718.47	1888.03	1873.15	2136.60	2220.44	2332.71	2095.65	2203.01
Spun Share	90.95	86.37	85.73	84.84	84.38	84.45	82.96	81.25	81.63	78.97	74.98	71.37	71.28
Count							**Total Filament Yarn Consumption**						
1-10					21.01	26.32	35.45	29.68	46.12	79.17	112.36	157.07	154.65
11-20					9.87	7.85	8.76	8.92	10.45	9.71	9.56	11.17	10.09
21-30					37.84	37.24	42.95	40.46	44.71	69.72	111.11	125.97	168.02
31-40					14.92	13.77	12.20	15.89	21.42	38.63	20.64	18.83	19.12
41-60					109-91	141.19	162.48	194.30	252.55	284.77	377.44	417.20	426.78
61-80					43.14	45.24	54.89	47.88	39.95	44.37	54.09	41.66	44.10
>80					54.45	55.37	62.56	58.93	63.20	62.16	69.67	64.32	52.48
Total	105.13	223.10	244.45	276.05	291.15	326.96	379.29	396.07	478.41	588.53	754.87	836.23	875.23
Average Count					60.75	56.52	56.18	55.05	53.02	48.29	46.87	44.10	43.09
Adjustment*	124.46	230.63	245.52	289.63	291.36	310.90	380.08	422.83	467.73	579.45	764.95	825.49	870.99
Polyprelene	*1.441	1.73	2.23	3.02	3.67	5.43	7.81	9.30	13.25	11.89	13.38	15.31	16.86
Adjustment**	125.90	232.37	247.75	292.65	295.03	316.33	387.89	432.13	480.97	591.34	778.34	840.80	887.85
Filament Share	9.05	13.63	14.27	15.16	15.62	15.55	17.04	18.75	18.37	21.03	25.02	28.63	28.72
*Acetate													
Count							**Total Yarn Consumption**						
1-10	—	—	—	—	210.20	251.37	297.48	290.36	333.12	514.19	570.14	564.24	611.85
11-20	—	—	—	—	352.72	353.75	401.23	413.12	466.34	465.11	507.37	500.57	517.39
21-30	—	—	—	—	338.32	362.33	412.67	438.21	534.17	554.03	630.55	644.74	741.05
31-40	—	—	—	—	519.49	575.54	607.37	580.04	639.66	672.23	684.43	606.43	633.56

(Contd...)

(Contd...)

Year	1983-84	1988-89	1989-90	1990-91	1991-92	1992-93	1993-94	1994-95	1995-96	1996-97	1997-98	1998-99	1999-2000
41-60	—	—	—	—	292.13	347.79	386.66	403.17	473.46	467.83	568.10	597.00	606.93
61-80	—	—	—	—	114.74	110.10	131.29	121.53	166.97	129.82	135.79	121.84	117.84
>80	—	—	—	—	87.28	86.45	98.51	96.89	97.18	99.62	103.20	99.34	84.42
Total	1370.93	1709.07	1752.88	1932.99	1914.88	2087.32	2335.21	2343.33	2710.91	2902.83	3199.59	3134.16	3313.04
Polyprelene	1.441	1.73	2.23	3.02	3.67	5.43	7.81	9.30	13.25	11.89	—	—	—
Adjustment*	1372.37	1710.80	1755.11	1936.01	1918.55	2092.75	2343.02	2352.62	2724.15	2914.72	3111.04	2936.44	3090.85
Adjustment**	1390.81	1705.29	1735.75	1930.58	1889.01	2034.80	2275.92	2305.28	2617.57	2811.78	3111.04	2936.44	3090.85
Fibre/Filament Requirement for Yarn Production													
Yarn Produced	1415.57	1812.41	1898.98	2102.95	2100.15	2273.69	2528.88	2605.33	2976.50	3394.37	3741.55	3659.33	3939.68
Cotton Fibre	1325.42	1583.24	1651.80	1818.82	1754.54	1893.51	2059.63	2062.63	2298.70	2612.10	2719.00	2485.00	2652.00
Other Fibre	198.73	258.27	265.54	295.84	335.32	351.40	414.48	474.05	563.21	614.84	769.00	780.00	875.00
Filament Inc. Polypre	105.13	224.83	246.68	279.07	294.82	332.39	387.10	405.37	491.65	600.42	768.25	851.54	892.09
Total Fibre & Filame	1629.28	2066.34	2164.02	2393.74	2384.68	2577.30	2861.21	2942.04	3353.56	3827.36	4256.25	4116.54	4419.09
Fibre/Yarn Ratio	1.15	1.14	1.14	1.14	1.14	1.13	1.13	1.13	1.13	1.13	1.14	1.12	1.12
Cotton Fibre Share	81.35	76.62	76.33	75.98	73.58	73.47	71.98	70.11	68.55	68.25	63.88	60.37	60.01

Note: (i) *Adjustments are made at each blend stage to work out total availability of yarn. This takes into account exports, charges in stocks etc.

(ii) **Adjustments which are not made at each blend stage due to lack of data are made at aggregate stage and include difference between opening and closing stock to work out total availability of yarn for production of fabrics.

(iii) The above data does not include yarn consumed in khadi, silk and wool sectors.

(iv) There are few gaps in anylsis for the period 1997-98 to 1999-2000, due to change in data structure and availability. We tried to reconcile under the constraints.

Source: Compendium of textile statistics, Office of the textile commissioner, G.O.I., Mumbai and Handbook of statistics on cotton textile industry, ICMF, TEXPROCIL and other figures are as derived by the author.

APPENDIX 3.2

Fibre-wise and Sector-wise Production of Fabrics Derived on the Basis of Delivery of Yarn

A) Cotton Sector **(Million Square Meter)**

Range	*1983*	*1988-89*	*1989-90*	*1990-91*	*1991-92*	*1992-93*	*1993-94*	*1994-95*	*1995-96*	*1996-97*	*1997-98*	*1998-99*	*1999-2000*
Count							**Consumption of Cotton Yarn in Mill Sector**						
0-10	77	63	68	64	59	50	59	61	61	72	73	66	65
11-20	648	531	530	521	475	394	433	408	401	434	440	395	393
21-30	1172	846	767	713	628	540	494	426	377	415	421	378	375
31-40	706	488	433	388	337	297	253	215	180	135	137	123	122
40-60	70	79	85	77	59	41	31	42	36	38	39	35	34
60-80	54	46	38	49	48	43	45	49	40	43	43	39	38
<80	54	46	38	49	48	43	45	49	40	42	43	39	38
Total	2781	2100	1958	1862	1654	1408	1359	1250	1135	1180	1196	1073	1067
Mill Share	29.80	18.59	17.18	15.02	14.37	11.20	10.03	9.68	7.47	8.39	8.49	8.46	8.07
Fabric Weight	130.90	131.63	133.36	133.25	133.89	133.53	136.92	137.00	139.74	141.85	141.85	141.85	141.85
Adjustment	2785	2100	1957	1859	1651	1407	1356	1247	1131	1193	1196	1073	1067
Count Range							**Production of Cotton Fabrics in Powerloom Sector**						
0-10	163	244	273	355	368	445	513	466	491	652	616	532	597
11-20	361	420	478	572	534	572	636	576	589	624	557	518	530
21-30	537	634	635	754	671	791	874	801	935	833	789	707	806
31-40	834	1471	1540	1705	1590	1864	1889	1611	1610	1454	1376	1147	1275
40-60	539	958	885	990	838	1069	1130	1020	1032	788	750	659	654
60-80	551	768	857	952	776	670	684	627	1241	674	525	478	426
>80	134	265	259	274	281	263	314	327	292	263	209	212	200
Total	3119	4760	4926	5601	5059	5674	6041	5429	6191	5289	4822	4253	4488
Powerloom Share	33.43	42.14	43.23	45.21	43.96	45.12	44.58	42.03	40.72	37.59	34.23	33.52	33.93
Fabric Weight	98.60	96.63	97.64	99.27	101.61	103.45	104.61	104.44	99.66	110.42	111.78	111.44	113.62

(Contd......)

(Contd...)

Year	1983	1988-89	1989-90	1990-91	1991-92	1992-93	1993-94	1994-95	1995-96	1996-97	1997-98	1998-99	1999-2000
Count Range	**Production of Cotton Fabrics in Hosiery Sector**												
0-10	3	4	5	6	7	9	11	11	16	25	28	26	28
11-20	115	143	175	207	218	233	285	291	390	497	521	532	510
21-30	121	151	163	191	192	225	274	284	434	465	517	508	543
31-40	523	1012	1135	1244	1311	1528	1707	1643	2149	2340	2597	2376	2475
40-60	81	170	168	186	178	225	263	268	354	326	364	351	327
60-80	36	59	70	77	71	61	69	71	184	121	110	110	92
<80	2	6	6	6	7	7	9	10	12	13	12	13	12
Total	881	1545	1721	1918	1984	2288	2618	2579	3539	3788	4150	3918	3986
Hosiery Share	9.44	13.68	15.10	15.48	17.24	18.19	19.32	19.96	23.28	26.92	29.45	30.88	30.13
Fabric Weight	103.94	101.60	102.28	102.70	103.31	103.15	103.51	103.55	102.30	105.08	105.07	105.41	105.62
Count Range	**Production of Cotton Fabrics in Handloom Sector**												
0-10	276	321	331	401	422	511	601	631	719	1216	1285	1110	1242
11-20	680	616	644	717	681	730	829	866	958	675	675	627	640
21-30	379	348	321	354	321	378	427	451	570	297	315	282	320
31-40	504	693	668	687	652	765	792	779	842	952	1008	841	932
40-60	414	574	488	507	437	557	602	627	686	316	336	296	292
60-80	251	273	280	289	240	207	216	228	489	211	184	167	149
)80	42	65	59	58	60	56	69	83	80	133	118	120	113
Total	2546	2890	2790	3012	2813	3206	3535	3664	4342	3799	3921	3443	3688
Handloom Share	27.29	25.59	24.49	24.31	24.45	25.49	26.09	28.36	28.56	27.00	27.83	27.14	27.88
Fabric Weight	112.20	109.00	111.10	113.56	116.59	117.59	119.38	119.55	116.07	136.61	137.71	137.37	139.38
Total Cotton Fabrics Production in Mill, Powerboom, Hosiery and Handloom Sector													
0-10	518	632	676	826	856	1015	1184	1169	1287	1966	2002	1734	1933
11-20	1804	1710	1827	2017	1909	1929	2183	2142	2338	2230	2194	2072	2073
21-30	2209	1980	1885	2012	1811	1935	2069	1962	2315	2010	2042	1875	2045
31-40	2567	3665	3776	4025	3890	4455	4641	4248	4780	4882	5118	4488	4804
40-60	1104	1781	1625	1760	1512	1892	2026	1957	5108	1469	1490	1341	1308

(Contd....)

(Contd....)

Year	1983	1988-89	1989-90	1990-91	1991-92	1992-93	1993-94	1994-95	1995-96	1996-97	1997-98	1998-99	1999-2000
60-80	892	1146	1245	1367	1135	981	1014	975	1955	1048	862	794	705
)80	233	382	361	387	395	369	436	468	423	451	381	384	363
Total	9327	11295	11395	12392	11510	12577	13554	12922	15207	14055	14089	12688	13229
Fabric Weight	112.45	106.98	107.77	108.38	110.20	110.37	111.49	111.69	107.95	118.70	119.57	119.19	120.67
Conversion Rate	8.89	9.35	9.28	9.23	9.07	9.06	8.97	8.95	9.26	8.42	8.36	8.39	8.29
Adjustment	9331	11296	11394	12390	11507	12575	3551	12918	15203	14068	14089	12688	13229
Cotton Share	66.67	62.30	61.95	60.71	58.06	59.43	56.46	53.03	54.47	50.57	44.75	42.51	42.50
Count Range							**Cotton Viscose**						
0-10	-	0	0	0	0	0	0	2	2	6	4	3	3
11-20	-	13	10	4	6	8	10	16	29	22	19	28	49
21-30	-	6	9	13	13	30	49	89	107	78	64	82	111
31-40	-	48	30	33	56	69	53	41	30	29	21	38	49
40-60	-	87	65	70	51	44	26	18	6	12	8	10	12
60-80	-	103	52	38	41	27	4	8	3	10	6	9	24
<80	-	47	20	17	15	16	10	9	11	6	4	7	8
Total	515	305	185	176	183	193	153	183	189	161	127	177	257
Fabric Weight	73.72	73.72	76.00	76.74	81.06	88.19	97.95	102.75	109.13	108.05	109.27	107.61	106.88
Count Range							**Cotton Polyester**						
0-10	-	1	1	2	3	7	5	8	11	9	13	24	26
11-20	-	19	36	56	49	70	83	125	146	145	203	213	238
21-30	-	53	66	84	115	126	176	198	225	278	300	356	517
31-40	-	105	88	101	88	96	148	149	122	193	255	236	198
40-60	-	411	373	437	468	390	454	346	311	295	309	352	327
60-80	-	175	149	187	257	264	484	489	567	619	678	652	548
<80	-	6	5	7	10	14	15	10	2	2	5.21	4.43	2.61
Total	330	771	719	875	991	966	1365	1325	1384	1541	1764	1837	1856
Fabric Weight	72.79	72.79	75.43	76.53	74.39	77.35	74.50	78.12	78.05	78.80	81.31	83.06	87.65
Adjustment	330	771	706	857	960	915	1301	1210	1165	1265	1764	1837	1856

(Contd....)

(Contd....)

Year	1983	1988-89	1989-90	1990-91	1991-92	1992-93	1993-94	1994-95	1995-96	1996-97	1997-98	1998-99	1999-2000
Count Range							**Cotton Blended Fabrics**						
1-10	-	2	1	2	3	8	8	15	16	18	25	34	36
11-20	-	33	46	61	56	82	116	160	187	179	250	292	341
21-30	-	67	82	102	141	168	239	312	351	375	402	530	729
31-40	-	169	133	144	155	173	213	207	156	225	300	307	299
41-60	-	518	455	517	531	444	490	367	322	311	333	380	357
61-80	-	279	203	229	299	292	493	497	574	632	694	673	579
>80	-	54	25	25	25	30	25	19	14	8	10	12	11
Total	1041	1122	945	1080	1210	1196	1585	1577	1619	1747	2014	2228	2351
Fabric Weight	75.87	73.60	76.05	76.74	75.89	79.82	78.49	82.76	82.68	83.60	84.89	87.68	92.11
After Adjustment	1041	1122	932	1061	1179	1145	1521	1462	1399	1471	2014	2228	2351
Count Range							**Polyester Viscose**						
0-10	-	2	1	2	1	1	1	2	4	7	26	36	41
11-20	-	107	98	87	79	83	117	174	261	382	598	626	649
21-30	-	97	164	319	459	515	678	940	1238	1512	1807	1727	1671
31-40	-	474	417	450	388	374	406	454	456	489	483	412	385
40-60	-	298	281	329	471	551	583	520	546	618	658	560	523
60-80	-	15	14	14	12	14	22	14	23	14	31	60	96
<80	-	5	0	0	0	0	0	0	0	7	3	7	4
Total	473	999	975	1201	1412	1538	1807	2104	2527	3029	3606	3427	3369
Fabric Weight	95.17	95.17	95.46	95.14	92.69	91.86	93.41	97.17	99.23	100.98	103.89	105.15	105.53
Count Range							**Total Blended Spun Fabrics Production**						
1-10	-	4	2	5	4	10	9	17	20	27	63	78	87
11-20	-	155	159	158	145	180	247	345	463	619	907	979	1068
21-30	-	177	265	459	642	706	952	1288	1616	2046	2319	2355	2561
31-40	-	673	580	624	575	571	643	687	631	761	876	824	783

(Contd...)

(Contd....)

Year	1983	1988-89	1989-90	1990-91	1991-92	1992-93	1993-94	1994-95	1995-96	1996-97	1997-98	1998-99	1999-2000
41-60	-	837	752	866	1033	1022	1112	922	900	977	1045	1017	973
61-80	-	296	218	244	321	340	537	523	630	679	781	802	746
>80	-	59	25	25	25	30	26	20	14	15	12	24	17
Total	1688	2200	2002	2380	2745	2859	3525	3802	4275	5124	6003	6079	6235
Fabric Weight	83.54	84.21	86.45	86.86	85.18	86.46	86.38	90.93	92.47	94.43	97.05	97.86	99.57
Conversion Rate	11.97	11.87	11.57	11.51	11.74	11.57	11.58	11.00	10.81	10.59	10.30	10.22	10.04
Adjustment*	1688	2200	1945	2318	2627	2707	3369	3553	3856	4636	6073	6146	6292
Others	-4.43	-32.65	-2.78	-5.99	-13.15	-57.25	-41.10	-106.68	-96.57	21.29	0.00	0.00	0.00
Adjustment**	1683	2168	1942	2312	2614	2649	3328	3446	3759	4658	6073	6146	6292
Blend Share	12.03	11.96	10.56	11.32	13.19	12.52	13.86	14.14	13.46	16.76	19.29	20.59	20.21
Count Range							**Viscose**						
0-10	-	2	2	1	1	1	1	1	1	1	2	3	6
11-20	-	122	146	154	159	148	124	124	141	90	97	82	94
21-30	-	111	119	92	123	153	156	188	230	128	158	145	181
31-40	-	327	360	350	323	299	324	305	295	176	196	171	163
40-60	-	14	13	17	36	20	24	16	14	6	7	6	5
60-80	-	0	0	0	3	0	2	0	0	0	0	0	0
<80	-	0	0	0	0	0	0	0	0	0	0	0	0
Total	543	576	641	614	645	620	631	635	682	401	461	408	448
Fabric Weight	112.43	112.43	113.36	113.84	112.58	113.38	111.04	111.68	112.56	113.76	113.29	113.18	114.58
Adjustment*	543	576	601	585	584	557	572	547	567	279	461	408	448
Count Range							**Polyester**						
0-10	-	0	0	0	1	2	3	4	7	5	27	44	53
11-20	-	5	2	3	3	9	14	31	62	59	100	146	189
21-30	-	4	10	11	22	30	39	64	97	114	211	429	638

(Contd....)

(Contd...)

Year	*1983*	*1988-89*	*1989-90*	*1990-91*	*1991-92*	*1992-93*	*1993-94*	*1994-95*	*1995-96*	*1996-97*	*1997-98*	*1998-99*	*1999-2000*
31-40	-	15	10	14	43	47	45	72	84	75	101	115	169
40-60	-	37	30	42	97	100	153	233	297	339	368	397	531
60-80	-	13	14	10	4	10	18	15	30	39	53	82	104
<80	-	0	16	16	1	1	0	0	0	31	68	70	58
Total	43	75	82	96	171	199	272	418	577	662	929	1284	1742
Fabric Weight	46.42	46.42	45.34	46.63	48.76	50.39	49.08	50.56	51.95	50.36	54.32	56.76	56.90
Adjustment*	43	75	75	87	103	105	183	332	443	471	929	1284	1742
Count Range Acrylic													
0-10	-	1	3	0	1	1	1	3	2	12	26	35	49
11-20	-	24	34	12	26	17	27	47	54	58	51	38	28
21-30	-	128	165	177	201	219	259	275	401	368	300	319	274
31-40	-	46	67	116	142	166	228	289	350	352	315	251	210
40-60	-	1	1	1	11	6	10	5	23	12	16	18	14
60-80	-	0	0	0	0	0	0	0	0	0	0	0	1
)80	-	0	0	0	0	0	0	0	0	0	0	4	0
Total	109	200	270	307	382	409	525	619	829	803	707	665	575
Fabric Weight	100.66	100.66	101.34	96.51	97.00	96.41	96.46	98.06	96.83	98.85	100.76	101.81	105.17
Adjustment*	109	200	269	305	376	400	506	560	793	731	707	665	575
Count Range						**100% Spun Fabrics Production M.S.Mt**							
1-10	-	3	5	2	3	4	5	8	11	19	55	82	109
11-20	-	155	186	173	194	179	172	210	263	210	252	271	322
21-30	-	257	308	289	362	429	494	559	792	638	685	908	1138
31-40	-	405	450	494	516	526	605	671	738	608	624	554	564
41-60	-	54	49	62	148	136	191	261	335	357	393	424	562
61-80	-	13	14	10	7	10	21	15	30	39	55	84	107

(Contd....)

(Contd...)

Year	1983	1988-89	1989-90	1990-91	1991-92	1992-93	1993-94	1994-95	1995-96	1996-97	1997-98	1998-99	1999-2000
>80	-	0	16	16	1	1	0	0	0	31	68	74	58
Total	714	888	1028	1047	1231	1283	1488	1725	2170	1902	2132	2396	2859
Fabric Weight	106.42	103.88	104.34	102.41	98.65	97.53	94.25	91.75	90.15	85.23	83.29	79.62	77.18
Conversion Rate	9.40	9.63	9.58	9.76	10.14	10.25	10.61	10.90	11.09	11.73	12.01	12.56	12.96
Adjustment*	714	888	980	1007	1095	1118	1320	1492	1884	1517	2169	2431	2894
Others	-4.98	-37.64	0.00	0.00	0.00	0.31	-21.01	-15.91	-29.73	68.29	0.00	0.00	0.00
Adjustment**	709	851	980	1007	1095	1118	1299	1476	1855	1586	2169	2431	2894
100% Spun Share	5.07	4.69	5.33	4.94	5.52	5.28	5.41	6.06	6.64	5.70	6.89	8.14	9.30
Count Range						**Nylon Filament Fabrics**							
1-10	-	-	-	-	12	15	14	17	7	12	0	0	0
11-20	-	-	-	-	0	0	0	0	0	0	1	2	2
21-30	-	-	-	-	23	29	52	53	56	59	55	39	33
31-40	-	-	-	-	5	0	0	0	0	0	0	0	1
41-60	-	-	-	-	59	83	68	76	77	73	77	74	58
61-80	-	-	-	-	32	35	20	35	31	25	21	24	23
>80	-	-	-	-	935	898	1109	1117	1296	1102	852	916	989
Total	932	1235	1338	1376	1066	1061	1262	1298	1467	1270	1007	1056	1106
Fabric Weight	28.95	28.95	28.95	28.95	28.95	30.59	29.58	30.32	28.34	29.88	29.65	27.11	25.89
Adjustment*	991	1289	1338	1340	1085	1035	1314	1318	1499	1254	1003	1027	1020
ConversionRate	34.54	34.54	34.54	34.54	34.54	32.69	33.81	32.98	35.29	33.47	33.73	36.88	38.63
Count Range						**Polyester Filament Babrics**							
1-10	-	-	-	-	72	93	128	97	181	301	497	703	695
11-20	-	-	-	-	0	0	0	0	0	0	0	0	0

(Contd...)

(Contd....)

Year	1983	1988-89	1989-90	1990-91	1991-92	1992-93	1993-94	1994-95	1995-96	1996-97	1997-98	1998-99	1999-2000
21-30	-	-	-	-	324	323	353	334	373	564	1024	1182	1603
31-40	-	-	-	-	55	68	56	93	127	286	118	98	121
41-60	-	-	-	-	1263	1684	1969	2336	3219	3424	5110	5676	5941
61-80	-	-	-	-	795	844	1077	918	752	793	1075	818	870
>80	-	-	-	-	407	442	477	441	456	453	665	579	400
Total	622	2008	2198	2603	2916	3454	4061	4219	5108	5821	8490	9055	9629
Fabric Weight	71.19	71.19	71.19	71.19	71.19	71.38	71.16	70.69	73.65	84.74	78.67	82.31	83.19
Adjustment*	774	2094	2293	2868	2947	3306	4096	4670	5035	5794	8634	9016	9526
Conversion Rate	14.05	14.05	14.05	14.05	14.05	14.01	14.05	14.15	13.58	11.80	12.71	12.15	12.02
Count Range						**Viscose Filament Fabrics**							
1-10	-	-	-	-	13	14	23	25	26	25	25	28	24
11-20	-	-	-	-	66	53	59	60	70	65	63	73	66
21-30	-	-	-	-	26	15	20	14	15	15	17	19	18
31-40	-	-	-	-	88	69	65	66	87	88	88	90	70
41-60	-	-	-	-	305	326	370	466	448	414	414	442	338
61-80	-	-	-	-	77	69	54	52	55	42	38	31	32
>80	-	-	-	-	38	26	25	1	0	5	6	3	4
Total	395	517	574	594	614	573	615	692	700	655	651	686	552
Fabric Weight	85.80	85.80	85.80	85.80	85.80	83.72	86.18	84.52	86.62	87.50	87.59	88.75	90.18
Adjustment*	0	0	0	0	0	0	0	0	0	0	0	0	0
Conversion rate	11.65	11.65	11.65	11.65	11.65	11.94	11.60	11.83	11.54	11.43	11.42	11.27	11.09
Count Range						**Total Filament Fabrics Production M.S.Mt**							
1-10	-	-	-	-	98	123	165	139	214	338	522	730	719
11-20	-	-	-	-	66	53	59	60	70	65	64	75	68
21-30	-	-	-	-	373	368	425	401	443	638	1095	1240	1653

(Contd....)

(Contd......)

Year	1983	1988-89	1989-90	1990-91	1991-92	1992-93	1993-94	1994-95	1995-96	1996-97	1997-98	1998-99	1999-2000
31-40	-	-	-	-	148	137	121	159	214	374	206	188	191
41-60	-	-	-	-	1627	2093	2407	2877	3744	3911	5602	6192	6337
61-80	-	-	-	-	904	948	1150	1004	838	860	1134	874	925
>80	-	-	-	-	1380	1366	1611	1569	1752	1560	1523	1498	1393
Total	1949	3761	4110	4572	4596	5088	5938	6209	7275	7746	10148	10798	11287
Fabric Weight	53.95	59.32	59.48	60.38	63.34	64.26	63.87	63.79	65.76	75.98	74.39	77.44	77.54
Conversion Rate	18.53	16.86	16.81	16.56	15.79	15.56	15.66	15.68	15.21	13.16	13.44	12.91	12.90
Adjustment**	2266	3928	4176	4802	4675	4942	6110	6758	7364	7787	10456	10866	11342
Filament Share	16.20	21.67	22.70	23.52	23.58	23.35	25.45	27.73	26.38	28.02	33.22	36.41	36.44
Count Range							**Total Synthetic Fabrics Production**						
1-10	-	7	8	7	105	137	180	164	245	384	640	890	916
11-20	-	310	345	331	45	411	477	615	796	895	1223	1324	1457
21-30	-	435	573	748	1377	1503	1871	2248	2852	3322	4099	4503	5352
31-40	-	1078	1030	1118	1239	1234	1369	1517	1584	1742	1706	1566	1538
41-60	-	891	800	928	2808	3251	3710	4060	4980	5245	7039	7633	7872
61-80	-	309	233	254	1233	1298	1708	1543	1498	1578	1970	1760	1777
>80	-	59	41	41	1406	1397	1636	1589	1766	1606	1604	1596	1468
Total	4351	6849	7140	7998	8573	9230	10952	11736	13719	14772	18282	19273	20381
Fabric Weight	74.04	40.53	39.26	39.24	75.41	75.76	75.25	76.69	77.94	83.57	41.58	40.77	41.29
Conversion Rate	13.51	24.68	25.47	25.48	13.26	13.20	13.29	13.04	12.83	11.97	24.05	24.53	24.22
Adjustment**	4659	6835	7001	8022	8317	8587	10455	11450	12716	13726	17392	17160	17898
Synthetic Share	33.30	37.70	38.06	39.30	41.95	40.58	43.55	46.99	45.55	49.38	55.25	57.49	57.50
Count Range							**Total Fabrics**						
1-10	-	-	-	-	961	1152	1364	1333	1532	2350	2642	2624	2849

(Contd...)

(Contd...)

Year	1983	1988-89	1989-90	1990-91	1991-92	1992-93	1993-94	1994-95	1995-96	1996-97	1997-98	1998-99	1999-2000
11-20	-	-	-	-	2314	2341	2660	2757	3135	3125	3417	3397	3530
21-30	-	-	-	-	3188	3438	3940	4210	5167	5331	6141	6378	7398
31-40	-	-	-	-	5129	5689	6011	5765	6364	6624	6824	6054	6342
41-60	-	-	-	-	4320	5143	5737	6017	7088	6714	8529	8974	9180
61-80	-	-	-	-	2368	2279	2722	2519	3453	2626	2832	2554	2482
>80	-	-	-	-	1802	1765	2072	2057	2189	2057	1985	1980	1830
Total	13678	18145	18535	20391	20083	21807	24506	24658	28926	28827	32371	31961	33610
Fabric Weight	100.23	94.19	94.57	94.80	95.35	95.72	95.29	95.04	93.72	100.70	98.84	98.06	98.57
Adjustment**	13989	18131	18395	20412	19824	21162	24006	24369	27919	27794	31481	29847	31127
Conversion Rate	9.98	10.62	10.57	10.55	10.49	10.45	10.49	10.52	10.67	9.93	10.12	10.20	10.14
Share of Various Sector in Total Fabric Production													
Mill	3604	2902	2667	2589	2376	2000	1990	1987	1727	1666	1658	1517	1457
Mill Share are	25.76	16.01	14.50	12.68	11.99	9.45	8.29	8.15	6.1	5.99	5.27	5.08	4.68
Powerloom	6251	10180	10648	12319	12007	13069	15153	15204	17171	17305	20789	19917	20932
Power Share	44.68	56.15	57.88	60.35	60.57	61.76	63.12	62.39	61.50	62.26	66.04	66.73	67.25
Handloom	3134	3316	3189	3355	3194	3603	3977	4197	5022	4470	4270	3783	4048
Hand Share	22.41	18.29	17.33	16.44	16.11	17.02	16.57	17.22	17.99	16.08	13.56	12.68	13.00
Hosiery	1001	1733	1892	2148	2247	2490	2885	2981	3999	4353	4764	4630	4690
Hosiery Share	7.15	9.56	10.28	10.53	11.33	11.77	12.02	12.23	14.32	15.66	15.13	15.51	15.07
Total	13989	18131	18395	20412	19824	21162	24006	24369	27919	27794	31481	29847	31127

Note : *(i)* The above data does not include the fabrics produced in Khadi, Silk and Wool Sector.

(ii) The above sector-wise analysis of production of fabrics is based on delivery of yarn to various sectors and subject to change as hank yarn is partially consumed in the powerloom sector.

(iii) Production of fabrics in the mill sector do not include production in non SSI weaving segment.

(iv) *The estimates derived fum count range-wise data are adjusted based on adjustments at each blend stage. This takes into account experts, changes in stock of yarn etc.

(v) **The adjustments which are not posible at each blend stage due to lack of data are made at aggregate level.

Source : As derived by the author.

APPENDIX 3.3

Ratio of Various Blends Taken to Work out Conversion Rates for Yarn and Fabrics

Cotton Polyester Blended Yarn: 40:60
Cotton Viscose Blended Yarn: 40:60
Cotton with Other: 40:60
Polyester Viscose: 40:60
Polyester with Other : 60:40
PVC Blended: 60:40

Others Blend: In this case, the average weight derived above for polyester cotton blend is used for each count range.

100 per cent Polyester (Carbonised): In the case of 100% Polyester carbonised, weight of fabrics is very light as cotton content in it, which is around 40 per cent is carbonised. Carbonised means burnt. This procedure require advance technology and is generally performed in mills sector.

The weight of cotton polyester blend in the count range 0-10s is estimated as (222.68x.4)+(222.68x.6x108/112)=217.91 gms/sq.mt. Similarly, one could estimate the weight for other count ranges and for other blends of fabrics.

The limitation in this analysis is that the same blend ratios are assumed for all the count ranges.

Source: Derived from SITRA and Experts Opinion.

4

Changes in Demand and Supply Pattern in Indian Textiles and Clothing Products

Having derived the production estimates of cotton, blended and synthetic fabrics, this chapter is devoted to an analysis of the changes in demand and supply pattern in Indian textiles and clothing products. The fabric produced in the country has to be ultimately used in some final forms such as fabrics, made-ups and garments. The fabric produced is either exported or consumed domestically or kept in stock to be sold during the next period. In case of consumption overshooting production in any year, the stocks should get depleted and vice-versa. In the long run, the estimates of production have to be balanced with its uses. If it is not true then either the production estimates are wrong or the estimates about its final uses are incorrect. Having already made an attempt to work out the production estimates of fabrics in Chapter 3, it is important to analyse its various uses (Figure 4.1) such as

(1) Direct fabrics export or consumed domestically in the form of garments in piece length. The garments in piece length do not require stitching and are used in the form of Sari, Dhoti etc.

(2) For manufacturing of made-ups, which are either exported or consumed domestically. Made-ups is product ready to use such as towels, chaddars, curtains etc.

(3) For manufacturing of garments, which are either exported or used domestically. Garments are products ready to wear such as trousers, shirts, t-shirts, pyjamas, etc.

The data regarding exports and consumption of fabrics in several forms such as fabrics, made-ups and garments are available in different units such as square metres, metres, kilograms, rupees and pieces. The data for exports is available from the Cotton Textiles Export Promotion Council (TEXPROCIL), Synthetic and Rayon Textile Exports Promotion Council (SRTEPC), Apparel Export Promotion Council (AEPC) and Handloom Export Promotion Council. The data for domestic consumption is available from consumer household survey and consumer non-household survey published by Textile committee, GOI. The analysis is done separately for cotton and synthetic products. An attempt is made in this study to convert the consumption of fabrics in all these forms for exports and domestic market into square metre equivalent by working conversion norms as explained later.

The total export of fabrics equivalent to square metres is subtracted from the total production of fabrics to find out the total fabrics equivalent availability for domestic consumption. An attempt is then made to include the import content of fabrics in various forms. The estimates about the domestic availability of fabrics are then compared with the square metre equivalent consumption estimate, which is derived from data available from Textile Committee. The estimates of fabrics equivalent demand in various forms derived this way are then extended for estimating the requirement of yarn and fibres. A two-step procedure is adopted for this purpose. First, an attempt is made to convert export of fabrics in square metres into kilograms by using fabrics to yarn conversion rates. Secondly, the yarn equivalent export is then converted into fibre equivalent export by using fibre to yarn conversion rates. The combed and carded yarn share consumed in different sector is different as explained in Chapter 2, and hence conversion rates for yarn to fibre are derived accordingly for each sector. The textiles and clothing exports are thus analysed in terms of yarn and fibre equivalent exports in kilograms in addition to fabrics equivalent exports in square metres. The total fabrics, yarn and its equivalent fibre exports are used to find out the domestic availability of various types of fabrics, yarn and fibres. From this analysis of exports, the per capita consumption of fabrics and fibre are worked out and compared with the related available information on consumption. These estimates of domestic consumption derived in this study are further split into fabrics use in the form garments in piece-length, made-ups, tailor-made and ready-made garments. Thus one could work out the total production of various varieties by combining the various uses in exports and domestic segment.

The overall comparison of production and total consumption estimates hides several discrepancies at sectoral level, which are mainly caused by diversion of hank yarn to powerloom sector. An attempt is made to find the revised estimates of sector-wise production of fabrics on the basis of extent of hank yarn diversion to powerloom sector. These revised estimates are then used to work out the estimates of values added in cotton and synthetic sector for textiles and clothing products. The results derived are thus comparable with CSO estimates of GDP in textiles and clothing sector. Similar estimates of sector-wise production of fabrics are used to work out the employment estimates in various sectors. The estimates of employment in textile sector by the Textile Ministry/Textile Commissioner are not observed and are derived from official estimates of production of fabrics, which are based on unscientific conversion rates.

Figure 4.1 gives an overview of the various stages of textiles and clothing production, and ultimate uses of these products.

We begin the analysis with cotton textiles and clothing products.

Cotton Textiles and Clothing Products

In this section an attempt is made first to work out the exports of cotton textiles and clothing products equivalent to fabrics,

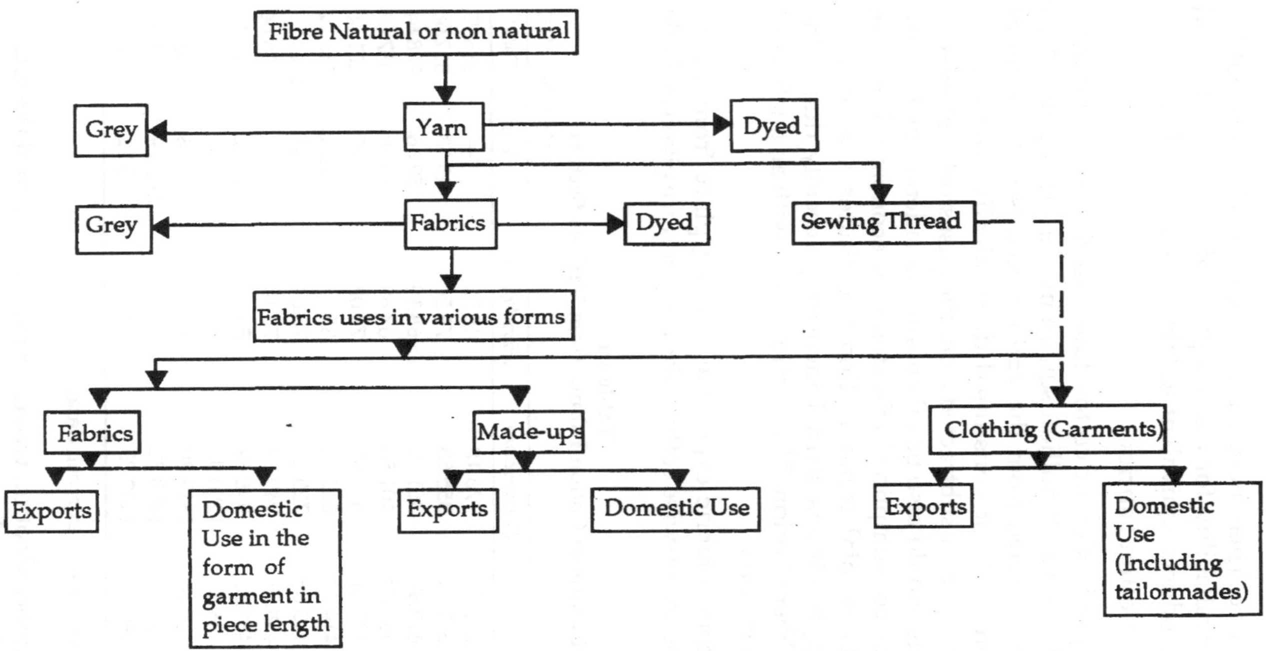

Figure 4.1. Stages of Production of Textiles and Clothing Products and their Ultimate Uses.

Note: The product on the left side of the doted lines are called textile products while product on the right side are called clothing or garment products.

yarn and fibre. Then these estimates are used to work out the domestic availability for consumption of cotton textiles and clothing products equivalent to fabrics, yarn and fibre.

Exports of Cotton Fabrics

The total production of cotton fabric in the country during 1999-2000 was 13229 million square metres. This production was either exported from the various sectors in the form of various products or consumed domestically. The balance should be added or subtracted from the past stocks. However, the imports should also be taken into considerations to work out the total consumption in the domestic economy. The share of imports in total consumption constitutes a very small percentage, but it has started increasing recently due to the impact of liberalisation. This section starts with an analysis of item-wise exports.

The cotton fabric exports are taking place from all the sectors. The sector-wise cotton fabric exports are given in Table 4.1.

Table 4.1
Exports of Cotton Fabrics from Various Sectors

(Mn. Sq. Mts)

Year	*Mill*	*Powerloom*	*Handloom*	*Hosiery*	*Total*
1983	272.87	73.18	40.72	—	386.77
1988-89	371.24	355.55	79.56	25.73	832.08
1989-90	418.87	361.92	68.19	59.66	908.64
1990-91	483.83	401.56	63.69	88.59	1037.67
1991-92	431.24	612.69	76.03	81.70	1201.66
1992-93	414.39	622.92	85.67	92.24	1215.22
1993-94	413.86	725.29	78.61	105.01	1322.77
1994-95	458.97	949.29	78.18	130.21	1616.64
1995-96	466.83	998.69	59.75	115.92	1641.19
1996-97	486.43	1270.94	47.69	130.56	1935.62
1997-98	476.14	1315.80	43.01	110.26	1945.22
1998-99	638.64	1458.82	39.90	107.29	2244.65
1999-2000	699.51	1432.05	40.07	95.22	2266.85

Source: Derived from Texprocil data.

The export of cotton woven fabric has grown at the fastest rate from the powerloom sector. The mill sector's exports are increasing while its total production is declining. One needs to go into details to find the reason behind these structural changes. However, it is clear that the overall exports are growing at a much faster rate of 9.07 per cent per annum compared with production of 0.73 per cent per annum (point to point annual compound growth rate) during 1990-91 to 1999-2000. This means share of direct cotton fabrics exports, as percentage of cotton fabric production, is increasing at a very fast rate over the period of time.

The share of mill sector and handloom sector in total exports of cotton fabric exports has declined steeply over the period of time. Their share has been taken by the powerloom sector in the woven cotton fabric exports. The hosiery sector is another sector for which share in total cotton fabrics exports has increased over the period of time. The trend of decline in mill sector share was quite smooth till the year 1997-98, but thereafter the share of mill sector showed a rise from 26.57 per cent in mill and powerloom sector exports of fabrics to 32.82 per cent during 1999-2000.

The exports and production data for fabrics is presented in terms of kilograms equivalent in the ICAC and FAO. The country-wise per capita domestic consumption is also given in terms of kilograms equivalent fibre/filament. The main purpose for this is to quantify the various linkages in the production process by expressing each of input and output in a common units namely kilogram equivalent. The fabric weight per square metre as well as conversion rate per kilogram are derived in chapter 3 for various sectors and fibres. The data for various sectors at various points of time is given in Table 4.2.

One of the issues to be discussed is whether the same conversion rates could be applied for exports as for domestic production. It is believed that international demand is for the heavier fabrics. To work out the approximate weight for exported fabric one could use data from monthly statistics of India's foreign trade published by the Directorate General of Commercial Intelligence & Statistics (DGCIS), Government of

Table 4.2
Sector-wise Weights and Conversion Rates of Cotton Fabrics

Sectors	*1988-89*	*1993-94*	*1996-97*	*1999-2000*	*1988-89*	*1993-94*	*1996-97*	*1999-2000*
	Fabrics Weight Gms. Per Sq. Mt				*Fabrics Conversion Rates*			
Mill	131.63	136.92	141.85	141.85	7.60	7.30	7.05	7.05
Powerloom	96.63	104.61	110.42	113.62	10.35	9.56	9.06	8.80
Handloom	109.00	119.38	136.61	139.38	9.17	8.38	7.32	7.17
Hosiery	101.60	103.47	105.08	105.62	9.49	9.66	9.52	9.47
Decentralised	101.97	108.96	106.47	118.81	9.80	9.18	9.39	8.42

Source: Derived from DGCIS data.

India for various years. We have calculated the share of fabric exports for 1993-94 and 1996-97 in categories such as >200 gms/square metre, <200 gms/square metre, >100 gms/square metre and 100 gms/square metre as given in Table 4.3.

Table 4.3
Percentage Share of Various Sectors in Square Metres Equivalent of Fabrics Exports

	Weight of Fabrics in Gm/Square Metre				
	≥ 200	*< 200*	*>100*	*<100*	*Total*
Sectors			**Period 1993-94**		
Mill	36.26	1.93	30.55	31.26	100
Powerloom	12.02	21.56	---	66.42	100
Handloom	16.67	2.17	12.59	68.56	100
Total	25.05	9.48	16.36	49.10	100
			Period 1996-97		
Mill	31.39	28.30	1.78	38.52	100
Powerloom	13.78	8.99	25.57	51.66	100
Handloom	9.02	2.16	18.27	70.54	100
Total	24.41	1.63	24.60	49.35	100

Note: In the above table, data is taken in terms of percentages deliberately as the total values are grossly underestimated in the case of DGCIS data compared to the TEXPROCIL data. DGCIS data expressed in percentage terms could give us rough idea about share of various varieties of fabrics exported from various sectors.

Source: Derived from DGCIS data and TEXPROCIL data.

The methodology used to derive average weight for these export categories of fabrics is similar to the one used for deriving average weight of fabrics derived in Chapter 3 for production of fabrics. This exercise has also been undertaken for different count ranges and in each count range the various varieties of fabric produced and their respective share have been taken into account. The weighted fabric weight per square metre for these categories of exports thus worked out are

≥ 200 Gms=226.4 gms/square metre,
< 200 gms/square metre =165.66 gms/square metre,
≥ 100 gms/square metre =122.22 gms/square metre,
< 100 gms/square metre =73.67 gms/square metre.

The average export weight for woven fabrics exports for the year 1993-94 works out to be 127.91 gms/square metre compared to average weight of 111.49 gms/square metre production for the same year. For the year 1996-97 for average weight of the export works out to be 123.87 gms/square metre compared to 118.70 gms/square metre for production. The sector wise analysis for fabric weight of production and export are given in Table 4.4

Table 4.4

Sector-wise Comparison of Fabrics Weight for Production and Exports

(Gms/Sq. Mt)

Sectors	*1993-94*	*1996-97*	*1993-94*	*1996-97*
	Production		*Exports*	
Mill	136.92	141.85	149.77	146.48
Powerloom	104.61	110.42	102.49	115.40
Handloom	119.38	136.61	107.11	98.09
Total	111.49	118.70	127.91	123.87

Source: Derived by the author by using data from DGCIS and Office of the Textile Commissioner.

The data in Table 4.4 shows that there are differences in weight both at sector as well as at aggregate level. It is possible to derive the sector-wise weights for exports for all the years by using DGCIS data. Keeping in mind, the wide fluctuations in the weight of fabrics for sector-wise exports, the weight for exports of fabrics should be worked over time. However, this exercise is quite complicated. More important, DGCIS data on exports do not tally with the data given by Export Promotion Council and are generally underestimated. However, for the handloom sector exports, DGCIS estimates are 3-4 times higher than the data given by the Handloom Export Promotion Council. This raises doubts about the reliability of DGCIS data. There is possibility that the cause of high exports of handloom fabrics reported by DGCIS than by Export Promotion Council may be due to misreporting of powerloom fabrics exports to a considerable extent as handloom fabrics exports in DGCIS data. Some studies argued that powerloom fabrics is being exported as handloom fabrics with a view to deriving advantage of quota free benefits (Bhide, 1996). In view of these limitations, the DGCIS data have not been used in the export analysis. Instead, the weight of fabrics as derived in Chapter 3 for workings out production of fabrics are used for analysis of exports also. This method seems to be more reliable despite limitations.[1]

The average weight of fabrics for exports and production derived this way differ due to the difference in share of various sectors in exports and production. The average conversion rates for various sectors vary quite a lot. As expected, the average weight of fabrics meant for export worked out to be heavier compared to fabrics meant for domestic production. However, in case one also includes made-ups and garments the weight of fabrics equivalent exports worked out to be approximately similar to those of domestic production, as we will see in subsequent sections.

Exports of Cotton Woven Fabrics in Kilograms

The data for cotton woven fabrics export is available in square metre (sector wise) as well as in Rupees. By using the conversion rates of sector-wise production of fabrics, one could calculate the woven fabric exports in million kilograms and compare it with the export of woven fabrics given by the ICAC in kilograms (Table 4.5).

The estimates of total exports of cotton fabrics in kilograms derived by the above method are quite close to those given by the ICAC. Because, the estimates derived by this method tally with ICAC study, it points out the reliability of conversion rates and other estimates derived in this study. It also points to the possibility that the composition of exports for various sectors is similar to the composition of production in various sectors.[2]

1. The sector-wise average weight of fabrics derived in Chapter 3 have some error margin due to possible diversion of hank yarns to the powerloom sector for production of fabrics.
2. This means sector-wise comparative advantage differs, but their production as well as exports consists of similar varieties. In fact, it is important to operate in both the markets mainly to exploit economies of scale.

Table 4.5
Exports of Cotton Woven Fabrics

	Derived in this Study using Sector-Wise Conversion Rates			*ICAC Data (C.Y.)*	*Derived Conversion Rate ICAC*
Year	*Mn. Sq. Mts*	*Gms/Sq. Mts*	*Mn. Kgs**	*Mn. Kgs**	*Gms/Sq. Mts*
1991-92	1119.96	115.05	128.85	132	117.86
1992-93	1122.84	115.63	129.83	137	122.01
1993-94	1217.76	116.57	141.96	159	130.57
1994-95	1486.43	115.33	171.43	163	109.66
1995-96	1525.37	112.63	171.80	175	114.73

Note: *Figures are equivalent yarn.
ICAC data is for calendar year.
Source: Derived by the author and compared it with ICAC Data.

The woven fabrics average weight for export ranges between 110-130 gms/square metre during the period 1991-1995. This analysis is also supported by the conversion rate of 117 gms/square metre taken for average garment export in the official analysis (Garment Export Entitlement Policy) and similar conversion rate taken for fabrics and made-ups in Textile Export Entitlement Policy. An attempt is also made to the estimates about the conversion rate of fabrics for various countries in Appendix 4.1.[3] The estimates derived in Appendix 4.1 also costs doubt about the low conversion rate assumed officially for the decentralised sector.[4]

Exports of Hosiery Fabrics

Having assumed that sector-wise export weight are not different from the sector wise production weights, one can derive the hosiery fabric exports in kilograms by using the hosiery sector conversion rate for production.

3. An attempt is also made to work out total production of fabrics in square metres in the world and conversion rate of fabrics for various countries.
4. The weight of fabrics for the decentralised sector is taken as 77.5 gms/square metres for official statistics, which is nowhere close to the weight of cotton fabrics exports.

Exports of Cotton Woven and Hosiery Fabrics

The data derived separately for the woven and hosiery sector could be added to work out the total exports of fabrics in kilograms Table 4.6).

Table 4.6
Total Exports of Woven and Hosiery Fabrics

Year	*Woven*	*Hosiery*	*Total*	*Total*	
		*Mn. Kgs**		*Gms/Sq. Mt*	*Mn. Sq. Mt*
1983	47.49	--	47.49	122.79	386.77
1988-89	91.88	2.61	94.50	113.58	832.08
1989-90	98.78	6.10	104.88	115.34	908.64
1990-91	111.57	9.06	120.63	116.25	1037.67
1991-92	128.85	8.44	137.29	112.99	1201.66
1992-93	129.83	9.51	139.34	114.68	1215.22
1993-94	141.96	10.87	152.83	115.54	1322.77
1994-95	171.37	13.48	184.85	114.34	1616.64
1995-96	171.80	11.86	183.66	111.90	1641.29
1996-97	214.92	13.72	228.64	118.12	1935.62
1997-98	220.54	11.58	232.13	119.33	1945.22
1998-99	258.64	11.31	269.96	120.26	2244.65
1999-2000	267.52	10.06	277.58	122.45	2266.85
Percentage Per Annum Compound Growth Rates					
1983 to 1990-91	12.98		14.24		15.14
1990-91 to 1999-2000	10.09	2.76	9.69	0.70	9.04
t-statistics	18.94	1.71	18.58	3.02	17.44

Note (*i*) *Figures are equivalent yarn.
(*ii*) Compound growth rate for the period 1983 to 1990-91 is worked on the basis of point to point in this chapter throughtout.
(*iii*) Compound growth rate for the period 1990-91 to 1999-2000 is worked on the basis of semi-log trend in this chapter throughout.

Source : Derived by the author from TEXPROCIL data.

The cotton fabrics exports from the country was only 386.77 million square metres, which accounted for 4.15 per cent of the total cotton fabrics production during 1983 before the introduction of New Textile Policy. In seven years period, export rose more than two and half times to 1037.67 metre by 1990-91 and export share in cotton fabrics production increased to 8.44 per cent. Export recorded an increase of 92.99 million square metres per year on an average *i.e.* at a rate of 15.14 per cent during first phase of reforms.

In the second phase during 1990-91 to 1999-2000, the increase was of 136.58 million square metres on an average per year, which means growth rate of 9.04 per cent per annum. The share of exports in production of fabrics increased from 9.06 per cent in 1990-91 to 17.14 per cent in 1999-2000.

The total exports of cotton fabric directly from all sectors amounted to 2266.95 million square metres during 1999-2000, which is equivalent to 277.58 million kilograms. In addition, the export of fabric also takes place indirectly in the form of made-ups and garments. In this study, an attempt is made to work out the content of fabric exported in other forms as well.

Export of Cotton Made-ups

The data on cotton made-up export is available in value terms from Cotton Textile Exports Promotion Councils Office (TEXPROCIL) (Table 4.7). The sector-wise made-ups exports in kilograms for the years 1996-97 and 1997-98 is made available on request (not published) from Cotton Textile Exports Promotion Councils Office, Bombay. One needs conversion rates to work out the exports in square metres equivalent from the kilograms data. We have used same weights for made-ups as for fabrics to convert it into metres. This is because the main counts which are used to produce made-ups ranges from 10 to 40s. One could say that 90 per cent of made-ups categories are produced from this count range and remaining counts share constitutes only around 10 per cent. By using this approximation in the production statistics, one could conclude that the sector-wise made-ups weight is not much different from the fabrics weight. Hence the conversion rates used for made-ups are same as in case of production of fabrics.

Once, square metre equivalent of made-ups exports are worked out for 1996-97 and 1997-98, one could derive the average price per square metre of made-ups. It could be assumed that the qualities as well as price of made-ups and fabrics are moving proportionally over period of time. Since the prices of fabrics exports are available over a period of time, the relationship between the two for the two years is used to derive the prices of made-ups exports.

Table 4.7
Exports of Cotton Made-Ups from Various Sectors

(Mn. Rs.)

	Mill	*Powerloom & Knitted*	*Handloom*	*Total*
1983	590.70	210.00	665.10	1465.80
1988-89	993.40	843.00	1684.40	3520.80
1989-90	1606.90	1281.30	2297.10	5185.30
1990-91	2553.80	2055.40	2845.60	7454.80
1991-92	3130.20	3212.20	5019.70	11362.10
1992-93	3248.80	5607.70	7606.30	16462.80
1993-94	3305.80	9466.50	10161.00	22933.30
1994-95	3653.60	13692.90	11794.00	29140.50
1995-96	4883.40	16213.40	12358.30	33447.10
1996-97	5409.10	20165.30	13847.90	39422.30
1997-98	7563.20	23463.70	16394.90	47421.80
1998-99	11363.50	26638.90	17843.60	55846.60
1999-2000	14829.10	28928.60	16851.10	60608.80

Note : The knitted made-ups export is included in the powerloom sector. This is because data for the knitted made-up export was not separately available before the year 1994-95. However, it would not make much difference as knitted made-ups export is only 0.92 million kilograms out of total 99.83 million kilograms export of powerloom and knitted made-ups for the year 1997-98 as per TEXPROCIL data received on request.

Source: TEXPROCIL data.

Cotton made ups exports from the country were only 241.83 million square metres during 1983. After the introduction of NTP, there was 17.38 per cent per annum growth rate during the period 1983 to 1990-91. During second phase of liberalisation, the rise in export continues at a fairly fast rate of 12.40 per cent. The increase in absolute terms was on average 71.53 million square metres per year during first

phase of liberalisation as compared to 187.59 million square metres on an average during the second phase of liberalisation.

Table 4.8
Exports of Cotton Made-ups from Various Sectors

(Mn. Sq. Mts)

	Mill	*Powerloom & Knitted*	*Handloom*	*Total*
1983	92.06	40.71	109.06	241.83
1988-89	98.27	96.01	278.23	472.51
1989-90	143.80	122.88	333.13	599.81
1990-91	198.09	192.01	352.42	742.52
1991-92	186.68	228.68	486.25	901.61
1992-93	165.66	340.73	569.30	1075.69
1993-94	142.23	554.76	676.38	1373.37
1994-95	138.04	696.13	691.73	1525.89
1995-96	155.33	734.80	655.29	1545.42
1996-97	165.28	962.90	604.03	1732.21
1997-98	215.37	1062.07	648.05	1925.49
1998-99	335.71	1194.17	643.39	2173.27
1999-2000	434.07	1336.99	659.76	2430.82
Percentage Per Annum Compound Growth Rates				
1983 to 1990-91	11.57	24.80	18.24	17.38
1990-91 to 1999-2000	7.91	22.08	4.76	12.40
t-statistics	2.34	11.11	2.73	14.59

Source: Derived by the author from TEXPROCIL data.

The made-ups segment is the one where the growth has been the most rapid. The powerloom sector has taken the maximum advantage of growth opportunities. Like in fabrics segment where powerloom sector outperformed the mill sector, in made up segment also its performance was far superior to that the mill and handloom sector. The sector-wise made-up exports in terms of kilograms worked out are given in Table 4.9. However, after the year 1997-98, the exports of mill made-ups increased at very rapid rate and grew at even faster rate than powerloom sector. The share of mill sector in powerloom and mill sector exports was 69.34 per cent during 1983 and declined to 50.78 per cent during 1990-91. There was steep decline in its share even after that till 1994-95 and it got down to 16.55 per cent. Its share increased to 17.45 per cent during 1995-96, but declined later to 14.65 per cent during 1996-97. There was again small increase in its share during 1997-98 to 16.86 per cent. However, years 1998-99 and 1999-2000 saw a very high rise in mill sector share in made-ups exports from mill and powerloom sector to 21.94 per cent and 24.51 per cent respectively. Similar analogies are reported in the behavior of mill sector exports of fabrics after the year 1997-98. The share of mill sector in mill and powerloom sector export of fabrics showed a rapid decline from 78.85 per cent during 1983 to 54.65 per cent during 1990-91 and further to 26.57 per cent during 1997-98. Thereafter, export of fabrics from mill sector showed rise in its share to 30.45 per cent during 1998-99 and further to 32.82 per cent during 1999-2000. This change in pattern needs to be analyzed carefully.

The non-SSI weaving units are included in composite sector to form the mill sector in the official definition since 1994-95. The official document is quite about the non-SSI weaving units exports. This in fact was earlier also treated as exports from the mill sector in most of the cases and thus share of exports was overestimated in mill sector to that extent. Since we maintained the definition of mill sector as composite units for our analysis to maintain consistency, the extent of overestimation will be there in our analysis throughout. However, the consequences of change in official definition appear to have facilitated the branding of powerlloom sector fabrics/made-ups as mill sector product to be sold in domestic or exports market to extract the high premium. This type of practice was always there, but it seems to have reached a high proportion after the year 1997-98.

It would be noticed that whereas the share of powerloom in made up exports was only 14 per cent in 1983, by 1999-2000 its share had increased to 55 per cent.

Table 4.9
Exports of Made-ups from Various Sectors

(Mn. Kgs.)

Year	*Mill*	*Powerloom & Knitted*	*Handloom*	*Total*
1983	12.05	4.01	12.24	28.30
1988-89	12.93	9.28	30.31	52.52
1989-90	19.18	12.00	35.14	66.31
1990-91	26.40	19.06	40.17	85.63
1991-92	24.99	23.24	52.00	100.23
1992-93	22.12	35.25	63.60	120.97
1993-94	19.49	58.03	79.00	156.52
1994-95	18.93	72.70	82.63	174.27
1995-96	21.74	73.23	76.06	171.03
1996-97	23.13	106.32	82.52	211.97
1997-98	30.55	118.72	89.25	265.17
1998-99	47.62	133.08	88.38	298.54
1999-2000	61.57	151.91	91.96	338.81

Figures are given in terms of yarn equivalent export.

Source: Derived by the author from TEXPROCIL data.

Exports of Cotton Garments

India's garment exports consist of both woven garments and knitted garments. The fabrics for woven garments originate from mill, powerloom and the handloom sectors. The mill sector garment exports means that the fabrics required for making garments originates from the mill sector and same implies for other sectors as well. This means sector here refers for fabrics and not garments. The sector of garment could be either large, medium or small size. The data for the mill and powerloom garment exports is not separately available in official statistics. The combined data for mill and powerloom sectors is referred to as mill-made garments in the official statistics. Handloom garment exports constitute a very small percentage of the total garment exports. The knitted garment exports constitute the largest share in total garment exports (Table 4.10).

The exports of garment have grown at very high rate since the introduction of NTP in 1985. To work out the share of exports in production, the quantity of garment exports needs to be expressed in terms of square metres by working out conversion rates from pieces to square metres.

DGCIS data provides information on item-wise exports from the country. The variety wise units of measurement in each item was converted into square metres on the basis of information collected from Garment Export Entitlement Policy and supplemented by garment manufacturer. The average weighted length per piece for exports is calculated as 1.66 square metres for woven garments. In the case of knitted garments, the average piece length for the exports of garments is estimated at 1.64 square metre.

Table 4.10
Exports of Garments

(Mn. Pieces)

Year	*Mill & Powerloom*	*Handloom*	*Knitted*	*Total*
1983	—	—	50.5	141.3
1988-89	—	—	125.1	328.0
1989-90	—	—	186.6	410.8
1990-91	249.9	2.0	223.5	475.4
1991-92	291.2	3.2	265.5	559.9
1992-93	312.8	4.9	349.2	666.9
1993-94	348.9	5.2	423.5	777.6
1994-95	399.1	7.5	385.7	792.3
1995-96	423.1	6.8	449.8	879.6
1996-97	446.8	7.5	512.5	966.8
1997-98	455.9	4.7	600.6	1062.0
1998-99	455.9	3.0	671.4	1130.2
1999-2000	440.9	2.3	722.2	1165.4

Source: Data from Apparel Export Promotion Council.

DGCIS data is used in the above analysis, as Garment Export Promotion Council data does not provide detailed information for variety-wise garments exports from India. It gives variety-wise exports of garments to various countries from India. An attempt is made to find the garments per piece length for some of major importers from India in the same manner as above. The results arrived are not much different than derived above for per piece length of woven and knitted garments.

Table 4.11
Exports of Garments

(Mn. Sq. Mts)

Year	*Mill & Powerloom*	*Mill*	*Power-loom*	*Handloom*	*Knitted*	*Total*
1983		104.59	46.25		82.75	233.59
1988-89		170.37	166.44		205.16	541.97
1989-90		200.68	171.49		306.02	678.19
1990-91	414.83	210.65	204.18	3.32	366.54	784.69
1991-92	483.39	217.25	266.14	5.31	435.42	924.12
1992-93	519.25	169.87	349.38	8.13	572.69	1100.07
1993-94	579.17	118.19	460.99	8.63	694.54	1282.35
1994-95	662.51	109.63	552.87	12.45	632.55	1307.50
1995-96	702.35	122.54	579.80	11.29	737.67	1451.30
1996-97	741.69	108.67	633.03	12.45	840.50	1594.64
1997-98	756.79	127.56	629.23	7.80	984.98	1749.58
1998-99	756.79	127.56	629.23	4.98	1101.10	1862.87
1999-2000	731.89	123.36	608.53	3.82	1184.41	1920.12

Source: Derived from Apparel Export Promotion Council data.

Since data on garment exports is not available separately for the mill and powerloom sector, an approximation is made to work out the rough share of these sectors in garments exports. By assuming that the share in garment exports of these two sectors is the same as their respective shares in made-ups exports, it is possible to work out their respective shares in garment exports (Table 4.11). For working out the mill sector exports of garments for the year 1998-99 and 1999-2000, the share of mill sector is taken same as was during the year 1997-98. This is because the shares of powerloom sector exports, which is branded as mill sector exports appears to have increased especially during these two years.

By using sector-wise conversion rates, we derived the garment exports in kilograms as given in Table 4.12.

Table 4.12
Exports of Garments from Various Sectors

(Mn. Kgs)

Year	*Mill*	*Powerloom*	*Handloom*	*Knitted*	*Total*
1983	13.69	4.56	---	8.60	26.85
1988-89	22.42	16.08	---	20.84	59.35
1989-90	26.77	16.74	---	31.30	74.81
1990-91	28.07	20.27	0.38	37.49	86.20
1991-92	29.09	27.04	0.62	44.98	101.73
1992-93	22.68	36.14	0.96	59.07	118.86
1993-94	16.19	48.22	1.03	71.89	137.34
1994-95	15.03	57.74	1.49	65.50	139.77
1995-96	17.15	57.78	1.31	75.46	151.70
1996-97	15.20	69.90	1.70	88.32	175.12
1997-98	18.09	70.34	1.07	103.49	192.99
1998-99	18.09	70.12	0.68	116.07	204.97
1999-2000	17.50	69.14	0.53	125.09	212.27

Figures are given in terms of yarn equivalent exports.
Source: Derived from Apparel Export Promotion Council and TEXPROCIL data.

An alternative would have been to use the share of these sectors in exports of fabrics to estimate their respective share in garment exports. The counterpart in made-ups ratios was preferred to fabrics because both made-ups and garments are final products. As can be noted from Table 4.3 and 4.12, share of mill sector in exports is declining as one move from fabrics to made-ups and garments. This is because mill sector products lose competitiveness as one move up towards further value-added products that require labour intensive technologies (Roy 1998).

Total Cotton Fabrics Equivalent Exports and Domestic Availability in the form of Fabrics, Made-ups and Garments

The fabrics equivalent of exports from all the sectors at various production stages such as fabrics, made-ups and garments is given in Table 4.13.

The growth of export in all the stages of production is quite high. The fabrics equivalent of export increased by 13.58 per cent during 1983 to 1999-2000. On the other hand,

Table 4.13
Exports of Cotton Fabrics in the Form of Fabrics, Made-ups and Garments

(Mn. Sq. Mts)

Year	Fabrics	Made-ups	Garments	Total	Production of Cotton Fabrics	Domestic Availability	Per Capita Domestic Availability Sq. Mt.	Exports as % of Production
(1)	(2)	(3)	(4)	(5)	(6)	(7)	(8)	(9)
1983	387	242	234	862	9331	8469	11.78	9.24
1988-89	832	472	542	1846	11295	9449	11.82	16.35
1989-90	909	583	678	2170	11394	9224	11.31	19.04
1990-91	1038	744	785	2566	12390	9824	11.80	20.71
1991-92	1202	861	924	2987	11507	8520	10.00	25.96
1992-93	1215	1047	1100	3363	12575	9212	10.62	26.74
1993-94	1323	1359	1282	3964	13550	9586	10.85	29.25
1994-95	1617	1525	1308	4450	12918	8469	9.41	34.44
1995-96	1641	1545	1451	4638	15203	10565	11.46	30.51
1996-97	1936	1732	1595	5262	14069	8807	9.37	37.40
1997-98	1945	1925	1750	5620	14089	8469	8.87	39.89
1998-99	2245	2173	1863	6281	12688	6407	6.60	49.50
1999-2000	2267	2431	1920	6618	13229	6611	6.70	50.02
CGR*	11.69	15.52	14.07	13.58	2.21	-1.54	-3.46	—

(Contd.....)

(Contd...)

(1)	(2)	(3)	(4)	(5)	(6)	(7)	(8)	(9)
Point to Point % p.a. Gr. Rt. 1983 to 1999-2000	11.69	15.52	14.07	13.58	2.21	-1.54	-3.46	—

* CGR is worked on the basis of point to point % p.a. compound Growth Rate during the period 1983 to 1999-2000.

Source: Derived by the author.

production of cotton fabrics increased by only 2.21 per cent per annum during the same period. This shows that share of export has increased quite rapidly over the period of time in total fabric production and reached slightly above than 50 per cent mark during 1999-2000. The made-ups registered the maximum growth. The made-ups share in total fabrics exports in all forms has initially declined from 28.0 per cent during 1983 to 36.7 per cent during 1999-2000. The change in the share of various products in total fabrics equivalent exports in the form of fabrics, made-ups and garments is given in Table 4.14.

Table 4.14
Percentage Share of Exports in the Form of Fabrics, Made-ups and Garments in Total Fabrics Equivalent Exports

Year	*Fabrics*	*Made-ups*	*Garments*	*Total*
1983	44.86	28.05	27.09	100.00
1988-89	45.06	25.58	29.35	100.00
1989-90	41.88	26.87	31.26	100.00
1990-91	40.44	28.99	30.58	100.00
1991-92	40.23	28.84	30.94	100.00
1992-93	36.14	31.14	32.72	100.00
1993-94	33.37	34.28	32.35	100.00
1994-95	36.33	34.28	29.39	100.00
1995-96	35.39	33.32	31.29	100.00
1996-97	36.78	32.92	30.30	100.00
1997-98	34.61	34.26	31.13	100.00
1998-99	35.74	34.60	29.66	100.00
1999-2000	34.25	36.73	29.01	100.00

Source: Derived by the author.

Total Cotton Yarn Equivalent Exports and Domestic Availability in the form of Yarn, Fabrics, Made-ups and Garments

The analysis so far was restricted to calculating the fabrics equivalent exports of various products such as fabrics, made-ups and garments in terms of square metre of fabrics and kilograms of yarn. The yarn exports to be added into fabrics equivalent to work out the total yarn equivalent exports in the forms of textiles and clothing products and is given in Table 4.15. The share of yarn equivalent exports is amazingly

Table 4.15

Yarn Equivalent Exports in terms of Yarn, Fabrics, Made-ups and Garments

(Mn. Kgs)

Year	*Yarn*	*Fabrics*	*Made-ups*	*Garments*	*Total Exports*	*Production of Cotton Yarn*	*Domestic Availability*		*Export as % of Production*
							Total	*Fabrics*	
1983	6.6	47.5	28.3	26.9	109.2	1092.0	973.2	955.8	9.74
1988-89	40.4	94.5	52.5	59.4	246.8	1310.0	1039.6	1029.3	18.84
1989-90	62.1	104.9	66.3	74.8	308.1	1372.0	1021.0	1023.9	22.46
1990-91	90.1	120.6	85.6	86.2	382.6	1510.0	1093.5	1084.4	25.34
1991-92	126.0	137.3	100.2	101.7	465.2	1450.0	967.8	944.8	32.08
1992-93	128.6	139.3	121.0	118.9	507.8	1569.0	1043.8	1026.2	32.36
1993-94	178.8	152.8	156.5	137.3	625.5	1697.0	1099.3	1025.5	36.86
1994-95	228.5	184.9	174.3	139.8	727.5	1696.0	990.3	922.5	42.89
1995-96	262.8	183.7	171.0	151.7	769.2	1894.0	1196.3	1063.8	40.61
1996-97	464.9	228.6	215.0	175.1	1083.6	2148.0	1116.7	997.4	50.45
1997-98	489.0	232.1	238.5	193.0	1152.6	2213.0	1088.0	993.4	52.08
1998-99	486.6	270.0	269.1	205.0	1230.6	2022.0	815.2	744.4	60.86
1999-2000	554.7	277.6	305.5	212.3	1350.0	2204.0	852.1	803.0	61.25

Figures are given in terms of yarn equivalent exports.
Source: Derived by the author.

reached a very high proportion and was 61.25 per cent of the total cotton yarn production in the country during 1999-2000.

The domestic availability of cotton yarn is worked out in two steps. Firstly, the domestic availability of fabrics in terms of yarn is worked out by subtracting the yarn equivalent fabrics exports in the form of fabrics, made-ups and garment from the consumption of yarn to produce the cotton fabrics. In the second step, this yarn equivalent fabrics in various forms for the domestic consumption is added into the use of cotton yarn for other purposes. In this methodology import content of cotton textiles and clothing products is not taken into account, which will be taken into account at latter stage. This would not make much difference as import of cotton textiles and clothing products accounts for a small proportion of total production of cotton textiles and clothing products. The share of various forms of exports in total yarn equivalent exports is given in Table 4.16. The yarn constitutes the maximum share, while the garments the lowest in total cotton yarn equivalent exports.

Table 4.16
Percentage Share of Yarn Equivalent Exports in terms of Yarn Fabrics, Made-ups and Garments

Year	*Yarn*	*Fabrics*	*Made-ups*	*Garments*	*Total*
1983	6.03	43.48	25.91	24.58	100.00
1988-89	16.36	38.30	21.28	24.05	100.00
1989-90	20.16	34.04	21.52	24.28	100.00
1990-91	23.55	31.53	22.38	22.53	100.00
1991-92	27.07	29.51	21.55	21.87	100.00
1992-93	25.33	27.44	23.82	23.41	100.00
1993-94	28.59	24.43	25.02	21.96	100.00
1994-95	31.41	25.42	23.95	19.21	100.00
1995-96	34.16	23.88	22.24	19.72	100.00
1996-97	42.90	21.10	19.84	16.16	100.00
1997-98	42.42	20.14	20.69	16.74	100.00
1998-99	39.54	21.94	21.87	16.66	100.00
1999-2000	41.09	20.56	22.63	15.72	100.00

Source: Derived by the author.

Total Cotton Fibre Equivalent Exports in the form of Yarn, Fabrics, Made-ups and Garments

This exercise now has to be taken one step back with a view to finding the fibre equivalent of all textiles and clothing exports. The yarn equivalent exports from various sectors are required to work out the fibre equivalent exports in textiles and clothing products, which is given in Table 4.17.

Table 4.17

Yarn Equivalent Exports from Various Sectors in the form of Yarn, Fabrics, Made-ups and Garments

(Mn. Kgs)

Year	*Mill*	*Powerloom*	*Handloom*	*Hosiery*	*Total*
1983	68.03	15.79	16.81	8.60	109.22
1988-89	124.59	59.72	38.98	23.46	246.75
1989-90	163.94	64.08	42.71	37.40	308.13
1990-91	209.05	79.19	47.78	46.55	382.57
1991-92	237.76	112.53	61.48	53.42	465.20
1992-93	228.76	135.82	74.63	68.58	507.80
1993-94	271.22	182.13	89.41	82.76	625.52
1994-95	325.44	229.59	93.47	78.98	727.48
1995-96	367.00	230.54	84.30	87.32	769.17
1996-97	571.30	316.56	93.73	102.04	1083.63
1997-98	605.19	336.13	96.24	115.07	1152.64
1998-99	642.91	365.79	94.55	127.38	1230.61
1999-2000	733.00	383.77	98.07	135.15	1350.00

Note: Figures are given in terms of yarn equivalent exports.
Source: Derived by the author.

From yarn equivalent of sector-wise export, one could work out the fibre equivalent export by finding out fibre to yarn conversion rate for each sector on the basis of analysis in Chapter 2. It was worked out in Chapter 2, the yarn consumed in mill and hosiery sectors have combed yarn content of around 50 per cent, powerloom sector 15 per cent and handloom sector around 4 per cent. At the current level of technology, the cotton fibre required to produce combed yarn has on an average wastage of 30.5 per cent and in the case of carded yarn a wastage of 13.5 per cent. The sector wise weighted wastage therefore work out as

22.00 per cent for mill and hosiery sector,
16.05 per cent for powerloom sector and
14.18 per cent for the handloom sector.

By using these conversion rates, total cotton fibre equivalent of exports have been calculated and is given in Table 4.18.

Table 4.18
Fibre Equivalent Exports in Cotton Textile and Clothing Products from Various Sectors

(Mn. Kgs)

Year	*Mill*	*Powerloom*	*Handloom*	*Hosiery*	*Total*
1983	82.99	18.32	19.19	10.40	131.00
1988-89	152.00	69.30	44.51	28.62	294.43
1989-90	200.00	74.37	48.77	45.63	368.77
1990-91	255.04	91.90	54.56	56.79	458.28
1991-92	290.07	130.60	70.20	65.18	556.04
1992-93	279.09	157.62	85.21	83.67	605.59
1993-94	330.88	211.36	102.09	100.97	745.31
1994-95	397.04	266.44	106.72	96.36	866.55
1995-96	447.74	267.54	96.26	106.53	918.08
1996-97	696.98	367.37	107.03	124.49	1295.87
1997-98	732.06	385.32	108.63	140.41	1366.42
1998-99	777.69	419.32	106.72	155.42	1459.14
1999-2000	886.66	439.93	110.70	164.90	1602.20

Note: (1) Figures are given in terms of fibre equivalent exports.
(2) Above fibre equivalent exports is of textiles and clothing items and do not include exports in terms of fibres.

Source: Derived by the author.

The fibre yarn ratio in yarn equivalent exports show that on an average around 36 per cent of our exports are of combed type during the period of study, while the content of combed yarn is higher in direct exports of cotton yarn and was around 54 per cent during 1997-98. On the other hand, content of combed yarn in the yarn produced domestically is approximately 27.5 per cent on an average. This means the combed share in the cotton yarn consumed for domestic purpose is less than 10 per cent during the period of study.

Table 4.18 gives the exports of total cotton equivalent fiber in 100% cotton textiles and clothing products. This does not include the export of raw cotton as the study is primarily concerned with textiles and clothing products. However, the export of cotton fibre in textiles and clothing products is also taking place in the form of cotton-blended textiles and clothing products. The cotton fibre content in the cotton blended textiles and clothing exports is worked out in section related with synthetic products and the total export of cotton in all textiles and clothing products thus worked out is given in Table 4.19.

Synthetic Textiles and Clothing Products

In this section an attempt is made first to work out the exports of synthetic textiles and clothing products equivalent to fabrics, yarn and fibre. Then these estimates are used to work out the domestic availability for consumption of synthetic textiles and clothing products equivalent to fabrics, yarn and fibre. This has been derived at various stages by subtracting exports from production. The detailed analysis has been undertaken to find the fibre/filament-wise content in export for the year 1995-96.

The year 1995-96 norms are used better on available data to derive estimates of fibre/filament-wise estimates for other years. The year 1995-96 is selected as lots of definational changes have taken place in official definations of various sections after this year.

Fibre/Filament-wise Production of Synthetic Fabrics During 1995-96

The fibre-wise production of synthetic fabrics (as derived in Chapter 3) is given in Table 4.20.

Synthetic Fabrics Equivalent Exports in terms of Fabrics, Made-ups and Garments During 1995-96

The detailed data on fibre-wise exports of synthetic fabrics are worked out for the year 1995-96. The fabrics export data is available in kilograms, square metres as well as in value terms from Synthetic Rayon Export Promotion Council.

Table 4.19

Total Exports of Cotton Equivalent Fibre in Cotton and Synthetic Textiles and Clothing Products

(Mn. Kgs)

Year	*Cotton Fibre Equivalent Exports in Various Products*			*Consumptin of Cotton Fibre Mn. kgs*		*Domestic Availability*		*Exports as % of Fibre Used*
	Cotton	*Blended*	*Total*	*Mill & SSI*	*Extra Factory*	*Total*	*Per Capita Kgs*	*%*
1983	131.00	1.19	132.19	1340.8	79.0	1287.6	1.79	9.86
1988-89	294.43	3.54	299.97	1622.3	110.5	1432.8	1.79	18.49
1989-90	368.77	7.15	375.92	1689.9	119.0	1433	1.76	22.25
1990-91	458.28	7.82	466.10	1822.1	127.5	1483.5	1.78	25.58
1991-92	556.04	11.16	567.20	1765.7	136.0	1334.5	1.57	32.12
1992-93	605.59	12.90	618.49	1823.5	136.0	1341.0	1.55	33.92
1993-94	745.31	14.86	760.17	1965.9	136.0	1341.7	1.52	38.67
1994-95	866.55	21.03	887.58	2087.5	161.5	1361.4	1.51	42.52
1995-96	918.08	24.60	942.68	2307.8	161.5	1526.6	1.66	40.85
1996-97	1295.87	27.58	1323.45	2565.4	201.6	1443.6	1.54	51.59
1997-98	1366.42	32.20	1398.62	2719.0	156.9	1477.3	1.55	51.44
1998-99	1459.14	33.49	1492.63	2485.0	231.0	1185.6	1.22	61.58
1999-2000	1602.20	41.98	1644.18	2652.0	187.0	1163.9	1.18	63.16

Note: 1. Figures are given in terms of fibre equivalent exports and do not include export in the form of raw cotton.
2. Exports of cotton fibre include exports in the form of cotton and blended textiles and clothing products. The quantum of cotton fibre exports in blended textiles and clothing products is worked in detail later in the chapter.

Sources: Derived by the author.

Table 4.20

Fibre/Filament-wise Production of Synthetic Fabrics during 1995-96

	Production 1995-96		
	Mn. Sq. Mts	*Mn. Kgs**	*Wt Gms/Sq.mt*
Viscose Filament	628	54.44	86.63
Viscose Spun	567	63.84	112.56
Nylon Filament	1499	42.47	28.33
Polyester Filament	5035	370.82	73.65
Polyester (Carbonised)	443	22.99	51.95
Polyester Viscose	2328	231.03	99.23
Polyester Cotton	1165	90.92	78.85
Viscose Cotton	189	20.63	109.13
Total Above	11854	897.14	75.68
Others	862	78.78	51.86
Total	12716	975.92	76.75

Note: * Equivalent yarn.

Source: As derived by the author from Man-made Textiles Statistics, Synthetic and Rayon Export Promotion Council.

The composition of various fibres/filaments in fabrics export is given in Table 4.21.

Table 4.21

Fibre/Filament-wise Exports of Synthetic Fabrics during 1995-96

	Mn. Sq. Mts	*Mn Kgs**	*Mn. Rs.*	*Gms/ sq. mt*
Viscose Filament	15.13	3.39	750.28	224.25
Viscose Spun	20.23	1.68	645.04	83.30
Nylon Filament	5.54	0.27	174.49	49.54
Polyester Filament	227.84	14.64	5447.80	64.27
Polyester (Carbonised)	104.89	5.55	2207.54	52.91
Polyester Viscose	85.01	1.56	587.73	136.02
Polyester Cotton	128.01	22.14	3219.40	172.94
Viscose Cotton	4.43	0.54	201.80	121.90
Others	19.89	3.58	1031.22	179.94
Total	610.95	63.37	17265.31	103.72

* Equivalent yarn.

Source: Man-made Textiles Statistics, Synthetic and Rayon Export Promotion Council.

The share of knitted fabrics in total exports of synthetic fabrics is negligible (0.40% in 1995-96) and hence we have not taken it separately. Synthetic knitted fabrics export is of quite heavy variety compared to woven as its weight comes to 166.66 gm/sq. mt. during 1995-96.

The weight of fabrics exported, changes over the period depending upon their blends and varieties and is therefore different than average production weight (Table 4.22). The exports constitutes a very small proportion and any change in its composition of various varieties being exported makes lots of difference on average weight or conversion rate of synthetic fabrics being exported. Thus year 1995-96 conversion rates may give misleading results if applied for other years to derive one indicator from the other.

So, the data on the actual quantity of synthetic fabrics being exported in terms of square metres, kilograms and value terms is being collected from Export Promotion Council for maximum numbers of years for which data was made available. For years before 1991-92, the data on fabrics in kilograms was not available and we used the conversion rate for the year

Table 4.22

Fibre/Filament-wise Comparison of Synthetic Fabrics Weight for Export and Production

(Gm/sq.mt)

	Exports 1996-97	*Production 1995-96*	*Exports 1995-96*
Viscose Filament	71.06	86.62	224.25
Viscose Spun	96.16	112.56	83.3
Nylon Filament	65.34	28.34	49.54
Polyester Filament	59.2	73.65	64.27
Polyester Spun (Carbonised)	57.53	51.95	52.91
Polyester Viscose	137.54	99.23	136.02
Polyester Cotton	161.29	78.05	172.94
Viscose Cotton	121.9	109.13	101.15
Others	98.92	91.39	180.22
Total	99.97		103.72

Source: Man-made Textiles Statistics, Synthetic and Rayon Export Promotion Council.

1991-92 to arrive the weight of fabrics being exported for those years.

Fibre/Filament-wise Synthetic Made-ups Exports During Year 1995-96

In the case of made-ups, the exports are available in kilograms and rupees equivalent for various fibres/filaments. To convert it into square metres equivalent exports, the conversion rates for each fibre/filament are taken as similar to the conversion rate derived for the production of fabrics for these fibres/filaments in Chapter 3 and are given in Table 4.23.

Conversion rates of production of fabrics are preferred to those of conversion rates of fabrics for exports. This is because exports of different fibres are very small and small changes in it affect the conversion rates widely. This therefore cannot be taken as representative for working out kilograms equivalent exports of made-ups or garments. Moreover, conversion rates of production of fabrics are preferred rather than the conversion rates of fabrics for exports to derive square metre equivalent exports of made-ups as made-ups and garments are produced from fabrics after further value addition.

Table 4.23

Fibre/Filament-wise Synthetic Made-ups Export during 1995-96

	Mn. Sq. Mts	*Mn Kgs**	*Mn. Rs.*	*Gms/ Sq. Mt*
Viscose Filament	10.57	0.92	608.02	86.63
Viscose Spun	10.71	1.21	1166.33	112.56
Nylon Filament	54.18	1.53	181.21	28.33
Polyester Filament	6.35	0.47	195.86	73.65
Polyester Spun (Carbonised)	40.16	2.08	702.85	51.95
Polyester Viscose	1.73	0.17	42.92	99.24
Polyester Cotton	7.83	0.61	123.83	78.04
Viscose Cotton	0.95	0.10	43.28	109.15
Others	21.3	1.95	438.89	91.39
Total	153.76	9.04	3503.2	58.8

Note: * Equivalent yarn.

Source: Man-made Textiles Statistics, Synthetic and Rayon Export Promotion Council.

The weighted conversion rate for the made-ups exports worked out is 58.80 gm/sq.mt for the year 1995-96. This conversion rate is used for all the years for which analysis is undertaken to work out the made-ups exports in square metres.

Fibre/Filament-wise Synthetic Garments Exports During Year 1995-96

In the case of garments, the data for fibre-wise exports is not available. The data for total garments exports is available in pieces, which is converted into square metres by using conversion rate of 1 piece=1.66 square metres and for knitted garments 1 piece=1.64 square metres. The methodology for working per piece equivalent square metres is explained in the case of cotton garments analysis for exports. To work out fibre-wise garment exports in square metres, it is assumed that the fibre-wise exports of garments is taking place in same proportion as that of fabrics. To convert it into kilograms, the conversion rates for each fibre/filament are taken as same as that of production.

The weight and conversion rate of garment exports on an average comes approximately the same as that of production of fabrics for the year 1995-96. Hence to work out year-wise exports of garments for various indicators, conversion rate of fabrics from yarn are taken same as that of production.

Fibre/Filament-wise Total Exports and Availability for Domestic Consumption of Synthetic Products in Various Forms During 1995-96

By using these approximations, fibre/filament-wise-total fabrics equivalent exports have been obtained. One could add yarn exports into yarn equivalent exports of fabrics, made-ups and garments to work out the total yarn equivalent exports of synthetic products. Further, this could be converted into equivalent of fibre exports by applying the fibre wise conversion rate of yarn from fibre. The synthetic fabrics, yarn and fibres/filaments equivalent exports in various synthetic textiles and clothing products during 1995-96 are given in Table 4.24.

Table 4.24

Fabrics, Yarn and Fibres/Filaments Equivalent Exports in Various Synthetic Textiles & Clothing Products during 1995-96

	Fabrics Equivalent	*Fabrics* Equivalent*	*Yarn**	*Total Yarn Equivalent**	*Fabre/Filament Equivalent#*
	Mn. Sq. Mt			*Mn. Kgs*	
Viscose Filament	33.74	5.66	9.17	14.83	14.83
Viscose Spun	41.69	3.56	12.87	16.43	17.93
Nylon Filament	62.66	1.91	0.33	2.23	2.23
Polyester Filament	355.25	20.95	14.76	35.71	35.71
Polyester Spun (Carbonised)	200.78	9.85	6.97	16.81	17.24
Polyester Viscose	131.91	16.35	19.76	36.10	37.96
Polyester Cotton	203.86	31.59	17.14	48.72	54.58
Viscose Cotton	7.73	0.86		0.86	1.00
Others	51.76	6.96	8.70	15.65	16.28
Total	1089.34	97.71	89.66	187.37	197.78

Note: (1) * Equivalent yarn.
(2) # Equivalent fibre/filament.

Source: As derived by the author from Man-made Textiles Statistics, Synthetic and Rayon Export Promotion Council.

The various fibre/filament blends could be segregated into each fibre/filaments as given in Table 4.25.

Table 4.25
Fibre/Filament-wise Exports of Various Synthetic Textiles and Clothing Products during 1995-96

Fibres/Filaments	*Mn. Kgs #*	*Share of various fibre/filaments*
Polyester	108.33	54.77
Viscose	52.47	26.53
Nylon	2.23	1.13
Other	10.15	5.13
Total	173.18	87.56
Cotton Fibre	24.6	12.44
Synthetic fibre/Filament	197.78	100.00

Note: # Equivalent fibre.
Source: As derived by the author from Man-made Textiles Statistics, Synthetic and Rayon Export Promotion Council.

From the above analysis it is clear that cotton holds important share even in exports of synthetic textiles and clothing products. Cotton fibre accounts for 12.4 per cent of total exports of synthetic fibre/filament in 1995-96. Polyester is the major fibre/filament used in exports of synthetic products with a share of 54.8 per cent. Viscose is another important fibre/filament being exported with a share of 26.5 per cent in the total exports of synthetic textiles and clothing products.

Exports of Cotton and Synthetic Textiles and Clothing Products Equivalent to Various Fibres/Filaments during 1995-96

In case, the cotton fibre content of 100 per cent cotton fabrics is also included, the fibres/filament-wise share in total textiles and clothing goods exports is given in Table 4.26.

The cotton fibre content in total cotton and synthetic product exports is as high as 84.5 per cent during the year 1995-96.

Table 4.26
Fibre/Filament-wise Export of Cotton and Synthetic Textile and Clothing Products during 1995-96

	Million Kgs#	*% Share*
Cotton	942.68	84.48
Polyester	108.33	9.71
Viscose	52.47	4.70
Nylon	2.23	0.20
Other	10.15	0.91
Total	1115.86	100.00

Note: (1) # Equivalent fibre/filament.
(2) Cotton fibre exports in 100% cotton textiles and clothing product accounts for 918.08 million kilograms as estimated earlier.

Source: As derived by the author from Man-made Textiles Statistics, Synthetic and Rayon Export Promotion Council.

Total Domestic Availability of Cotton and Synthetic Products in Various forms during 1995-96

Having worked out the synthetic exports in various forms, one could find out the domestic availability of synthetic fabrics by subtracting fabrics equivalent exports from production. Similarly, by subtracting fibre/filament-wise exports from total fibres/filament-wise in mill, SSI and for ex-factory consumption, one could work out synthetic fibre/filament-wise. The yarn availability for domestic consumption is worked out by adding other uses of yarn in the total yarn equivalent fabrics available for domestic consumption.

The domestic availability of synthetic textiles and clothing products equivalent to fabrics, yarn and fibre are added to their counterpart for 100% cotton to arrive at fibre filament-wise (Table 4.27) domestic availability of cotton and synthetic products were domestic availability.

Among the synthetic fibres, the maximum consumption is that of polyester filament/fibres mainly in the form of sarees, which is generally purchased by the poor population.

The per capita availability of fabrics is worked out by dividing their respective quantities with the mid year population (Table 4.28).

Table 4.27
Domestic Availability of Cotton and Synthetic Products during 1995-96

	Domestic Availability of Textiles and Clothing Products Equivalent to		
	Fabric Mn. Sq. Mts	*Yarn Mn. Kgs*	*Fabre/Filament Equivalent Yarn Mn. Kgs*
Cotton	10565	1196.3	1470.96
Viscose Filament	594.26	48.78	48.78
Viscose Spun	525.31	60.28	65.71
Nylon Filament	1436.34	40.56	40.56
Polyester Filament	4679.75	349.87	349.87
Polyester Spun (Carbonised)	242.22	13.14	13.47
Polyester Viscose	2196.09	214.68	225.63
Polyester Cotton	961.14	59.33	65.20
Viscose Cotton	181.27	19.77	22.50
Others	810.24	95.82	103.74
Total	22191.62	2098.53	2406.42

Source: As derived by the author from Man-made Textiles Statistics, Synthetic and Rayon Export Promotion Council and Compendium of Textile Statistics, Textile Committee.

Table 4.28
Per Capita Domestic Availability of Textiles and Clothing Products in the form of Fabrics and Fibre during 1995-96

	Fibre/Filament-wise Per Capital Equivalent Availability		*Share of various Fibre/Yarn Equivalent-wise in Per Capita Equivalent Availability*	
	Fabrics Sq. Mts	*Fibre in Kgs#*	*Sq. Mts Fabrics*	*Kgs#*
	(1)	*(2)*	*(3)*	*(4)*
Cotton	11.46	1.60	47.61	61.13
Viscose Filament	0.64	0.05	2.68	2.03
Viscose Spun	0.57	0.07	2.37	2.73
Nylon Filament	1.56	0.04	6.47	1.69
Polyester Filament	5.08	0.38	21.09	14.54
Polyester Spun (Carbonised)	0.26	0.01	1.09	0.56

(Contd...)

(Contd.....)

	(1)	(2)	(3)	(4)
Polyester Viscose	2.38	0.24	9.90	9.38
Polyester Cotton	1.04	0.07	4.33	2.71
Viscose Cotton	0.20	0.02	0.82	0.93
Others	0.88	0.11	3.65	4.31
Total	24.07	2.61	100.00	100.00

Note: # Equivalents Fibre/Filament.
Source: As derived by the author from Man-made Textiles Statistics, Synthetic and Rayon Export Promotion Council and Compendium of Textile Statistics, Textile Committee.

The per capita availability of fabrics is estimated at 24.07 square metre equivalent. The share of cotton fabrics in it is estimated to be 47.61 per cent in terms of square metre. Polyester filament accounts for 5.08 square metre having a share of 21.09 per cent in per capita domestic availability of fabrics. The other fibres/filaments having more than 1 square metre share in per capita domestic availability include polyester viscose, nylon filament and polyester cotton.

The fibre/filament equivalent domestic availability worked out is given in Table 4.29.

Table 4.29
Share of Various Fibres/Filament in Domestic Availability during 1995-96

	Total Mn. Kgs#	*Per Capita Kgs#*	*Percentage Share of Various fibres*
Cotton	1526.62	1.66	63.44
Viscose	252.33	0.27	10.49
Polyester	546.58	0.59	22.71
Nylon	40.56	0.04	1.69
Other	40.32	0.04	1.68
Total	2406.42	2.61	100.00

Note : # Equivalent fibre/filament.
Source: As derived by the author from Man-made Textiles Statistics, Synthetic and Rayon Export Promotion Council and Compendium of Textile Statistics, Textile Committee.

The above results shows that cotton content was very high in India's domestic availability of fibre/filament as compared to cotton content in world consumption during 1995-96. The cotton fibre content in India's domestic availability of fibre/filament was 63.44 per cent even during 1995-96. This is far higher than 44 per cent content of cotton in World fibre/filament consumption.

A detailed analysis has been undertaken above for the year 1995-96 to know the kind of synthetic fabrics, yarn and fibre/filament being exported and domestically consumed from the country. The norms on share of cotton fibre in total synthetic fibre exports for year 1995-96 are used for other years in the following section to work out the domestic availability as well as exports of cotton and synthetic fibres/filaments over the period of time.

Year-wise Exports of Synthetic Fabrics

For fabrics exports the data is available in kilograms, square metres and rupees for the period 1991-92 to 1999-2000. The conversion rate of total synthetic fabrics for earlier period is taken as the same as for the period 1991-92 to work out exports of fabrics for these years in terms of kilograms. The weight of synthetic fabrics varied between 99 gm/sq.mt to 141.60 gm/sq.mt. for the period 1991-92 to 1999-2000. This means average weight for synthetic fabrics is heavier in case of exports than production. The dominance of heavier blends as well as higher mill sector share for exports may be the reason for it as in case of cotton fabrics. However, the limitation is that sector-wise data is not available in the case of synthetic fabrics. Moreover, the period 1983-84, we have data only in value terms on exports of fabrics. The price per square metre of fabrics for year 1983-84 was estimated by the assumption that the yearly prices variations during the period 1988-89 to 1983-84 remain the same as during 1998-99 to 1993-94. This means it has been assumed that quality of fabrics as well prices have changed in similar manner over the period 1983 to 1998-99.

Table 4.30
Exports of Synthetic Fabrics during 1983 to 1999-2000

	Fabrics Exports				
	Mn. Sq. Mts	*Mn. Kgs*	*Wt. (Gm/sq.mt)*	*Mn. Rs.*	*Rs/Sq. Mts*
1983#	33.17*	3.65*	110.06*	192.70	5.81*
1988-89	85.30	9.39*	110.06*	1074.90	12.60
1989-90	163.40	17.98*	110.06*	2476.40	15.16
1990-91	207.79	22.87*	110.06*	3463.50	16.67
1991-92	285.11	31.38	110.06	6154.98	21.59
1992-93	324.47	35.49	109.37	8080.74	24.90
1993-94	430.86	48.62	112.84	11775.19	27.33
1994-95	538.28	61.11	113.52	14991.69	27.85
1995-96	610.95	63.37	103.72	17265.31	28.26
1996-97	601.88	60.17	99.97	16915.06	28.10
1997-98	616.01	69.97	113.59	18991.30	30.83
1998-99	562.00	71.65	127.49	20115.00	35.79
1999-2000	537.00	76.04	141.60	20979.00	39.07

Note: (1) Exports are in term of yarn equivalent, (2) * estimated., (3) # Financial Year.

Source: As derived by the author from Man-made Textiles Statistics, Synthetic and Rayon Export Promotion Council.

Year-wise Exports of Synthetic Made-ups

The synthetic made exports data is available in rupees and kilograms for the period of 1991-92 to 1999-2000. We have derived the average made-ups export in square metres by using the conversion rate for the year 1995-96 derived in our earlier analysis. For the remaining years 1983-84, 1988-89 to 1991-92 quantity data on made-ups exports are not available. The quantity data for remaining years were worked out from values at current prices by applying per unit price for the year 1991-92 and applying on it the assumption that price variations in made-ups during the period 1983 to 1991-92 are similar to that in the case of fabrics for the same period. The yearly made-ups exports as worked out are given in Table 4.31.

Year-wise Exports of Synthetic Garments

The total garments exports is given in pieces for both knitted and woven garments (Table 4.32). The knitted constitute small percentage share in garments exports, but are much larger than in the case of fabrics.

Table 4.31

Exports of Synthetic Made-ups during 1983 to 1999-2000

	Mn. Rs.	*Mn. Sq. Mts*	*Mn. Kgs*	*Rs./Sq.Mt*
1983#	236.60	45.81*	2.69*	5.16
1988-89	667.80	59.62*	2.91*	11.20
1989-90	1522.00	112.97*	6.04*	13.47
1990-91	1366.40	92.22*	5.42*	14.82
1991-92	1896.90	98.84*	5.81*	19.19
1992-93	2097.20	94.73	5.57	22.14
1993-94	2648.20	120.07	7.06	22.06
1994-95	2899.50	134.52	7.91	21.55
1995-96	3503.20	153.76	9.04	22.78
1996-97	3816.10	173.81	10.22	21.96
1997-98	5189.50	226.26	13.30	22.94
1998-99	7052.30	240.48	14.14	29.33
1999-2000	10071.20	327.48	19.25	30.75

Note: (1) # Financial year.
(2) * Estimated.

Source: As derived by the author from Man-made Textiles Statistics, Synthetic and Rayon Export Promotion Council.

The exports of synthetic garments mainly takes place of such products for which fabrics originates from the mill and powerloom sectors. However, as sector-wise detail is not available for exports of synthetic fabrics and made-ups, the analysis for garments exports is also undertaken for overall knitted and woven garments exports.

The piece length for garments is worked out as 1 piece=1.66 square metres for woven garments and 1 piece=1.64 square metres for knitted garments as derived in case of cotton garments exports. The conversion rates or weight of garments exported for various years are taken same as that of their respective conversion rates for production of fabrics during respective years. The results derived are given in Table 4.33.

Table 4.32
Exports of Synthetic Garment in Pieces during 1990-91 to 1999-2000

(Figures are in Mn.)

	Knitted		*Handloom*		*Mill & Powerloom*		*Total*	
	Pieces	*Rs.*	*Pieces*	*Rs.*	*Pieces*	*Rs.*	*Pieces*	*Rs.*
1990-91	7.3	637.8	Neg.	3.2	132.3	15112.9	139.6	15754.0
1991-92	5.6	586.0	Neg.	4.5	137.2	18123.2	142.8	18713.7
1992-93	7.5	813.2	Neg.	12.4	133.2	21533.8	140.7	22359.4
1993-94	9.1	1533.6	0.20	28.2	125.5	23292.2	134.8	24854.0
1994-95	9.8	1616.4	0.50	74.8	169.7	34585.8	180.0	36277.0
1995-96	11.5	1580.5	0.20	31.0	184.0	37537.9	195.7	39149.5
1996-97	16.5	2712.6	0.10	18.3	186.4	38635.4	203.0	41366.3
1997-98	18.7	2364.4	0.10	16.5	197.8	43614.6	216.6	45995.5
1998-99	29.7	43737.0	0.30	52.9	208.8	53085.8	238.8	57512.4
1999-2000	43.5	56077.0	0.10	45.5	214.2	57830.3	257.7	63483.5

Source: Apparel Export Promotion Council.

Table 4.33
Exports of Synthetic Garments during 1983 to 1999-2000

Year	*Knitted Garments Export Mn. Pieces*	*Total Garments Export Mn. Pieces*	*Total Garments Exports Mn. Sq. Mts*	*Total Garments Exports in Mn. Kgs*
1983			25.17	1.86
1988-89	3.8	62.4	103.51	7.57
1989-90	3.6	110.0	182.53	13.42
1990-91	7.3	139.6	231.59	17.08
1991-92	5.6	142.8	236.94	17.87
1992-93	7.5	140.7	233.41	17.68
1993-94	9.1	134.8	223.59	16.82
1994-95	9.8	180.0	298.60	22.90
1995-96	11.5	195.7	324.63	25.30
1996-97	16.5	203.0	336.65	28.04
1997-98	18.7	216.6	359.18	29.77
1998-99	29.7	238.8	395.81	33.45
1999-2000	43.5	257.7	427.08	36.14

Source: As derived by the author from Apparel Export Promotion Council.

Synthetic Textiles and Clothing Products Exports and Domestic Availability Equivalent to Fabrics, Yarn and Fibre/ Filaments

From the above analysis of exports of fabrics in various stages of production, one could workout the total exports of fabrics in the form of fabrics, made-ups and garments. By adding the synthetic yarn exports in it, one could work out the total exports of synthetic yarn in the form of yarn, fabrics, made-ups and garments.

The exports of various synthetic textiles and clothing products equivalent to yarn at various stages of production are given in Table 4.35.

The yarn export constitutes the maximum share in total yarn equivalent exports and made-ups the lowest. Using earlier information on the production of synthetic fabrics and yarn, the share of exports in various forms could be worked

Table 4.34

Fabrics, Yarn and Fibre Equivalent Exports in the form of Various Synthetic Textiles & Clothing Products during 1983 to 1999-2000

Year	*Fabrics Equivalent Exports*	*Fabrics Equivalent Exports*	*Yarn Export**	*Total Yarn Equivalent Exports*	*Total Fibre Equivalent Export*	*Cotton Content in Exports*	*MMF/Filament Contet in Export*
	Mn.Sq. Mt.	*Mt Mn.Kgs*					
1983	104.14	8.21	0.93	9.14	9.59	1.19	8.40
1988-89	248.42	20.46	8.61	29.07	30.68	3.54	27.14
1989-90	458.90	38.04	16.5	54.54	57.56	7.15	50.41
1990-91	531.60	45.37	14.47	59.84	63.15	7.82	55.33
1991-92	620.89	55.06	30.36	85.42	90.15	11.16	78.99
1992-93	652.61	58.74	40.02	98.76	104.23	12.9	91.33
1993-94	774.51	72.5	41.3	113.8	120.10	14.86	105.24
1994-95	971.41	91.92	69.1	161.02	169.93	21.03	148.90
1995-96	1089.34	97.71	89.66	187.37	197.78	24.6	173.18
1996-97	1112.34	98.43	112.74	211.17	222.85	27.58	195.27
1997-98	1201.45	113.04	133.27	246.31	259.94	32.2	227.74
1998-99	1198.29	119.24	137.16	256.4	270.50	33.49	237.01
1999-2000	1291.56	131.43	190	321.43	339.10	41.98	297.12

Note: (1) * Filament yarn exports is included as it is important to calculate the domestic availability of yarn. However, for projecting future demand in Chapter 5, it is not covered. It was important to excluded it in Chapter 5 to make the export data in quantity terms comparable with the world data available from FAO and analysis undertaken in TOI.

(2) Exports in the form of fibre are not included as main purpose is to assess the potential for textiles exports.

Source: As derived by the author.

out. The domestic availability of synthetic fabrics and yarn could also be worked out by subtracting the exports from production.

Table 4.35
Yarn Equivalent Exports in Various Synthetic Textiles and Clothing Products during 1983 to 1999-2000

(Mn. Kgs)

Year	*Yarn**	*Fabrics*	*Made-ups*	*Garments*	*Total*
1983	0.93	3.65*	2.69*	1.86	9.14
1988-89	8.61	9.39*	2.91*	7.57	29.07
1989-90	16.50	17.98*	6.04*	13.42	54.54
1990-91	14.47	22.87*	5.42*	17.08	59.84
1991-92	30.36	31.38	5.81*	17.87	85.42
1992-93	40.02	35.49	5.57	17.68	98.76
1993-94	41.30	48.62	7.06	16.82	113.80
1994-95	69.10	61.11	7.91	22.90	161.02
1995-96	89.66	63.37	9.04	25.30	187.37
1996-97	112.74	60.17	10.22	28.04	211.17
1997-98	133.27	69.97	13.30	29.77	246.31
1998-99	137.16	71.65	14.14	33.45	256.40
1999-2000	190.00	76.04	19.25	36.14	321.43

Note: * Include filament yarn exports.
Source: As derived by the author from various Export Promotion Councils.

The exports of synthetic fabrics in various forms thus worked out is 1292 million square metres, which comes to around 7.22 per cent of total production of synthetic fabrics during 1999-2000. The export of synthetic yarn in various forms constitutes 18.72 per cent of total production during 1999-2000 (Table 4.36).

The methodology used here to work out yarn available for production of synthetic fabrics takes into accounts the stock depletion/addition of total synthetic yarn and import of filament yarn. However, the import of non-100% cotton spun yarn in various forms is ignored at that stage as it constitutes small share of total yarn. This import content in the form of various textiles and clothing products is taken into account at later stage. This methodology is similar to the methodology used for the cotton segment.

Table 4.36
Synthetic Fabrics and Yarn Equivalent Exports and Domestic Availability during 1983 to 1997-98

Year	Fabrics Production	Fabrics Exports	Fabrics Exports as	Domestic Availability of Fabrics		Yarn Production	Yarn Exports	Yarn Exports as
	Mn.Sq.Mts		% of Production	Total Mn.Sq.Mts	Per Capita Sq. Mt	Mn. Kgs		% of Production
1983	4659	104	2.24	4555	6.34	323.57	9.14	2.82
1988-89	6835	248	3.63	6587	8.24	502.41	29.07	5.79
1989-90	7001	459	6.55	6542	8.02	526.98	54.54	10.35
1990-91	8022	532	6.63	7490	9.00	592.34	59.84	10.10
1991-92	8317	621	7.47	7696	9.04	650.51	85.42	13.13
1992-93	8587	653	7.60	7934	9.14	704.69	98.76	14.01
1993-94	10455	775	7.41	9680	10.95	831.88	113.80	13.68
1994-95	11450	971	8.48	10479	11.64	909.33	161.02	17.71
1995-96	12716	1089	8.57	11627	12.61	1082.5	187.34	17.31
1996-97	13726	1112	8.10	12614	13.43	1246.37	211.17	16.94
1997-98	17392	1201	6.91	16191	16.95	1528.09	246.31	16.12
1998-99	17160	1198	6.98	15962	16.44	1621.94	256.40	15.81
1999-2000	17898	1292	7.22	16606	16.83	1716.68	321.43	18.72

Source: As derived by the author.

The total availability of synthetic yarn for domestic consumption is given in Table 4.37. The synthetic yarn available for domestic consumption is converted to fibre/filament equivalent domestic availability by applying the conversion rates of yarn from fibre as explained in Chapter 3.[5] The methodology is similar to the one adopted for the year 1995-96.

The comparison of per capita availability estimates derived above tally with the existing estimates on consumption. FAO data for the year 1990,1991,1992 is given in Table 4.38. FAO data for synthetic products includes domestic consumption of cellulosic products as well. The per capita availability data derived above also tallies with the ICACA available data on India's per capita 0.5 kilograms consumption of synthetic fibre for the year 1986 (Table 4.38).

Total Exports and Domestic Availability of Cotton and Synthetic Textiles and Clothing Products

The total exports and domestic availability of cotton and synthetic fabrics in textiles and clothing products is given in Table 4.39.

The made-ups grew at the fastest rate over the period of time. However, share of fabrics is still the dominant one. The share of exports in total production of fabrics has increased from 6.9 per cent during 1983 to 15.2 during 1990-91 and further to 25.4 per cent during 1999-2000.

The total domestic availability of cotton and synthetic fabrics has increased from 13024 to 17314 million square metres from 1983 to 1990-91, which further increased to 23217 million square metres during 1999-2000 (Table 4.40). The per capita availability of fabrics has increased from 18.12 to 20.80 square metre from 1983 to 1990-91 and further to 23.53 square metres during 1999-2000. Thus, the availability of fabrics for domestic

5. Another way could have been adopting consumption of fibre/filament in mill and SSI sector. However, this method is adopted as data is not very reliable, specially in the case of filament yarn, which is raw material for production of fabrics.

Table 4.37

Domestic Availability of Yarn in Synthetic Products

Year	*Total Yarn Required for Production of Synthetic Fabric*	*Synthetic Fabric Equivalent Exports*	*Other Use of synthetic yarn*	*Domestic Availability of Synthetic Yarn*	*Per Capita Availability of Synthetic Yarn*
		Mn. Kgs			*Kgs*
1983	342.00	8.21	0.00	333.79	0.46
1988-89	493.29	20.46	10.00	482.83	0.60
1989-90	508.75	38.04	9.00	479.71	0.59
1990-91	587.58	45.37	9.00	551.21	0.66
1991-92	622.01	55.06	6.00	572.95	0.67
1992-93	646.80	58.74	11.00	599.06	0.69
1993-94	775.92	72.50	25.00	728.42	0.82
1994-95	861.98	91.92	21.00	791.06	0.88
1995-96	975.92	97.71	24.00	902.21	0.98
1996-97	1143.43	98.43	28.00	1073.00	1.15
1997-98	1281.78	113.04	37.00	1131.74	1.18
1998-99	1365.54	119.24	73.00	1173.30	1.21
1999-2000	1395.25	131.43	63.00	1200.82	1.22

Source: As derived by the author.

Table 4.38

Estimates of Consumption of Man-made and Cotton Fibre for Domestic Use in the form of Synthetic Products

Year	*Synthetic Fibre/Yarn Ratio**	*Synthetic Fibre Requirements Mn. Kgs*	*Cotton Fibre Mn.Kgs*	*MMF/Filament Content Mn. Kgs*	*Per Capita MMF/Filament Consumption Kgs*	*Per Capita MMF Consumption Kgs#*
1983	1.060	353.82	32.41	321.41	0.44	0.5
1988-89	1.044	483.19	33.40	470.68	0.58	
1989-90	1.041	480.64	27.59	471.79	0.57	
1990-91	1.040	554.54	32.44	540.81	0.65	0.80
1991-92	1.040	583.39	34.06	561.81	0.66	0.70
1992-93	1.039	599.57	34.21	588.21	0.68	0.80
1993-94	1.039	704.88	45.89	710.93	0.80	
1994-95	1.039	778.27	47.59	774.32	0.86	
1995-96	1.037	885.82	46.91	888.54	0.97	
1996-97	1.033	1050.56	62.42	1045.99	1.12	
1997-98	1.030	1165.69	70.91	1094.78	1.146	
1998-99	1.027	1204.98	82.16	1122.82	1.156	
1999-2000	1.026	1232.04	84.98	1147.06	1.163	

Note: (1) * Ratios derived from data on production of yarn from fibre as worked in Chapter 3 by undergoing fibre-wise analysis.

(2) # FAO Estimates. These estimates includes cellulosic.

Source: As derived by the author.

consumption grew at slcw rate both during eighties and ninties.

However, the Textile Commissioner's data gives higher estimates compared to the one derived in this study, and growth rate is also high. The per capita availability grew from 21.29 to 23.74 square metres during 1985-86 to 1990-91, which further it reached a level of 30.55 square metres by 1999-2000.

In fact, a lot of literature discussed the cause of slow down in per capita household consumption during eighties on the basis of Textile Committee data on household consumption. Desai (1983) argued that although the per capita consumption stagnated during eighties, the fabrics available with consumers increased as there was shift in consumption pattern towards synthetic products, which is more durable. An attempt is thus made to find the estimates of stocks with consumers by providing 2.5 times durability to synthetic fabrics compared to cotton fabrics on the basis of estimates of quantity derived in this study. The results show that per capita availability of the stock increased at approximately 4.23 per cent per annum from 1990-91 to 1999-2000. These results broadly tally with the results obtained regarding per capita consumption growth in value terms derived by using prices from Textile Committee. Thus the increase in per capita consumption and availability of fabrics in real terms is higher than pointed out in this study by the estimates of quantity of fabrics.

It is possible to make a comparison of estimates made in this study with Textile Committee estimates. The Textiles Committee estimates are given in metres, which are converted into square metres by deriving conversion rates using item-wise analysis. From the item-wise analysis of the household consumption of fabrics, which takes into account the composition of various products, the width of fabric is estimated equal to 1.11 square metre approximately. By using this conversion rate, the comparison of our estimates with the Textile Committee estimates shows that the results derived are close to each other, which provide credential to the estimates of production of fabrics derived in our study.

The explanation for the small difference could be that the derived estimates are regarding availability of fabrics and the Textile Committee's estimates are regarding consumption of fabrics. Besides, the textile Committee estimates about consumption are for calendar year, while the estimates derived in this study is for financial year. Anyway, the difference is not large and this much difference is understandable in derived estimates and survey estimates.

The data in Tables 4.40 point out that the non-household consumption has more or less remained at same level as percentage of the total domestic availability of fabrics, when the average of three years is taken. This is likely as the purchases of fabrics by several government departments such as military, police and offices, which constitute the major purchases, have been cut down in recent times. On the other hand this is compensated by rise in demand in hotels and non-institutional areas for fabrics.

However, the overall comparison at aggregate level hides wide discrepancies existing at fibre-wise analysis as well as sector level analysis. We discuss below the magnitude of these discrepancies and reason for the same.

Discrepancies at fibre level Availability of Fabrics for Domestic Consumption and Estimates of Consumption Derived from Textile Committee Data

There exist wide discrepancies in the estimates of production of fabrics derived in this study and Textile Committee data on consumer household and non-household purchases for individual blends separately. This is expected, as it is not possible for the consumers to able to identify the exact blend of fabrics purchased by them. The specifications of fabrics are not generally mentioned in the absence of mandatory rules.

Thus, the analysis below is restricted to two main fibres, which are easy to distinguish namely 100% cotton and synthetic fabrics.

The comparison shows that the estimates about domestic

Table 4.39

Exports of Cotton and Synthetic Fabrics in the form of Fabrics, Made-ups and Garments

Year	*Fabrics*	*Made-ups*	*Garments*	*Total Exports*	*Production of Fabrics*	*Fabrics*	*Made-ups*	*Garments*	*Total Exports*
	In Mn. Sq. Mts					*% Share in Production*			
1983	420	288	259	966	13989	3.0	2.1	1.9	6.9
1988-89	917	532	646	2094	18131	5.1	2.9	3.6	11.6
1989-90	1072	696	861	2629	18395	5.8	3.8	4.7	14.3
1990-91	1246	836	1017	3098	20412	6.1	4.1	5.0	15.2
1991-92	1487	960	1161	3608	19824	7.5	4.8	5.9	18.2
1992-93	1539	1142	1333	4016	21162	7.3	5.4	6.3	19.0
1993-94	1754	1479	1506	4739	24006	7.3	6.2	6.3	19.7
1994-95	2155	1660	1607	5421	24369	8.8	6.8	6.6	22.2
1995-96	2252	1699	1776	5727	27919	8.1	6.1	6.4	20.5
1996-97	2538	1906	1932	6374	27794	9.1	6.9	6.9	22.9
1997-98	2561	2151	2109	6821	31481	8.1	6.8	6.7	21.7
1998-99	2807	2413	2259	7479	29847	9.4	8.1	7.6	25.1
1999-2000	2804	2758	2347	7910	31127	9.0	8.9	7.5	25.4
Compound % p.a. Gr. Rt. 1983 to 1999-2000	12.6	15.2	14.8	14.0	5.1	—	—	—	—

* Data is in Square Metres.

Source: Derived by the author.

Table 4.40
Domestic Availability and Consumption of Cotton and Synthetic Products

Year	Domestic Availability	Consumption Household & Non-Household	Per Capita Domestic Availability		Per Capita Household Consumption		Non-household Availability/Consumption		
		Textile Committee	Derived	Official	Textile Committee		Derived	Textile Committee	Derived as % of Domestic Availability*
	Mn.Sq.Mts	Mn.Sq.Mts	Sq.Mts	Sq.Mts	Mts	Sq.Mts		Mn.Sq.Mts	
(1)	(2)	(3)	(4)	(5)	(6)	(7)	(8)	(9)	(10)
1983	13024	12609	18.12	14.82*	13.21	14.66	2485	2070	19.1#
1988-89	16037	15346	20.07	22.46	12.52	13.90	4928	2799	30.7#
1989-90	15766	15901	19.33	22.08	12.40	13.76	4541	2905	28.8#
1990-91	17314	15591	20.80	23.74	11.83	13.13	6382	3269	32.3
1991-92	16216	16252	19.04	22.40	12.39	13.76	4497	3255	31.3
1992-93	17147	17009	19.76	24.39	12.68	14.08	4928	3532	31.2
1993-94	19266	17490	21.80	26.02	13.71	15.21	5822	3630	29.0
1994-95	18949		21.06	25.65	12.89	14.31	6071		30.4
1995-96	22192		24.07	28.35	13.25	14.71	8629		34.0

(Contd....)

(Contd....)

(1)	(2)	(3)	(4)	(5)	(6)	(7)	(8)	(9)	(10)
1996-97	21421		22.80	30.03	13.21	14.66	7648		35.7
1997-98	24660		25.82	30.92@	15.65	17.37	8068		35.7
1998-99	22369		23.04	28.19@	13.21	17.55	5330		30.7
1999-2000	23217		23.53	30.55@					30.7a

Note: @ Official figures of domestic availability are repeatedly changed. The latest years data is based on latest estimates.

Figures are for one year rather than three years averages, a is assumed on the basis of last years value.

* Figures are worked out on the basis of average of three years.

Source: As derived by the author.

availability of synthetic fabric are higher than that of the Textile Commissioner's Consumer Household and Non-household Survey. On the other hand it is lower in the case of cotton. The prime reason for the difference seems to be problem faced by consumer in distinguishing between 100% cotton fabrics and cotton blended fabrics. However, the difference seems to be widening as is clear from data in Table 4.41 and Table 4.42, as the composition of cotton blended has increased over the period of time. The cotton blended fabrics share in total production of fabrics was 7.44 per cent during 1983, which declined to 5.20 per cent during 1990-91, and remained at almost same level till 1996-97. However, it increased at fast rate from 5.29 per cent level during 1996-97 to 7.55 per cent during 1999-2000 due to shortage of cotton. The consumers are either are not very aware about the fibre content or they are misled by the shopkeeper to satisfy the demand gap caused due to shortage of cotton. Thus the estimates derived in this study regarding fibre-wise production of fabrics seem to be reliable and the discrepancies are primarily due to identification problem faced by the consumers.

In the first phase of reforms after 1985, the growth in production of cotton fabrics was sufficient to meet the high growth in demand from exports of fabrics in various forms, while the per capita consumption of cotton fabrics was maintained. However, in the second phase of reforms during 1990-91 to 1999-2000, the high growth in exports of cotton equivalent fabrics has caused decline in domestic availability of cotton fabrics, not only in per capita terms but even in absolute terms. The per capita domestic availability of cotton fabrics as per our estimates declined from 11.80 square metre during 1990-91 to 6.70 square metre during 1999-2000.[6]

6. The estimates about production of fabrics derived in this study do not cover production of fabrics in the khadi sector. On the other hand, the estimates about the consumption of fabrics include that as well. It would not make much difference, as production of khadi sector constitutes around 0.6 per cent during 1999-2000.

Table 4.41

Estimates of Domestic Availability and Consumption of Cotton Fabrics in Various Forms

Year	*Cotton Domestic Availability*	*Total Consumption (Textile Committee)*	*Per Capita Domestic Availability Derived*	*Per Capita Household Consumption*	*Ratio of Derived Availability to Consumer household*
	Mn. Sq.		*Mt Sq. Mts*		
1983	8469		11.78	11.23	1.05
1988-89	9450	9972	11.82	10.18	1.16
1989-90	9224	9479	11.31	9.32	1.21
1990-91	9824	8963	11.80	8.26	1.43
1991-92	8520	9096	10.00	8.35	1.20
1992-93	9213	9594	10.62	8.56	1.24
1993-94	9586	9747	10.85	8.61	1.26
1994-95	8470		9.41	7.77	1.21
1995-96	10565		11.46	7.79	1.47
1996-97	8807		9.37	7.69	1.22
1997-98	8469		8.87	7.85	1.13
1998-99	6407		6.60	7.09	0.93
1999-2000	6611		6.70		
Percentage Per Annum Compound Growth Rates					
1990-91 to 1999-00	-3.65 (-2.66)		-5.54 (-4.11)		
t-statistics					
R^2					

Note : Figures in bracket indicate t-statistics.

Source: Derived by the author.

Table 4.42

Estimates of Domestic Availability and Consumption of Synthetic Fabrics in Various Forms

Year	*Domestic Availability*	*Total Consumption (Textile Committee)*	*Per Capita Domestic Availability Derived*	*Per Capita Household Consumption*	*Ratio of Derived Availability to Consumer Household*
	Mn. Sq.		*Mt. Sq. Mts*		
1983	4555		6.34	3.43	1.85
1988-89	6587	3936	8.24	3.72	2.22
1989-90	6542	4651	8.02	4.44	1.81
1990-91	7490	5238	9.00	4.87	1.85
1991-92	7696	5879	9.04	5.41	1.67
1992-93	7934	6156	9.14	5.52	1.66
1993-94	9680	7327	10.95	6.60	1.66
1994-95	10479		11.64	6.54	1.78
1995-96	11627		12.61	6.92	1.82
1996-97	12614		13.43	6.97	1.93
1997-98	16191		16.95	9.52	1.78
1998-99	15962		16.44	10.46	1.57
1999-2000	16606		16.83		
	Percentage Per Annum Compound Growth Rates				
1990-91 to 1999-00 t-statistics	10.14 (15.05)		8.24 (12.22)		

Note: Figures in bracket indicate t-statistics.

Source: Derived by the author.

Yarn Equivalent Exports and Domestic Availability in Various Forms

The above analysis is regarding the fabrics equivalent exports and domestic availability. It is important to find out the yarn and fibre equivalent domestic availability to link up the requirements at various production stages. The analysis is thus extended to yarn equivalent exports and domestic availability of textiles and clothing products as given in Table 4.43.

Thus the share of exports in total production of yarn has increased at a very rapid rate over the period of time. It increased from 8.36 per cent during 1983 to 21.05 during 1990-91 and further to 42.63 during 1999-2000. This is because the Indian textile exports has grown at, much higher rate than production over the entire period. However, the worrisome picture emerges as none of the segments, whichever way they are defined, do the country's exports show signs of moving up the value chain. Unit values, which can be interpreted as the average price of exported items show declines, or at best remained stable over time for the entire range of segments. The maximum exports of textiles and clothing items are taking place in terms of yarn.

Fibre/Filament Equivalent Exports and Domestic Availability in Various Forms

The cotton and synthetic fibre analysis is combined and then used to work out the share of cotton in exports, domestic availability and production for various textiles and clothing products as given in Table 4.44.

It has been worked out that the share of cotton in exports has come down to much lesser extent compared to share in domestic consumption. The similar pattern has emerged for the yarn and fabrics equivalent textiles and clothing exports and domestic availability as shown in Table 4.44. Howevr, the changes in fibre-composition in the domestic segment has been so far been discussed without taking into consideration the import content.

Table 4.43
Yarn Equivalent Exports and Domestic Availability in Various Textiles and Clothing Items

Year	Yarn	Fabrics	Maee-ups	Garm-ents	Total Export	Yarn Produc-tion	Domestic Availabi-lity	Yarn	Fabrics	Made-ups	Garm-ents	Total Export
	Million Kilograms							Item-wise Percentage share of exports in Production				
1983	7.5	51.2	31.0	28.8	118.3	1415.6	1307.0	0.53	3.61	2.19	2.03	8.36
1988-89	49.0	103.9	55.4	67.0	275.9	1812.4	1522.4	2.70	5.73	3.06	3.70	15.22
1989-90	78.6	122.9	72.3	88.2	362.6	1899.0	1500.7	4.14	6.47	3.81	4.65	19.10
1990-91	104.6	143.5	91.0	103.3	442.4	2102.3	1644.7	4.97	6.82	4.33	4.91	21.05
1991-92	156.4	168.7	106.0	119.6	550.6	2100.5	1540.8	7.44	8.03	5.05	5.69	26.21
1992-93	168.6	174.8	126.6	136.6	606.6	2273.7	1642.9	7.42	7.69	5.57	6.01	26.68
1993-94	220.1	201.4	163.6	154.1	739.3	2528.9	1827.7	8.70	7.96	6.47	6.09	29.23
1994-95	297.6	246.0	182.2	162.7	888.5	2605.3	1781.4	11.42	9.44	6.99	6.24	34.10
1995-96	352.5	247.1	180.0	177.0	956.6	2976.5	2098.5	11.84	8.30	6.05	5.95	32.14
1996-97	577.6	288.8	225.2	203.1	1294.8	3394.4	2189.7	17.02	8.51	6.64	5.98	38.14
1997-98	622.3	302.1	251.8	222.8	1398.9	3741.1	2219.7	16.63	8.07	6.73	5.95	37.39
1998-99	623.8	341.7	283.2	238.5	1487.0	3643.9	1988.5	17.12	9.38	7.77	6.54	40.81
1999-2000	744.7	353.6	324.8	248.4	1671.4	3920.7	2052.9	18.99	9.02	8.28	6.34	42.63

Figures are given in terms of yarn equivalent.
Source: Derived by the author.

Table 4.44
Fibre/Filament Content in Textiles and Clothing Exports and Domestic Use

(Mn. Kgs.)

Year	*Fibre/Filaments Equivalent*			*%Share of Cotton in Fibre/Filaments Equivalent*			*% Share of Cotton in Yarn Equivalent*		*Share of Cotton in Fabrics Equivalent*	
	Exports	*Domestic*	*Total*	*Exports*	*Domestic*	*Total*	*Exports*	*Domestic*	*Exports*	*Domestic*
1983	140.6	1609.0	1749.6	94.0	80.0	81.1	92.28	74.46	89.2	65.0
1988-89	327.1	1903.5	2230.6	91.7	75.3	77.7	89.46	68.29	88.2	58.9
1989-90	426.3	1904.8	2331.1	88.2	75.2	77.6	84.96	68.03	82.5	58.5
1990-91	521.4	2024.3	2545.7	89.4	73.3	76.6	86.48	66.49	82.8	56.7
1991-92	646.2	1896.3	2542.5	87.8	70.4	74.8	84.49	62.81	82.8	52.5
1992-93	709.8	1929.2	2639.0	87.1	69.5	74.3	83.72	63.54	83.7	53.7
1993-94	865.4	2052.6	2918.0	87.8	65.4	72.0	84.61	60.15	83.6	49.8
1994-95	1036.5	2135.7	3172.2	85.6	63.7	70.9	81.88	55.59	82.1	44.7
1995-96	1115.9	2406.4	3522.3	84.5	63.2	69.9	80.41	57.01	81.0	47.6
1996-97	1518.7	2489.6	4008.3	87.1	58.0	69.0	83.69	51.00	82.6	41.1
1997-98	1626.4	2572.1	4198.4	86.0	57.4	68.5	82.39	49.01	82.4	34.3
1998-99	1729.6	2308.4	4038.1	86.3	51.4	66.3	82.76	41.00	84.0	28.6
1999-00	1941.3	2311.0	4252.3	84.7	50.4	66.0	80.77	41.51	83.7	28.5

Source: As derived by the author.

Table 4.45

Cotton and Synthetic Fibre Content in Textiles and Clothing Products Available for Domestic Use

Year	*Domestic Availability of Fibre/Filaments in Mn. Kgs*			*Per Capita Domestic Availability in Kgs*			*Share of Cotton Fibre*
	Cotton	*Synthetic*	*Total*	*Cotton*	*Synthetic*	*Total*	
1983	1288	321	1609	1.79	0.45	2.24	79.91
1988-89	1433	471	1904	1.79	0.59	2.38	75.21
1989-90	1433	472	1905	1.76	0.58	2.33	75.54
1990-91	1484	541	2024	1.78	0.65	2.43	73.25
1991-92	1335	562	1896	1.57	0.66	2.23	70.40
1992-93	1341	588	1929	1.55	0.68	2.22	69.82
1993-94	1342	711	2053	1.52	0.80	2.32	65.52
1994-95	1361	774	2136	1.51	0.86	2.37	63.71
1995-96	1527	879	2406	1.66	0.95	2.61	63.36
1996-97	1444	1046	2490	1.54	1.11	2.65	58.11
1997-98	1477	1095	2572	1.55	1.15	2.69	57.62
1998-99	1186	1123	2308	1.22	1.16	2.38	51.26
1999-2000	1164	1147	2311	1.18	1.16	2.34	50.43

Source: As derived by the author.

Import Content

In the analysis so far, we have not taken into account the import content of any textiles and clothing products. The only import, which is taken into consideration, was of filament yarn, which is not covered under textiles and clothing products. The inclusion of import of textiles and clothing products at various stages would not make much difference to the analysis so far as imports of textiles and clothing items holds a very small proportion of the total domestic consumption. However, imports are bound to increase with the MFA phase out. The fibre-wise equivalent import of various textiles and clothing items analysed by us for the year 1993-94 to 1996-97 is given in Table 4.52.

From the above analysis, it is clear that the import content in various textiles and clothing items was only 0.05 kg during 1996-97, which is approximately 1.84 per cent of the total per capita domestic availability of fibre, which is 2.72 kg (2.67+0.05=2.72 kg) during 1996-97. The import content was only 0.75 per cent of total domestic availability of fibre during 1995-96. There was thus 150 per cent growth in terms of fibre filament equivalent import of textiles and clothing products from 1995-96 to 1996-97.

The estimates for the year 1997-98, 1998-99 and 1999-2000 show that the import content of yarn in cotton textiles and clothing items was 6.6, 7.7 and 6.6 million kilograms respectively. The same figures for synthetic textiles and clothing products are estimated at 50.18, 55.67 and 65.08 million kilograms. The fibre/filament content could be worked out using conversion rate of yarn.

This means that share of cotton fibre in the domestic consumption (textiles and clothing products and other items) still accounts for 49.19 per cent of the total consumption of cotton and synthetic fibre in the country. Cotton fibre share was 79.91 per cent in 1983 and was declining throughout eighties. However, ninties saw a step decline in share of cotton fibre in domestic consumption especially after the year 1995-96. The share of cotton fibre declined from 73.25 during 1990-

91 to 62.88 during 1995-96 and further to 49.19 per cent during 1999-2000.

Table 4.46
Per Capita Equivalent Import of Cotton and MMF in Textile and Clothing Products

	Yarn Equivalent	*Fibre Equivalent*	*Population*	*Per Capita Fibre*
	Mn. Kgs		*Mn.*	*Kgs*
1993-94				
Cotton Items	1.49	2.49	883.9	0.00
Synthetic Items	8.08	7.79	883.9	0.01
Total	9.57	9.28	883.9	0.01
1994-95				
Cotton Items	1.42	2.80	899.9	0.00
Synthetic Items	13.98	13.52	899.9	0.02
Total	15.40	16.32	899.9	0.02
1995-96				
Cotton Items	1.03	2.20	916	0.00
Synthetic Items	14.43	14.06	916	0.02
Total	15.46	16.26	916	0.02
1996-97				
Cotton Items	4.41	8.01.	932	0.01
Synthetic Items	40.77	40.33	932	0.04
Total	45.18	48.34	932	0.05

Source: As derived by the author from DGCIS data.

As per ICACA data, India's per capita apparel cotton fibre consumption was 1.8 kg in 1986. The per capita cotton fibre availability for domestic consumption as worked out in this study is not much different compared to the one estimated by ICACA data. The above estimates also mach with the FAO estimates regarding synthetic fibre/filament consumption in the country. FAO estimated the synthetic fibre/filament consumption as 0.5 kgs during 1983, 0.80 during 1990-91, 0.70 kgs during 1991-92 and 0.8 kgs during 1992-93.

In case, share of silk and wool fibre is also taken into account, which constitutes around 2.4 per cent of the total fibre consumption, the share of cotton fibre in domestic consumption is further reduced to 48.22 per cent during 1999-

Table 4.47

Per Capita Availability of Cotton and MMF/Filament Including Import Content

Year	*Per Capita Domestic Availability Sq. Mts*			*Per Capita Domestic Availability of Fibre Kgs*		
	Total	*Cotton*	*Cotton share*	*Total*	*Cotton*	*Cotton share*
1983	18.12	11.78	65.03	2.24	1.79	79.91
1988-89	20.07	11.82	58.93	2.38	1.79	75.21
1989-90	19.33	11.31	58.51	2.34	1.76	75.21
1990-91	20.80	11.80	56.74	2.43	1.78	73.25
1991-92	19.04	10.00	52.54	2.23	1.57	70.40
1992-93	19.76	10.62	53.73	2.23	1.55	69.51
1993-94	21.92	10.85	49.48	2.33	1.52	65.24
1994-95	21.30	9.41	44.20	2.39	1.51	63.18
1995-96	24.31	11.46	47.14	2.64	1.66	62.88
1996-97	23.36	9.45	40.47	2.70	1.55	57.41
1997-98	26.50	8.92	33.66	2.76	1.56	56.42
1998-99	23.79	6.66	28.00	2.45	1.23	50.22
1999-00	24.38	6.75	27.71	2.41	1.19	49.19

Source: As derived by the author.

2000. This means we are fast approaching the world average share of cotton in total fibre/filament consumption, which is estimated at 44 per cent. The decline in cotton share in world total fibre/filament consumption is not much and is estimated to be 43.17 per cent by 2005-06 by FAO and ICAC.

The share of synthetic products in total fibre/filament consumption in India could further be increased by lowering excise duties on synthetic products, on custom duties intermediary and machinery products required to produce the synthetic products. This has been already taken place with considerable success during ninties.

Discrepancies at Sector level

The above analysis reflects the reliability of fibre-wise estimates of fabrics production derived in Chapter 3. However, already the sector-wise estimates about production of cotton fabrics derived from delivery of yarn to various sectors need to be verified. There are four sectors of production of fabrics namely mill, powerloom, handloom and hosiery.

The fabrics produced from these sectors could be classified into two main segments namely hosiery and woven fabrics. From the comparison of consumption data with estimates of production of hosiery fabrics, it appears that the consumer household survey data by the Textile Committee is not able to capture the sudden shift in consumption pattern from woven fabrics to hosiery fabrics. One of the possible explanations for it could be the fact that earlier hosiery sector data used to be clubbed with the powerloom sector data. It seems confusion still persist regarding the definition of hosiery fabrics and there may be interviewers as well as consumers, which may be continuing clubbing the data with the powerloom sector. Thus, in this regard the estimates of fabrics production in hosiery sector as derived in Chapter 3 are taken as reliable.

In the case of woven fabrics, the main difference in production and consumption estimates seems to be due to the divergence of hank yarn to powerloom sector. The extent of divergence of hank yarn to powerloom sector is studied in detail and based on these revised estimates of sector-wise production of fabrics are worked out.

Estimates About Diversion of Cotton Hank Yarn to Powerloom Sector

An attempt is made in this section to find out the extent of hank yarn diversion to the powerloom sector, as it is believed that lots of hank yarn which is meant to be consumed in the handloom sector is being actually consumed in the powerloom sector. The hank yarn delivery in the total production of yarn remains more or less constant due to government regulations.

Initially, the total consumption of handloom fabrics in exports and domestic market is worked out and compared it with the estimates of production of handloom fabrics derived in Chapter 3 from the delivery of hank yarn.

The estimates about the exports of handloom fabrics in various forms such as fabrics, made-ups and garnets have already been worked out. The data regarding the domestic consumption of handloom fabrics in the household sector are available from the *Consumer Household Survey* published by Textile Committee. However, there are certain inherent problems in the consumer household survey, such as identification of fabrics produced in various sectors as well as errors due to memory lapse. So consumer household data for various sectors could be used only after careful scrutiny. However, it is easy to distinguish fabrics produced in handloom sector from the fabrics produced in mill and powerloom sector. Thus it is safe to assume that the data derived from consumer household survey regarding handloom sector may not be very much off the mark.

The data regarding consumption of household sector is available in million metres from the consumer household survey. The consumption of handloom fabrics in the household sector is then converted into square metres by using the item-wise conversion rates available from garment export entitlement policy, textile export entitlement policy and opinions of experts regarding piece and metre length for each item. The total consumption of handloom fabrics in the domestic segment is then worked out by assuming that the share of various sectors in household and non-household consumption is similar. The consumption of handloom fabrics arrived then is added into the square metre equivalent exports of handloom fabrics in textiles ad clothing products to arrive at the total consumption of handloom fabrics in the country over time as given in Table 4.48.

These estimates of consumption of handloom fabrics are then compared with the production of handloom fabrics arrived in Chapter 3 on the basis of delivery of hank yarn (Table 4.49).

The difference between consumption estimates and estimates about the production of handloom fabrics based on delivery of hank yarn are approximately 1509 million square metres during 1999-2000. The difference increased mainly after 1991-92. In fact the handloom sector was producing more fabrics than would have been possible with the delivery of hank yarn during eighties and even during 1991-92. This means the availability of hank yarn was imposing a constraint on the expansion of handloom sector during eighties. With the introduction of economic reforms during 1991, the demand of hank yarn from handloom sector squeezed considerably, as the sector found it difficult to survive in the open environment.

On the other hand, production of hank yarn remained a fixed percentage of the total yarn production, which is obligatory. One could work out the diversion from the gap between the consumption and production estimates of handloom fabrics derived in Chapter 3 on the basis of delivery of hank yarn. These gaps are then multiplied with weight of fabrics to estimate the approximate diversion of hank yarn to the powerloom sector. The total hank yarn diversion to powerloom sector during 1999-2000 is estimated at 210 million kilograms, which is 41 per cent of the total production of hank yarn.

From above estimates, one could also conclude that hank yarn is presently produced far in excess than the demand in handloom sector. But in that case the price of hank yarn should have declined considerably. But this is not the case. Hank yarn prices are rising at similar rate as that of cone yarn. Does that mean that there is too much demand of hank yarn in powerloom sector to get excise concession? This is likely as Small Spinning Units are also producing a fair amount hank yarn in addition to production of hank yarn in mill sector as brought out in Table 4.50.

Table 4.48
Consumption of Handloom Equivalent Cotton Fabrics in the Household, Non-household and Export Segments

Year	*Household Consumption Mn. Mts*	*Share of Non-household (%)*	*Exports Mn.Sq. Mts*	*Total Mn. Sq. Mts*
1983	2866	19.1#	149.78	3692
1988-89	2543	30.7#	357.63	4027
1989-90	1729	28.8#	384.45	2813
1990-91	1643	32.3	420.78	2848
1991-92	2025	31.3	527.33	3475
1992-93	1151	31.2	634.65	2308
1993-94	1471	29.0	748.99	2821
1994-95	1223	30.4	781.82	2539
1995-96	1252	34.0	726.33	2623
1996-97	1207	35.7	664.17	2541
1997-98	1423	35.7	698.86	2912
1998-99	1000	30.7	688.27	2131
1999-2000		30.7a	703.65	

Note: "a" means taken as same as of adjacent year for which data is available.

Source: As derived by the author from Textile Committee and TEXPROCIL data.

SSI sector data is only available since 1992-93. It is therefore, obvious that this extra production of hank yarn by SSI along with production by the mill sector is being consumed on a large scale by the powerloom sector. The fact that the hank yarn prices are rising in accordance to the rise in prices of cone yarns is the indication that the demand of hank yarn by the powerloom sector is quite large (Table 4.51).

Table 4.49

Comparison of Production and Consumption Estimates for the Cotton Handloom Fabrics

Year	Consumption of (Exports Plus Domestic)	Production Derived from Hank Yarn Delivery	Difference between production & consumption	Cotton Hank Yarn Delivery	Hank Yarn Requirement	Diversion of Cotton Hank Yarn	
	Mn. Sq. Mts			Mn. Kgs		% of Production	
1983	4545	3134	-1411	289	415	-128.8	-44.6
1988-89	4620	3316	-1305	315	439	-123.9	-39.3
1989-90	3215	3189	-26	310	313	-2.5	-0.8
1990-91	3173	3355	183	342	323	18.7	5.5
1991-92	3946	3194	-752	328	405	-77.2	-23.5
1992-93	2594	3603	1009	377	271	105.6	28.0
1993-94	3174	3977	803	422	337	85.3	20.2
1994-95	2908	4197	1289	438	304	134.5	30.7
1995-96	3034	5022	1988	504	305	199.5	39.6
1996-97	2990	4470	1480	519	347	171.8	33.1
1997-98	3171	4270	1099	540	401	139.0	25.7
1998-99	2342	3783	1442	473	293	180.2	38.1
1999-2000	2391*	4048	1656	514	304*	210.3	40.9*

* Estimated.

Source: As derived by the author from Textile Committee and Texprocil data.

Table 4.50

Hank Yarn Delivery to the Decentralised Sector

(Mn. Kgs)

	Cotton	*Synthetic*	*Total*	*Cotton*	*Synthetic*	*Total*
	Includes delivery by SSI spinning units			*Excludes delivery by SSI spinning units*		
1983-84	289	53	342	289	53	342
1988-89	315	39	354	315	39	354
1989-90	310	38	348	310	38	348
1990-91	342	33	375	342	33	375
1991-92	328	36	364	328	36	364
1992-93	377	38	415	348	38	386
1993-94	422	42	464	376	42	418
1994-95	438	52	490	370	52	422
1995-96	504	67	571	435	67	502
1996-97	519	71	590	469	67	536
1997-98	540	58	598	N.A.	N.A.	N.A.
1998-99	473	56	529	N.A.	N.A.	N.A.
1999-2000	514	60	574	N.A.	N.A.	N.A.

Note: Data for SSI sector is only available after year 1992-93. N.A. means not available.

Source: Handbook of Statistics on Cotton Textile Industry, The Indian Cotton Mills Federation.

The comparison for wholesale price index however do not reveal variations for various counts. The prices per kilogram of hank and cone yarn for various counts reveal that prices of hank yarn are lower mainly for higher counts. In fact, the hank yarn prices are higher for counts up to 20s compared to cone yarn (Tables 4.52 and 4.53). So the diversion of hank yarn to powerloom sector must be taking place of counts above than 20s.

One could question the reason for rise in diversion of hank yarn to powerloom sector over time. One of the important reasons for rise in diversion seems to be the fact handloom sector has become non-competitive in open environment. This is because of non-availability of adequate and timely credit facility, lack of marketing facility, replication of handloom products on powerlooms at a lower cost, and

Table 4.51
Wholesale Prices Index of Cotton Hank and Cotton Cone Yarn

Year	*Cone*	*Hanks*	*Year*	*Cone*	*Hanks*	*Year*	*Cone*	*Hanks*
	Base 1981-82 = 100					*Base 1993-94=100*		
1983	103.9	108.4	1990	189.9	194.2	1994-95	137.38	136.56
1984	115.5	118.2	1991	233.2	230.7	1995-96	149.58	145.79
1985	113.0	114.9	1992	252.7	252.8	1996-97	134.02	140.47
1986	102.3	104.3	1993	271.3	269.2	1997-98	138.42	144.96
1987	136.9	141.3	1994	368.0	364.2	1998-99	137.76	149.25
1988	164.3	171.4	1995	397.1	389.0	1999-00	140.72	145.28
1989	188.1	193.9	1996	374.1	378.2			

Source: Wholesale Price Index.

Table 4.52
Prices of Cotton Hank and Cotton Cone Yarn for 20s Carded

(Rs. per Kgs)

Month/Year	*Hank* 91-92	*Cone* 91-92	*Hank* 96-97	*Cone* 96-97	*Hank* 97-98	*Cone* 97-98	*Hank* 99-2000	*Cone* 99-2000
April	44.53	41.55	91.08	83.80	85.63	75.00	82.60	80.88
May	44.69	42.26	90.93	83.80	84.09	80.80	81.60	80.88
June	44.90	42.50	88.77	81.90	85.08	82.00	79.20	80.88
July	46.39	42.50	88.27	80.00	86.78	82.00	78.80	80.88
August	51.61	50.32	85.37	80.00	86.83	82.20	78.20	80.88
September	53.89	51.43	86.12	80.00	86.34	83.75	78.60	76.13
October	51.39	47.20	85.68	78.25	86.45	84.00	80.00	76.13
November	51.91	49.60	85.37	75.00	86.30	84.00	80.80	76.13
December	56.98	52.53	85.24	75.00	86.84	84.00	80.20	76.13
January	59.87	51.00	85.63	75.00	87.05	84.40	78.80	79.13
February	59.06	52.50	84.09	75.00	87.39	88.00	77.20	79.13
March	57.21	49.70	85.08	75.00	88.99	88.00	76.40	79.13

Note: (1) Hank prices are exclusive of excise duties and sales tax, while cone prices are inclusive of excise duty and sales tax.

(2) Hank yarn prices are for Coimbatore market and cone yarn prices are for Mumbai market.

Source: Handbook of Statistics on Cotton Textile Industry, The Indian Cotton Mills Federation.

Table 4.53
Prices of Cotton Hank and Cotton Cone Yarn for Finer Counts

(Rs. per Kgs)

	Hank	Cone	Hank	Cone	Hank	Cone	Hank	Cone
	60s Carded	60/63s Warp Carded	60s Carded	60/63s Warp Carded	60s Carded	60/63s Warp Carded	60s Carded	60/63s Warp Carded
Month/Year	*1991*	*1991*	*1996*	*1996*	*1997*	*1997*	*2000*	*2000*
January	68.04	81.30	129.49	186.33	126.87	135.65	620.00	785.89
February	67.41	81.20	130.96	188.53	126.98	135.25	624.00	785.44
March	66.03	81.20	129.43	185.90	129.07	135.55	624.00	764.22
April	66.88	81.20	127.97	182.64	133.70	137.72	621.00	759.44
May	67.73	81.20	127.84	182.64	134.01	136.57	625.00	756.13
June	67.85	81.20	126.27	181.26	136.51	139.67	629.00	818.25
July	68.72	81.20	126.32	194.12	153.08	148.02	631.00	824.63
August	76.31	86.45	127.09	205.09	135.33	149.47	644.00	833.13
September	75.50	86.50	129.07	209.18	139.37	151.40	645.00	823.63
October	72.46	85.80	130.47	208.81	139.74	150.58	641.00	808.63
November	71.93	85.64	130.13	208.81	139.92	149.63	643.00	820.63
December	74.53	86.47	127.59	208.81	139.59	153.71	674.00	851.63

Note: (1) Hank prices are exclusive of excise duties and sales tax, while cone prices are inclusive of excise duty and sales tax.

(2) Hank yarn prices are for Coimbatore market and Cone yarn prices are for Mumbai market.

Source: Handbook of Statistics on Cotton Textile Industry, The Indian Cotton Mills Federation.

the gradual phasing out of the Janata Cloth Scheme. In brief the following important factors have been identified, which have encouraged the diversion of hank yarn to powerloom sector over the period of time. These are

1. Non-availability of adequate and timely credit facilities and lack of marketing infrastructure.
2. Obsolete technology and traditional production techniques were suicidal in a changing environment of rising demand for ready-made garment. The garment exporters were allowed to sell 50 per cent of their products in the domestic market.
3. Inadequate availability of inputs like standard dyes and chemicals in small packs.
4. Easing of monitoring at several stages of production.
5. Decline in competitiveness of handloom sector over the time due to production of similar products by the powerloom at a lower cost.
6. Data about production (delivery) of hank and other cone yarn in SSI spinning units was not available before the year 1992-93. Hence the diversion of hank yarn during earlier period might have been underestimated to that extent. The share of SSI spinning units in the total delivery of hank yarn accounts for 9.63 per cent during 1996-97.
7. The Handloom (Reservation of Articles for Production) Act, 1985, enacted by the Parliament reserved 22 textile articles for exclusive production by handloom sector. The numbers of textile articles exclusively reserved for the productions by handloom sector were lowered to 11 vide notification dated July 26, 1996.

Sector-wise Revised Estimates of Production of Cotton Fabrics

The sector-wise estimates of production of cotton fabrics (derived in this study in Chapter 3) are revised on the basis of total consumption estimates of cotton handloom fabrics (exports plus domestic consumption). The revised estimates of production of handloom fabrics are taken as same as that of total estimates of consumption of handloom fabrics. The cotton fabrics production of powerloom sector has been revised by adding the difference between production and consumption estimates of cotton handloom fabrics in the estimates of production of fabrics in the powerloom sector. This is based on the assumption that the hank yarn, which is not consumed in the handloom sector, is actually used to produce fabrics in the powerloom sector.[7] The sector-wise revised estimates about the production of cotton fabrics are given in Table 4.54.

The estimates derived in this study (Table 4.54) about the production of fabrics in the powerloom and handloom sectors are compared with the official estimates (Table 3.18). The estimated production of cotton fabrics in powerloom sector worked out in this study is 5997 million square metre as against official estimates of 6329 million square metre during 1999-2000. However, the growth rate in estimates of powerloom fabrics is estimated at 1.43 per cent per annum during 1990-91 to 1999-2000 compared with -2.62 per cent derived from official data. On the other hand, in case of production of fabrics in the handloom sector, the estimates derived in this study of 2179 million square metres is almost one third compared with the Textile Commissioner's estimates of 6376 million square metre. Moreover the growth rates in case of handloom sector is estimated at -2.62 per cent during 1990-91 to 1999-2000 compared with 5.32 per cent growth rate obtained in case of official statistics. The growth rate of production of fabrics is only 1.28 per cent per annum in our study compared with 2.87 per cent as derived from official statistics.

7. There is some difference between the reed and picks used to produce fabrics in handloom and powerloom sector and difference is very low in finer counts. The difference in reeds and picks at various count ranges in the two sectors to produce fabrics from the hank yarn consumed in powerloom sector would not make much difference in the total estimates about production of fabrics.

Table 4.54
Sector-wise Revised Estimates of Production of Cotton Fabrics

Year	Mill		Powerloom		Handloom		Hosiery		Total
	Mn.Sq. Mt	% Share	Mn.Sq. Mt	% Share	Mn.Sq. Mt	% Share	Mn.Sq. Mt	% Share	Mn. Sq. Mt
1983	2785	29.85	1973	21.14	3692	39.57	881	9.44	9331
1988-89	2100	18.59	3623	32.08	4027	35.65	1545	13.68	11295
1989-90	1957	17.18	4903	43.03	2813	24.69	1721	15.10	11394
1990-91	1859	15.00	5765	46.53	2848	22.99	1918	15.48	12390
1991-92	1651	14.35	4397	38.21	3475	30.20	1984	17.24	11507
1992-93	1407	11.19	6572	52.26	2308	18.35	2288	18.19	12575
1993-94	1356	10.01	6755	49.85	2821	20.82	2618	19.32	13550
1994-95	1247	9.65	6554	50.73	2539	19.65	2579	19.96	12919
1995-96	1131	7.44	7910	52.03	2623	17.25	3539	23.28	15203
1996-97	1193	8.48	6547	46.53	2541	18.06	3788	26.92	14069
1997-98	1196	8.49	5831	41.39	2912	20.67	4150	29.46	14089
1998-99	1073	8.46	5565	43.86	2131	16.80	3918	30.88	12688
1999-2000	1067	8.07	5997	45.33	2179	16.47	3986	30.13	13229
Percentage per Annum Compound Growth Rates in Mn. Sq Mts									
1983 to 90-91	9.61		25.78		15.84		27.58		16.85
90-91 to 99-00	-6.13		1.43		-2.62		9.54		1.28
t-statistics	-6.56		0.65		-1.55		9.19		1.60

Source: As derived by the author from Textile Committee and TEXPROCIL data.

Total Production of Fabrics Based on Revised Estimates of Hank Yarn Diversion

Due to lack of data on sector-wise domestic consumption of synthetic fabrics in the household and non-household sector, it has been assumed that diversion of hank yarn to powerloom sector is same for synthetic and cotton yarn.[8] The extent of total hank yarn (cotton and synthetic) diversion to powerloom sector on this basis is estimated to be 234.5 million kgs (Table 4.55).

Based on these estimates of diversion of cotton and synthetic hank yarn, the sector-wise production of fabrics are worked out as in the case of cotton fabrics. The results thus derived are given in Table 4.56. The fibre-wise estimates shows that the production of cotton fabrics derived in this study are much different than official estimates due to difference in conversion rates. Textile Commissioner's estimates of production of cotton fabrics during 1999-2000 are 5760 million square metres (43.5 per cent) higher compared with estimates derived in this study during the same period. The production of woven cotton fabrics has slowed down considerably (Table 4.54). The substitution of cotton woven fabrics with fabrics made from other fibres and shifts in demand in favour of hosiery fabrics are the possible reasons for the same.

The total production of fabrics derived in this study is 7500 million metres lower compared with the official estimates during 1999-2000. This means the official estimates are 24.1 per cent higher compared with estimates derived in this study during 1999-2000. The growth of total fabrics production derived in this study is lower at 5.59 per cent compared with derived from official estimates at 6.41 per cent during 1990-91 to 1999-2000. The sector-wise comparison for the year 1999-2000 shows that official estimates are 1684 million square metres higher for production of hosiery fabrics. The revised estimates

8. The divergence of synthetic hank yarn is very small share of total hank yarn consumption.

Table 4.55
Diversion of Cotton and Synthetic Hank Yarn to Powerloom Sector

Year	*Consumption (exports Plus Domestic)*	*Production Derived from Hank Yarn Delivery*	*Difference between production & Consumption*	*Hank Yarn Delivery*	*Hank Yarn Requirement*	*Diversion of Hank Yarn*	
	Mn. Sq. Mts			*Mn. Kgs*		*% of Production*	
1983	4545	3134	1411	342	491.7	-149.7	-44.6
1988-89	4620	3316	1304	354	493.3	-139.3	-39.3
1989-90	3215	3189	26	348	351.3	-3.3	-0.8
1990-91	3173	3355	-182	375	354.2	20.8	5.5
1991-92	3946	3194	752	364	449.5	-85.5	-23.5
1992-93	2594	3603	-1009	415	298.4	116.6	28.0
1993-94	3174	3977	-803	464	370.5	93.5	20.2
1994-95	2908	4197	-1289	490	340.0	150.0	30.7
1995-96	3034	5022	-1988	571	345.5	225.5	39.6
1996-97	2990	4470	-1480	590	394.5	195.5	33.1
1997-98	3171	4270	-1099	598	444.1	153.9	25.7
1998-99	2342	3783	-1441	529	327.7	201.3	38.1
1999-2000	2391*	4048	-1657	574	339.5	234.5	40.9*

Note : *Projected.
Source: As derived by the author from Textile Committee and TEXPROCIL data.

of production of fabrics in the powerloom sector was 22589 million square metre during 1999-2000, which is 855 million square metre lower than Textile Commissioner's estimates. This is despite the fact that the revised estimates in this study takes into account the production of fabrics in the powerloom sector from the yarn initially packed in hank form and later diverted to powerloom sector. The official estimate of production of fabrics in powerloom sector (including non-SSI weaving mills) is estimated at 23444 million square metres during 1999-2000 on the basis of delivery of yarn, which do not take into account the diversion of hank yarn to powerloom sector.

The production of fabrics in handloom sector is estimated at 2391 million square metre during 1999-2000, which is only 32.5 per cent of the Textile Commissioner's estimates of 7352 million square metre during the same year. Moreover the growth rate in case of handloom sector is –3.23 per cent during nineties on the bases of estimates derived in this study compared with 6.72 per cent growth rate obtained in case of official statistics.

The data in Table 4.56 reveal that the performance of mill and handloom sector is poor and performance of powerloom and hosiery sector is quite good. Thus the social objective of increasing the employment by imposing a restriction of producing a certain minimum percentage of yarn in hank form remains unfulfilled. Moreover, the New Textile Policy (NTP 1985) and later Economic Reforms introduced during 1991 also failed to bring the required level of technology progress in the weaving, dying and garment segment. Bedi (2000) observed that the quality of overall cotton fabrics produced in the country in fact deteriorated over the period of time. Calculating quality indices using following formula has derived this

Index of Quality of fabrics = Σ (Prices of fabrics in Sector i x Weight of Sector i)/ (Whole Sale Price Index of Fabrics in sector i)

Table 4.56
Production of Cotton and Synthetic Fabrics

(Mn.Sq.Mt.)

Year	Mill	Powerloom		Handloom		Hosiery		Total		Cotton Total	
		Derived	Official	Derived	Official	Derived	Official	Derived	Official	Derived	Official
1983	3604	4840		4545	—	1001	—	13989	13137	9331	10130
1988-89	2902	8876	10974	4620	3993	1733	2149	18131	20018	11296	13658
1989-90	2667	10622	11632	3215	3924	1892	2375	18395	20598	11394	13936
1990-91	2589	12502	13348	3173	4295	2148	2696	20412	22928	12390	15431
1991-92	2376	11255	13262	3946	4123	2247	2827	19824	22588	11507	14647
1992-93	2000	14079	14644	2594	5219	2490	3182	21162	25045	12575	16343
1993-94	1990	15957	15994	3174	5851	2885	3637	24006	27472	13551	17790
1994-95	1987	16493	16260	2908	6180	2981	3748	24369	28175	12918	17019
1995-96	1726	19159	17494	3034	7202	3999	5038	27919	31460	15203	18900
1996-97	1666	18785	19643	2990	7456	4353	5533	27794	34298	14068	19841
1997-98	1658	21888	21241	3171	7603	4764	6394	31481	36896	14089	19992
1998-99	1517	21358	20957	2342	6792	4630	6277	29847	35543	12688	17948
1999-2000	1457	22589	23444	2391	7352	4690	6374	31127	38627	13229	18989
Percentage Per Annum Compound Growth Rates											
1990-91 to 1999-2000	-6.02	8.16	6.56	-3.23	6.72	10.22	11.13	5.59	6.41	1.28	2.87
t-statistics	-11.88	8.89	18.45	-2.31	5.68	10.61	12.55	10.12	14.50	1.60	4.13

Note: The data for mill sector is exclusive of non-SSI weaving units and that of powerloom sector is inclusive.

Source: Official data taken from Handbook of statistics on Cotton Textile Industry, ICMF and other figures are as derived by the author.

Time series data of value of output at constant prices captures qualitative changes in the composition of textile output. The quality index obtained by deflating the ex-factory price of fabrics with its wholesale price index captures all changes that occur at the fabric stage including its product composition. The analysis brings out that there was a quality improvement in cotton fabrics in the mills and handloom sector, although the variations were very high during the nineties. On the other hand, quality of fabrics seems to have deteriorated in the powerloom sector. Because of the large weight of the powerloom sector, the overall quality of fabrics deteriorated in all the sectors over this period of time. This was mainly due to a shift in production from the mill and handloom sectors to the powerloom sector. It seems that the change in production of cotton fabrics from one sector to another has taken place mainly on cost considerations rather than on the basis of quality improvement. The deterioration in quality of woven fabrics over time could also be explained by the shift in production towards coarser count composition in all the sectors of production especially towards 0-10s count range.

Sector-wise qualitative changes for the exports segments were worked out in a similar manner by deflating dollar price of exports by relevant international price index of fibres. It comes out that the quality index for exported fabrics did not improve over time after the fibre stage.

The limitations of such qualitative indices are that they do not capture the impact of technological progress on cost reduction. Another problem appears in measuring the quality in case prices are deliberately cut to increase the turnover. In fact, the cost reduction due to technological change would be reflected in the wholesale price index. Similarly, the items included in WPI may change over the period of time as some of commodities earlier produced are wiped out. Thus the value of fabrics produced in each sector may not be true representative of its quality. The brand name of mill products and other factors may be responsible for extracting higher price in the mill sector despite comparatively low difference in quality of fabrics. In case of exports, one could even lower the dollar price realisation and still be able to get higher profit margins in rupee terms at constant prices. However, in such a case, the depreciation of domestic currency should take place at a higher rate compared with the relative difference in the inflation rate between the exporting and the importing countries. The results are thus to be interpreted keeping in mind these limitations. This along with the shift toward coarser count composition could explain the decline in quality index for export of cotton yarn, despite the fact that modernisation in spinning industry took place at a very rapid rate during the nineties. Despite these limitations the above quality index is useful in reflecting most of the qualitative changes, which takes place over the period of time.

The following facts can highlight the state of technology in the installed weaving capacity. The share of shuttleless looms in mill sector was only 5.05 per cent during March 1997, as per ITMF data. The total installed looms in the mill sector by March 1997 were 12,415,000 out of which only 716,000 were shuttleless looms. In addition, there were at the end of 1995, approximately 1.7 million powerlooms in the decentralised sector, of which some 3,000 were of the shuttleless type. This means shuttleless looms were 0.18 per cent of the total installed looms in the powerloom sector. Furthermore, there were approximately 3.9 million handlooms in the handloom sector (ITMF Volume 20/1997 Shipment Statistics). This means there was only limited use of latest technology in all the sectors. In a decade, from 1988 to 1997, the cumulative shipments of shuttleless looms to India numbered 7804 and that of shuttle looms 27013. This was 1.49 per cent of total shuttles looms and 21.64 per cent of total shuttle looms installed respectively in the world.

It seems that despite the fact that some modernisation has taken place to get benefits of rise in exports, the disincentives to gradually transform from small scale to large-scale sector hindered the rapid growth of technology development in weaving sector. Thus even after the end of nineties, the technological development could not develop to the desired level due to irrational excise duty structure.

Relative Performance of Various Sectors in Export Segment

The analysis of relative performance of various sectors is restricted to cotton segment alone as sector-wise domestic consumption or exports for synthetic products is not available. The performance of these sectors in exports and domestic segments are analysed one by one.

Export Segment

The sector-wise exports of cotton equivalent fabrics in the form of fabrics, made-ups and garments as derived in the earlier section are reproduced along with their respective growth rates in Table 4.57. The exports of fabrics in the form of fabrics, made-ups and garments from mill sector grew at the rate of 3.56 per cent per annum during nineties, as against 10.33 per cent for all the sectors during 1990-91 to 1999-2000. The performance was 15.93 per cent for the powerloom sector, 11.17 per cent for the hosiery sector. The handloom sector with 3.51 per cent per annum growth rate during 1990-91 to 1997-98 performed poorly in the export segment.

The slow growing sectors in the export segment are mill and handloom sectors. If garment exports are excluded, the share of handloom in the export of fabrics and made-ups is higher than the mill sector. Handloom sector exports are almost negligible in the garment sector, yet the sector's growth rate for overall exports was quite high. The share of handloom sector in total exports remained more or less constant till the year 1992-93, but showed signs of a decline thereafter. The exports of handloom sector during 1999-2000 were lower compared with the level achieved during 1993-94 and 1994-95. On the other hand, the pattern was different for the mill sector exports. The exports from the mill sector during 1997-98 were also lower compared with the exports during 1991-92 and picked up at very fast rate after 1997-98. This has raised the share of mill sector in total exports. However, the growth of fabrics from powerloom sector continued to grow at high rate.

Table 4.57
Sector-wise Total Exports of Cotton Fabrics in the Form of Fabrics, Made-ups and Garments

Year	*Mill*		*Powerloom*		*Handloom*		*Hosiery*		*Total*
	Mn.Sq. Mt	*% Share*	*Mn.Sq Mt*	*% Share*	*Mn.Sq. Mt*	*% Share*	*Mn.Sq. Mt*	*% Share*	*Mn. Sq. Mt*
(1)	*(2)*	*(3)*	*(4)*	*(5)*	*(6)*	*(7)*	*(8)*	*(9)*	*(10)*
1983	470	54.46	160	18.57	150	17.37	83	9.60	862
1988-89	640	34.66	618	33.47	358	19.37	231	12.51	1846
1989-90	763	34.91	656	30.02	401	18.35	366	16.73	2186
1990-91	893	34.80	798	31.11	419	16.35	455	17.75	2565
1991-92	835	27.59	1108	36.59	567	18.74	517	17.08	3027
1992-93	750	22.12	1313	38.72	663	19.55	665	19.61	3390
1993-94	674	16.95	1741	43.77	763	19.19	800	20.10	3978
1994-95	707	15.88	2198	49.41	782	17.57	763	17.14	4450
1995-96	745	16.06	2313	49.90	726	15.65	854	18.39	4638
1996-97	760	14.45	2867	54.48	664	12.62	971	18.45	5262
1997-98	819	14.57	3007	53.50	699	12.43	1095	19.49	5620
1998-99	1102	17.54	3282	52.26	688	10.96	1208	19.24	6281
1999-2000	1257	18.99	3378	51.04	704	10.63	1280	19.34	6618

(Contd....)

(Contd.....)

(1)	(2)	(3)	(4)	(5)	(6)	(7)	(8)	(9)	(10)
		Percentage per Annum Compound Growth Rates in Mn.Sq. Mts							
83 to 90-91	9.61		25.78		15.84		27.58		16.85
90-91 to 99-00	3.56		15.93		3.51		11.17		10.33
t statistics	1.82		10.83		2.04		14.09		20.61
R^2	0.21		0.93		0.26		0.96		0.98

Note: (1) Powerloom made-ups exports include knitted made-ups exports as well, which are insignificant. It is derived that knitted made-ups exports were less than 9 million square metres for the period 1997-98.

(2) The mill sector's exports are overestimated to some extent as data for exports from the non-SSI weaving units is not separately available and is treated as mill sectors exports. The production of the non-SSI weaving units is estimated at only 2.5 per cent during 1996-97. However, it is rising over time.

Source: As derived by the author.

The very high growth rate of the exports of fabrics from the powerloom sector was instrumental in bringing down the share of the remaining sectors in woven fabrics till 1997-98. On the other hand, the exports of hosiery fabric grew at a higher rate than the exports of woven fabrics.

The high growth of exports from mill sector is inconsistent with its overall performance in the production of fabrics. It appears that after the inclusion of non-weaving units into the official definition as Mill sector, it become easier for the fabrics produced in powerloom sector to be branded/stamped as mill sector fabrics. In fact, there was always overestimation of exports from mill sector and in fact exports of non-SSI units were always treated as exports from mill sector, though production was not. But, the reporting of exports of powerloom sector as mill sector exports becomes convenient after the change in official definition of the mill sector. This belief gets strengthened, as the exports of fabrics from the mill sector are reported to be higher than the production of fabrics not only in mill sector as defined in this study but also from mill and non-SSI weaving units. This explains the negative share of mill sector in the demand of fabrics in the domestic segment.

Domestic Segment

From the analysis of export data, it seems that the powerloom sector has grown at the cost of both mill as well as the handloom sector and unless there is some compelling reason, the same should apply in case of the domestic segment. One could work out the domestic availability of fabrics produced in various sector by taking out sector-wise exports from production (Table 4.58). On the basis of revised estimates of production in the powerloom and handloom sectors in this study, it has been worked out that share of powerloom sector is increasing at a very high rate even in the domestic segment. However, the results would have been different in case the analysis would have been taken on the basis of sector-wise estimates of production of cotton fabrics derived on the basis of delivery of cotton yarn to various sectors as derived in

Chapter 3.[9] This strengthens the widespread belief that a large proportion of hank yarn is actually consumed in the powerloom sector and strengthens the revised estimates derived in this study.

Thus on the basis of revised data, it could be concluded that the performance of mill and handloom sector is poor in all segments and that of hosiery and powerloom sector is good. We try to link the reasons behind these structural changes in the following section.

Hosiery Sector

This is the sector with high growth as demand shifted from woven fabrics to hosiery fabrics. However, quality improvement and technology progress did not take place much in this sector due to barrier to entry for large-scale sector, which continued even after NTP 2000.

Handloom Sector

Handloom sector exports of total fabrics in various forms increased at a rate 3.51 per cent during 1990-91 to 1999-2000.

However, the exports from handloom sector grew at higher rate of 5.72 per cent per annum during the period 1990-91 to 1996-97. The rate of the growth was much higher compared to negative growth in the mill sector. This indicates the competitiveness of the handloom sector in the international market. However, the consumption of handloom fabrics in the domestic market declined at 8.05 per cent per annum during the period 1983 to 1996-97. A detailed analysis is required to understand the divergent behaviour of the handloom sector in the export and domestic markets till year 1999-2000.

---

9. The estimates about the domestic availability of fabrics derived by subtracting exports of fabrics from production of fabrics derived in Chapter 3 do not support the facts that powerloom sector is growing fast in domestic segment. The estimates of production of fabrics are derived in Chapter 3 on the basis of delivery of yarn to various sectors. The poor performance of powerloom sector despite very high growth rate in exports raises doubt about the production estimates derived in Chapter 3.

Table 4.58
Sector-wise Revised Availability of Cotton Fabrics for Domestic Consumption

Year	Mill		Powerloom		Handloom		Hosiery		Total
	Mn.Sq. Mt	% Share	Mn.Sq. Mt	% Share	Mn.Sq. Mt	% Share	Mn.Sq. Mt	% Share	Mn.Sq. Mt
(1)	(2)	(3)	(4)	(5)	(6)	(7)	(8)	(9)	(10)
1983	2315	27.33	1737	20.51	3618	42.72	798	9.42	8469
1988-89	1460	15.45	3215	34.02	3459	36.61	1314	13.91	9449
1989-90	1194	12.97	4299	46.69	2360	25.63	1355	14.72	9208
1990-91	966	9.83	5115	52.06	2281	23.22	1463	14.89	9825
1991-92	816	9.62	3357	39.59	2840	33.49	1467	17.30	8480
1992-93	657	7.15	5290	57.59	1614	17.57	1623	17.67	9185
1993-94	682	7.12	5004	52.28	2068	21.60	1818	18.99	9572
1994-95	540	6.38	4382	51.74	1731	20.44	1816	21.44	8469
1995-96	386	3.65	5722	54.16	1772	16.77	2685	25.41	10565
1996-97	433	4.92	3848	43.69	1709	19.41	2817	31.99	8807
1997-98	377	4.45	3025	35.72	2012	23.76	3055	36.07	8469
1998-99	71	1.09	2311	35.52	1415	21.75	2710	41.65	6407
1999-2000	-190	-2.87	2648	40.05	1446	21.87	2706	40.93	6611

(Contd....)

(Contd....)

(1)	(2)	(3)	(4)	(5)	(6)	(7)	(8)	(9)	(10)
			Percentage per Annum Compound Growth Rates in Mn.Sq. Mts						
1983 to 1990-91	-11.74		16.68		-6.38		9.05		2.14
1990-91 to 1999-00	-23.60*		-7.18		-5.11		8.91		-3.61
t-statistics	-4.07		-2.68		-2.97		6.42		-2.63

Note:
1. Negative availability of mill sector fabrics for domestic consumption is explained by over reporting of exports by the mill sector. The powerloom fabrics is also branded as mill sectors exports.
2. Hosiery fabrics domestic availability is marginally overestimated as exports of knitted made-ups are excluded from the production of cotton fabrics.
3. * means growth rate worked for the period 1990-91 to 1998-99.

Source: As derived by the author.

The performance of the handloom sector in exports could be linked to various incentives given to the sector in successive trade agreements. Bhide (1996) in her thesis reported that India often agreed to lower base levels for quota as a trade-off for continued exemption for handloom products. In the early years of MFA, this negotiating strategy seems to have had some justification for two reasons. Firstly, handloom exports did expand rapidly. Secondly, since MFA quotas were not being fully utilised especially in the 1970s, the country's interests were not actually affected by the trade-off.

However, one adverse consequence of the strategy was that the country did not build up high quota levels in the early years. This affected exports from other sectors later in the 1980's when some Indian textiles and clothing products gained competitiveness and the quotas became binding.

Several exporters and importers confirmed during interviews that certain quantity of powerloom cloth is indeed being exported as handloom cloth. Bhide further states that the extent to which this substitution has been taking place is not easy to establish. Firstly, because no statistical survey has been conducted on the subject though it has generated a great deal of controversy in the country. Secondly, because powerloom manufacturers have mastered the technique of producing cloth on powerloom which is virtually indistinguishable from handloom cloth even by scientific testing processes. Bhide, (1996) argued that to take advantage of various incentives in trade agreements offered to the handloom sector, powerloom fabrics are being exported as handloom fabrics.

The analysis of product-wise exports from the handloom sector show that the major increase in exports mainly took place in the form of made-ups. In fact, the export of fabrics from the handloom sector has declined in absolute terms, while exports of garments from the handloom sector are almost negligible.

The extent of duplication does not seem to be large in case of data reported by the Handloom Export Promotion

Council. Otherwise, the increase in handloom exports would not have taken place in the made-ups sector alone. In fact, if we look at the quota utilisation for the country as a whole with different quota countries, it is higher in the case of fabrics compared to made-ups. Hence, the substitution would have been more in case of fabrics, where the demand is higher. So it indicates that if at all the powerloom duplication is taking place, it cannot be a significant proportion of the total exports as given by the Export Promotion Council. This indicates the handloom sector competitive advantage in made-up products, while it has lost to other sectors, especially the powerloom sector, in other products.

However, the counter argument could be that as the quota level for handloom sector exports is high for made-ups goods, duplication must be taking place mainly in these products. But, the decline in overall exports from the handloom sector from 782 million square metre equivalent fabrics during 1994-95 to 664 million square metre in 1996-97 indicates that duplication if at all is taking place cannot be significant in the export segment. Otherwise, the substitution would have been taken place even after the year 1994-95, and decline in overall gabrics equivalent handloom exports would not have taken place.

In the domestic market, however, the powerloom sector has very limited scope to pass off its production as handloom sector. This, for example, is relevant in those cases where the categories of products are exclusively reserved for the handloom sector and several institutions purchasing fabrics have been asked to buy only handloom production. It is not easy to sell fabrics through duplications to these institutions. This is anyway not applicable in case of household purchases, which constitutes the major share of domestic consumption. Hence, the duplication even if it is taking place is not on a large scale. Powerloom sector is in fact adopting the easier way out in the domestic market by consuming hank yarn and utilising excise benefits meant for the handloom sector rather than attempting to produce fabrics which looks alike the handloom sector.

Thus the data provided by the Handloom Export Promotion Council on handloom exports and that of the Textile Committee on consumer purchases could be considered reliable for the handloom sector. The prime reason which could be atributed to this is that fabrics produced in handloom sector is easily distinguishable from the fabrics produced by the other sectors.

An attempt is thus made on the basis of the Textile Committee data to consider changes in the domestic consumption pattern household for analysing the performance of handloom sector (Tables 4.59, 4.60 and 4.61).

Household consumer purchase survey indicate the broad trend prevailing in the domestic sector as a whole. The analysis has been undertaken on the basis of household consumer survey data for three periods 1983, 1992 and 1998. These years have been chosen as year 1983 being the first year, year 1992 was the first year after the 1991 reforms and 1998 the last year at the time of analysis for which we got detailed data on item-wise consumption for each sector.

The trends show that the domestic consumption of handloom fabrics is on the decline in all the segments, except the made-ups. In the made-ups segment, handloom sector is able to increase its production of total made-ups. A similar pattern emerged in the export segment.

The handloom sector is continuously losing its competitiveness as is clear from its declining share in consumption pattern and there was a steep decline after 1992. It is clear from the data that despite tall claims by the government, nothing much has been done for the benefit of this labour intensive sector. The cotton yarn cone price was Rs. 400 as compared to cotton hank price of Rs. 404 during July 1998 for 20s carded. The prices of hank yarn for coarser counts remained high compared with cotton cone yarn for most of the years. The high prices of coarser hank counts compared with cone prices along with other reasons mentioned for diversion of hank yarn to powerloom sector earlier explain the decline in production of handloom fabrics after the

Table 4.59

Item-wise Share of Handloom Sector in Cotton Woven Fabrics Available for Domestic Consumption during 1983

Items	*Woven Fabrics*		*Handloom*		*Handloom Share in Woven Fabrics*
	Share	*Mn.Sq. Mts*	*Share*	*Mn.Sq.Mts*	
Made-ups	7.42	569	8.44	305	53.60
Piece length	29.74	2281	6.91	250	10.96
Readymade Garment	9.37	719	12.63	457	63.56
Garments in Piece length	53.47	4102	72.02	2606	63.53
Total	100.00	7671	100.00	3618	47.16

Source: Derived from Textile Committee data.

Table 4.60

Item-wise Share of Handloom Sector in Cotton Woven Fabrics Available for Domestic Consumption during 1992-93

Items	*Woven Fabrics*		*Handloom*		*Handloom Share in Woven Fabrics*
	Share	*Mn.Sq. Mts*	*Share*	*Mn.Sq.Mts*	
Made-ups	10.90	824	19.23	310	37.66
Piece length	18.00	1361	4.10	66	4.86
Ready-made Garment	12.40	938	13.35	215	22.98
Garments in Piece length	58.70	4438	63.32	1022	23.03
Total	100.00	7561	100.00	1614	21.35

Source: Derived from Textile Committee data.

Table 4.61

Item-wise Share of Handloom Sector in Cotton Woven Fabrics Available for Domestic Consumption during 1998

Items	*Woven Fabrics*		*Handloom*		*Handloom Share in Woven Fabrics*
	Share	*Mn.Sq. Mts*	*Share*	*Mn.Sq.Mts*	
Made-ups	16.25	903.03	40.22	431	47.68
Piece length	16.23	901.97	4.87	49	5.38
Ready-made Garment	20.27	1126.44	4.08	44	3.88
Garments in Piece length	47.25	2625.41	50.83	544	20.71
Total	100.00	5556.85	100.00	1071	19.27

Source: Derived from Textile Committee data.

introduction of economic reforms during 1991. This marked a decisive departure from the earlier policies. For the first time in the post-independence period, in the textile industry emphasis has been placed on productivity, in sharp contrast to the hitherto thrust on employment. On the other hand, low prices of hank yarn for medium and finer varieties are in fact benefiting the powerlooom sector. Hank yarn is increasingly being diverted for the consumption in the powerloom sector and the diversion must be taking place in those varieties where it is beneficial.

The cost of production is high in handloom sector as analysed in various studies related with sector-wise cost of production. The advantage of handloom is linked to certain type of yarn or certain type of loom-woven design, which is more common in made-up varieties. Thus the survival of handlooms depends upon the segmented market in these varieties as well as ensured supply of related inputs. The handloom sector may further suffer in case the excise benefit is taken away. However, a large portion of hank yarn meant for consumption in the handloom sector is actually consumed in the powerloom sector, causing unnecessary burden on the exchequer in the form of excise relief. So should the Government continue to pursue the policy of mandatory proportion of hank yarn production and if so at what level. This is very crucial question for any policy formulation and which is even ignored during NTP 2000. This sector cannot survive in new economic environment except in a few varieties of Saris, made-ups etc. In case of saris even cone yarn is requirement and the sector is competitive despite that.

Mill Sector

The growth in exports of fabrics in various forms from mill sector was at the rate of 3.56 per cent during the same period. The growth in exports from mill sector was negative in consonance with the performance of production in the mill sector till year 1997-98. As discussed earlier the spurt in export growth from the mill sector after 1996-97 is nothing to do with the rise in competitiveness of the sector, but is mainly caused by change in definition of mill sector. The official definition of mill sector is changed to include non-SSI weaving units in addition to composite mills, which facilitate the exports of fabrics from the powerloom sector to be branded as mill sector fabrics. Though it was taking place earlier as well, it got facilitated, as the mil sector definition does not necessarily mean consumption of its own yarn. Thus the analysis is made till year 1996-97, till the impact of branding powerloom fabrics as mill sector exports was not significant.

In all categories of production of fabrics, the mill sector is losing its share and is unable to compete with the decentralised sector. In coarser and superfine varieties mills have relatively better chance to establish in case the new policy regime become conducive to their survival. The slow pace of investment, in shuttleless looms, by the mill sector may be an indication that mills were no longer interested in modernisation. The Mills seems to be better in heavier varieties as they are consuming their own yarn. On the other hand, to meet the demand for some high end products, mills are using latest technology. In fact, the latest trend in the mill sector of having various profit centres in the same unit may further reduce the share of sector, as even heavy cloth may not be profitable if profit at the spinning stage is taken off.

Powerloom Sector

From the above analysis, it seems that the powerloom sector is efficient in both the domestic and export markets. The obvious reason for it could be the cost of production. Mazumdar (1984) suggests that at identical wages,[10] mills are more efficient than powerlooms.[11] Misra (1993) uses somewhat

10. Wages are also different due to difference in cost of living among different cities.

11. It is argued that in actual practice the main benefit like concessional loans and subsidies were also taken by the mill sector. Against this, the powerloom sector has to borrow money from the money single space required lenders at very high rate in the absence of getting it from financial institutions. Hence, the policies are not only biased against mill sector,

(Contd.....)

different data set from that of other studies to argue that, in fact, the difference between mill and powerloom favours the mills at pre-tax prices. But when the excise on fabrics is added to mills, the balance tilts in favour of powerlooms because of the alleged tax evasion by them. But this view has also been disputed. The arguments advanced by Misra and Mazumdar are based on several cost studies of mill and powerloom sectors. It is, however, argued that these databases are not reliable. This is because these studies have taken data from best practice mills and compared it with the data for average powerlooms. However, this procedure may not be inappropriate to find the impact of Economic Reforms on the modernisation in weaving sector. In the existing environment (especially till NTP 2000 announced the dereservation of garment sector for the large scale sector), the market cost of production in mill sector turns out to be comparatively high and mills are not allowed to close down due exit barriers. Neither the new mills nor modern capacity is coming in mills in this kind of scenario. Thus it is sensible to compare new mills with modern technology with average powerlooms, as it is this new machinery regarding which the decision to invest in mill sector has to be taken by comparing its competitiveness in the powerloom sector.

(Contd....)

but also not very conducive in certain matters for the powerloom sector (T. Roy 1998b). One of the recent examples of policy biasedness in favour of mill sector is disbursement of Technological Upgradation Fund (TUF). As per policy TUF worth Rs. 25000 crore is to be disbursed in the textile sector in the next five years at an interest rate subsidy of 5 per cent point. Whereas financial Institutions like the Industrial Development Bank of India (IDBI), Industrial Finance Corporation of India (IFCI) and Industrial Credit and Investment Corporation of India (ICICI) will be lending about Rs. 17500 crore to medium and large companies. Small Industries Development Bank of India (SIDBI) the nodal agency for distributing loans to the small-scale industries would be lending Rs. 8000 crore only. This is despite the fact that the decentralised sector is the largest producer in the fabrics segments where modernisation is required. The NTP 2000 has also failed to address these important issues.

The most disturbing factor however is the fact that policy till recently failed on account of both technology improvement and employment generation in the handloom sector during eighties and nineties. The shift in production of fabrics from mill and handloom sector to powerloom sector mainly took place not on quality consideration but on the basis of cost consideration. The relatively better performance of powerloom sector in exports of grey and dyed fabrics raises doubts on the argument generally forwarded that this sector is competitive due to excise avoidance. The share of mill sector in exports of grey fabrics declined from 50 per cent in 1992 to 31 per cent in 1999-2000 and that total handloom and powerloom fabrics exports from 40 per cent to 36 per cent during the same period. This indicates that the mill sector is increasingly becoming non-competitive not only in dyed fabrics but also in grey fabrics as its share in both is declining. There were no excise duties on grey fabrics till recently.

The high growth in exports from powerloom sector is the indication of cost competitiveness of this sector in international market. However, India's exports mainly confined to grey low value added products. The slow growth of technology progress in the weaving segment is caused by several factors. The technological progress in mill sector is not taking place due to relatively disadvantageous position of this sector compared with powerloom sector. On the other hand, the powerloom sector does not have much incentive to bring technological progress in a situation where the labour is very cheap and modernisation after a stage could lead to disqualification from the benefits of SSI sector.

The technology progress in dyed segment did not take place as grey fabric was always taxed at lower rate compared to dyed fabrics. The escalating duty on additional value added discourage investment in large dyeing units. These go on splitting into smaller units and quality was compromised to get advantage of excise benefits meant for smaller units. The high price of better quality dyed fabrics was putting a constraint on the demand for them. The exports of better-dyed products was also suffering, as exports alone are generally not attractive. Exports of grey fabrics constitutes around 50 per cent of country's total fabric exports.

Thus irrational excise along with excise evasions, and numerous restrictions imposed in the path of gradual transformation of SSI into the medium and large-scale sector are among the important reasons generally forwarded for the slow technological improvement in weaving and dyeing segment.

The prime factor affecting the competitiveness of mill sector is the demand of fabrics in smaller lots by small garment units spread all over the country. The production of fabric in smaller lots is not very conducive for the mill sector, especially for units operating with modern technology such as air jet or shuttle less looms, having very high speed. Thus, modernisation could not take place in weaving units except for in those mills producing denim for exports or super fine verities, which is demanded in larger lots. The relatively high share of the mill sector in exports is explained by the fact that production is concentrated in heavy fabrics for which there is demand in larger lots in the international market. The most significant feature of the New Textile Policy announced on November 2, 2000 has been dereservation of garment from the small-scale sector. The dereservation of the garment industry will, over time, induce restructuring in the entire textile and clothing industry after the spinning stage. As was expected as a follow-up step after dereservation, the finance bill 2001 introduced MODVAT from the fibre to the garment stage with a 16 per cent excise duty. However, certain exemptions in the form of excise concession for hank yarn meant to be consumed in the handloom sector and for manual dyeing break the chain in MODVAT process. Similarly, the duty at the processing stage by independent processing houses for the small units is shifted away from ad valorem to specific duties. Thus the purpose of introducing MODVAT has been diluted. Moreover, excise duty avoidance at the fabrics stage by various units mainly in the decentralised sector could contribute to the slow growth of the organised garment industry. As most of yarn is consumed for production of fabrics, a possible solution is to impose excise duty at yarn stage even for value addition from fabrics stage with some possible options including the reimbursement of excise at later stage.

The garment industry also has several options by which it can avoid excise duty. Job work is exempted from any excise duty and hence a unit can evade taxes by mis-reporting in-house production. Similarly, the garment exporters need not pay any excise duty if their domestic sales are less than Rs. 10 million. These exemptions increase the evasion and hence weaken the impact of MODVAT.

Cotton Vs. Synthetic Products

One problem area, which is not addressed even in the finance bill 2001, is the relatively high excise and custom duty on synthetic yarn compared to cotton yarn. On the other hand, the excise duty on synthetic and cotton fabrics is currently at same rate. This causes tax escalation on the cotton products at the value-added stages. The new policy may not be adequately able to induce the desired modernisation at the weaving and dying stages unless a uniform rate of excise duty is imposed on cotton and synthetic yarn. India is presently a major exporter of cotton yarn and cotton fabrics but not of cotton made-ups or synthetic products. A rational policy demands equalisation of duty rates across cotton and synthetics at all stages of production.

Thus the textile policies introduced till 2000 has caused stagnation in technology progress both in weaving and dyeing units. In brief not much progress in technology have taken place in these sectors of production after the spinning stage. The policies till recently failed on account of both technology improvement and employment generation in handloom sector during eighties and nineties. The decline in handloom sector may continue with reforms and phasing out of export quota. The low technology development in dyeing units is responsible for the low per unit export price realisation. This is the cause for India's low share in world textile exports in value terms despite high share in quantity terms. We still have manual dyeing units and although we are able to export made-ups and garments due to our low labour cost and fabric competitiveness, we are not able to attract remunerative prices for the same. Hence, our products are basically of low quality.

The industry is set to face a dramatically new environment when domestic markets are opened up to imports. While this was expected to happen this year with the elimination of the final set of quantitative restrictions, the government has postponed the lifting of these restrictions citing the possibility of substantial damage to the livelihood of workers employed in this industry. However, this is only a postponement and at best buys time for the industry to push through a very quick process of restructuring for improved efficiency.

Changes in Pattern of Domestic Consumption in the form of Fabrics, Made-ups and Garments

The analyses so far was confined to quantitative changes in consumption and production pattern. This brings out that the total domestic availability of fabrics has increased from 18.12 square metre to 24.38 square metre during 1983 to 1999-2000 showing a rise of 1.87 per cent per annum. The fibre-wise analysis shows that per capita availability of cotton fabrics has declined, while that of synthetic fabrics has increased. However, quantitative data on availability of fabrics fail to capture several other noticeable changes that took place over the period of time. Due to shift in composition in favour of synthetic products, the per capita consumption at constant price increased at much higher rate then quantity due to shift in composition in favour of synthetic products. An attempt is made in the following section to work out whether or not there occurred any qualitative changes in consumption or production pattern. This analysis is important, as there are no reliable estimates regarding the extent of production of various fabrics such as garments, made-ups and others in the country.

The production data is available in two forms such as woven and hosiery. One has to rely on the data on consumer survey on household consumption of cotton and synthetics fabrics to find the variety-wise share within the woven fabrics. To apply it on the total fabrics available for domestic consumption, two assumptions are made. It is first assumed that the consumption pattern in the non-household sector is similar to the household sector. Secondly, it is further assumed that the production of fabrics in various qualities is identical to the consumption.[12] The woven cloth could be subdivided into following four varieties.

(1) Piece length
(2) Garments in piece length
(3) Readymade garments
(4) Household varieties.

Piece Length

The fabrics purchased by the consumer are in the form of piece length, which are then stitched by the tailor to produce various products such as garments, made-up or piece cloth. The fabrics purchased by the consumers in piece length form is in dyed form.

Garments in Piece Length

The fabrics purchased by the consumer for various uses such as sarees, dhoti, lungi, turban, angavastra, odhni, dupatta etc are called garments in piece length, as these are in the form of fabrics but ready to wear.

Readymade Garments

Ready-made garments are the garment products available in market in the form of ready to wear such as shirt, bush shirt, trouser, coat, half pant, frocks, and school uniforms.

Made-ups or Household Varieties

Made-ups or Household verities are the products available in the form of ready to use such as chaddar, bed sheet, bedcover,

12. The variety-wise exports of fabrics have already been discussed earlier.

blanket/rajai, pillowcase, khadi/carpet matt, towel and others.

Hosiery Garments

The hosiery processing is entirely different from weaving activity. The main hosiery items are towels and undergarments.

Share of Various Varieties in the Fabrics Available for Domestic Consumption

The domestic availability of cotton and synthetic fabrics worked out in the earlier analysis, could be further segregated into knitted and woven fabrics both for cotton and synthetic products. The results arrived are given in Table 4.62.

The woven fabrics consist of four varieties as discussed above. The Textile Committee data on household consumer survey provide details regarding various varieties of purchases of woven fabrics over time. The data on household consumption is converted into square metre equivalent by using conversion rates. The variety-wise consumption is available in pieces, metres etc. The conversion rates on piece and metre length equivalent to square metres are obtained from garment export entitlement policy, textile export entitlement policy, as well as using experts opinion. These are then applied on variety wise consumption of various items to work out weighted conversion rates. The respective shares of various varieties in the total consumption of woven products in household sector as obtained from Textile Committee data are given in Table 4.63.

The above data show that the share of made-ups (household variety) in the total domestic availability of woven fabrics has not changed much over time. The combined share of readymade garment and piece length also has not changed much over the period of time. However, the separate shares of readymade garments and piece length have undergone a significant change over the period of time. The share of readymade garments in total woven fabrics has more than doubled from 7.69 per cent in 1983 to 18.43 per cent in

Table 4.62

Knitted and Woven Fabrics Equivalent Availability of Cotton and Synthetic Products for Domestic Use

(Mn. Sq. Mts)

Year	*Cotton Total*	*Cotton Knitted*	*Cotton Woven*	*Synthetic Total*	*Synthetic Knitted*	*Synthetic Woven*	*Cotton & Synthetic Total*	*Cotton & Synthetic Knitted*	*Cotton & Synthetic Woven*
1983	8469	798	7671	4555	100	4455	13024	898	12126
1988-89	9448	1314	8134	6587	169	6418	16035	1483	14552
1989-90	9207	1355	7852	6542	133	6409	15749	1488	14261
1990-91	9825	1463	8362	7490	201	7289	17315	1664	15651
1991-92	8480	1467	7013	7696	224	7472	16176	1691	14485
1992-93	9184	1623	7561	7934	154	7780	17118	1777	15341
1993-94	9572	1819	7753	9680	215	9465	19252	2033	17218
1994-95	8469	1816	6653	10479	341	10138	18948	2157	16791
1995-96	10565	2685	7880	11627	373	11254	22192	3058	19134
1996-97	8807	2816	5991	12614	467	12147	21421	3284	18137
1997-98	8469	3054	5415	16191	484	15707	24660	3538	21122
1998-99	6407	2710	3697	15962	558	15404	22369	3268	19101
1999-00	6611	2707	3904	16606	490	16116	23217	3197	20020
Percentage Per Annum Compound Growth Rates									
1990-91 to 99-00	-3.61	8.91	-8.25	10.14	13.67	10.04	4.37	9.53	3.66
t-statistics	-2.63	6.43	-4.79	15.05	6.13	15.08	6.40	7.18	5.69

Source: As derived by the author.

1999-2000, correspondingly the share of piece length fabrics has declined. This means consumers' preference for the readymade garments has increased a lot, over the period, and correspondingly the tailor made stitching is losing ground. This pattern will further be strengthened with the recent decision of government in NTP 2000 to de-reserve the garment industry.

The quantity of fabrics consumed in each of these varieties is obtained by multiplying the total domestic availability of woven fabrics with the share of each variety and is given in Table 4.64.

Cotton Products

The variety-wise estimates of production for the cotton sector could be made in similar manner. The product-wise detailed data on cotton fibre is available from the Textile Committee Consumer Household Survey, Volume 2. The data is converted into square metre equivalent by analysing variety-wise household consumption data for year 1983, 1992 and 1998. Once the variety wise share of cotton textile products is worked out for these years, the share for other years is worked out by assuming constant annual growth rate between two years data for each variety. The values then arrived at are adjusted proportionally for total cotton fabrics available for domestic consumption. The variety-wise availability of cotton woven fabrics is given in Table 4.65.

The data in Table 4.66 shows that the share of piece lengths is declining, while the share of other varieties is increasing over the period of time.

Synthetic Products

The variety-wise quantum of synthetic products available for domestic consumption can be found by subtracting variety-wise cotton quantity from the total quantity of cotton and synthetic fabrics available for domestic consumption (Table 4.67).

Table 4.63

Various Varieties Share in Domestic Consumption of Woven Fabric

Year	*Household Variety*	*Readymade Garments*	*Piece Length*	*Readymade Garments & Piece Length*	*Garment in piece length*
1983	5.21	7.69	33.70	41.39	53.40
1988-89	6.01	10.26	29.62	39.88	54.11
1989-90	5.69	10.80	30.56	41.36	52.95
1990-91	5.56	11.44	31.03	42.47	51.97
1991-92	6.12	13.07	27.00	40.07	53.81
1992-93	5.42	12.48	26.77	39.25	55.33
1993-94	5.85	13.68	26.57	40.25	53.90
1994-95	6.30	14.96	26.33	41.29	52.40
1995-96	6.78	16.34	26.04	42.37	50.85
1996-97	7.28	17.80	25.69	43.49	49.24
1997-98	7.79	19.35	25.29	44.64	47.57
1998-99	6.32	16.92	24.92	41.84	51.84
1999-2000	6.78	18.43	24.59	43.03	50.19

Source: As derived by the author from Textile Committee data.

Table 4.64
Variety-wise Availability of Woven Fabrics for Domestic Use

(Mn. Sq. Mts)

Year	*Household Variety*	*Readymade Garment*	*Piece Length*	*Readymade Garments & Piece Length*	*Garment in Piece Length*	*Woven Fabrics*
1983	632	932	4086	5019	6475	12126
1988-89	875	1493	4310	5803	7874	14552
1989-90	811	1540	4358	5898	7551	14261
1990-91	870	1790	4857	6647	8134	15651
1991-92	886	1893	3911	5804	7794	14485
1992-93	831	1915	4107	6021	8488	15341
1993-94	1007	2355	4575	6931	9280	17218
1994-95	1059	2512	4421	6933	8799	16791
1995-96	1297	3126	4982	8107	9729	19134
1996-97	1320	3228	4659	7887	8930	18137
1997-98	1646	4086	5343	9429	10048	21122
1998-99	1207	3232	4761	7992	9901	19101
1999-2000	1358	3690	4924	8614	10049	20020

Source: As derived by the author from Textile Committee.

Variety-wise Estimates of Production of Fabrics

The above analysis is about the item-wise consumption in the domestic market. One could work out the item-wise production of fabrics from this data by combining the item-wise export analysis undertaken earlier. This will give us the total production of fabrics in various stages such as Piece length, Garment in Piece Length, made-ups and Readymade Garments.

Total Value of Cotton and Synthetic Textiles Products

The estimates of production have been revised in this study in quantity terms. The accurate estimates of production of fabrics are not only important to analyse the structural changes and future growth potential but also has important implications for policy perspective. Moreover, these estimates are used to derive the estimates of value added and employment.

An attempt is made in this study to find the value of output as well as value added in textiles and clothing sector based on these revised estimates of production of fabrics by applying ex-factory prices. This exercise of reworking the value added and value of output in textiles and clothing industry was initiated long back in the context of my Ph.D. work and in the meantime Central Statistical Organisation (CSO) has also revised its estimates of GDP in various sectors on the basis of revised methodology and come out with a new series with a base year 1993-94. The CSO based on old data and methodology estimated the share of textiles and clothing (excluding tailoring activity) in country's GDP at 4 per cent level during 1995-96 at 1980-81 prices. The share of textiles and clothing in GDP is reduced to half the old series estimates in the new CSO series based at 1993-94 prices.

The estimates derived in this study are compared with the CSO estimates and the methodologies adopted by CSO is thoroughly explained and examined. The method used to work out value of output for textile and garments sector is different in this study compared to the one used by CSO in new 1993-94 base series.

Table 4.65
Variety-wise Availability of Cotton Woven Fabrics for Domestic Use

(Mn. Sq. Mts)

Year	*Cotton Made-up*	*Cotton Readymade Garments*	*Cotton Piece Length*	*Cotton Garment & Piece Length*	*Garment in Piece Length*	*Total Woven*
1983	569	719	2281	3000	4102	7671
1988-89	756	900	1846	2746	4631	8134
1989-90	762	894	1683	2576	4513	7852
1990-91	846	980	1691	2672	4846	8362
1991-92	738	845	1337	2182	4093	7013
1992-93	824	938	1361	2299	4438	7561
1993-94	909	1049	1380	2429	4415	7753
1994-95	837	981	1168	2149	3668	6653
1995-96	1060	1262	1362	2624	4196	7880
1996-97	861	1040	1016	2057	3073	5991
1997-98	829	1017	900	1916	2670	5415
1998-99	601	749	600	1349	1747	3697
1999-2000	672	851	617	1468	1763	3904

Source: As derived by the author from Textile Committee.

Table 4.66
Percentage Share of Various Varieties in Cotton Woven Fabrics for Domestic Use

Year	*Cotton Made-up*	*Cotton Readymade Garments*	*Cotton Piece Length*	*Cotton Garment & Piece Length*	*Garment in Piece Length*	*Total. Woven*
1983	7.42	9.37	29.74	39.11	53.47	100.00
1988-89	9.30	11.06	22.70	33.76	56.94	100.00
1989-90	9.71	11.39	21.43	32.81	57.47	100.00
1990-91	10.12	11.72	20.22	31.95	57.95	100.00
1991-92	10.53	12.05	19.06	31.11	58.36	100.00
1992-93	10.90	12.40	18.00	30.40	58.70	100.00
1993-94	11.72	13.54	17.80	31.33	56.95	100.00
1994-95	12.57	14.74	17.56	32.30	55.13	100.00
1995-96	13.46	16.02	17.28	33.30	53.24	100.00
1996-97	14.37	17.37	16.96	34.33	51.30	100.00
1997-98	15.31	18.78	16.61	35.39	49.30	100.00
1998-99	16.25	20.27	16.23	36.50	47.25	100.00
1999-2000	17.22	21.80	15.81	37.61	45.17	100.00

Source: As derived by the author from Textile Committee.

Table 4.67
Variety-wise Availability of Synthetic Fabrics for Domestic Use

(Mn. Sq. Mts)

Year	*Synthetic Made-ups*	*Synthetic Readymade Garments*	*Synthetic Piece length*	*Synthetic Garment & Piece length*	*Garment in Piece Length*	*Total Woven*
1983-84	63	214	1805	2019	2374	4455
1988-89	118	593	2464	3057	3243	6418
1989-90	49	646	2675	3322	3039	6409
1990-91	24	810	3166	3975	3288	7289
1991-92	148	1048	2574	3622	3702	7472
1992-93	7	977	2746	3723	4050	7780
1993-94	99	1306	3196	4501	4865	9465
1994-95	222	1532	3253	4785	5131	10138
1995-96	237	1863	3620	5483	5534	11254
1996-97	459	2187	3643	5830	5857	12146
1997-98	817	3069	4443	7512	7378	15707
1998-99	606	2482	4161	6643	8154	15404
1999-2000	686	2839	4306	7145	8285	16116

Source: As derived by the author from Textile Committee.

Central Statistical Organisation (CSO) Methodology

Central Statistical Organisation (CSO) publishes the estimates of value added in textiles and garments in National Accounts Statistics (NAS). As per CSO, the share of textiles and clothing (excluding tailoring activity) in country's GDP was estimated at 4 per cent during 1995-96 as per the old base 1980-81. CSO explained the methodology in its publication Source and Methods 1989 and used Textile Commissioner's data on production of fabrics to work out value of output and value added in the unregistered sector. The production of fabrics data for cotton blended and manmade fabrics were obtained from the reports of the Textile Commissioner and for woollen, acrylic, polyester woollen, pure silk and hosiery were available in the reports of the *Consumption Panel Project,* All India Annual Survey of Textile Committee. CSO changed this methodology in between after it got realised that the conversion rates of fabrics to yarn adopted by Textiles Commissioner are arbitrary.

CSO has changed its methodology several times for working out GDP in textiles and clothing sector. Before shifting to current methodology CSO was using NSS survey results for unregistered manufacturing for year 1984-85 to work out the production and value added in the unregistered sector over time. For the registered manufacturing sector, CSO continued to use Annual Survey of Industries results. However, the data source for output of clothing for estimating the Private Final Consumption Expenditure (PFCE) continued to be office of the Textile Commissioner. The estimates of PFCE were not consistent with the estimates of GDP in textiles and clothing sector. CSO further changed its methodology during 1999 and shifted to a new series presently in use with base 1993-94. In the new series the PFCE estimates of textile products for unregistered manufacturing in consonance with the GDP estimates, are based on results of ASI, SSI and enterprises survey of unregistered manufacturing. This change in methodology has resulted in substantial downward revision of PFCE of clothing (Rs. 221290 million during the base year

1993-94). The present methodology adopted by CSO is discussed in detail below.

In its present method based on 1993-94 base year, the data used for registered sector continued to be of Annual Survey of Industries (ASI). The estimates of Gross Value Added (GVA) for the unregistered units belonging to Small Scale Industries group have been worked out by using the estimates of GVA per worker based on the results of *Second All-India Census on Small Scale Industrial Units,* 1987-88 published by Development Commissioner, Small Scale Industries and the corresponding work force. This GVA per worker has been duly inflated for the base year 1993-94 using WPI and the corresponding work force has been duly extrapolated using the inter-survey growth rate of the working force of the 43rd round and 50th round of NSS. The estimates of other unregistered manufacturing units *i.e.* the units other than the one belonging to SSI group mentioned above, have been compiled using the information on GVA per worker from the follow-up surveys of the *Economic Census for Directory Manufacturing Establishment (DMEs)* and from the results of NSS 51st round (1994-95) for *Non-Directory Manufactory Establishments (NDMEs)* and *Own Account Enterprises (OAEs).* The GVA per worker from the 51st round of NSS that relates to the year 1994-95 is suitably deflated to the year 1993-94. The estimates of work force for this portion of unregistered manufacturing *i.e.* for the units neither belonging to ASI nor to SSI, has been obtained from the total work force on manufacturing activities subtracting the work force relating to ASI and SSI (non-ASI) segments. In this method, the estimates of GDP from textiles sector get revised downward. The figures for latter years are then calculated by using Index of Industrial production for various commodities. Thus one of the limitations of CSO methodology is to depend upon the Index from Textile Commissioner for textile commodities to work out the production and value added over the period of time from the base year 1993-94 values. These limitations are discussed in detail along with the related issue.

Comparison of Coverage Adopted by CSO and in this Study

This study basically deals with cotton and synthetic textiles and clothing products. However, the fibre-wise and product stage-wise estimates derived in this study are not exactly comparable with the CSO estimates.

The prime reason for this is that as per this NIC classification, not only fabrics and related products are covered in it, but include all textiles and related activities such as ropes, blankets, carpets, coir etc. On the other hand, in our study, only fabrics related products are covered, which constitutes major share of textiles and clothing products. Moreover, the tailoring activity in NIC classification is covered under the service activity, the data for which is available separately. The other differences are NIC although define 23 as cotton textiles, but covers in it cotton blended and other products as well. This is because a unit which is dominantly cotton producing, all its products are put under the cotton textiles including those of non-cotton and *vice-versa* as a unit could only be classified under one head. There are several dominantly cotton producing units, which are producing other than 100 per cent cotton products also in large quantity. Similarly not only textiles but other products are also included in this industry in case the unit is dominantly cotton producing. This is major limiation of CSO data. However, in the method adopted by us in this study, only 100 per cent cotton products are covered in the cotton textiles.

Similarly, comparing the estimates for Synthetic products, care has to be taken that the estimates derived in this study covers all spun (excluding 100% cotton textiles and clothing products) and filament textiles and clothing products. On the other hand, CSO estimates for NIC 24 covers in it cotton and other products as well. This is because a unit which is dominantly synthetic producing, all its products are put under the synthetic textiles including those of non-cotton and *vice-versa* as a unit could only be classified under one head. In addition, this industry as per NIC classification is also meant to include data for wool and silk textile product, while we in our study have only taken synthetic textiles.

The estimates of CSO for textile and clothing products at two-digit NIC classification are categorised into following groups.

NIC Code	Description of Industry
23	Manufacture of Cotton Textiles
24	Manufacture of Wool, Silk and Synthetic Fibre Textiles.
25	Manufacture of Jute, hemp and Mesta Textiles and
26	Manufacture of textile Products

Comparison of Estimates Derived in this Study with CSO

Cotton Textiles

In this study, an attempt is made to arrive at production values of cotton textiles by using sector-wise revised estimates of production of fabrics and sector-wise ex-factory prices. The sector-wise analysis is important as average price differ quite a lot among various sectors. The sector-wise ex-factory price as well as market price is available over time[13] for the fabrics produced in mill sector from the Compendium of Textile Statistics, Textile Commissioner. However, for the powerloom sector and handloom sector, the ex-factory price is not available while the market price is available for the powerloom sector in Textile Commissioner's report. The ex-factory price for the powerloom sectors is obtained by working out the ex-factory and retail price ratio for mill sector over time and applying the same proportion for the powerloom fabrics.[14] In the case of handloom sector, the ratio of retail prices paid by consumers for the cotton fabrics of handloom sector compared to mill and powerloom sectors jointly is multiplied with the combined ex-factory prices of mill and powerloom sectors to

13. The ex-factory prices for years 1983 and 1988-89 for mill sector are worked out by assuming changes in ex-factory price pattern similar to exports prices for the sector.
14. For the years 1983 and 1988-89, the procedure adopted for powerloom sector is similar to the procedure in case of mill sector.

work out the ex-factory price for the handloom sector. The data for retail prices for these sectors during the year 1994 is worked out from the average price paid during five years period 1992 to 1996 available from Consumer Household Survey, Textile Committee to take out the impact of yearly fluctuations. To work out the ex-factory price for the cotton handloom fabrics over the period of time from the year 1994-95 (1994) data, it is assumed that the quality and prices in the exports and domestic segment are moving in the same proportion. Similar procedure is adopted for working out the ex-factory price for the hosiery sector. The sector-wise prices derived thus are then multiplied by the production of fabrics in various sectors to derive the value of cotton fabrics produced in the country.

The estimates derived this way only account for 50 per cent of the dyed fabrics value for various sectors. This is because 50 per cent of dyeing of fabrics is taking place outside these sectors in independent processing units.[15] To work out the total value of fabrics production, the dyeing cost of roughly 20 per cent of the grey fabrics cost (derived from Werner International data) should also be included for the remaining 50 per cent grey fabrics. After working out the total value of fabrics produced in the country, one needs to add into it the value of cotton yarn export at ex-factory price to arrive at the total production in the cotton textile sector. The value of yarn consumed for other than fabrics use is not included in these estimates, as most of it is consumed as the input in garment industry as sewing thread. This is automatically to be taken care off, while one works out the tailoring charges for ready-made garments and stitched cloth. However, the value added in the textile sector will be underestimated to that extent, which is anyway a very small proportion.

To work out the value added from the estimates of value of output derived above, the value added share is worked out. The value added shares from raw cotton to yarn and

15. The export of fabrics in grey form is approximately 50 per cent of the total direct exports of fabrics.

raw cotton to fabrics worked out are 38.18 per cent and 41.06 per cent respectively during 1999. These shares changes over the period of time. The value-added share in output for different years are worked out by using average share for the period 1989 to 1999 from the data of Cost of Production data from International textile manufacturing federation, Zurich. The values thus arrived are given in Table 4.68.

The value added for cotton textiles derived in this study is much lower compared to CSO estimates, primarily due to the difference in definition. This is because lots of non-cotton textile products are covered as cotton textile products according to CSO definition as explained earlier.

Synthetic Textiles

Sector-wise and fibre-wise analysis for the synthetic segment is not possible as detailed required for the same is not available. A few assumptions have been made even to arrive at the estimates of total value added in synthetic sector. The average ex-factory price for synthetic fabrics is worked out by using the average export price of synthetic fabrics and multiplying it with the ratio of average ex-factory and exports price of cotton fabrics. This has been worked over the period of time. The ex-factory prices worked out this way reflect average prices for around 50 per cent of grey and 50 per cent dyed fabrics. The total value of output for dyed fabrics is obtained by applying similar methodology as in the case of cotton textile. However, adjustments have been made for filament yarn both for exports and production. Filament yarn is raw material for textiles industry unlike spun yarn in which fibre is raw material. The results derived this way are given in Table 4.69.

The share of value added for synthetic textiles in GDP derived in this study is much higher compared to CSO estimates. This is because of difference in definition as explained earlier as lots of non-synthetic textile products are falling in NIC code 24(CSO data), which has been the closest in CSO data for comparison as synthetic products.

Table 4.68
Total Production and Value Added in India's Cotton Textile Sector

(Mn. Rs.)

Year	*Value of Output*	*Value Added*		*Value of Output*	*Value Added*	*CSO Value Added*	*Value Added share in GDP (%)*	*CSO Value Added share in GDP (%)*
		Total	*Mill Sector Share %*					
	At Current Prices			*At 1993-94 Prices*			*At 1993-94 Prices*	
1983-84	44593	19881	45.06	96242	42908		0.91	
1988-89	72664	32289	51.55	121158	53838		0.88	
1989-90	84043	37297	46.71	123151	54653		0.83	
1990-91	100671	44618	42.23	136675	60575		0.87	
1991-92	118639	52388	46.44	140783	62166		0.89	
1992-93	129121	56966	50.54	140630	62044		0.84	
1993-94	154347	68007	45.06	154347	68007	90380	0.87	1.16
1994-95	166705	73015	51.18	125830	55112	94990	0.66	1.13
1995-96	201405	88130	52.67	138904	60781	88630	0.68	0.99
1996-97	208528	90281	55.87	150507	65161	107520	0.67	1.11
1997-98	208528	103229	47.35	146502	72524	109600	0.71	1.08
1998-99	217861	98496	57.24	150510	68046	101130	0.63	0.93
1999-2000	240560	95646	59.61	166750	66300		0.58	

Note: WPI at 1993-94 prices for years before 1993-94 is worked out by using WPI 1980-81 base data.

Source: As derived by the author

Table 4.69
Total Production and Value Added in India's Synthetic Textile Sector

(Mn. Rs.)

Year	Value of Output	Value Added: Total	Value Added: Mill Sector Share %	Value of Output	Value Added	CSO Value Added	Value Added share in GDP (%)	CSO Value Added share in GDP (%)
	At Current Prices			At 1993-94 Prices			At 1993-94 Prices	
1983-84	17927	7723	61.50	27670	11920		0.25	
1988-89	57390	24640	36.14	80227	34445		0.56	
1989-90	70858	30379	29.23	88014	37734		0.57	
1990-91	95927	41194	24.94	116031	49827		0.72	
1991-92	137607	58825	23.54	154748	66153		0.94	
1992-93	114054	48410	30.65	120072	50965		0.69	
1993-94	167557	71555	23.29	167557	71555	53140	0.92	0.68
1994-95	175056	74227	28.69	165399	70132	56000	0.84	0.67
1995-96	178116	74798	32.53	157262	66041	49740	0.73	0.55
1996-97	204259	86428	23.13	213210	90215	66140	0.93	0.68
1997-98	203606	84108	23.29	234528	96881	64100	0.95	0.63
1998-99	232198	94856	22.48	284463	116207	65890	1.07	0.61
1999-2000	219008	88706	23.41	264736	107227		0.93	

Note: CSO Value Added at 1993-94 base for year before 1993-94 are converted by using values of 1980-81 base.
Source: As derived by the author.

Value Added Estimates in Cotton and Synthetic Textiles Sector

Thus the fibre-wise estimates derived in this study differ widely compared with the National Accounts Statistics (CSO). However, the difference is not that wide for total value added in cotton and synthetic textiles derived in this study (Table 4.70) compared to CSO (NAS) estimates (NIC code 23 & 24). CSO estimates are expected to be 10 per cent higher due to inclusion of silk and wool products. Moreover, CSO estimates include all bases of yarn such as production of ropes etc. The gap varies for various years due to the approximations used in CSO method to arrive at various years values from base year data by using Index of Industrial production (IIP). In the case of textiles products, the IIP is based on production data available from Textile Commissioner. So even in revised estimates, the CSO has to depend upon the sector-wise production of fabrics available from Textile Commissioner. CSO has infact stopped using Textile Commissioner's data as it was felt that there estimates of production of fabrics are not scientifically drawn.

The Textile Commissioner assumes a fixed conversion rate from yarn to fabrics, while the actual conversion rate should depend upon the weight of each sector and count composition of yarn used within the sector. Moreover, the diversion of hank yarn to powerloom sector is taking place on large scale, which also affects conversion rates. Moreover, the IIP based on Textile Commissioner data cannot capture qualitative changes in fabrics. Under these limitations, it seems that the methodology used in this study has comparative advantage compared to the methodology used by CSO.

Total Value of Stitching for Ready-made Garments and Tailor-made Products

To work out the stitching charges, it is important to know the total fabrics being stitched in the country. The piece-length and readymade garments go through stitching process in the woven fabrics. In addition knitted fabrics go through stitching process. The total fabrics ultimately go through the stitching

Table 4.70
Total Value of Cotton and Synthetic Textiles at 1993-94 Prices

	Share of Various sectors in value added contribution from Yarn to Fabrics					*Total Value Added in Textile sector*			*CSO estimates*	
	Mill	*Power-loom*	*Hand-loom*	*Hosiery*	*Total*	*Mn Rs. current prices*	*Mill Sector share*	*Mn. Rs. at 93-94 prices*	*Mn. Rs. 93-94 prices*	*CSO/our estimates*
1983-84	31.67	18.14	46.58	3.61	100.00	27604	49.66	54828	—	—
1988-89	24.73	36.05	32.47	6.75	100.00	56929	44.88	88283	—	—
1989-90	23.17	43.64	25.46	7.73	100.00	67676	38.87	92387	—	—
1990-91	22.23	45.43	24.61	7.73	100.00	85812	33.93	110403	—	—
1991-92	20.38	41.38	30.09	8.15	100.00	111213	34.33	128319	—	—
1992-93	17.07	50.56	23.37	8.99	100.00	105376	41.40	113008	—	—
1993-94	16.40	48.53	26.24	8.83	100.00	139562	33.89	139562	143520	1.03
1994-95	16.30	50.30	24.23	9.17	100.00	147242	39.84	125244	150990	1.21
1995-96	13.70	53.45	21.61	11.24	100.00	162928	43.42	126822	138370	1.09
1996-97	13.91	50.48	23.88	11.73	100.00	176709	39.86	155377	173660	1.12
1997-98	11.80	48.20	28.95	11.05	100.00	187337	36.55	169405	173700	1.03
1998-99	12.68	46.52	29.98	10.82	100.00	193352	40.19	184253	167020	0.91
1999-2000	10.85	49.32	28.78	11.05	100.00	184352	42.19	173527		

Note: WPI at 1993-94 prices for years before 1993-94 is worked out by using WPI 1980-81 base data.
Source: CSO and as derived by the author.

process both for domestic and export segment is worked out in quantity terms earlier and are combined in Table 4.71.

Per unit stitching charges are worked out by applying the International Werner data for year 1994. The ratio of tailoring cost to fabrics cost for shirt available from International Werner data is used and applied on average per unit price of dyed fabrics in India to find the per square metre tailoring cost for shirts during 1994. For working out the stitching charges for other products, the ratio of export prices of these products to export price of shirt is applied on tailoring cost for shirt. The stitching charges thus worked out for each product are applied on the quantity of each items used for stitching as available from consumer household survey and is given in Table 4.72. The average tailoring charges per square metre of fabrics thus worked out is Rupees 16.71 during the year 1994-95. To work out the tailoring cost per square metre over the period of time, the tailoring cost for year 1994-95 is inflated/deflated with the comparative per unit export prices of garments during the period.

The stitching charges are then applied on the total quantity of fabrics being stitched over the period of time. The value-added share in stitching charges for the unregistered sector in the new series as obtained from CSO records is 58 per cent. This ratio is used to work out the value added in tailoring cost in our study. There exist difference between the share of value added in registered and unregistered sector. This is due to different composition and integration of production stages. However, some difference in share of value added in output in registered and unregistered sector is due to higher use of inputs in registered sector compared to unregistered sector. Thus the share of value added in output should be higher for unregistered sector compared to registered sector, but due to lack of data, we used same ratio. The results regarding the total value added in tailoring activity including garment industry are given in Table 4.73.

Table 4.71
Type of Fabrics Stitched in Domestic and Export Market

(Mn. Sq. Mts)

	Woven Garments and Piece Length					Knitted Garments					Total	
	Domestic		Exports*		Total	Domestic		Exports		Total	Total	Mill Sector Share in Total
	Cotton	Synthetic	Cotton	Synthetic		Cotton	Synthetic	Cotton	Synthetic			
1983	3000	2019	151	23	5193	798	100	83	1	982	6175	44.14
1988-89	2746	3057	337	97	6237	1314	169	205	6	1694	7931	43.74
1989-90	2576	3322	372	177	6447	1355	133	306	6	1800	8247	44.83
1990-91	2672	3975	418	220	7285	1463	201	367	12	2043	9328	43.56
1991-92	2182	3622	489	228	6521	1467	224	435	9	2135	8656	43.66
1992-93	2299	3723	527	221	6770	1623	154	573	12	2362	9132	43.15
1993-94	2429	4501	588	209	7727	1819	215	695	15	2744	10471	43.62
1994-95	2149	4785	675	283	7892	1816	341	633	16	2806	10698	43.90
1995-96	2624	5483	714	306	9127	2685	373	738	19	3815	12942	46.36
1996-97	2057	5830	754	310	8951	2816	467	841	27	4151	13102	47.14
1997-98	1916	7512	765	329	10522	3054	484	985	31	4554	15076	47.89
1998-99	1349	6643	762	347	9101	2710	558	1101	49	4418	13519	45.29
1999-00	1468	7145	736	356	9705	2707	490	1184	71	4452	14157	45.48

Note: * Exports data in this column includes only garments exports.
Source: As derived by the author.

Table 4.72
Main Varieties Consumed in Domestic Household Sector during 1998

(Sq. Mts)

Shirt/Bush Shirt Manila	*Coat/Suit*	*Trouser*	*Half Pant/Short Quarter Pant*	*Pajama Salwar Churidar*	*Kurta/ Zubba Kameez*	*School Uniform*	*Blouses/ Choli*	*Frock*
0.35	0.02	0.12	0.09	0.06	0.04	0.07	0.10	0.26
Skirt/Midi	Petti Coat	Brassier	Night Suit Dressing Gown/Night Gown	Maxi	Baba Suit	Others		Total
0.04	0.41	0.01	0.64	0.04	0.14	0.34		2.72

Source: As derived from Textile Committee data.

Table 4.73

Value Added in Tailoring Sector including for Ready-made Garments

Year	*Value Added at 1993-94 price (Mn. Rs.)*			*Ready-made Garments at 1993-94 Prices (Mn. Rs.)*			*Tailoring sector value added share in GDP at 1993-94 Prices*		
	Cotton	*Synthetic*	*Total*	*Value*	*Share*	*CSO*	*Cotton*	*Synthetic*	*Total*
1983-84	14655	7790	22446	7593	33.83	—	0.31	0.17	0.48
1988-89	24123	17449	41573	18982	45.66	—	0.39	0.28	0.68
1989-90	25413	20060	45472	21446	47.16	—	0.39	0.31	0.69
1990-91	31077	27844	58921	28241	47.93	—	0.45	0.40	0.85
1991-92	33970	30330	64301	35248	54.82	—	0.48	0.43	0.92
1992-93	46439	38006	84445	46470	55.03		0.63	0.51	1.14
1993-94	49011	43773	92783	52237	56.30	50860	0.63	0.56	1.19
1994-95	41733	42937	84670	49676	58.67	49900	0.50	0.51	1.01
1995-96	49706	45442	95148	58525	61.51	55470	0.55	0.51	1.06
1996-97	50467	51761	102228	65876	64.44	56040	0.52	0.53	1.05
1997-98	49921	62074	111994	72304	64.56	58950	0.49	0.61	1.10
1998-99	49289	63230	112519	72891	64.78	56870	0.46	0.58	1.04
1999-2000	50105	66275	116380	75915	65.23		0.43	0.58	1.01

Note: WPI at 1993-94 prices for years before 1993-94 are worked out by using WPI 1980-81 data.

Source: As derived by the author.

Total Value Added in Textiles and Clothing Sector for the Cotton and Synthetic Products

The value added share of textiles and clothing sector in GDP is estimated at 2.52 per cent during 1999-2000 (Table 4.74). It's share was 2.44 per cent of the GDP during 1990-91. The share of mill sector in total textiles and clothing value added worked out is 42.29 per cent during 1999-2000. The value added in textiles and clothing sector has grown by 6.1 per cent per annum during 1990-91 to 1999-2000 as against the GDP growth of 6 per cent per annum during the same period. The production of fabrics in quantity terms grew by 5.59 per cent during the same period.

The share of textiles is 1.51 per cent and of stitching for ready made and tailoring goods is 1.01 per cent of GDP. The total value added in the cotton segment accounts for 1.01 per cent of the GDP and that of synthetic segment 1.51 per cent. Thus the share of cotton products is low compared to synthetic products in total textiles and clothing production (including tailoring service) in the estimates derived in this study.

The results derived in this study are comparable with CSO estimates and the small difference is expected due to change in definition of various products. However, there is difference in pattern over time in the estimates derived in this study and CSO estimates, as the CSO estimates over time are based on the Index of Industrial Production (IIP) based on production data from Textile Commissioner. The difference could widen over time as Textile Commissioner's data could deviate from actual depending upon change in count composition of yarn used in various sectors. Thus in the long run, there is possibility that the method adopted by the CSO (NAS) to work out value added over the period of time may give results widely different than the actual.

An attempt is also made to find the share of mill sector in total value added in textiles and clothing sector. Mill sector share is estimated at 42 per cent during 1999-2000. CSO data is available for the latest year 1997-98 as tailoring service value added is not available so far the year 1998-99. The share of

Table 4.74
Value Added in Textiles and Clothing Sector

(Mn. Rs.)

	Cotton	Synthetic	Textiles	Clothing	Total		Total		Cotton	Synthetic	Textiles	Clothing	Total
	Value Added at 1993-94 Prices*					Mill's Share$	CSO	CSO Regs. Sec. Share	Value Added Share in GDP at 1993-94 Prices				
(1)	(2)	(3)	(4)	(5)	(6)	(7)	(8)	(9)	(10)	(11)	(12)	(13)	(14)
1983	57563	19710	54828	22445	77273	40.86	—	—	1.22	0.42	1.16	0.48	1.64
1988-89	77961	51894	88283	41572	129855	38.55	—	—	1.27	0.84	1.44	0.68	2.11
1989-90	80066	57794	92387	45473	137860	34.61	—	—	1.22	0.88	1.41	0.69	2.10
1990-91	91652	77671	110402	58921	169323	31.04	—	—	1.32	1.12	1.59	0.85	2.44
1991-92	96136	96483	128319	64300	192619	33.28	—	—	1.37	1.37	1.83	0.92	2.74
1992-93	108483	88971	113009	84445	197454	37.94	—	—	1.47	1.21	1.53	1.14	2.68
1993-94	117018	115328	139562	92784	232346	33.29	24130	51.71	1.50	1.48	1.79	1.19	2.97
1994-95	96845	113069	125244	84670	209914	38.44	25039	52.48	1.16	1.35	1.49	1.01	2.50
1995-96	110487	111483	126822	95148	221970	41.94	24530	44.70	1.23	1.24	1.41	1.06	2.47
1996-97	115628	141976	155376	102228	257604	40.29	28343	47.70	1.19	1.46	1.60	1.05	2.66
1997-98	122445	158955	169405	111995	281400	37.96	29247	46.07	1.20	1.56	1.67	1.10	2.77
1998-99	117335	179437	184253	112519	296772	40.65	—	—	1.08	1.66	1.70	1.04	2.74
1999-2000	116405	173502	173527	116380	289907	42.29	—	—	1.01	1.51	1.51	1.01	2.52

(Contd....)

(Contd...)

(1)	(2)	(3)	(4)	(5)	(6)	(7)	(8)	(9)	(10)	(11)	(12)	(13)	(14)
				Percentage Per Annum Compound Growth Rates									
1990-91 to 99-00	2.57 (3.43)	9.14 (10.38)	5.43 (5.83)	7.19 (7.68)	6.06 (9.49)	—	—	—	—	—	—	—	—

Note:
1. $ This is share of mill sector and ready-made garments in total textiles and clothing value added at constant prices.
2. CSO (NAS) estimates include NIC code 23, 24, 26 and Service activity. Textile products in CSO (NAS) refers to clothing and garments
3. * means CSO data for tailoring service is not available for year 1998-99 so far.

Source: As derived by the author.

registered sector in total textiles and clothing value added worked out is 46 per cent. There is both of difference between mill sector and registered sector.

Expenditure on Textiles and Clothing Final Consumption in the Country

After working out the total value of textiles and clothing production in the country, it is possible to work out estimates of final consumption on textiles and clothing products. As our estimates of value added are not much different from CSO estimates, the total private final expenditure should also not be much different.

This is particularly true as our estimates of total fabrics available for domestic consumption is almost same as derived by Textile Committee survey on household and non-household sector. However, the estimates of total private consumption on textile goods as derived by Textile Committee data are much different than the CSO estimates.

The estimates of Textile Committee are worked out by using consumers survey data, while those of CSO are worked out by using retail prices and domestic availability of textile products. Thus there is need to go into the detail of these differences by analysing the methodology used by CSO.

CSO derives consumption estimates by using the value of production at ex-factory prices in each industry. The share of final products in the total value of production for each industry is worked out by identifying the products used for final consumption. The consumption by the government and non-profit institutions departments is taken out of it. The excise and sales duties paid under the industry head and other costs such as trade and transport margins are then added up to find the market value of final products in each industry. The export of final products is then excluded from it to work out the domestic availability for private consumption. This is added up for the industries NIC code 23, 24 and 26 to find the total value of private final consumption expenditure on textiles and clothing products. The crucial limitation in CSO estimates is regarding the assumption of share of final products in each industry and the estimate of trade and transport margin.

Another limitation of CSO estimates seems to be decision regarding market prices to work out private final consumption. CSO seems to be guided by Textile Commissioner data on retail price. Textile Commissioner data on retail prices seems to only relevant for large towns and cities and do not represent the actual price spent by the consumers in rural and far flung areas. The final market prices paid by the consumer depend upon the number of intermediaries at different stages and trade and transport margin for each of them. The final prices paid by the consumers in several cases even exceed the three times the ex-factory prices of the products. This gets confirmed when one compares the ex-factory price data available from Textile Commissioner and market price as available from Textile Committee data on household survey. Thus, Textile Committee data on consumption in both quantity and value terms seems reliable. Thus, the issue regarding the appropriate market prices should be looked more carefully by CSO and Ministry of Textiles. The definition of retail price published by Textile Commissioner should be made clearer and centres and products surveyed should be clearly specified from which the price data is collected.

An attempt has been made in this study to work the total expenditure incurred by consumers on textiles and garments products in the country by using two sets of prices provided by the Textile Committee and the Textile Commissioner. The two market prices adopted in this study give wide differences in the estimates of total expenditure on textiles and clothing goods in the country. The share of textile and clothing (government and non-profit institutions is not taken out) in private final consumption expenditure worked out by two methods is approximately 5.6 per cent and 10.1 per cent respectively. This difference due to the prices needs to be looked into by the CSO and the Ministry of Textiles.

Employment

Employment is one of the most important parameter as it has major economic socio implications. It needs special attention as labour reforms are going to be introduced soon. An attempt is made in this study to work out the estimates of employment in textiles and clothing sector. This is important, as estimates of employment provided by Textile Commissioners are not observed but are derived from these estimates of production of fabrics. The Textile Commissioner's estimates of production of fabrics are controversial as these are based on unscientific conversion rates of fabrics from yarn. The estimates of employment in textiles and clothing sector provided by Textile Commissioners need to be critical examined, as these estimates are much higher and growing over time compared to NSS and Economic Senses data. Thus the issue has been discussed in detail in this section and attempt is made in this study to estimates the employment in textiles and clothing sector on the basis of revised estimates of sector-wise production of fabrics derived in this study earlier.

Employment Coefficients

To work out the employment estimates from sector-wise production of fabrics, it is important to know the employment requirement per unit of production of fabrics in various sectors. Mazumdar (1991) study provided the detailed data on the requirement of workers per shift in various sectors. The employment co-efficient for the handloom and powerloom sectors are derived from a World Bank Survey of a textile town, MAU, in Uttar Pradesh. For the mill sector ASI factory sector data is taken. The study also undertook cost-benefit analysis of weaving technology in the three sectors of the industry (mentioned in Review of literature),[16] but we are concerned with the employment estimates.

16. In this analysis of cost-benefit, the cost of weaving yarn of 40s*40s count is worked out both from private and social profitability angle. Mazumdar estimated that powerloom sector is most profitable in the interest rate of 13-46 per cent. This explains the phenomenal growth

(Contd...)

Handloom Sector

In the handloom sector, 2 adult male equivalent worker are required (one adult male, which is assisted by other family members casually) per loom per 8 hours to produce 11 metres of cloth. Handloom sector works 1 shift per day. Thus, 2.0 adult workers produce 11 metres of fabrics in the handloom sector per day per loom. Thus 2.0 employees could produce 11x365=4015 metre of fabrics. There is need of 1.07 million employees at full capacity utilisation.

To work out the employment in the handloom sector, various assumptions/modifications have been made. Handloom sector on an average works 9 months per year, as weavers do not operate in rainy seasons. It can work only for one shift per day during the daylight. Thus the estimates of total main employment in this sector are estimated at 1.43 million.

Further, the utilisation level may be around 60 per cent even for 9 months period for which it works, due to closures or under-utilisation. This may be due to various socio-economic reasons such as attending marriages and other ceremonies and non-availability of raw material. Based on these assumptions, the estimates of main employment generated in the handloom sector is 2.38 million.

The estimates of employment derived above are indication of main employment generated in this sector. However, other members of the family meet the requirement of one worker. These members of the weaver are casually employed. As

---

(Contd...)

of powerloom sector. However, at shadow wages (assuming mills wages are high due to institutional influence), the switchover value of rate of interest at which mills become profitable relative to powerloom is in the range of 13.2 to 30.1 per cent. Thus the rate of interest over which powerloom sector is profitable is greatly reduced after accounting for shadow costs. For handloom sector, after accounting for the shadow wages and cost of land and building, the switchover interest rate at which it become profitable relative to powerloom falls in the range of 34.7 to 46 per cent.

mentioned above, other family members. (around three number) on the average assist one adult male weaver. Thus, it could be argued that instead of 2 workers including the weaver, the actual worker employed including casual worker may be arround 4 on an average. Thus, the estimates of main and casual employment generated in the handloom sector is 4.77 million during 1999-2000. Same procedure is applied for other years and estimates derived are given in Table 4.75.

Powerloom and Hosiery Sector

In case of powerloom and hosiery sector 1.6 adults male equivalent workers (one weaver and others) are required per loom to produce 33 metre fabrics per 8 hours shift. Powerloom sector works 1.5 shifts on an average per day. Thus, 2.4 adult workers produce on an average 49.5 metre of fabrics in the powerloom sector per day per loom.

To work out employment estimates in powerloom and hosiery sector, the various assumptions/modifications have been made. The powerloom and hosiery sector is unorganised and workers are employed only in case there is work. The workers only get one-day holiday in a week in addition to some other holidays and hence 90 per cent utilisation is expected. These workers derive their main earnings from this occupation.

Mill Sector

In the case of mill sector, the official estimates of employment are taken, which include employment in spinning and weaving[17] segment. By adding the employment generation in the mill, powerloom, hosiery and handloom sectors, the total employment in textile sector is worked out in Table 4.75.

---

17. In case of mill sector 0.8 adult male equivalent workers are required per loom to produce 33 metre fabrics per 8 hours. Mill sector works 2.5 shifts on an average per day. Thus, 2.0 adult workers are required to produce 82.5 metres of fabrics in the mill sector per day per loom. In addition, the workers are required in mill sector for spinning the yarn. But there are number of workers employed in mill sectors are far more in excess due to low utilisation. The official data for mill sector is reliable and is given in Table 7.

Output and Employment Relation in Various Sectors

It has been estimated from the above analysis that to produce the same amount of fabrics in handloom, powerloom and mill sector, the employment generation differ quite a lot. Powerloom sector needs to employee 2 times the worker needs required needs in the mill sector to produce the same amount of fabrics, while handloom sector needs to employee 7.5 times for the same amount of quantity. Moreover, the handloom sector works only 9 months and that too at not more than 60 per cent utilisation due to various socio-economic factors. The numbers of casual workers employed are also very large. This is the reason that this sector is not economical, but for the same reason employees around 12 to 15 times more workers than mill sector and 6 to 7 times more workers than powerloom sector to produce the same amount of fabrics. The gap is expected to further widening with the technology progress in various sectors.

These ratios could be worked out in terms of value added as well. The value added per unit of fabrics in mill sector is 3.16 times and 3.02 times in powerloom and hosiery sector compared to handloom sector during 1999-2000. Thus the employment per unit of value added in handloom sector is expected to be 12.5 to 16 times higher at 1999-2000 prices compared to only 2 to 2.5 times in case of powerlom sector. This is better measure of labour intensity.

Garment Sector

An attempt has also been made to work out estimates of employment in garment segment, both for ready-made and tailor-made products. The estimates of fabrics consumed in quantity terms in the form of made-ups, piece-length (which is latter stitched), garment piece-length and read-made garment are worked out earlier. These estimates are then used to work out employment by working out employment-output ratio for the garment sector. The data on wages share in cost of production of garments is available from Werner International Inc. Management Consultants, Brussels, Belgium and wage rate data is available from International Textile

Manufacturing Federation, Zurich (Chapter 5). Thus number of workers required to produce per unit and hence per square metre of garment are estimated. This is turn is used to find the total workers required in garment segment to stitch the given amount of fabrics.

Total Estimates of Employment in Textiles and Clothing Segment

Using the above coefficients for each of the sectors, the employment estimates in textiles and clothing sector for various sectors are worked over time out in Table 4.75. The estimates derived in this study are comparable with the CSO estimates available for the year 1993-94. The estimates of main employment in textile and ready-made garment sector as derived in our study are 8.15 million during 1993-94 as compared to CSO estimates of 7.30 million (NIC 23, 247, 248, 260, 263, 265, 266, 267 & 268) (Table 4.75, Column 6). However, the estimates differ widely from the textile ministry estimates. In case the estimates of employment during 1993-94 in tailor segment are added, the total main employment generated by textiles and clothing segment adds up to 9.20 million and main and casual add to 12.37 million during 1993-94. These estimates are 10.17 million (main) and 13.14 million (main and casual) respectively during 1999-2000, which are much lower compared to Textile Ministry estimates of 21.75 million. An attempt is made to find the possible reasons for so high estimates predicted by the Ministry. By applying the sector-wise employment coefficient used above on the Textile Commissioner's sector-wise data of production of fabrics, the employment estimates worked out are 19.23 million in Textiles (main and casual) and 20.99 million in Textiles and clothing (main and casual) sectors during 1996-97.

Ministry estimates of 21.75 million employment are revised downward recently to 17.97 million based on certain survey results undertaken by Ministry. For the year 1998-99, the revised estimates of employment by the Ministry are 17.40 million as against 12.69 million derived in this study. Ministry estimates of employment for the year 1999-2000 are still awaited, while estimates derived in this study are 12.87 million. Thus, the prime reason for difference in estimates derived in our study and Textile Ministry estimates was the difference. These estimates are close to estimate of sector-wise production of fabrics. Thus the Ministry slowly seems to be realising the mistake. However, Ministry estimates still are higher both according to estimates derived in this study and CSO estimate. It is suggested that the discrepancies in Ministry estimates caused due to wrong estimates of sector-wise production of fabrics should be corrected at all stages in a logical manner.

To conclude, one could say that the estimates of main employment in textiles and clothing sector grew by only 2.93 per cent per annum and main and casual by 1.47 per cent during 1990-91 to 1999-2000. This is against the high growth of value added in textiles and clothing sector. The GDP in textiles and clothing sector grew by 6.1 per cent per annum during 1990-91 to 1999-2000 as against the overall GDP growth of 6 per cent per annum during the same period. Thus the share of textiles and clothing in total GDP grew marginally to 2.52 per cent during 1999-2000 from 2.44 per cent during 1990-91. The production of fabrics in quantity terms also grew by 5.59 per cent per annum during the same period. Thus the employment per unit of output has come down and the labour productivity has increased due to shift in production from handloom to powerloom sector during nineties. However, considering the fact that the growth in overall registered manufacturing sector was jobless during nineties despite 7 to 8 per cent growth in its value added, the performance of textile and clothing sector seems not bad. However, looking at the entire period 1983 to 1999-2000, the growth in employment has taken place at a very marginal rate. The growth in employment in textiles and clothing sector including tailor made products is estimated to grow by 0.15 per cent during 1983 to 1999-2000 as against 1.48 per cent per annum during 1990-91 to 1999-2000. These estimates are based on the assumption that additional outputs in a sector generate same amount of employment and growth in labour productivity is mainly caused by sectoral shifts.

Table 4.75
Employment Estimates in Textile and Clothing Sector
Million Equivalent Workers

Year	Handloom Main	Power-loom & Hosiery	Mill	Textiles Main	Ready-made Garment	Textile & Ready-made garment (main)	CSO Estimate of Textile & Ready made garment	Tailor-ing	Textiles & Clothing (main)	Textiles & Clothing (main & casual)	Ministry Estimates* Million Equivalent Workers	Ministry Estimate (Revised)
1983	4.54	0.81	1.18	6.53	0.51	7.04		0.98	8.02	12.56	11.18	
1988-89	4.61	1.47	1.1	7.18	0.88	8.06		1.03	9.09	13.69	14.64	
1989-90	3.20	1.72	1.16	6.08	0.93	7.01		1.05	8.06	11.27	15.54	
1990-91	3.17	2.01	1.1	6.28	1.07	7.35		1.17	8.52	11.69	16.49	
1991-92	3.94	1.84	1.06	6.84	1.14	7.98		0.95	8.93	12.87	17.8	
1992-93	2.59	2.25	1.1	5.94	1.21	7.15		0.98	8.13	10.72		
1993-94	3.17	2.54	1	16.71	11.44	8.15	7.3	1.05	9.20	12.37		
1994-95	2.90	2.62	1	6.52	1.52	8.04		1.00	9.04	11.94		
1995-96	3.03	3.10	1	7.13	1.84	8.97		1.30	10.27	13.29	21.04	
1996-97	2.98	3.08	1.03	7.09	1.91	9.00		1.17	10.17	13.14	21.75	17.97
1997-98	3.16	3.20	1.03	7.39	2.09	9.48		1.49	10.97	14.12		
1998-99	2.33	3.60	1.01	6.94	2.11	9.05		1.30	10.35	12.69		17.40
1999-2000	2.38	3.47	1.04	6.89	2.2	9.09		1.40	10.49	12.87		
Percentage Per Annum Compound Growth Rates												
1990-91 to 99-00	-3.27	7.34	-0.66	1.38	8.83	2.79		3.93	2.93	1.47		
t-statistics	-2.35	9.66	-1.81	2.41	14.15	5.06		3.26	5.23	2.02		
Rsq.	0.33	0.91	0.20	0.35	0.96	0.73		0.52	0.75	0.25		
1983 to 1999-2000	-3.96	9.52	-0.79	0.33	9.57	1.61		2.25	1.69	0.15		

Note: *Employment estimates by using Textile Commissioner's data on Sector-wise Production of Fabrics
Ministry estimates of employment were 21.75 million, which are revised downward to 17.97 million for the year 1996-97, based on certain survey results undertaken by Ministry.

Source: CSO and as derived by the author.

However, the labour productivity must have increased in the sector due to capital deepening and technology progress. The technology progress has taken place in the powerloom sector after mid eighties to take benefit of the export opportunities, while it could not persist for long at the same rate due to fear of losing incentives of SSI sector. Considering the possibility of growth in labour productivity within each sector, the actual growth in employment must have taken place at lower rate than projected above. Thus the policies pursued till now failed to bring the desired technology progress in textiles and clothing sector and the growth in employment in this labour intensive sector were also not to the expected level.

In the handloom sector, the policies failed to not only generate employment growth, but the level of employment declined atthe rate of (-) 3.27 per cent per annum during ninties. The growth in employment has mainly taken place in powerloom and ready-made garment segment. Thus the policy to protect the handloom sector by imposing restriction on the imposition of hank yarn production did not work. The employment per unit value added is 12.5 to 16 times higher in case of handloom sector compared to powerloom sector. However, it is important to be kept in mind that despite decline in employment in the handloom sector, it still accounts for 2.38 million main employees and 4.76 million main and of casual employees during 1999-2000. Thus there is need to show some caution while taking decision on the removal of hank yarn obligations and excise concessions on hank yarn. One possible way is to subsidise the handloom fabrics or provide concessions to handloom weavers directly. The other option is to provide training to handloom weavers to help them find an alternative employment.

The recent government decision to de-reserve garment sector for the exclusive production in the SSI sector to meet the domestic demand may also be crucial in displacing the employment especially in the short run by way of modernisation. However, the modernisation is crucial for the growth of this sector and in the long run the high value addition and rise in growth may be able to raise the growth in employment.

Thus the anticipated squeeze in employment especially in the short run is a serious socio-economic matter, especially because the existence of a vast army of workers is at stake. Therefore, the state has to intervene in a decisive manner. Perhaps, the government has to provide, inter alia, training infrastructure for the workers employed in the small garment and handloom units to help them find an alternative employment.

Summing Up

- Of the 31,127 million square metres of fabrics produced in the country in 1999-2000, exports in the form of fabrics, made-ups and garments were estimated to be 7,910 million square metres 6,618 million square metres of cotton fabrics and 1,292 million square metres of synthetic fabrics. Domestic availability of fabric thus worked out to be 23,217 million square metres during 1999-2000, which is broadly in consonance with the estimates of total consumption provided by the Textile Committee.
- It is estimated that around 234.5 million kilograms of cotton and synthetic hank yarn is being diverted to the powerloom sector during 1999-2000. The production of cotton fabrics in the powerloom and handloom sectors is reworked in the light of this diversion, although the overall estimates of production of fabrics remain same as derived in Chapter 3.
- The revised estimate of cotton fabrics production in the handloom sector of 2,373 million square metre during 1999-2000 is almost one-third compared with the Textile Commissioner's estimates of 6,376 million square metres during the same year. Moreover, the growth rate in the case of the handloom sector is negative (-3.23) in the estimates obtained in this study compared with high growth rate of 5.32 per cent per

annum obtained from official statistics. On the other hand, the revised estimate of production of cotton fabrics in the powerloom sector was 5,997 million square metres as against official estimate of 6,329 million square metres (including non-SSI weaving units) during 1999-2000. However, the growth rate of 1.43 per cent per annum during the period 1990-91 to 1999-2000 differs widely from the negative (-1.18 per cent) growth rate obtained by using official estimate of production of fabrics in powerloom sector. Thus the official statistics shows high growth for the handloom sector and negative growth for the powerloom sector in case of cotton fabrics, which is anyway against the general opinion that powerloom sector is growing.

➡ The estimated production of cotton and synthetic fabrics in the handloom sector was 2,391 million square metres during 1999-2000 is less than one third compared with the Textile Commissioner's estimates of 7352 million square metres during the same year. Moreover, the growth rate in the case of handloom sector is negative (-2.72 per cent per annum) in the estimates obtained in this study compared with the high growth rate of 6.72 per cent per annum obtained from official statistics. On the other hand the estimates of cotton and synthetic fabrics production in the powerloom sector was 22,589 million square metres as against the official estimates of 23,444 million square metres during 1999-2000. The production in the powerloom sector grew at the rate of 8.16 per cent per annum during 1990-91 to 1999-2000 in the estimates derived in this study as against 6.56 per cent per annum as per official estimates for the same period.

➡ The shares of various sectors in total production of fabrics thus worked out are 4.68 per cent for mills, 72.57 per cent for powerlooms, 7.68 per cent for handlooms and 15.07 per cent for hosiery sector during

1999-2000, as against official estimates of 3.77 per cent, 60.69 per cent, 19.03 per cent and 16.50 per cent for these sectors, respectively, for the same period.

- The share of cotton fibre in per capita total fibre consumption has declined from 79.91 per cent in 1983 to 73.25 per cent during 1990-91 and further steeply to 49.19 per cent during 1999-2000. This means we are fast approaching the world average share of cotton in total fibre/filament consumption, which is estimated at 44 per cent. The cotton share in world total fibre/filament consumption is not declining much and is estimated to decline to 43.17 per cent by 2005-06 as per FAO and ICAC predictions.

- The value of output and value added in cotton and synthetic textiles and clothing sectors are worked out in this study by using ex-factory prices, revised estimates of fabrics production and share of readymade garments and tailor-made garments. The share of textiles in total GDP worked out to be 1.51 per cent and that of clothing 1.01 per cent during 1999-2000. These are close to CSO (NAS) estimates for industry groups NIC code 23-24 and 26 (including tailoring activity) respectively. Thus the estimates of value added in textiles and clothing industry derived in this study; based on the conversion rate worked out in this study, tally with the CSO (NAS) estimates, which are based on different data sources. However, share of cotton textiles products worked out in this study is lower compared to the CSO (NAS) estimates, while the share of synthetic textile products is higher than CSO estimates. The basic reason for difference at disagregate level, while tallying at aggregate level seems to be the inclusion of total production and value added of those mills in cotton industry in CSO (NAS) methodology, which are predominantly producing cotton products and similarly for other industries and products.

- There is however a major lacuna in the methodology used by the CSO, which may in the long run lead to wide disparities in the estimates of GDP in textile industry. This is because subsequent values over time are derived from the base year values by applying the Index of Industrial Production (IIP) trend, which in turn are based on production data of Textile Commissioner. CSO infact stopped using Textile Commissioner estimates of production of fabrics to derive value added in the sector as it felt that the conversion rates of yarn to fabric taken by the Textile Commissioner are not appropriate. As it has been demonstrated in this study that the growth rates and quantities derived on the basis of Textile Commissioner's production index deviate too much from the actual estimates. The actual weighted conversion rates depends upon the share of various sectors, count composition, and construction parameters of fabrics.

- The total expenditure incurred by consumers has been worked out by using two sets of prices provided by the Textile Committee and the Textile Commissioner. As estimated in this study, these two sets of official data on market prices give wide differences in the estimates of total expenditure on textiles and clothing goods in the country. The share of textile and clothing (government and non-profit institutions purchase is not subtracted) in private final consumption expenditure based on these prices is estimated to be 10.1 and 5.6 per cent respectively. This difference due to the prices needs to be looked into by the CSO and the Ministry of Textiles.

- Total employment in the textile and clothing sector (main and casual) worked out on the basis of revised estimates of production of fabric was 12.69 million during 1998-99 and 12.87 million during 1999-2000. The estimate is much higher compared with the Ministry of Textiles estimate (revised) of around 17.4 million during 1998-99. However, the estimate of employment derived in this study for textiles and ready-made garment industry (main) of 8.15 million are close to CSO estimates of employment of 7.3 million as on October 1, 1993, for industry group NIC code 23, 24, 25 and 26.

➡ The estimates of main employment in textiles and clothing sector as derived in this study is estimated to grew by only 2.93 per cent per annum and main and casual by 1.47 per cent during 1990-91 to 1999-2000. This is against the high growth of value added in textiles and clothing sector. The GDP in textiles and clothing sector grew by 6.1 per cent per annum during 1990-91 to 1999-2000. Thus the share of textiles and clothing in total GDP grew marginally to 2.5 per cent during 1999-2000 from 2.4 per cent during 1990-91. The production of fabrics in quantity terms also grew by 5.59 per cent per annum during the same period. Thus the employment per unit of output has come down and thus the labour productivity has increased due to shift in production from handloom to powerloom sector during ninties. However, considering the fact that the growth in registered manufacturing sector was jobless during nineties despite 7 to 8 per cent growth in GDP, the performance of textile and clothing sector seems not bad. This cannot be considered good either as the industry is highly labour intensive especially garment sector, which has high potential for growth. The entire period 1983 to 1999-2000, infact reflect the very nominal growth of 0.15 per cent per annum in employment in textiles and clothing industry.

➡ In the handloom sector, the policies failed to not only generate employment growth, but it declined by (-) 3.27 per cent per annum during ninties. The growth in employment has mainly taken place in powerloom and ready-made garment segment. Thus the policies to protect the handloom sector by imposing obligations on the production of hank yarn production did not work. The employment per unit value added is 12.5 to 16 times higher in case of handloom sector compared to powerloom sector. But it should also be kept in mind that despite decline in employment in the handloom sector, it still accounts for 2.38 million equivalent main employees during 1999-2000 and additional same amount are equivalent main and casual workers. Thus although it is important to take decision on the removal of hank yarn obligations and excise concessions on hank yarn as significant part of it is being diverted to powerloom sector is necessary. Subsidising the handloom fabrics or providing concessions to handloom weavers directly is one possible alternative in the short run. However, providing training to weavers to help them find an alternative employment is the solution in the long run.

➡ The recent government decision to de-reserve garment sector for the exclusive production in the SSI sector to meet the domestic demand may be crucial in displacing the employment especially in the short run by way of modernisation. However, the modernisation is crucial for the growth of this industry. In the long run the high value addition may lead to high growth in employment. However, the anticipated squeeze in employment especially in the short run is a serious socio-economic matter, as the existence of a vast army of workers is at stake. Therefore, the state has to intervene in a decisive manner. Perhaps, the government has to provide, inter alia, training infrastructure for the workers employed in the small garment and handloom units to help them find an alternative employment.

APPENDIX 4.1

Various Countries / Regions Production of Cotton Fabrics

Country	Year	Mn.Mt	Mn.Sq.Mt	Gms/Sq.Mt	Mn.Kgs.	MnKgs95
(1)	(2)	(3)	(4)	(5)	(5)	(6)
1. AFRICA	1994		1467	180.16	264	255
Algeria	1992	70		117.65	8	6
Cameroon	1987	16		251.53	4	4
Egypt	1994		494	191.09	94	90
Ethiopia	1994		61	239.34	15	14
Kenya	1994		43	183.72	8	8
Madagascar	1993	35	42	100.00	4	3
South Africa	1994		162	164.81	27	31
Total Available	1994		888	180.29	160	155
2. AMERICA	1994					1415
USA	1994		3740	220.51	825	828
Brazil	1994	1300		215.35	280	279
Total Available	1994		5040	219.18	1105	1107
3. ASIA/CIS/OCENIA						2721
Australia	1994		50	132.00	7	8
Thailand 1	1992		1863	204.52	381	315
Taiwan 2 *	1990	729		357.20	260	195
Pakistan 3	1995		3101	208.21	646	889

(Contd....)

(Contd...)

(1)	(2)	(3)	(4)	(5)	(5)	(6)
China	1994	21124		106.90	2258	2385
India 4	1993	19648	17679	80.61	1425	1570
Bangladesh	1994	32		239.75	8	8
Japan 5	1994		1180	179.77	212	186
Korea Republic	1993		480	118.96	57	44
Hong Kong	1994		692	138.73	96	90
Uzbekistan	1993	517		60.90	32	21
Turkey	1994	362		777.32	281	275
Azerbaijan	1994	89	87	59.77	5	5
Kazakhstan	1994		85	101.18	9	3
Kyrgystan	1994	46	49	97.96	5	4
Total Available			48030	118.28	5681	5997
Total Available (except)			30351	140.22	4256	4427
4. EUROPE						1115
UK	1988		240	130.42	31	15
Belgium	1993		331	162.54	54	45
Germany including DR GER	1994		635	207.24	132	123
Austria	1994	55	83	120.48	10	10
Norway	1988	12		168.07	2	1
Switzerland	1990	87		221.71	19	52
Czec Republic	1994		365	127.67	47	49
Belarus	1994	20	25	292.00	7	6

(Contd...)

(Contd....)

(1)	(2)	(3)	(4)	(5)	(5)	(6)
Bulgaria	1993	72		170.63	12	14
Hungary	1994		76	198.68	15	13
Litthuania	1994	32		108.36	4	4
Poland	1994	256	321	106.85	34	29
Romania	1994		294	124.15	37	34
Rusian Fed.	1994	1506	1631	125.44	205	168
Yugosalavia 2	1990		266	186.19	50	4
Ukraine	1993		262	111.07	29	25
Total Available			4732	145.13	687	591
Grand Total Available (country-wise)			58690	130.05	7632	7850
World Fabrics Production & % available share			77108			78
Total Available (country-wise except India)			41011	151.36	6207	6280
World Fabrics Production & % available share			66250			63
Total Available (country-wise & Africa region)			59269	130.53	7737	7949
World Fabrics Production & % available share			76820			79

(Contd....)

(Contd......)

(1)	(2)	(3)	(4)	(5)	(5)	(6)
Total Available (country-wise & Africa region except			41590	151.76	6312	6379
World Fabrics Production & % available share			66077	151.76		64
World Fabrics Production			76820	130.53		10028

Note: 1. Sq.Mt = taken as 1 Sq.Mt for addition (in case data is not available).
2. Gms/Mt is calculated, where Sq.Mt data is not available
3. *Spun Fabrics

Source: 1. I.C.A.C. (International Cotton Advisory Committee)
2. U.N. (Industrial Commodity Statistics Year Book 1994)
3. The Asian Cotton Textile Outlook
4. Textile Statistics Bureq (TSB) UK
5. All Pakistan Textile Mills Association (APTMA)
6. Indian Cotton Mills Federation (ICMF)
7. Japan Textile News (JTN)

5

Prospects for India's Textiles and Clothing Sector by the Years 2005-06 and 2010-11

This chapter deals with the prospects for India's Textiles and Clothing Sector by the year 2005-06 and 2010-11. The item-wise exports and domestic demand analysis worked out till year 1999-2000 in previous chapters is used along with item-wise share in world trade and demand to work out future projections. This is in this regard that impact of restrictions on India's and world export has been reviewed both in terms of quantity and quality. India's relative competitiveness position at various stages of production and India's share of export in various countries including quota countries is also analysed. The impact of MFA phase out and other reforms is analysed to work out the future requirement of various fibres/ filaments, yarns, fabrics and ready-made garments in India. These are then used to work out the future investment requirement in Indian spinning sector by using productivity and age-composition-wise analysis undertaken in Chapter 2 of this study.

Methodology Used

We begin the analysis with the impact of restrictions on world trade and demand. Textile Outlook International TOI (Economic Intelligence Unit, EIU) analysis regarding World Textiles and Clothing Scenario by 2005-06 is studied in detail and the data is adjusted according to latest available information and model is extended to capture the impact of

MFA and to study the prospects for India. TOI analysis is based on the article by John Coker (Coker, 1997) on World Textile and Clothing Consumption Forecasts to 2005 in Textile Outlook International (TOI), the Economic Intelligence Unit, March 1997. TOI (EIU) projected total demand and supply of various textiles and clothing goods in various Countries/ Regions by the year 2005. The Demand predictions in various Countries/Regions are based on expected growth in per capita consumption based on the income ranges (average) of various countries. On the other hand supply of various products is worked out on the basis of shipment of various machinery and fibres. The gap between supply and demand is used to work out Net trade (Exports minus Imports) in various countries/regions. The study goes into detail regarding item-wise demand and supply scenario for these countries/regions.

The item-wise demand and supply analysis regarding World and South Asia's is used to draw the item-wise demand and supply scenario for India by taking into account intra-regional trade, fibre-wise analysis and modifications in the data and model used. The data used by TOI is modified based on information from other sources as well as available information for the latest year. The analysis in this study is not restricted to net trade as in case of TOI analysis, but is extended to cover gross exports.

TOI model regarding item-wise trends are revised for various countries/regions on the basis of share in world trade and competitiveness of these countries/regions after MFA phase out. Future scenario worked out in this manner is carefully examined especially in case of India, by looking at various possible aspects and by adjusting and readjusting at each possible stages to synchronize for world and India's scenario. Thus India's demand and supply scenario worked out by applying price and income elasticises and India's competitiveness in world scenario fits well with the overall world and South Asia's scenario.

To work out India's competitiveness in world, an attempt is made in this study to find the item-wise major importers and exporters in world. India's share in these countries imports is analysed in this regard. The other major markets for India's exports are also analysed. The impact of trade restrictions on quality and quantity of exports especially from India is worked out. India's relative cost competitiveness at several stages of production is also analysed. India's present and future advantageous regarding availability of raw material, major producer of spun yarn in wide count ranges, and cheap availability of labour is discussed in detail in this study.

We begin our analysis with the identification of major importers and exporters of textiles and clothing goods in the world. Further an attempt is made to analyse the protection policies pursued by these importers and their impact on world and various countries exports.

Major Trading Countries of Textiles and Clothing Items in the World

Major Importers

The three major countries identified as major importers are EU, US, and Japan. These three countries import account for 67.85 per cent of the total world textiles and clothing exports during 1996, despite restrictive policies pursued by these countries. The main net importers were US, EU, Japan, United Arab Emirates, Canada and Switzerland.

Major Exporters

The top ten exporters of textiles and clothing items to world were EU, China, South Korea, US, Taiwan, Hong Kong, India, Turkey, Pakistan and Indonesia. Thus countries of Asia region are among the top exporters. Nine of these top ten exporters also fall among the top ten exporters to three main importers of textiles and clothing namely EU, US, and Japan. Among the top ten exporters, four countries namely EU, China, South Korea, and Hong Kong were also among the top ten importers in the world.

The main net exporters were China, Taiwan, South Korea, India, Turkey, Pakistan, Hong Kong, Indonesia and Thailand. Thus India as country is one of the potential exporters in world.

Protectionist Policies among the Major Importers

After the MFA phase out, the competitiveness of country will play a dominant role in determining its share in the international trade. The impacts of present protectionist policies pursued by major importers in the world is important to analyse in this regard.

EU Imports and Restrictions

More than half of the EU (15)'s trading is taking place within the European Union countries itself due to intra-regional free trade zone. In textiles intra European trade is to the extent of 68.59 per cent of total imports and in clothing it accounted for 44.53 per cent, which added up to 54.35 per cent for combined textiles and clothing imports. China is second largest exporter after intra-EU trade with a share of 5.56 per cent in total textiles and clothing exports to EU during 1996. In 1996, the other major exporters to EU were Turkey and Hong Kong having a respective share of 4.71 per cent and 3.21 per cent. India was exporting US $ 4471 million worth of goods and ranked fifth with the share of 3.36 per cent in total EU (15) imports. The other major exporters to EU were USA, Tunisia, Morocco, Poland and Switzerland. They are placed sixth, seventh, eighth, ninth and tenth respectively. Pakistan was not included in the top ten and was placed eleventh in the terms of exports to EU.

The extent of restrictions on developing countries imports could be judged by classifying EU's imports into MFA and non-MFA trade. 61.9 per cent of EU import volume and 86.7 per cent in value terms were covered by MFA quota. The exports from quota countries may not be falling under MFA, but face other kinds of restrictions. Moreover, the high value added products face higher restrictions. The clothing items share is much higher compared to textiles items under MFA quota as 97.86 per cent of the clothing exports volume falls under MFA quota as against 47.85 per cent for textiles items. Further, even in textile items, the share of high value added items seems much higher—compared with low value added items under MFA quota. The other instruments used for restrictions by EU are given in Appendix 5.1.

The impact of these restrictions was mainly felt by the non-industrial countries. The non-industrial countries accounts for 88.76 per cent of items in quantity terms and 88.73 per cent in value terms originate falling under MFA quota countries. Non-industrial countries share in non-MFA items is also high and accounts for 72.69 per cent of EU non-MFA import in quantity terms and 67.97 percent in value terms. The industrial countries seems to have comparative advantage in better quality products as their per unit value is higher in both MFA as well as non-MFA items as compared with other countries.

The analysis of top ten suppliers of MFA Textiles to EU reveals that India ranked no 1 both in terms of quantum and value of MFA imports during 1995. In fact India's ranking was 5th in volume terms and eighth in quantity terms during 1989. India's growth rate was very high especially in low end products as is clear from the fact that though the exports increased by 18.24 per cent per annum in volume terms, in value terms these increased by only 11.75 per cent from 1989 to 1995. India accounts for 12.80 per cent of EU's MFA quota volume as compared with 10.11 per cent in value.

The analysis of top ten suppliers of MFA Clothing to the EU reveals that India ranked fifth as far as quantum of MFA imports during 1995 was concerned and 7th in terms of value. In fact, India's ranking was 8th in volume during 1989 and 7th in value. India's growth rate was high especially in low end products in clothing as is clear from the fact that though the export increased by 15.25 per cent per annum in volume terms, the increase was only 10.67 per cent in value terms during 1989 to 1995. India accounts for 5.67 per cent of EU's MFA quota volume as compared to 6.30 per cent in value terms during 1995. China, Turkey and Hong Kong were ranked first, second and third respectively in value terms during the same period.

These restrictions on the developing countries' imports would have definitely reduced the extent of penetration into developed countries market. However, despite these restrictions, the imports from Extra-EU are growing. EU imports of textiles and clothing items in dollar value terms increased at 3.65 per cent per annum from 1990 to 1995, while the Extra-EU import increased at much higher rate of 6.12 per cent per annum during the same period. In case of MFA products, the EEC imports grew at a rate of 3.34 per cent from 1989 to 1995.

USA Imports and Restrictions

In case of USA, China was one of the largest exporters having 14.28 per cent share in its imports. The other countries with high share include Mexico 8.84 per cent, EU (15) 8.54 per cent, Hong Kong 8.1 per cent, Taiwan 5.31 per cent, Canada 4.43 per cent and South Korea 4.31 per cent. India was ranked eighth with exports worth US$ 2150 million having a share of 3.98 per cent. Philippines and Indonesia were ranked ninth and tenth in USA imports having their respective share of 3.13 and 3.12 per cent. Pakistan ranked eleventh below Thailand, Malaysia, Honduras, Bangladesh and Sri Lanka respectively. Pakistan accounts for US$ 1142 million worth of exports having 2.11 per cent share and is ranked sixteenth in U.S. imports.

The USA total imports grew by 8.18 percent per annum during 1990 to 1996. The clothing trade from Latin America to North America grew at much higher rate at 20 per cent from 1990 to 1996. In case of MFA products, the USA imports grew at a rate of 8.64 per cent from 1989 to 1995. Thus the restrictions imposed by developed countries are able to restrict the growth of products falling under MFA to almost the same level as that of overall imports in these countries, despite higher potential for growth in MFA products.

India's growth of textiles and clothing exports to USA grew by 13.81 per cent per annum during 1989 to 1995 in value terms and 12.17 per cent in quantity terms. The growth is much higher compared to USA imports of MFA items. India's export of MFA items grew at a rate of 8.64 per cent in value terms (US $) and 7.09 per cent in quantity terms.

The impact of restrictions depends upon several factors such as quota and other restrictions level and comparative competitiveness of that country in various products, etc. So impact of quota and other restrictions varies for different countries from item to item. The restrictions affect both the quantity and quality of goods exported.

Quantify the Impact of Protectionist Policies on World Trade

In estimating the impact of the MFA, the crucial difficulty arises in estimating the supply curve due to quota regime. Some authors chose quota rents to compute the supply price. Such information is available for Hong Kong, where export licences are openly traded. Hamilton (1991) extended his approach to the main European countries and found that on average between 1980 and 1989 the import tariff equivalent of MFA restrictions was equal to 15 per cent. However, Ricardo Faini *et al.* (1992) found out quota utilisation rates well in excess of 100 per cent were not uncommon. Hence, it is more appropriate to assume that supply becomes lesser prices elastic with a tightening of trade restrictions and vice-versa. Other factors which influence the supply curve are inefficiencies in the distribution of quotas across firms, constraints on substitute products, etc. Faini's (1995) findings suggest that a 10 per cent reduction in developing countries exports prices would lead to a significant increase in trade flows, on an average of more than 30 and 10 per cent respectively for their apparel and textile exports."[1]

Erzan *et al.* (1991) and in Goto (1990) and Trela and Whalley (1988, 1990) built a world general equilibrium model to analyse the effects of MFA. They concluded that elimination of both tariff and quotas on Textile and Clothing trade would lead to global gains of more than $17 billion, of which $11 billion would flow to developing countries.

1. In related study, Cline (1987) uses a simple model of production, employment and trade in T&C to assess the causes of employment decline in the sector and projects its future evolution. In his simple partial equilibrium model, he evaluated the welfare cost of protection.

ESCAP study made projections under the current arrangement of quota acceleration. These projections are based on the findings of Hertal and others, supplemented by UNCTAD statistics for 1995 ESCAP (1996b). The long-term effect of the MFA phase out is likely to be much stronger, although there is also uncertainty over the possibility of new forms of trade barriers after MFA is expected to phased out. The major impact of restriction according to this study was on labour intensive and mainly cotton-based products. Thus in the case of MFA phase out, the major beneficiary is going to be South Asia as it has a strong comparative advantage in these products. It was however further argued in the study that most of cotton textiles and clothing exports from ESCAP region are of low quality. The relatively demand in these products is inelastic and world price may decline steeply with the further increase in exports. The empirical evidence of EC, US shows that these restrictions have caused the expected shift from constrained exporters to domestic producers and from constrained exporters to unconstrained exporters. Thus the restrictions have arrested the growth of exports from LDC to developed countries. The development of labour-saving technology in textiles sector has reduced the comparative advantage of developing countries in textile products and hence the major impact of restrains was felt in garment segment.

Faini and Heimler (1994) expressed similar views in a related study. According to this study, MFA has only succeeded in slowing down rather than halting or even reversing the process of shifting comparative advantage in Textiles and Clothing towards developing countries. In fact, developing countries account for a larger share of world exports of Textiles and Clothing today than they did 20 years ago at the onset of the MFA. It has been especially true in case of clothing for which restrictions are higher compared to textiles. It has been argued that despite restrictions, developing countries have made particularly conspicuous gains and their share of world exports has soared from 15 per cent in 1963 to 43.5 per cent in 1989. On the other hand, in textiles, industrial countries have managed more successfully to retain their competitive position because the sector has been amenable to technological labour-saving innovations. Remarkably, around 77 per cent of developed countries textile exports originate from other developed countries. The fact that the pattern of trade among various countries does not differ substantially also support the fact that MFA could not completely reverse the process of shifting comparative advantage. The pattern of Less Developed Countries trade in fibre, yarns, textiles and clothing for Australia and New Zealand (that apply global quantitative restrictions) are broadly similar to those for the United States and EC (which apply discriminatory quantitative restrictions) (Faini, R., J. DE Melo and W. Takacs, 1992).

Impact of Protection on Quality of Output

Falvey's, 1979 analysed that in heterogeneous goods the protection is likely to influence not only the quantity and the price of such goods, but also the choice of quality. The proportional increase in the domestic price of the higher quality goods is smaller. This is based on the assumption that initially prices of higher quality goods are higher. It has been argued that once quota is imposed, under plausible assumptions about the price responsiveness of demand, imports of high quality goods will decline less and the average quality of imports will increase.

Later contributions have extended Falvey's approach to non-competitive conditions. Faini and Heimler 1994 argued that the impact of protection on the quality levels of both domestic and foreign production will depend on several factors, including demand conditions, market structure and technology. Even at an empirical level, results are mixed.

In this analysis Faini & Heimler choose to use the index number approach to measure quality. They then compute multilateral price indices to measure the price and quality of textile and clothing imports from Tunisia, Morocco, Korea, China, Taiwan, Singapore and Hong Kong into the four major European Community (EC) countries (Italy, France, Germany and United Kingdom). In textiles, the analysis of the quality content shows mixed results. The quality of exports from developing countries remains much lower than that of imports from Italy. Quality upgrading in clothing was much more widespread. It comes out that these developing countries are improving the quality of their exports to European countries at rates similar to those experienced by Italian producers. Since constraints from the MFA are more likely to have occurred in clothing than in textiles, these results tend to confirm the hypothesis that at least for these countries, a binding quota has led to quality upgrading. Morocco and Tunisia offer no support to the hypothesis of quality upgrading for imports as these countries were not subject to MFA or any other binding restrictions on their clothing exports to the EC during these years.[2] All these measures have limitations in measuring the quality or competitiveness of a product and hence it is not easy to work out the competitiveness of a country. Bhide (1996) expressed that it is not easy to establish the hypothesis that Indian goods are competitive in quality or in price, as there exist a very wide range of products, which are highly differentiated, especially in clothing. Secondly, there is no single internationally accepted index of quality. Thirdly, the market for textiles and clothing is highly segmented. There is also a fair element of quality, design and fashion trends. India's per unit export price for textiles and clothing items is among the lowest in the top ten MFA clothing exporters to EU and USA. However, for proper comparison, the price of each variety should be compared with other countries. The price

2. Similar results are obtained in case of India. Bedi (2000) find out the qualitative changes during the liberalisation period in India. Qualitative changes are defined as changes in product composition or variety compared with the base year and it is assumed that the relative prices of various varieties reflect their quality. A time period series of these values when deflated at constant prices captures qualitative changes in the composition of textile output. In the case of exports qualitative index is prepared by deflating the per unit dollar value realisation of exports of cotton products with Cotton look Index (ICAC) and synthetic products with other textile fibre price index (ICAC).

movement of cotton yarn for both 20s and 30s counts for India is among the low value realisation countries.

These facts indicate that MFA has slowed the growth in exports from developing countries and the pattern of trade is still guided by comparative advantages. This means despite quota level, one need to be competitive to materialise exports. However quota could act as binding constraint to further increase the level of exports. Thus, the competitive strengths of a country is important to promote future exports specially after MFA phase out.

After analysing the protection policies pursued by the developed countries and its impact, an attempt is made in the following section to find the impact of quota acceleration due to MFA phase out.

Impact of Quota Acceleration due to MFA Phase out on Various Countries' Exports with Special Reference to India

To know about the impact of MFA phase out on various countries' exports, it is important to study how the MFA is going to be phased out and what are going to be its impacts on the growth prospects of various countries during the intermediary period.

According to the Agreement on Textile Clothing (ATC), bilateral quotas under the MFA will be enlarged progressively in three stages. In the first stage, during 1995 to 1998 not less than 16 per cent of the total volume of 1990 imports will be integrated into the GATT, in the second stage, during 1998 to 2002 not less than a further 17 per cent and in the third stage not less than a further 18 per cent will be integrated into the GATT. The balance will be integrated by 2005 immediately after the expiry of the Agreement on Textiles and Clothing.

In the first stage, the growth rate in quotas will be 16 per cent. For smaller suppliers, the increase could be 27 per cent. In the second stage, the growth rates will be further increased by 25 per cent. In the last stage, the growth rates will be raised to 27 per cent. The ATC defines small suppliers as those whose restricted exports amounted to 1.2 per cent of the total volume of restrictions applied by an importing country on 31 December 1991 (ESCAP, 1996a).

The tariffs will remain at very high rate despite Uruguay round agreement in the textiles and clothing sector. The average tariff rate in the post-Uruguay round will be 12 per cent in textiles and clothing goods, which is three times the average tariff for all goods. The average tariffs in pre-Uruguay round is 16 per cent and in case of India 25 per cent.

The USA has already come out with a full list of products, which it intends to integrate during the three stages of MFA phase out. The number of restrained items and their growth in imports varied for various supplier countries to USA. The number of restrained products in the case of India was 13, Bangladesh 14, Thailand 21, and the Philippines 27. The quotas for these countries on most products were allowed to grow a much more generous 6-7 per cent.

EU has bilateral textile and clothing agreements with 49 countries at present, although not all of them are under the MFA or subject to quotas. Many suppliers' countries are subject to "surveillance". This means that imports are monitored to identify sudden surges, which may require action, and to prevent and detect fraudulent imports. In these cases, the main aim is to identify goods and the country of origin of the products.

The growths of quota items to EU vary for various items and countries. The comparison of various Asian countries growth to EU shows that India's growth for most of items falls in higher range.

- Vietnam has 27 clothing products under quota for the 1996-97 period, of which 17 are confined to growth of 2 per cent or less.
- Macau has 17 clothing products under restriction fr the period 1996-97, of which 14 are confined to growth of 2 per cent or less.
- India has ten clothing products under restriction for

the period 1996-97, none of which is subject to growth of 2 per cent or less.

- The Philippines has 12, Pakistan 8 and Thailand 11 clothing products under restriction for the period 1996-97, mostly in the higher band of 2.1-6.0 per cent

ESCAP study estimated the impact of quota growth of EU, USA, Canada and Norway on exports from Asian countries (Appendix 5.2). In this study, the total quota level have been converted to tons equivalent to make the comparison more meaningful by applying ICAC conversion rate of 7194.24 square metres per tons for quota of USA and Norway. In the case of exports from India also the conversion rates used is same to make the compasrion more meaningful with other countries. This explains the quota level of 268 million kilograms (Appendix 5.2), which is estimated to be around 15 million kilogram higher compared with what its conversion rates of fabrics being exported from India.

If quota acceleration would not be imposed as per WTO agreement, then India's growth rate in quota items would have been at constant level of 6 per cent per annum for Canada, 3.5 per cent per annum for EU, 2.0 per cent per annum for Norway and 5.5 per cent per annum for USA. The quota level would have reached from 268 million kilograms to 417 million kilograms by the end of phase out period at a annual compound growth rate of 4.52 per cent per annum. On the other hand, acceleration of quota growth would cause around 61 million kilograms of additional exports to India during the last year of the phase out. India's export of quota items is expected to rise from 268 million kilograms to 478 million kilograms in case the acceleration of quota takes place as per agreement. Thus overall growth rate of Textiles and Clothing exports will increase from 4.52 to 5.96 per cent per annum due to quota acceleration. The agreement allows the acceleration of quota growth from various countries in such a manner that India's share is expected to remain at almost the same level among the quota countries during the transitional phase.

However, this is not really a substantial gain in the intermediate period considering the fact that India's textiles and clothing items have achieved in the past much higher growth rate than the above growth rate with the quota acceleration. India's exports of textiles and clothing items for restricted items to USA and EU grew by 8.11 per cent per annum during 1990-91 to 1997-98. India's exports to these countries of total textiles and clothing items grew at 8.83 per cent per annum and to World at 16.43 per cent per annum during 1990-91 to 1997-98 in kilogram equivalent terms.

By making assumption similar to the one made by Global Trade Analysis Project (GTAP) model, one can estimate the total yarn equivalent exports from India by 2005. It has been recently pointed out by the GTAP that the overall export growth from restricted exporting countries is likely to be underestimated if the agreed quota acceleration is imposed on all exports, as unrestricted products tend to grow more rapidly. However, since the growth of indirect exports to likely to decline as a result of quota acceleration, the underestimation will offset to some extent. Even at the expected growth rate of 5.96 per cent per annum during the period 1997-98 to 2005 on the basis of quota acceleration, India's yarn equivalent export would grow from 1338.9 million kilograms (excluding Filament yarn) in 1996-97 to 2128 million kilograms by 2005-06.

The analysis about quota acceleration due to MFA phase out only tells us the expected level of quota at the end of MFA phase out. However, the actual level of exports after the phase out may widely differ depending upon the competitiveness of a country. The exact level of various countries exports is thus questionable. The prime factor supposed to play the dominant role in determining the share of a country seems to be its relative competitiveness in future. It is in this regard that an attempt is made to find out India share of textiles and clothing exports in various countries and items trade, and cost competitiveness and other strengths and weaknesses of India textiles and clothing industry vis-a-vis other countries.

We begin our analysis based on TOI analysis and modification made in it regarding demand and supply in various courtiers/regions.

International Textiles and Clothing Scenario by 2005

An attempt is made in this study to find textile and clothing demand in world by 2005. The study is based on the analysis of per capita consumption and total demand of fibre in various countries/regions. The net export of fibre in each country/region is worked out on the basis of difference between mill fibre consumption and total domestic demand. The analysis is based on the article by John Coker (Coker, 1997) on World Textile and Clothing Consumption Forecasts to 2005 in Textile Outlook International (TOI), the Economic Intelligence Unit, March 1997. The data in this study is updated on the basis of latest available information and revised estimates are worked out for world trade. Once revised estimates about world trade are worked out, the share of South Asia and then India is worked out in the context of revised estimates about world trade, past performance and future competitiveness. Several changes, which have been made in this study compared with TOI analysis, are listed below.

Firstly, the TOI study is based on FAO data for year 1992. We have taken into accounts some of the differences with item-wise data taken in the TOI analysis. In addition to this, the changes are made as per the available information from ICAC data for cotton products as this seems to be more reliable data as it tallies with Export Promotion Council data of various countries and is available till 1995. The projections by 2005-06 in this study are revised on the basis of these changes and available information regarding the latest year. The revised estimates are worked out for world trade from the base year information on the basis of growth rate projected in TOI analysis. Once revised estimates about world trade are worked out, the share of South Asia and then India is worked out in the context of revised estimates about world trade, past performance and future competitiveness. For working out the country-wise per capita consumption, population figures were also revised on the basis of latest information from World Bank Report.

Secondly, an attempt is made to project world trade in gross terms, as net trade projections do not give separate figures about quantum of actual exports and imports. So the gross trade estimates are projected for world, South Asia and India.

Thirdly, TOI projections for these regions are only worked out for total net trade. No attempt was made to project the share of cotton and synthetic products. In this study, an attempt is made to project the world and India's trade separately for cotton and synthetic products both for gross and net trade.

Fourthly, the item-wise composition for South Asia has been reworked on the basis of latest information and considering the impact of MFA phase out on commodity trade composition and exports through indirect routes.

Fifthly, the TOI study made projections only for South Asia. In this study India's share of various items in South Asia and world trade is worked out separately in this study on the basis of past trends and potentials. India's data for exports is available till 1999-2000, which is used as base for future projections.

Sixthly, in this study, two alternatives are worked out for world, South Asia and India. As discussed Alternative I is where projections are based on TOI analysis after the above modification in TOI analysis have been made. In Alternative II, it is assumed that the per capita consumption of developed countries may continue to grow at a rate achieved during 1980 to 1995, while maintaing the modification made in TOI in Alternative I. Thus the Alternative II is basically optimistic scenario. Thus in Alternative II, it is assumed that despite higher increase in per capita consumption in eastern countries, the per capita consumption of developed countries can also grew simultaneously.

The two alternatives projected by 2005 are discussed in detail one by one.

Alternative I (Alt I)

Demand Pattern

The analysis in TOI regarding world demand in various countries/regions is based on the income and consumption per head for various countries. According to TOI, there exists close relationship between income per head and consumption per head. The analysis for various countries shows that as per capita income rises from less than US$ 1,000 to US$ 5000, fibre consumption rises quickly from 1 kg to 5-10 kg. In the case of annual income of US$ 5,000 to US$ 20000, fibre consumption rises much more slowly from 10 kg to 15-20 kg only. At higher income levels US$ 20,000 to US$ 30,000 or more, there is no discernible increase in consumption per head. The pattern is consistent and very strong except for a few countries such as USA, Switzerland and South Korea. The USA continues to display an apparently limitless appetite for textile consumption at all income levels.

Except of Singapore, Hong Kong and South Korea most of the major exporting countries are in the income group of less than US$ 5000 per annum.

World demand for apparel fibres is expected to rise at annual growth rate of 3.76 per cent during 1995-2005 from 38750 million kilograms to 56059 million kilograms as per TOI estimates. However, this is faster than the 2.4 per cent growth rate experienced in the previous ten years. The acceleration is based on the expectation that countries in the former eastern block will recover rapidly from their current decline towards the end of forecast period. Excluding the countries of Eastern Europe and the former USSR, which are expected to recover rapidly from their current very low levels, the growth rate is rather lower at 2.6 per cent.

Total demand in Japan and Western developed countries, other than the USA, will rise more slowly over the ten years to 2005 than during the 1980-95 period. This represents a break with the past, when most of the impetus for increased consumption came from developed countries. In part, this is due to economic slowdown. This shows that outside the USA, expenditure on textiles and clothing slows down very rapidly after personal incomes pass the US$ 20,000 mark. Demand growth will average 2.0 per cent a year in these developed countries. In USA, consumption per head is forecast to finally slow down with consumption per head to grow only by 0.8 per cent. This is based on the assumption that consumption is already unusually high relative to the country's income and it will conform to the general pattern before 2005. Demand in developing countries, on the other hand, is forecast to rise by a faster 3.2 per cent a year over the same period.

Supply Pattern

Notwithstanding the above trend in demand, the shift in the location in primary processing is expected to continue. Excluding the former Eastern bloc, the developed countries share of mill consumption will fall from 34 per cent to 26 per cent, while that of the developing countries will rise from 66 per cent to 74 per cent during 1995 to 2005. Mill consumption in Western developed countries is expected to stabilise at 12.9 million tons and all extra demand will be met from developing countries import.

These estimates are based on the fact that the mill consumption of fibre is declining continuously in developed countries since 1980. At the beginning of 1980s, developed countries processed 58 per cent of total world fibre. By 1985 this share had fallen to 51 per cent, and by 1995 to an estimated 38 per cent. Within this broad picture there are however wide variations. The USA showed remarkable ability to retain its market share. However, according to figures from ITMF, new shipments of spindles into the USA have fallen recently, which suggests that American spinners have some doubts about the immediate outlook. The other two major developed countries (primary processors), the EU and Japan, both have already lost considerable ground. In 1995, shipments of spindles into the EU and Japan were only 60 per cent and 30 per cent respectively of their average for previous ten years.

The benefit of this goes to Asia. This is underlined by the ITMF figures showing that 62 per cent of all short-staple spinning capacity shipped in 1999 went to Asia. In 1989 shipments to Asia were double those to the USA and Western Europe combined. India was main benefitory of developments in Asia, as India's share was 53 per cent of the total spindles shipped in Asia during 1990-99. These ratios for Asia however underestimate the extent of the gap between Western developed countries and Asia as they exclude deliveries within China. With some variations these trend are expected to continue.

The impact of it could be seen on yarn export. Among the principal yarn exporting countries the sharpest increase in recent years comes from India, Pakistan, Thailand and Indonesia. In contrast, those countries which established substantial export surpluses have recorded much lower growth or decline in recent years-notably China, South Korea, Turkey, Brazil, Hong Kong and Egypt.

On the other hand, the fabrics net exports from South Asia and to a lesser extent from East and South East Asia have continued to grow at a higher rate than net exports from China. Both yarn and fabrics trade have grown at faster rate than has total world consumption. Net imports of fabrics into Western Developed countries and Japan grew by an average of 8.5 per cent between 1985 and 1995. Thus, the potential countries for future growth in exports seem to be Asian Countries.

TOI estimated production at various stages of production. The production of garments and other textile products is worked out by adding net fabrics imports figure in total production of fabrics.[3] Nearly all the growth took place in developing countries. As in the case of mill consumption and yarn available, only the USA among developed countries has managed to enlarge its fabrics production base to some extent. Until 1990, this was rising in both the EU and Japan, but since then there has been a decline in both regions. Thus, the

3. For India, we adopted similar methodology in Chapter 4.

industry is dying in the developed countries despite protections.

Between 1985 and 1995, yarn imports into Western developed countries and Japan grew by 4.9 per cent per annum while fabrics trade expanded annually by 8.5 per cent. Over the same period, clothing imports grew by over 12 per cent a year. As a percentage of final consumption, net clothing imports have now reached 16 per cent in USA, 20 per cent in Japan, and other Western Europe and 21 per cent in the EU. Together, these three regions/countries account for over 91 per cent of the net clothing imports into the developed countries (excluding former eastern block countries). These are major importing countries and hence share of value added products in world trade is rising and expected to continue so with the decline in indirect routes caused by removal of restrictions.

Modifications in TOI Model

Estimates of Gross World Trade by 2005 on the Basis of TOI Estimates of Net World Trade

TOI projections about trade are undertaken in net terms. We in this analysis tried to find out the projections regarding item-wise gross trade based on the available data on gross trade till 1995 and projections of net trade till 2005 from TOI. The modifications in TOI net trade data and projections are made based on latest available data from ICAC, FAO and other sources. This is important to view both gross and net trade projections for proper analysis.

The net trade analysis is useful to find the gap between net demand, supply and trade. On the other hand, the gross trade analysis is useful to find the future potential for exports from the country, but this also has limitations. It does not convey the difference between potential exports and re-export of the country after no. of some value addition. So both net and gross trade are important from different angles. Table 5.1 gives figures for item-wise net imports of various countries/ region in the world without modification in TOI analysis. The figures are calculated by adding gross imports of various Regions/Countries. Negative figures for each country indicate

Table 5.1
Product-wise Net Imports and Exports from Developed and Developing Countries during 1980-1995

(TOI estimates)

	All Developed Countries Net Trade					*Mn. Kgs.*		*CGR 1995 to 2005*
	1980	1985	1990	1993	*1995	**2000	**2005	% p.a.
Yarn	272	522	678	625	728	883	935	2.53
Fabric	145	405	567	682	951	1104	1308	3.24
Other	20	92	289	393	401	589	841	7.69
Clothing	814	1221	2370	3234	3649	4783	6262	5.55
Total	1251	2240	3904	4934	5729	7359	9346	5.02
Fibre/Yarn	1.13	1.15	1.16	1.19	1.23	1.24	1.25	
Fibre Equivalent	1416	2586	4516	5876	7070	9093	11710	5.18
	Developing Countries Net Trade							
Yarn	-286	-565	-697	-588	-627	-889	-1007	4.85
Fabric	-255	-809	-1348	-1385	-1569	-1926	-2215	3.51
Other	109	-38	-214	-270	-314	-518	-806	9.89
Clothing	-777	-1311	-2229	-2296	-2719	-4074	-6042	8.31
Total	-1209	-2723	-4487	-4539	-5229	-7407	-10070	6.77
Fibre/Yarn	1.16	1.14	1.13	1.17	1.16	1.16	1.16	
Fibre Equivalent	-1404	-3097	-5063	-5293	-6080	-8613	-11710	6.77

Note: (1) *Estimates, (2) **Predicted, (3) Weights are actual weights rather than fibre/filament equivalent, (4) In this entire Chapter 5 Tables, Fibre/Yarn means Fibre/Filament over Yarn Ratio. This is written like this to same space, (5) For the same reason of space in Chapter 5 Tables, Fibre Equivalent is written for Fibre/Filament Equivalent, (6) CGR in this Chapter 5 Tables are worked on the basis of point to point data unless other-wise specified t-statistics are given.

Source: Derived from TO.

trade surpluses (*i.e.* where imports are less than exports) and positive figures indicate trade deficits (where exports are less than imports).

TOI analysis of data for the period 1980 to 1995 for gross trade (Table 5.2) reveals that gross and net figures are not comparable but trends in the gross and net imports have certain similarities. One can derive the gross trend from net in case changes in trade structure are available. The world gross trade data is available till year 1995, which showed lower growth rates compared to net trade due to higher base levels. The gross exports in textiles grew by 4.12 per cent per annum and clothing by 8.85 per cent per annum during 1980 to 1995. Yarn and fabrics account for much higher proportion of intra-trade between developed countries.

The share of net trade was very low in gross world trade during 1980, but has risen since then. The net trade share in gross trade was 16.32 per cent in 1980, 24.66 per cent in 1985, 29.96 per cent in 1990, 30.69 per cent in 1993 and 32.74 per cent in 1995. This indicates that net trade share in gross trade is growing continuously, but at a slower rate. This is understandable as trade through indirect routes may be lower with the removal of restrictions. However, it is going to be partially compensated by increase in trade of intermediate products to get advantage of lower cost of production at several places. Considering these assumptions, the share of net trade in gross trade is expected to be 33.70 per cent by the year 2005-06.

From these gross trade estimates, item-wise gross exports could be worked out by analysing the past trend and future expectations. For the item-wise analysis, the past trend reveals net clothing trade two-thirds of total net imports during 1995. This is much higher than its proportion in gross trade. The share of clothing trade in gross textiles and clothing trade was only 40.5 per cent in 1995, which reflects the fact that yarn and fabric account for a much higher proportion of exports which is re-traded after some or no value addition to get advantage of low conversion cost. The developed countries trade policies are designed to suit such flows. However, with the MFA phase out, the share of yarn and fabrics in total gross trade is going to be reduced. The item-wise gross trade for the year 2005 is worked out on the basis of TOI net trade data is given in Table 5.2.

In terms of fibre equivalent the gross trade is estimated at 31955 million kilograms, which is 49.46 per cent of the expected world fibre consumption by 2005. The gross world trade during 1995 was 42.27 per cent of the total fibre consumption in the world. The share of trade in fibre consumption is continuously on the rise. In the eighties, the share of world trade was only 25.64 per cent, which rose to 32.72 per cent in 1985 and then to 35.22 per cent in 1990 and further to 40.56 per cent in 1992. This means the maximum rise in share of trade in total fibre consumption has taken place during the eighties. However, trade as well as fibre consumption have both grown at higher rate during the nineties. The share of gross trade in world fibre consumption increased to 48.71 per cent in 1995. The share of trade in total fibre consumption cannot increase indefinitely at very high rate. Gross world trade share in total fibre consumption is expected to reach at level of 57 per cent by 2005.

Extension for Fibre-wise Analysis from TOI Aggregate Analysis

Coker (1997) in his article in TOI analysed the aggregate demand and supply scenario for textiles and clothing products without segregating it for various fibres. In this study we felt it important to extend the analysis fibre-wise to work out the future demand for spindles, etc. The fibre-wise trade and consumption requirement are worked out in Table 5.3 from the FAO data, which is available for the latest year 1992.

The filament is not included in total trade yarn as it is not textile product although filament fabrics, made-ups and garments are included. However, data on filament yarn is separately mentioned to get an idea about the extent of trade in this product. This is important as WTO data covers it for exports of textiles trade in value terms.

Table 5.2

World Gross Trade in Textile and Clothing Products during 1980-95

	TOI Analysis (Mn. Kgs.)					*Predicted*	*CGR % p.a.*	
	1980	*1985*	*1990*	*1992*	*1995*	*2005*	*1980 to 1995*	*1995 to 2005**
Yarn	1614	2019	2612	2846	2970	3814	4.15	2.53
Fabric	2655	3003	4301	4867	5340	7345	4.77	3.24
Clothing	1986	2696	4306	5605	7090	12167	8.85	5.55
Other	1409	1367	1810	2039	2100	4404	2.70	7.69
Total	7664	9085	13029	15357	17500	27730	5.66	4.71
Fibre Equivalent	8831	10469	15014	17696	20166	31955	5.66	4.71
Trade share %	29.55	31.99	40.58	46.74	48.71	57.00		
Fibre Consumption	29887	32723	36996	37861	41400	56059	2.20	3.08

Note: Item-wise weights are actual weights rather than fibre/filament equivalent.
Trade share % in entire Chapter 5 Tables means Trade space percentage in Total Fibre/Filament Consumption for production.

Source: Textile outlook international, March 1997.

Table 5.3
Fibre-wise Import of Various Products in World (1992)

(Mn. Kgs)

	Cotton	*Non-Cellulosic*	*Cellulosic*	*Wool*	*Flax*	*Total*	*Filament*	
							Non-Cellulosic	*Cellulosic*
Yarn	1573.5	691.5	145.9	523.2	25.2	2959.3	3742.9	857.9
Fabric	2309.1	1882.8	520.3	171.8	45.8	4929.8		
Other	936.6	830.8	111.2	184	15.9	2078.5		
Total Textiles	4819.2	3405.1	777.4	879	86.9	9967.6		
Textiles Share	62.07	66.05	72.28	73.40	68.86	65.07		
Clothing	2944.7	1749.9	298.1	318.6	39.3	5350.6		
Textile & Clothing	7763.9	5155	1075.5	1197.6	126.2	15318.2		
Fibre Equivalent	9242.5	5602	1173.9	1330	210	17558.4		
Fibre/Yarn	1.19	1.09	1.09	1.11	1.66	1.15		
Trade Share %	49.15	36.42	47.74	70.51	40.02	44.96		
Fibre Consumption	18804.8	15380.6	2459	1886.3	524.8	39055.5		

Note: (1) Weights are actual weights, rather than fibre equivalent.
(2) Filament yarn is given separately as it is generally considered as raw material.

Source: FAO, Consumer Purchase Textile Survey, 1996.

Table 5.4

Fibre-wise Import of Yarn by Selected Countries and Regions (1992)

(Mn.Kgs)

Major Importers	*Cotton*	*Cotton Share %*	*Spun Yarn*		*Wool*	*Flax*	*Total*	*Filament*	
			Non-Cellulosic	*Cellulosic*				*Non-Cellulosic*	*Cellulosic*
USA	45.7	56.49	21.6	5.5	7.4	0.7	80.9	269.1	15.3
EU (15)	549.9	48.91	227.7	90.7	240.3	15.7	1124.3	1364.7	303.4
Norway	2.5	54.35	0.8	0.1	1.2	0	4.6	7	1.3
Canada	24	48.68	21	0.8	3.6	0	49.3	87.5	2.6
Japan	190.8	71.57	29.5	0.3	45.2	0.8	266.6	78.5	3.8
L. America	14	37.43	14.7	1.7	5.2	1.8	37.4	157.7	36
South Asia	20.4	76.12	5.3	0.3	0.7	0.1	26.8	130.4	38.6
E&S Asia	557	55.95	242	20.2	171.3	5	995.5	795.2	206.9
Total Above	**1404.3**	**54.32**	**562.6**	**119.6**	**474.9**	**24.1**	**2585.4**	**2890.1**	**607.9**
Exporters									
India	0.2	33.33	0.1	-	0.3	-	0.6	47.6	2.6
China	170.4	58.38	22.3	0.3	98.9	-	291.9	198	62.6
Hong Kong	262.5	58.10	130	8.5	48.3	2.5	451.8	164	18.2
Rep Korea	75.9	51.70	40.5	8.8	19.3	2.3	146.8	102.8	62.5
Pakistan	0.1	11.11	0.4	0.1	0.2	0.1	0.9	46.5	26.9
Total Above	**509.1**	**57.07**	**193.3**	**17.7**	**167**	**4.9**	**892**	**558.9**	**172.8**

Source: FAO, Consumer Purchase Textile Survey, 1996.

The cotton share constitutes 50.68 per cent of the total yarn equivalent world trade during 1992. In terms of fibre equivalent the cotton trade share is even higher at 52.64 per cent of the total world trade during 1992 as the wastage in cotton is more.

Table 5.4 indicates that most of the developed countries are major net importer of cotton items for final consumption and India is one of the major exporters of cotton products. The fibre wise textiles and clothing trade in USA is analysed over the period of time to establish the trend in cotton fibre trade (Table 5.5).

Table 5.5
Share of Cotton Fibre in USA's Import Over Time
(Share worked out from total Sq. Mt Quantity Equivalent Import)

Cotton Share in	*1978*	*1983*	*1992*	*1993*	*1994*
Apparel	32.4	35.9	48.9	50.8	51.8
Total MFA Product	38.6	38.9	46.9	46.5	45.5

Source: Computed from US official Statistics.

The data in Table 5.5 indicates that trade in cotton fibre is growing at a faster rate, which is beneficial for India's exports. This trend is likely to continue and hence it is possible that cotton items in developing countries may be mainly meant for export purposes. The growth in domestic demand of developing countries may be met by increasing use of man-made fibres, which may be facilitated by lowering of excise duties on synthetic products in developing countries.

Discrepancies in FAO and ICAC data and Other Adjustments in TOI Analysis

Before we incorporate the fibre-wise analysis in TOI projections, the other changes required are also looked into. For any accurate estimates, it is important to have better understanding of the present status. TOI analysis is based on FAO data. However, an attempt is made by us to compile the country-wise and item-wise data available from FAO for year 1992 and compare it with TOI estimates of item-wise world trade. The figures thus arrived are slightly different than given in TOI study. The required modifications are thus made in the TOI analysis for this study. Moreover, data from another alternative source ICAC is used for further modifications. There are some discrepancies in the FAO data and ICAC data for cotton yarn and cotton fabric products. The ICAC data gave higher quantity for cotton yarn exports compared to FAO data, while the cotton fabrics exports are lower in case of ICAC. We have made these adjustments in TOI analysis (Table 5.6), as data published by various countries Export Promotion Council tally with ICAC statistics.

The fibre and item-wise trade figures for the year 1995 are obtained by using the latest available information from various sources. The synthetic yarn and fabrics trade estimates for year 1995 are based on available data for most of important countries and for others on the basis of growth rate expected in TOI analysis. ICAC data for cotton yarn and cotton fabrics are available for the year 1995. The data for clothing and other products for the year 1995 are arrived at by assuming the same growth rate for cotton and other fibres trade.

On the basis of revised estimates of world gross trade during 1995, the estimates for the 2005 are worked out by assuming the item-wise growth rates similar to the one as projected in TOI analysis.

The growth of trade for cotton and synthetic items (Table 5.8) are taken same, despite the fact that the growth rate in world consumption of synthetic products is expected to be higher than cotton fibre. This is based on the assumption that growth in cotton demand is going to be increasingly meant for exports from developing countries to developed countries. The demand for cotton products in developing countries would be mainly restricted to a few essential goods or to those customers who could afford to pay high prices. The synthetic products are expected to replace the cotton products both for existing demand and increase in demand in developing countries. This means cotton exports as percentage of total cotton fibre consumption will further increase.

Table 5.6
Revised Estimates of World Gross Trade during 1992

(Mn. Kgs)

	1992 Gross Trade TOI data	*1992 Cotton Trade FAO data*	*1992 Other Fibres Trade FAO data*	*1992 Gross Trade Data FAO*	*Revised Cotton Trade 1992 (ICAC & FAO data)*	*1992 Revised Total Trade data*
Yarn	2846	1574	1386	2959	1605	2991
Fabrics	4867	2309	2621	4930	2160	4781
Other	2039	937	1142	2079	937	2079
Clothing	5605	2945	2406	5351	2945	5351
Total	15357	7646	7554	15318	7646	15200
Fibre Equivalent	17696	9380	8316	17696	9102	17418

Note: Item-wise weights are actual weights, rather than fibre/filament equivalents.
Source: TOI estimates for 1992 are revised on the basis of ICAC and FAO data.

Table 5.7
Revised Estimate of World Gross Trade during 1995 and 2005

(Mn. Kgs)

	1995 Gross Trade	*1995 Cotton Trade*	*1995 Other Fibre Trade*	*2005 Gross Trade*	*2005 Cotton Trade*	*2005 Other Fibre Trade*
Yarn	3447	*2036	1411	4427	2615	1812
Fabrics	5461	*2593	2868	7511	3566	3945
Other	2141	965	1176	4490	2024	2466
Clothing	6768	3725	3043	11614	6392	5222
Total Yarn Equivalent	17817	9320	8497	28042	14597	13445
Fibre Equivalent	20442	11095	9347	32133	17377	14756
Trade Share %	49.38	60.96	40.29	56.99	75.23	44.34
Fibre Consumption	41400	18200	23200	56380	23100	33280

Note: (1) *ICAC data
(2) Item-wise weights are actual weights, rather than fibre/filament equivalents.

Source: TOI estimates are revised on the basis of data from ICAC, FAO and Association of Yarn Industry Synthetic Fibre Industry, Mumbai.

Table 5.8
Revised Gross World Trade Projection 2005

(Mn. Kgs)

	2005 Gross Fibre Trade	*2005 Cotton Fibre Trade*	*2005 Other Fibre Trade*
Yarn	4427	2615	1812
Fabrics	7511	3566	3945
Other	4490	2024	2466
Clothing	11614	6392	5222
Total Trade	28042	14597	13445
Fibre Equivalent	32133	17377	14756
Trade Share %	56.99	75.23	44.34
Fibre Consumption	56380	23100	33280

Note: Item-wise weights are actual weights, rather than fibre/filament equivalents.

Source: TOI estimates are revised on the basis of data from ICAC, FAO and Association of Yarn Industry Synthetic Fibre Industry, Mumbai.

South Asia

After reworking the item-wise world trade, TOI estimates for South Asia are reworked in the revised framework of world trade. As per, the TOI analysis, South Asia's net trade in terms of yarn equivalent weight was expected to increase from 1650 million kilograms in 1995 to 2370 million kilograms in 2000 and further to 3000 million kilograms in 2005. South Asia's net fibre trade equivalent are expected to increase from 1920 M Kg in 1995 to 2800 million kilograms in 2000 and further to 3549 in 2005.

The net trade figures are modified after taking into account the discrepancies in TOI data for South Asia. For the year 1992 and 1995, the Mills associations and official data for Pakistan and India's is used along with ICAC data to arrive at the item-wise revised estimates of South Asia's gross and net trade. The gross over net trade ratio is estimated at 1.17 during 1995 in South Asia region compared to 1.13 during 1992.

The estimates of TOI regarding growth of yarn equivalent net trade are 1.818 per cent during 1995 to 2005 from 1650 million kilograms to 3000 million kilograms. By assuming the similar growth rate as assumed in TOI, the revised estimates of yarn equivalent net trade for South Asia are expected to be 3313 million kilograms during 2005. Using conversion rates as worked out in Chapter 2 and Chapter 3, the net trade of fibre is estimated to be 3822 million kilograms. We have assumed that gross to net ratio may increase from 1.17 in 1995 to 1.22 in 2005. Similarly composition of various items is expected to change. Item-wise net and gross exports of textiles and clothing goods from South Asia are given in Table 5.9.

These changes in pattern of trade are based on following assumptions. The share of yarn is assumed to be lower than expected by the TOI analysis and that of made-ups and clothing would be higher. These changes are expected on the assumption that there is a limit to which yarn export from South Asia could be raised further as its share in world trade is already very high. Moreover, as the custom duties are expected to be lower, the impact of preference treatment given especially for value added products originally exported from same countries would become less effective. This would raise the share of developing countries' export especially of value added products in the world trade. As the indirect routes applied by various developing countries to avoid restrictions would no more be relevant, the share of intermediary goods trade will decline. Otherwise also, the next stage for developing countries is to shift to value added products exports. This has already happened in case of China, which was once considered a major cotton yarn exporter is now the net importer of cotton yarn. Considering all these aspects, it is possible that after reaching a peak level, the net export of yarn from South Asia may ultimately decline. The expected item-wise shares in net trade of South Asia are given in Table 5.10.

In addition to the changes in composition of trade, the other possible changes include the rise in export of synthetic products at all stages of production. Moreover, the indirect trade routes applied by exports originated from India and

Table 5.9
South Asia's Revised Estimate of Trade

	Net Trade Mn. Kgs			*Gross Trade Mn. Kgs*			*Gross/Net Trade Ratio*		
	1992	*1995*	*2005*	*1992*	*1995#*	*2005*	*1992*	*1995*	*2005*
Yarn	651	786	994	677	861	1143	1.04	1.10	1.15
Fabrics	319	427	828	464	636	1284	1.46	1.49	1.55
Other	235	259	663	247	266	734	1.05	1.03	1.11
Clothing	276	350	828	282	369	878	1.02	1.05	1.06
Total	1482	1822	3313	1671	2132	4039	1.13	1.17	1.22
Fibre/Equivalent	1734	2120	3822	1955	2481	4645	1.13	1.17	1.22

Note: Item-wise weights are actual weights, rather than fibre/filament equivalents.
Source: FAO revised data on the basis of India's data from official source and Data from ICAC, Handbook of statistics on cotton textile industry, ICMF and IPMA.

Pakistan's are expected to shift from newly advanced countries, as wages are going to rise there, to low wage cost countries in South Asia such as Bangladesh, Sri-Lanka, and Nepal. These countries of South Asia have already become quite competitive in clothing products and demand of fabrics and yarn is expected to increase further in these countries. These all explain the possible rise in gross to net trade ratio over time at higher rate in South Asia at compared to world. The expected share of South Asia in world trade for various textiles and clothing items is given in Table 5.10.

The above analysis fits in the country/region-wise framework for the overall world demand and supply as is given in Table 5.11. The analysis undertaken above shows considerable increase in South Asia's share in World Trade. It is possible only if these economies remain competitive by formulating policies conducive for their growth. Once the analysis has been revised for World and South Asia, it is easy to draw demand and supply scenario for state of Indian Textile and clothing industry. Before, we extend the world and South Asia's analysis for India, it is important to look at competitiveness of India's textile and clothing industry compared to other countries in the World.

To begin with, it is important to study the India's present state of textiles and clothing industry and item-wise share in various countries import, to find the potential markets for future growth etc. India's cost competitiveness of various products compared to other countries along with impact of quota restrictions, present share of each item in world trade and past growth pattern need to be also analysed to predict the future scenario.

India's Textiles and Clothing Exports to Major Importers in the World

India's textiles and clothing exports to top 20 importing countries in the world account for US$ 7267.48 and 76.77 per cent of India's exports. An attempt is also made to find the top fifteen countries to which India is a major exporter in textiles and clothing. These include EU, USA, Bangladesh,

Table 5.10
South Asia's Share in World Trade Projections 2005

	World Gross Trade of various items (Mn. Kgs.)			*South Asia's Gross Trade of Various Items (Mn. Kgs.)*			*South Asia's Share in World Trade*		
	1992	*1995*	*2005*	*1992*	*1995*	*2005*	*1992*	*1995*	*2005*
Yarn	2991	3447	4427	671	861	1143	22.6	25.0	25.8
Fabrics	4781	5461	7511	464	636	1284	9.7	11.6	17.1
Other	2079	2141	4490	247	266	734	11.9	12.4	16.3
Clothing	5351	6768	11614	282	369	878	5.3	5.5	7.6
Total	15202	17817	28042	1671	2132	4039	11.0	12.0	14.4
Fibre Equiv.	17418	20442	32133	1955	2481	4645	11.2	12.1	14.4

Note: (1) Item-wise weights are actual weights, rather than fibre/filament equivalents.
Source: TOI estimates are revised on the basis of data from ICAC, FAO and Association of Yarn Industry Synthetic Fibre Industry, Mumbai.

UAE, Hong Kong, USSR, Japan, Canada, Korea Republic, Australia, Switzerland, Mauritius, Taiwan, Saudi Arabia and Sri-Lanka.

Eleven countries are common among the major importers of Textiles and clothing in the world and India. The four countries that are not considered as major importer in the world, but are placed as major importers of Indian textiles and clothing goods include Bangladesh, USSR (Russia), Mauritius, and Sri Lanka. The markets where India's Textiles and Clothing have high share and are also growing include Hong Kong, Russia, Japan, Korea, Australia, Switzerland, Mauritius, Taiwan and Saudi Arabia.

Hence, the Indian exports are not only concentrated to major importers in the world or quota countries alone, but are spread to other countries as well. The import intensity and growth was also high especially for intermediary items such as yarn and fabrics to the non-quota countries such as Bangladesh, Hong Kong, Korea Rep, Sri Lanka, and Taiwan. All this points to India's competitive strength. This means India's standing is not only based on existing quota level but on competitiveness.

India's share in three countries EU, USA and Japan analysed in this study accounts for 3.26 per cent as against 3.15 per cent in case of World. Thus, it is possible that as tariffs on import from developing countries is expected to decline a major part of intra-EU trade may be shared by other exporters including India. The intra regional trade is very high and is 54.35 per cent in case of EU. In textiles intra-European trade account for 68.59 per cent and in clothing 44.53 per cent.

Thus, one can expect that India could gain substantially in case the custom duties and quotas will be removed on the exports from developing countries.

India's Item-wise Exports

India has more than 5 per cent share in world trade in cotton fabrics, textiles article not elsewhere classified, and floor covering, which is higher than India's overall share in world

Table 5.11
Fibre Consumption in Major Countries and Regions, 1980-95 and Projection for 2005

	Per capita fibre consumption					*Alt I*		*Alt II*		*Net Alt I*	*Imports Alt II*	*Domestic Consumption*	*Alt I*	*Alt II*
	1980	*1985*	*1990*	*1993*	*1995*	*2000*	*2005*	*2000*	*2005*	*2005*	*2005*	*1995*	*2005*	*2005*
			Kilograms					*Kilograms*		*Mn. Kgs.*			*Mn. Kgs.*	
I. Developed Countries						Textile Outlook International								
(a) Western Developed and Japan														
USA	20.90	22.20	26.00	29.00	29.90	31.00	32.50	33.69	37.96	3383	4564	7900	9702	11199
EU (15)	15.40	15.00	18.00	16.70	19.10	20.00	21.50	20.52	21.90	4521	4368	7120	8432	8475
Other Wewstern Europe	13.50	14.20	14.40	9.70	11.30	13.50	16.00	13.50	16.00	299	271	400	589	576
Japan	16.80	17.70	21.90	21.30	22.20	24.00	26.00	24.36	27.09	1682	1686	2800	3456	3549
Other	13.20	12.80	13.10	14.00	14.50	17.00	18.50	17.00	18.50	1563	1497	1500	2252	2220
Total	16.80	17.20	20.20	20.30	21.90	23.20	24.90	24.29	26.85	11448	12386	19720	24431	26019
(b) Eastern Developed														
Eastern Europe	12.60	12.10	9.80	5.60	6.70	10.00	14.00	10.00	14.00	-266	-270	670	1474	1470
Former USSR	14.70	14.60	14.70	8.10	6.70	8.60	14.50	8.60	14.50	802	797	1980	4457	4452
Total	14.10	14.00	13.30	7.50	6.70	9.00	14.40	9.00	14.36	536	536	2650	5931	5931
Total Developed	16.00	16.20	18.20	16.40	17.30	18.90	21.70	19.67	23.11	11984	12913	22370	30362	31941
II. Developing Countries														
China	4.00	5.00	4.70	5.30	5.60	5.80	6.40	6.26	6.40	-4368	-4707	6820	8736	8736
Latin America	5.50	5.00	5.30	6.10	6.60	7.00	7.60	7.01	7.60	0	0	3150	4407	4408
South Asia	2.00	2.10	2.60	2.60	2.80	3.00	3.30	3.13	3.50	-3822	-4119	3450	4732	5025.
East and South East Asia	3.50	3.60	5.70	6.10	6.60	7.50	9.00	8.15	9.00	-3628	-3910	2550	4031	4032
Other	3.50	3.10	2.80	2.90	3.20	3.30	3.50	3.11	3.50	-164	-177	3060	4113	4113
Total Developing	3.40	3.60	3.80	4.10	4.50	4.70	5.20	4.89	5.26	-11983	-12913	19030	26019	26313
World Total	6.80	6.80	7.20	7.20	7.50	7.80	8.83	8.21	9.12	1	0	41400	56381	58254
World Excluding Former Eastern Block										-535	-536	38750	50450	52323

Source: Derived for FAO and Textile Outlook Estimates.

textiles and clothing trade of 3 per cent. The analysis in Table 5.12 is based on SITC broad classification.

Table 5.12

India's Item-wise Export Share in the World Import during 1994

(US$ Mn.)

	World	*India*	*India Share in World*
Textile Yarn	29525	1051	3.56
Cotton Fabrics	17728	913	5.15
Man Made Fabric	28235	354	1.26
Other Woven Fabric	8973	203	2.27
Knitted Fabrics	8864	72	0.82
Lace, Ribon	3631	30	0.85
Special Textile Fabric	14004	49	0.36
Textile Art nec	11133	543	4.88
Floor Covering	8219	610	7.43
Total	13024	3829	2.94

Source: UN Trade Statistics.

The further analysis is undertaken at more disaggregate level. At disaggregate level, the items in which India has high share are cotton yarn, cotton sewing thread, artificial filament yarn, cotton fabrics woven unbleached, other 85 per cent cotton fabrics of less than 200 gms/smt, fabrics woven jute, sacks bags, textile material, curtains, other furnishing material, carpets, etc., woven, men's shirts, knit and non-knit and men's overcoat, women's dresses, skirts and divided skirts, blouses, shirt blouses, underwears, nightwears, etc., and women's non-knit under garments. Further, it has been found that those items where the quota utilisation is high are exported in large quantities to non-quota countries as well.

The share of India's exports of cotton yarn and cotton fabrics have been increasing over time in world cotton yarn and cotton fabrics trade respectively is brought out in Table 5.13. India has highest share in cotton yarn trade. However, India's share in textile yarn export is small (Table 5.12), primarily because of inclusion of filament yarn in this item.

The rapid rise in India's share of cotton yarn export has slowed down since 1996-97. However, it recovered during

1999 as cotton yarn exports increased from 473.54 million kilograms during 1998 to 534.83 million kilograms during 1999. The slow down was caused due to various factors staring from the East Asia countries crisis and slow down in World demand. On the other hand, cotton fabrics export has been registering an increase since 1995. The share of India in world cotton fabrics exports has increased from approximately 6.7 per cent in 1995 to approximately 8.8 per cent in 1998-99. It appears that India's share in the world cotton yarn export has already reached a very high level and may soon achieve peak. Thus only marginal increase in quantity is possible in the long run. However, in the short run the cotton yarn exports may increase at high rate for some more time. In the long run, in order to increase its exports of value added products strategy has to be shifted to increase exports of cotton fabrics, made-ups and garments. All efforts should be made to make the fabrics and dying activity more competitive.

Table 5.13

India's Share in World Trade of Cotton Yarn and Cotton Fabrics

(% Share)

Year	*1975*	*1980*	*1985*	*1990*	*1995*	*1996-97**	*1997-98**	*1998-99**	*2005-06* Alt I#
Cotton Yarn	0.7	0.9	1.0	4.2	12.9	22.3	22.7	22.2	19.7
Cotton Fabrics	4.8	4.8	5.1	6.9	6.7	8.6	8.3	8.8	11.5

* Approximation
# Projected on the basis of analysis later.
Source: WTO.

The items-wise analysis brings out one important conclusion that India's exports are predominantly of cotton products and its share in world export of many items like yarn, cotton woven grey fabrics, made-ups is quite high and is increasing over time. But the same is not true for dyed products as competitiveness gets eroded at dyeing stage. In the garments sector the non-availability of low quality fabrics as well barriers to entry for large sector in domestic segment (till New Textile Policy 2000) were responsible for low value added products. These factors come into the way for developing broad base export potential for India.

Thus it is to be noted that in some items, India is quite competitive as is clear from the fact that despite high quota level the utilisation is also high. These are items where there are chances of increase in India's share with the phasing out of MFA. On the other hand in some items, despite low quota base, utilisation is low. These are categories such as dyed products such as dyed yarn, dyed fabrics, high value made-ups and garments and synthetic products. Thus improvement in technology is must to increase India's share in high value added items. This is specially important as India is going to face a tuff competition in future among low value added products from countries like Sri Lanka, Bangladesh etc. In fact, China has already shifted away from low value added products towards higher value added products to increase its share in world textiles and clothing exports.

India's Export to Quota and Non-quota Countries

An attempt has been made to work out the yarn equivalent textiles and clothing exports of two major quota countries EEC and USA and compares it with the total exports from India.

Despite these constraints, India's exports share in world quantity trade of Textiles and Clothing products is quite high and is growing. But India's share in world value trade is low. An attempt is made in this study, to find the reasons that how it has happened that despite several restrictions, the growth in quantity exports in high.

The result shows that the growth in quota items is much lower compared to overall growth of exports from India. The growth of non-quota items to quota countries is even higher compared to growth of quota items, despite higher potential in quota items.[4]

4. An attempt is also made to find India's exports of quota items to two other quota countries namely Canada and Norway. It has been estimated that approximately 5.83 million kilograms of quota items are exported from India to Canada and Norway during 1995, 4.95 *(Contd...)*

The analysis of growth in exports of quota and non-quota items reveal that the notably good performance of India's exports of textiles and clothing could only happen because of high growth in exports to non-quota countries. Moreover, it was able to exploit other possible options. These include

Firstly, over-utilisation of quota levels since 1990. However, the problem is that quotas cannot be over utilised to an unlimited extent.

Secondly, exploitation of the non-quota items to quota countries has also been done to some extent. The growth of non-quota items to quota countries was higher compared with the quota items. However, it has been a practice in the past that in case a country export of certain item grew at a very high rate, the item is placed under quota restriction. It has been done several times in the past that several non-quota items have been brought under quota restrictions. In fact, even during the MFA phase out period, the developed countries have kept that option very much open. Moreover, in Table 5.14 data few more countries have included over the period of time in EEC list as mentioned below in the Table note. Thus the growth rates observed above of quota items do not reflect growth of same items and for same countries over time as these items and countries go on increasing over the period of time. Thus the actual growth rate of fixed number of items may be much lower and those of non-quota items may be much higher than reflected by figures given in Table 5.14. This has happened despite the fact that growth potential is much higher for quota items. This means quota regime has severely hindered India's potential growth in the past and free trade regime is likely to trigger India's export

(Contd...)

million kilograms in 1996, and 4.34 million kilograms in 1997. This means these two countries constitute very small share of total quota exports from India. These countries total imports are also comparatively small. Thus it would not make much difference in the share of quota countries in India's exports in case these two quota countries exports are also included.

Table 5.14

India's share of Textiles and Clothing Exports to EEC and USA

(Estimated Equivalent to Million Kilograms)

Year	*Quota Base*	*Shipment of Quota items*	*Quota Percentage utilisation*	*Total restricted items*	*Total restricted items share in exports to EEC and USA*	*Total exports to EEC and USA*	*EEC and USA exports share in India's Exports*	*Total Exports from India*
1987	87	84	96	84	47.82	175	—	—
1988	125	95	77	95	84.78	113	41.12	274
1989	128	97	76	97	73.60	131	36.83	356
1990	132	140	106	150	77.35	194	44.34	438
1991	143	141	99	153	75.76	202	37.27	543
1992	147	149	102	163	78.39	208	35.05	594
1993	159	165	103	185	79.48	233	32.09	727
1994	166	174	105	197	79.80	247	28.53	866
1995	186	198	106	218	76.91	284	30.42	932
1996	201	222	110	245	75.06	326	25.93	1257
1997	209	221	106	248	71.92	345	24.84	1389
CGR 1990 to 97	6.75	7.58	—	8.11	—	8.83	—	16.43
t-statistics	20.37	12.11	—	16.10	—	12.91	—	23.42

Note: (1) * means data is for year 1983 instead of year 1987.

(2) EEC consists of Germany, France, Italy, Benelux, Denmark, Ireland, UK, Greece, Spain and Portugal before 1993. However, exports of Sweden, Finland and Austria are also included in EEC exports since 1993.

(3) CGR in this Chapter 5 Tables are worked out using trend semi-log method in case t-statistics are also given.

performance. However, a word of caution here is that the growth of exports to non-quota countries is likely to decline after the NPFA phase out as the indirect export through these countries to quota countries is likely to decline.

The quota regime affect on the performance of India's exports was not much till mid eighties. In fact during the 1970s and the first half of 1980s, India's exports of cotton fabrics to the EEC and USA were less than half the quota for most years. However, condition changed in the mid-1980s as exports of cotton fabrics increased and was utilised quota. It need to be however pointed out that the utilisation of overall quota need not to be 100 per cent to be binding. This is because a country may be finding the quota in a few items binding despite the fact that its quota is unutilised in few other items. Therefore, an increase in the categorisation or number of restrictions may lead to low utilisation of overall quota. The other ways through which this quota regime affects the trade is by way of deciding the quotas on the past performance of each exporting country. This kind of quota regime causes a major constraint in case of fashion goods, where demand in particular goods appears for short period. Similar, the rise in order towards low price products under the quota regime affects the performance in terms of value.

Thus, the high growth of overall Indian exports in the past in quantity terms as shown in Table 5.14 has been mainly achieved by acquiring a very high growth rate of exports to non-quota countries. The very high growth of cotton yarn export to Asian countries during nineties is most suitable example of it.

Competitive Advantage of a Nation

According to Porter (1990), the competitiveness advantage of nation is the ability of nations/firms to compete in world markets. We in this study try to look into various parameters, which shows the ability of Indian textiles and clothing industry to compete in the world.

India's Position in World Textile Industry

India has a fairly strong base in textile production is brought out in Table 5.15. India's investment is lacking in shuttleless looms, which are considered modern looms for weaving. This may not be good, especially in the new economic environment. On the other hand, presently Indian spinning industry has the maximum number of modern spindles in the world.

Table 5.15
India's Ranking Regarding Various Parameters during 1996

	India	*India's Rank*	*Top Rank Country*
Installed Spindles (Million)	31.84	2	41.71 (China)
Installed Looms (Million)	India Ranks 1st in case looms*		
O.E. Rotors (000)	230	8	968 (USA)
Shuttleless Looms	10	15	113 (Russia)
Cotton Production (M. Tonnes)	2.98	3	4.2 (China)
Cotton Consumption (M. Tonnes)	2.7	3	4.6 (China)
Man Made Fibres/Filaments Production (Million Tonnes)	1.2	7	3.44 (USA)
Man Made Fibres/Filaments Consumption (Million Tonnes)	1.01	7	3.85 (China)
Exports of Textiles (Billion US Dollar)	4.85	•13	14.15 (Hong Kong)
Exports of Clothing (Billion US Dollar)	4.85	11	25.03 (China)

Note : *Installed in Decentralised sector are also included.
Source: International Textile Manufacturing Federation, Zurich and ICMF.

After discussing the state of factors of production, it is important to analyse the cost competitioned of Indian Textile and Clothing products.

Cost Comparison

Hourly Labour Cost (in US$)

As per Werner International survey data, the hourly labour cost in case of India was US $ 0.55 during 1991 and India ranked 45th in descending order among a survey of 52 countries. Seven countries in which labour cost were lower than India were Egypt 0.43, Sri Lanka ($0.39), Pakistan ($0.38), China PR ($0.34), Tanzania ($0.32), Nigeria (0.30) and Indonesia (0.28). This indicates that although labour cost in India is low, but main competitors of India in textiles and clothing are having even lower wages than India. Bangladesh, another competitor was not surveyed during the year 1991. However, by 1996 India's competitive position improved as hourly cost in China became higher than that in India. India's hourly labour cost was US$ 0.50 in 1996, while that of China was US$ 0.58. Bangladesh cost at US$ 0.44 was lower than that of India in this list.

It is important to analyse the various stages of production to arrive at the proper conclusions about the competitiveness of the country.

Cost of Cotton Yarn Production

For the year 1989, ITMF studied the cost structure for cotton yarn spinning for six countries namely Brazil, Germany, India, Japan, Korea and USA. During the course of time, Germany was dropped and was replaced by Italy in 1993. Later on by 1997, Thailand, Indonesia, and Turkey were also brought into the analysis Table 5.16a. A comparison of cost of production of 30s cotton yarn for various countries is given during the year 1999 in Table 5.16b.

For other year, the data is also available. From this, it is clear that India's cost of yarn production remained lowest throughout nineties till 1997. However, the manufacturing cost from raw cotton to yarn was not the lowest throughout. Even during 1997, Indonesia's manufacturing cost was lower than India. However, since Indonesia has to import cotton at higher prices, its total yarn cost is higher than India. Among the countries analysed for ring spinning Korea, Thailand and Turkey pose potential threat to India. The data for cost of cotton yarn production is analysed for 20s for the years 1989 and 1991 and for 30s for the years 1993 & 1997. Japan is competing with India in open-end rotor system.

However, the competitiveness of various countries has undergone a major change after the South Asian Crisis. India's cost of cotton yarn production no longer remained the lowest among the countries for which analysis was undertaken. It was shifted to number three places after the Brazil was placed

Table 5.16a

Total Ring Yarn Costs in Various Countries: Spinning for Ne 30 Combed Cotton during 1997

(US $)

Cost Element US$ per Kg of Yarn	*Brazil*	*India*	*Italy*	*Indonesia*	*Korea*	*USA*	*Turkey*
Labour	0.22	0.06	0.89	0.03	0.25	0.52	0.13
Power	0.19	0.33	0.27	0.19	0.18	0.17	0.23
Auxiliary Material	0.12	0.11	0.12	0.12	0.13	0.12	0.15
Depreciation & Int.	1.02	1.01	0.87	1.1	0.95	0.88	1.02
Manufacturing Cost	1.55	1.51	2.15	1.44	1.51	1.69	1.53
Cost Index	102.65	100.00	142.38	95.36	100.00	111.92	101.32
Waste	0.37	0.29	0.35	0.37	0.36	0.32	0.37
Raw Material	1.8	1.44	1.75	1.82	1.79	1.59	1.83
Total Yarn Costs	3.73	3.24	4.26	3.63	3.65	3.6	3.73
Yarn Cost Index	115.12	100.00	131.48	112.04	112.65	111.11	115.12

Source: International textile manufacturing Federation, Zurich and ICMF.

Table 5.16b

Total Ring Yarn Costs in Various Countries: Spinning for Ne 30 Combed Cotton during 1999

(US $)

Cost Element *US$ per Kg of Yarn*	*Brazil*	*India*	*Italy*	*Indonesia*	*Korea*	*USA*	*Turkey*
Labour	0.1	0.05	0.01	0.78	0.18	0.12	0.52
Power	0.1	0.3	0.1	0.26	0.14	0.19	0.17
Auxiliary Material	0.1	0.1	0.1	0.1	0.1	0.1	0.11
Depreciation & Int.	0.9	1.08	1.55	0.67	0.8	1.09	0.74
Manufacturing Cost	1.2	1.53	1.76	1.81	1.22	1.5	1.54
Manufacturing Cost Index	78.43	100.00	115.03	118.30	79.74	98.04	100.65
Waste	0.18	0.17	0.21	0.18	0.18	0.24	0.21
Raw Material	1.26	1.26	1.39	1.29	1.29	1.45	1.36
Total Yarn Costs	2.64	2.96	3.36	3.28	2.70	3.18	3.11
Yarn Cost Index	89.19	100.00	113.51	110.81	91.15	107.43	105.07

Source: International textile manufacturing Federation, Zurich and ICMF.

first with lowest cost and Korea the second best. But India's cost of production was still low compared to EU and South Asian Countries to which India is major exporter.

Doubt is expressed in several quarters that India will lose its competitiveness, once all kinds of subsidise are removed and free exports of cotton is allowed. As we see from the year 1999 analysis of spinning cost that raw material prices in India are US$ 0.13 per kg lower than Italy. In case we also include the wastage cost, Indian industry gets raw cotton at around US$ 0.17 lower than Italy cotton price. On the other hand, Indian cotton yarn cost is US $ 0.40 lower than Italy, the main producer of cotton yarn in developed countries.

However, it is a mattee of concern that we are no longer the lowest cost producers of cotton yarn in the world. What would happen in case we have to import cotton and the cost of transportation would also be included. In that case, we may end up producing just at the same cost as the most of other producers. This means, we wouldn't be able to export much of cotton yarn.

The above analysis clearly points to the fact that in order to remain competitive in international market, we should pay sufficient attention to cotton production and its productivity. The farmers should be given sufficient incentive to raise their productivity.

ITMF data provide information regarding important variables of cost of production such as capital interest rate, cost of electric power per unit and cost of building (m2). The comparison of these variable over time has been made in terms of US $ for all countries to draw meaningful conclusions. The cost of electric power per KWH has risen maximum in India and is highest among the countries for which the comparison has been made. Another factor which raises India's cost of production is relatively very high interest rates. India's cost of building is also high compared to Indonesia and Turkey. Thus, attention has to be paid to these factors in case India wants to remain competitive. Efforts should be made to lower manufacturing cost of production by lowering interest rates as well as improving power and other infrastructure facilities. By paying attention in this direction, we could remain competitive in the international market even if we have to import raw cotton.

Cost of Cotton Fabrics Production

India's cost of production of fabrics from cotton remained among the lowest throughout the nineties till 1997 except for the year 1993, when Korea's cost of fabric production was marginally lower than India's. However, the manufacturing cost was not the lowest throughout. Even during 1997, Indonesia and Turkey's costs of manufacturing were lower than India's Table 5.17a. Other countries posing potential threat to India, among the countries analysed for weaving are Turkey, Indonesia, Thailand, and Korea. This analysis was undertaken for the 100 per cent cotton fabrics, 60/60, Ne (count) 20 warp & weft, 63' width for years 1989 and 1991 and for the 100 per cent cotton fabrics, 70/70, Ne 30 warp and weft, 66" width for the years 1993 and after.

However, during 1999, the cost of fabrics was lower in Brazil and Korea compared to India (Table 5.17b). As was relevant in case of cotton yarn, the reduction in interest rates, cost of capital and rents and development of infrastructure are important to improve India's compositeness. In fact, consensus has already emerged that the interest rates in India may be lowered to the level of Developed Countries in the medium to long run and process has already begun in that direction.

Synthetic Products

The cost of manufacturing yarn and fabrics is similar in case of cotton and synthetics. The cost is different mainly because of raw material cost. India has already established big plant in MMF, which can economically produce at international cost. The higher excise and custom duties on synthetic products compared to cotton products seems to the prime reason for low share of synthetic products. With liberalisation, the excise and custom duties on synthetic products are becoming rational and hence its share in production and exports is rising in India.

Table 5.17a
1997 Total Fabric Costs in Various Countries: Weaving Grey 100 per cent Cotton 70/70, Ne 30 Warp & Weft, 66" Width

(US $)

Cost Element US$ per Yard of Fabric	*Brazil*	*Italy*	*India*	*Indonesia*	*Korea*	*USA*	*Turkey*
Labour	0.125	0.378	0.032	0.016	0.155	0.241	0.045
Power	0.069	0.107	0.113	0.067	0.065	0.063	0.075
Auxiliary Material	0.075	0.071	0.069	0.048	0.077	0.06	0.062
Depreciation & Int.	0.355	0.346	0.36	0.37	0.321	0.319	0.372
Total Manufacturing Costs	0.624	0.902	0.574	0.501	0.618	0.683	0.554
Manufacturing Cost Index	108.71	157.14	100.00	87.28	107.67	118.99	96.52
Waste	0.064	0.061	0.05	0.064	0.063	0.056	0.064
Raw Material	0.314	0.305	0.251	0.318	0.312	0.277	0.319
Total Costs	1.002	1.268	0.876	0.882	0.992	1.015	0.937
Fabrics Cost Index	114.38	144.75	100.00	100.68	113.24	115.87	106.96

Source: International Textile Manufacturing Federation, Zurich.

Table 5.17 b

1999 Total Fabric Costs in Various Countries: Weaving Grey 100 per cent Cotton 70/70, Ne 30 Warp & Weft, 66" Width

(US $)

Cost Element US$ per Yard of Fabric	*Brazil*	*Italy*	*India*	*Indonesia*	*Korea*	*USA*	*Turkey*
Labour	0.052	0.333	0.031	0.007	0.092	0.243	0.044
Power	0.043	0.109	0.114	0.04	0.057	0.072	0.074
Auxiliary Material	0.043	0.058	0.057	0.039	0.056	0.051	0.046
Depreciation & Int.	0.244	0.215	0.263	0.387	0.226	0.22	0.306
Total Manufacturing Costs	0.382	0.715	0.465	0.473	0.431	0.586	0.47
Manufacturing Cost Index	82.15	153.76	100.00	101.72	92.69	126.02	101.08
Waste	0.031	0.032	0.030	0.037	0.032	0.237	0.041
Raw Material	0.22	0.225	0.220	0.243	0.225	0.037	0.253
Total Costs	0.633	0.973	0.716	0.753	0.688	0.86	0.764
Fabrics Cost Index	88.43	135.90	100.00	105.20	96.12	120.15	106.73

Source: International Textile Manufacturing Federation, Zurich.

In the fiscal year 2001-2002, the excise duty on cotton and synthetic products are made similar except at yarn stage. This may be corrected over the period of time. However, the custom duties are still high on synthetic products. With the MFA phase out, these duties are likely to get reduced substantially.

Considering all this, it appears India can become competitive even in synthetic products during medium to long run.

Garments

Werner International compared various countries cost of production from yarn to manufacturing of shirt. The cost of production is lowest in the case of India at $3.88 per shirt. The raw material, depreciation and energy cost are higher in India compared to the USA. Despite that, India is competent as far as garment production is concerned as it is dominantly labour intensive industry and labour cost is low in India. The labour cost component at various stages of production from yarn to garment is given in Table 5.18.

This shows that US cost of production is higher by US$ 3.32 per shirt during 1994 due to labour cost difference. The process wise analysis of cost comparison shows that India is competitive at various stages of production such as spinning, weaving and stitching of garments. However, the cost of dyeing and finishing is slightly higher compared to Thailand. The total manufacturing cost per shirt in case of India was US$ 3.88 compared with US$ 4.26 in case of Thailand, US$ 4.37 in case of Mexico and US$ 7.11 in case of US.

India's competitive advantage is not lost even if we include the sales and general administrative expense or profit margins incurred at various stages. However, another scenario is added into the above analysis. This scenario consider the option of importing garment to USA from Mexico, the fabrics for which is exported earlier to Mexico from USA (Table 5.19).

Table 5.18
Country-wise Cost of Production per Shirt from Yarn

(US $)

	Cost of Production at Various Stages of Production from Yarn to Made Up Shirts							
	USA	%	MEX	%	INDIA	%	THAI	%
(1)	(2)	(3)	(4)	(5)	(6)	(7)	(8)	(9)
Yarn Cost/Shirt	1.27	17.86	1.26	28.83	1.17	30.15	1.23	28.87
Weaving Added Value/Shirt	0.61	8.58	0.5	11.44	0.48	12.37	0.48	11.27
Dyeing & Finishing Added Value/Shirt	0.48	6.75	0.45	10.30	0.43	11.08	0.42	9.86
Making-up Added Value/Shirt	4.74	66.67	2.16	49.43	1.8	46.39	2.13	50.00
Total Mfg. Cost/shirt	7.11	100.00	4.37	100.00	3.88	100.00	4.26	100.00
Mfg. Cost Index	100		61		55		60	
Mfg. Cost Differential with USA	0		2.74		3.22		2.85	
	Cost of Various Inputs and Factors of Production from Yarn to Made Up Shirts							
Raw Material	1.6	22.50	1.66	37.99	1.66	42.78	1.72	40.38
Personnel	3.57	50.21	0.7	16.02	0.25	6.44	0.7	16.43
Energy	0.26	3.66	0.57	13.04	0.56	14.43	0.41	9.62
Mfg. Expenses	1.04	14.63	0.62	14.19	0.58	14.95	0.64	15.02
Depreciation	0.64	9.00	0.82	18.76	0.85	21.91	0.8	18.78

(Contd....)

(Contd....)

(1)	*(2)*	*(3)*	*(4)*	*(5)*	*(6)*	*(7)*	*(8)*	*(9)*
Total Mfg. Cost/Shirt	7.11	100.00	4.37	100.00	3.88	100.00	4.26	100.00
Mfg. Cost Index	100		61		55		60	
Mfg. Cost Differential with USA	0.00		2.74		3.22		2.85	
Labour Cost/Shirt from Spinning to Manufacturing of Shirt								
Spinning	0.21	5.88	0.04	5.71	0.02	7.60	0.05	6.8
Weaving	0.25	7.00	0.05	7.14	0.02	8.70	0.05	7.9
Dyeing and Finishing	0.1	2.80	0.04	5.71	0.02	7.00	0.04	5.4
Sub-Total	0.56	15.69	0.13	18.57	0.06	23.30	0.14	20.1
Making-Up	3.01	84.31	0.57	81.43	0.19	76.70	0.56	79.9
Total	3.57	100.00	0.7	100.00	0.25	100.00	0.7	100
Labour Cost Differentials with USA			-2.87		-3.32		-2.87	
Labour Cost % of F.O.B. Cost	41.75	100.00	12.87	100.00	5.09	100.00	13.06	100.00

Source: Werner International Inc. Management Consultants, Brussels, Belgium.

Table 5.19
Country-wise Comparison of per Shirt Domestic Sale Cost

(US $)

	USA	%	*MEX*	%	*INDIA*	%	*THAI*	%	*USA-MEX*	%
Manufacturing Cost Fabric/Shirt	2.37	27.7	2.21	40.5	2.09	42.5	2.13	39.8	2.37	41.4
Sales and G & A/Shirt	0.17	1.3	0.15	2.8	0.15	2.97	0.16	2.79	0.17	2.9
Profit	0.25	3	0.24	4.3	0.22	4.54	0.23	4.26	0.25	4.43
Total Fabric Cost/Shirt	2.79	32.6	2.6	47.7	2.45	50	2.51	46.8	2.79	48.7
Making-up Added Value/Shirt	4.73	55.4	2.16	39.7	1.8	36.6	2.13	39.7	2.16	37.8
Sales and G & A/Shirt	0.25	2.9	0.19	3.5	0.21	4.33	0.23	4.33	0.25	4.33
Profit	0.78	9.1	0.5	9.09	0.45	9.09	0.49	9.09	0.52	9.09
Total F.O.B. Cost/Shirt	8.55	100	5.44	100	4.91	100	5.36	100	5.72	100

Source: Werner International Inc. Management Consultants, Various Issues, Brussels, Belgium.

Considering all the possible alternatives, India's cost remains competitive in garment industry. Despite the cost advantage, India's share of textiles and clothing export is still very low in the world trade. The cause being, there are additional costs involved such as freight, insurance, custom duties, custom clearance, agency fees, and inventory carrying cost etc. In case, these additional costs are added, the cost to retailer of fabrics shipped from various countries is given in Table 5.20.

Table 5.20
Retailer Cost in USA of Shirt Produced in Various Countries

(US $)

	USA	*MEX*	*INDIA*	*THAI*	*USA-MEX*
Total F.O.B. Cost/Shirt	8.55	5.44	4.91	5.36	5.72
Import Costs	0.00	1.22	2.18	2.21	0.47
Cost to Retailer	8.55	6.66	7.09	7.57	6.19

Note: *MEX means Married and THAI means Thailand.*
Source: Werner International Inc. Management Consultants, Various Issues, Brussels, Belgium.

Thus, Indian shirts are competitive compared to products from other countries. The high cost of import and inventory to retailer for Indian products takes away the benefit at the cost of production stage. The preferential treatment given to Mexico for products originated from USA further increases the margin to retailer for shirts shipped from India and Mexico. Thus Indian shirts cost 15 per cent more to retailer compared to Mexican shirts whose fabrics originate from USA during 1994 as per Werner International data. This has been possible due to lower cost of transport and the preferential treatment given by USA to those products, which originate from Mexico. This is visible from the rising share of Mexican garment imports from USA. The stiching changes in Mexico are lower compared to USA due to cheap labour availability. In fact, after NAFTA trade with all North American countries has been completely freed.

On the other hand, cost of US products is higher in USA

compared to the landed cost of shirt manufactured in India. Further analysis shows that despite the cost advantages compared to USA, the retailer in USA may not prefer the Indian product. This is because the retailer may not only considers the gross margin per shirt but also looks at the gross margin per dollar of sale as the domestic product could be considered as easily available and require almost half inventories compared to imported products. According to Werner's calculation, based on some approximation, the impact of less inventories on retailer's gross margin per capital employed would be higher for US and Mexican products than for to Indian or Thai products.

To sum up, India definitely have the low cost of manufacturing advantage. In case, custom duties are reduced in developed countries, India's exports are likely to rise as it may reduce the benefit of preferential treatment to a few countries. The above analysis clearly points to the fact that after the MFA phase out, Indian exports could rise at steeper rate. However, it is important that we should take steps to compensate for the increase in cost caused due to rise in cotton prices and pay attention for lowering interest rates and developing infrastructure. This is essential in case India wants to remain competitive in the new economic environment.

Another important point from the policy prospective is to increase competitiveness in Indian garment industry. The competition within large and small producers in garment sector would not only increase the technological progress in garment industry but also in the fabrics industry. This is because the small producers of garment were spread all over the country and were demanding fabrics in smaller lots. The production of fabrics in smaller lots is not conducive for the shuttles looms. This clearly points to the fact that technological progress in weaving sector was also affected due to reservation of garment industry for SSI sector. The fiscal budget 2001-2002 addressed this problem and de-reserved the garment sector.

The analysis so far explains the reason for low base of Indian textiles and clothing exports despite its low cost of production. Indian exports mainly remained confined to low value added cotton products. The recent policy changes are in the right direction and India may be able to achieve the high share in World textiles and clothing trade after MFA phase out. However, there are several areas of concern for which India has to look into.

Some key concerns for India

The key concerns in Indian textile industry are divided into numerous operational, strategic and regulatory factors. The operational ones include low quality exports, weak work culture, poor skills of workers, poor ginning facility, poor agriculture practices for cotton products, inadequate transport facilities, excessive dependence on powerloom for small delivery, and above all outdated and technological backwardness mainly in weaving, dyeing and garment units.

The strategic ones include lack of resources mainly in the dominant sector of weaving production *i.e.* powerloom sector for the investment in new technology. Moreover, high pre-shipment and post-shipment export credit rates and high Interest rates in general are making the things more difficult. The entrepreneurs behaviour is short term, inward looking and opportunistic and are unable to re-locate with the changing cost environment. The high water and rental charges specially in Mumbai, the order based product mix and lack of idea about long term demand for various products are some of the examples. On the other hand European and North American producers are quick to re-locate and are shifting production base to Morocco, Tunisia, Portugal, Turkey, Mexico, Honduras, Czech Republic, Hungary and other low wage CIS Countries to meet the challenge from developing countries. And finally, some of inhibitory regulatory factors are minimum hank yarn obligation, essential commodities act, restrictions on import of raw material, irregular power availability, and cascading taxes and local levies of around 10 per cent. In addition, the non-tariff barrier to export exists. The reservations and other restrictions imposed by the government are forcing people to cheat or behave in a manner, which is un-economical in the long run. Thus these measures are ultimately leading to evasion of excise and false branding, etc.

Before arriving at India's textiles and clothing export potential, it is important to review other competitive strengths of overall Indian economy, which could affect the performance of textiles and clothing industry. Chandra Pankaj and Shukla P.R. (1994) analysed India's competitiveness related with labour, product quality, on time delivery, after sales distribution, worker's motivation, and labour flexibility, total expenditure on R & D compared to various competitors such as Brazil, Thailand, South Korea, Canada, USA, Japan, Germany, France and Netherlands. India's is ranked poorly in most of these variables during year 1990. This study analysed that a strategy merely based on exports to combat the might of multinationals can prove to be dangerous, causing erosion in the strength of Indian companies in the home market. Thus, a quality nurturing of home market by the Indian companies prior to their being flooded with assorted consumer items by foreign companies is essential.

Chandra Pankaj, (1999) in a related study, namely competing through capabilities, compared India's competitiveness with China and Canada. India was placed much below in the parameters such as infrastructure, regulatory regime, quality of home market, quality of work environment, absenteeism, R & D investment, quality of operator, Extent of investment in technology, type of technology available, etc.

On the other hand, it was placed better as far as size of home market, quality of managerial and technical staff is concerned.[5] In the study Pankaj Chandra argued that competitiveness of Indian firms would be contingent on developing long term distinctive capabilities. Three key strategies, namely, commitment, co-ordination and

---

5. However, in a recent analysis KSA Technopak has analysed that various companies/firms have overestimated domestic demand in India on the basis of assuming large proportion of people in the middle class segment.

co-operation, for developing distinctive capabilities are provided.

After reviewing the world trade prospects, South Asia's share in it and analysis of India's strengths, weaknesses and opportunities, an attempt is made to find India's future prospects by the year 2005-06 and 2010-11 on the basis of above analysis.

Estimates for India

The item-wise world trade is worked out for the 1999-2000 by assuming constant Annual growth rate for the period 1995 to 2005. As the item-wise data for India is also available for the year 1999-2000, an attempt is made to find India's item-wise share in world trade. Hence, the base year is shifted to year 1999-2000 rather than year 1995-96 to make the analysis more meaningful and capture the latest changes in pattern. Infact the highest increase in the cotton yarn export took place during 1996-97. Though the growth is not maintained latter, but it provides India a better base for future growth. South Asia's export is also calculated for the year 1999 by assuming the constant annual growth rate as projected for the period 1995 to 2005 (Table 5.21).

India's exports in future are expected to grow at comparatively much lower rate than in the past. This is because it is not possible to maintain the past trend due to demand constraints and non-availability of raw material. The policy changes since 1985 and especially after 1991 brought boom in India's exports. India's exports in terms of yarn equivalent grew at 14.87 per cent per annum during 1990-91 to 1999-2000. The growth at the past trend rates may not be sustainable especially in cotton products. However, growth may be still higher than projected for South Asia after the MFA phase out, as India's exports in the past were more restricted. The exports from India by year 2005-06 are worked out from the base year 1999-2000 considering the past trends and future world and South Asia's trade scenario as well as present status. The results obtained are given in Table 5.22.

Table 5.21
India's Share in World and South Asia's Gross Trade 1999-2000

	1999-2000 India's Export Mn. Kgs.	*1999 World Exports Mn. Kgs.*	*1999-2000 India's Share in World Trade (%)*	*1999 South Asia's Exports Mn. Kgs.*	*1999-2000 India's Share in South Asia's (%)*
Yarn	675	3810	17.72	964	70.00
Fabrics	354	6204	5.71	842	42.02
Other	325	2879	11.29	399	81.41
Clothing	248	8400	2.95	522	47.52
Total	1602	21292	7.52	2728	58.19
Fibre Equivalent	1872	24429	7.66	3174	58.98

Note: (1) Item-wise weights are actual weights, rather than fibre/filament equivalents.
(2) Yarn export here is taken exclusive of filament yarn, as is the case in world Trade. The export of filament yarn is estimated at 69 million kilograms in case of India.
(3) India's export data are exclusive of silk and wool products.

Source: Estimates are derived on the basis of analysis from TOI and data from ICAC, FAO and Association of Synthetic Fibre Industry, Mumbai.

These results are arrived at mainly by considering the fact that how India's share in various items has increased in the past.[6] India's data is available for the year 1983 and then for the period 1988-89 to 1999-2000. The years for which analysis is done in this study are not matching with the years for which world trade data is available in TOI report. The item-wise world trade exports for the years 1983, 1988-89, 1990-91, 1995-96, 1997-98 and 1999-2000 are found out by using

6. The estimates of 2470 million kilogram of yarn equivalent export by 2005-06 derived in this study are higher than the estimates derived by allowing overall growth at the rate of quota acceleration. Due to quota acceleration, it is estimated that the exports would grow from 1339 Million kilograms (excluding filament yarn export) in 1997-98 to 2128 Million kilograms by 2005-06. Generally growth of non-quota items is higher than growth of quota items.

Table 5.22
India's Share in World and South Asia's Gross Trade by 2005-06

	India's Exports Mn. Kgs.	*World Trade Mn. Kgs*	*India's Share in World Trade (%)*	*South Asia's Exports Mn. Kgs*	*India's Share in South Asia's Trade (%)*	*India's Growth Rate 1990-91 to 1999-2000*	*India's Growth Rate 1999-2000 to 2005-06*	*World Trade Growth Rate 1999 to 2005*	*South Asia's, Trade Growth Rate 1999-2000 to 2005-06*
Yarn	809	4427	18.27	1143	70.8	21.73	4.50	2.53	2.87
Fabrics	590	7511	7.86	1284	46.0	10.23	8.85	3.24	7.28
Other	535	4490	11.92	734	72.9	13.77	10.02	7.68	10.68
Clothing	536	11614	4.62	878	61.0	9.75	11.66	5.55	9.06
Total	2470	28042	8.81	4039	61.2	14.68	7.95	4.67	6.60
Fibre Equivalent	2865	32133	8.92	4685	61.2	14.87	7.35	4.67	6.70

Note: (1) Item-wise weights are actual weights, rather than fibre/filament equivalents.
(2) Yarn export here is taken exclusive of filament yarn, as is the case in world Trade. The export of filament yarn is estimated at 69 million kilograms in case of India during 1999-2000.
(3) India's export data are exclusive of silk and wool products.
(4) CGR for the period 1990-91 to 1999-2000 is based on semi-log trend line.

Source: Estimates are derived on the basis of analysis from TOI and data from ICAC, FAO and Association of Synthetic Fibre Industry, Mumbai.

the constant annual growth rate for the nearest two years for which world trade data in TOI is available. India's item-wise exports share in world over time is given in Table 5.23.

Table 5.23
Item-wise India's share in World Trade Over Time

	Percentage Share of Various Items						
	1983	*1988*	*1990*	*1995*	*1997-98*	*1999-2000*	*2005-06**
Yarn	0.42	1.91	3.72	11.00	15.70	17.72	18.27
Fabrics	1.79	2.79	3.34	4.21	5.14	5.71	7.86
Other	2.24	2.95	5.03	8.41	10.02	11.29	11.92
Clothing	1.20	1.34	2.40	2.62	2.94	2.95	4.62
Total	1.21	1.88	2.90	4.55	6.88	7.52	8.81

* Projected

Note: (1) India's export data is exclusive of silk and wool products, while world trade data is inclusive of all fibre/filaments. However, yarn export here is taken exclusive of filament yarn, as is the case in world trade.

(2) Item-wise weights are actual weights, rather than fibre/filament equivalents.

Source: Estimates are derived on the basis of analysis from TOI and data from ICAC, FAO and Association of Synthetic Fibre Industry, Mumbai.

India's share in world trade is estimated to increase from 7.52 per cent to 8.81 per cent during 1999-2000 to 2005-06. This seems feasible considering the rise in India's share in the past. The slow down in growth is obvious, as India has already achieved very high growth during nineties and there is limit to which India could acquire share in world trade. With the expected growth rates given above, India's share in South Asia's gross trade may increase from 59 per cent to 61 per cent.

The estimates for India's exports are also made separately for cotton and synthetic fibres products. The world trade for cotton and synthetic items separately is required for the year 1999-2000 to find India's fibre-wise share in world trade. The fibre-wise world trade worked out on the basis of per cent per annum growth rate projected for the period 1995-96 to 2005-06 is given in Table 5.24 for the year 1999-2000.

Table 5.24
Fibre-wise Gross World's Export in 1999-2000

(Mn. Kgs)

	1999-2000 Total	*1999-2000 Cotton*	*1999-2000 Other fibre*
Yarn	3810	2250	1560
Fabrics	6204	2946	3258
Other	2879	1298	1581
Clothing	8400	4623	3777
Total Trade	21292	11174	10187
Fibre Equivalent	24460	13302	11157

Note: (1) Item-wise weights are actual weights, rather than fibre equivalents.
(2) Direct yarn exports here have been taken exclusive of filament yarn.

Source: TOI estimates are revised on the basis of data from ICAC, FAO and Association of Synthetic Fibre Industry, Mumbai.

The item-wise pattern of growth in case of India seems to be different. India's export of cotton products may increase at around 6 per cent per annum, while that of cotton yarn only moderately. Several EOU units came up during this period especially of cotton yarn and cotton fabrics. Thus, potential level has already been achieved in low value added items such as cotton yarn. Thus the export of value added products is expected to grow at higher rate. On the other hand, the exports of all synthetic products may continue to increase at a fast rate. In fact the lowering of excise and custom duties on synthetic products would lead to increase in their use for domestic consumption as well. This would make it possible to utilise full economies of scale, which may further boost export of synthetic products. Several studies including that of BICP's have pointed out that if restrictions in various forms are lowered, synthetic products could be made internationally competitive. India's expected export of cotton and synthetic products by 2005-06 is given in Tables 5.25 and 5.26.

The cotton yarn exports is expected to be 515 million kilograms by 2005-06. However, it has already achieved the level of 555 million kilograms during 1999-2000. This is assumed on the basis that the export of yarn may decline latter to increase export of value added products under raw material constraint.

India's yarn equivalent gross export of cotton and synthetic products are expected to be 2470 million kilograms by 2005-06. India's yarn equivalent export was 1602 million kilograms during 1999-2000. For the purpose of arriving at raw material and investment requirement, it is important to work out item-wise net export content. In the case of South Asia, the gross over net trade ratio is expected to increase from 1.17 to 1.21 during 1995 to 2005.

India's imports are expected to take place mainly from developed countries. The imports are expected to be high in the case of cotton yarn and cotton fabrics items. The raw material constraint may force India to become both major exporter and importer of cotton yarn and cotton fabrics as is the case for China. Moreover, the import of high quality cotton fabrics may increase to meet the requirements of garment producers. The item-wise estimates of India's net export (Gross exports minus imports) derived in this study are given in Table 5.27. In synthetic products imports are expected to increase at all the stages of production.

This means India's import of textiles and clothing items (cotton and synthetic) are expected to grow at a very high rate of more than 22 per cent per annum as these are expected to increase from 45 million kilograms (yarn equivalent) in 1997-98 to 278 million kilograms in 2005-06.

Alternative II (Alt. II)

In Alternative II, it is assumed that the developed countries per capita consumption may continue to grow at a rate achieved during 1980 to 1995, despite higher increase in per capita consumption in eastern countries. Another modification is made regarding estimates of per capita consumption in South Asia in the light of past trend, expectations and detailed

Table 5.25

India's Gross Export of Cotton Products : 1999-2000 to 2005-06 (Alternative I)

	1999-2000 Mn. Kgs.	*1999-2000 Share in World Trade (%)*	*2005-06 Mn. Kgs*	*2005-06 Share in World Trade (%)*	*India's Growth rate 1999-2000 to 2005-06 Alt I*	*India's Growth rate 1990-91 to 1999-2000*
Yarn	555	24.65	515	19.69	-1.24	21.52
Fabrics	278	9.42	411	11.53	6.73	9.69
Other	306	23.54	466	23.02	7.26	13.75
Clothing	212	4.59	435	6.81	12.73	9.85
Total	1350	12.08	1826	12.51	5.16	14.52

Note: (1) Item-wise weights are actual weights, rather than fibre equivalents.
(2) The above trade statistics do not include data on filament yarn export.

Source: Estimates are derived on the basis of TOI analysis and data from ICAC, FAO and Association of Synthetic Fibre Industry, Mumbai.

Table 5.26
India's Gross Export of Synthetic Products : 1999-2000 to 2005-06 (Alternative I)

	1999-2000 India's Gross Export Mn. Kgs.	*1999-2000 India's Share in World Trade (%)*	*2005-06 India's Gross Exports Alt I Mn. Kgs.*	*2005-06 India's Share in World Trade (%)*	*India's Growth rate 1999-2000 to 2005-06 Alt I*	*India's Growth rate 1990-91 to 1999-2000*
Yarn	120	7.71	294	16.23	16.06	26.07
Fabrics	76	2.35	179	4.54	15.25	12.52
Other	20	1.23	70	2.84	23.74	14.08
Clothing	36	0.95	101	1.93	18.93	9.32
Total	252	2.47	644	4.79	16.93	16.48

Note: (1) Item-wise weights are actual weights, rather than fibre/filament equivalents.
(2) India's export is exclusive of silk and wool products, while world trade data includes all fibres.
(3) The above trade statistics do not include data on filament yarn export.

Source: Estimates are derived on the basis of TOI analysis and data from ICAC, FAO and Association of Synthetic Fibre Industry, Mumbai.

analysis undertaken for India and data available for other countries of the region.

Table 5.27
India's Net Trade by 2005-06

	2005-06 Net Trade Mn. Kgs			2005-06 Gross over Net Trade Ratio		
	Total Items	*Cotton Items*	*Synthetic Items*	*Total Items*	*Cotton Items*	*Synthetic Items*
Yarn	666	386	280	1.21	1.33	1.05
Fabrics	450	350	100	1.31	1.17	1.79
Other	508	452	56	1.05	1.03	1.25
Clothing	506	426	80	1.06	1.02	1.26
Total	2130	1614	516	1.16	1.13	1.25
Fibre Equivalent	2446	1916	530	1.17	1.14	1.28

Note: (1) Item-wise weights are actual weights, rather than fibre equivalents.
(2) The above trade statistics do not include data on filament yarn export.

Source: Estimates are derived on the basis of TOI analysis and data from ICAC, FAO and Association of Synthetic Fibre Industry, Mumbai.

With these changes, the estimates for world fibre consumption may rise to 58254 million kilograms during 2005 as against 56380 million kilograms in Alternative I. The net trade in Alternative II will also increase significantly. As shown in Table 5.11, we expect that the net world trade to be 12913 million kilograms, which is around 16 per cent higher compared with Alternative I. This rise in net trade is possible only if the prices of textiles and clothing products in world market will decline as is possible with the lowering of various trade restrictions by developed countries. This may led to significant decline of products imported and exported by way of preferential treatments as the difference between the custom duties on import from developing countries and countries given preferential treatment commodities will be reduced. This may result in further increase in share of clothing in total trade in Alternative II, the lowering of preferential treatment is expected to mainly hit intermediary goods trade. These facts indicate that there may be only marginal rise in the share of gross trade in total fibre consumption from 57 per cent in Alternative I to 58 per cent in Alternative II. Thus, the gross trade is expected to be 29334 million kilograms in terms of yarn equivalent during 2005 in Alternative II, instead of 28043 million kilograms in Alternative I. In terms of fibre equivalent the gross trade is expected to be 33803 million kilograms instead of 32133 million kilograms (Table 5.28).

For South Asia, it appears that net fibre equivalent export from South Asia would increase from 3822 million kilograms to 4119 million kilograms. The rise in exports for Alternative II compared to Alternative I for South Asia is higher compared to expected increase in overall world trade. This is based on the assumption that the rise in net world export will be mainly met from developing countries. In case of India, the rise may be even higher than South Asia in the expanded opportunities, due to its relatively strengths compared with other countries of South Asia (Table 5.29).

It is expected that India's fibre equivalent net export may increase to 2656 million kilograms during 2005-06 instead of 2446 million kilogram in Alternative I. The fibre-wise composition of India's gross export and growth during the period 1997-98 to 2005-06 is given in Tables 5.30 and 5.31.

The projections for net yarn equivalent exports for cotton and synthetic fibre are also worked out. It is possible that the import proportion of cotton textiles and clothing products may turn out to be proportionately higher than the synthetic products in Alternative II compared with Alternative I. This is likely scenario in the event of cotton raw material constraint. The fibre-wise yarn equivalent net trade is given in Table 5.32.

The estimates derived above are based on several assumptions. These include increase in our industry's competitiveness, lowering of interest rates, rationalisation of excise duties, and increase in infrastructural facilities, etc. There is possibility that in case these conditions are not meet, India may not be able to achieve these targets.

Table 5.28
World Gross Trade in Yarn, Fabric, Clothing & Other Products : 1980-2005

	TOI Analysis						Revised Estimates	
	1980	*1985*	*1990*	*1992*	*1995*	*2005**	*Alternative I*	*Alternative II*
Yarn	1614	2019	2612	2846	2970	3814	4427	4471
Fabric	2655	3003	4301	4867	5340	7345	7511	7661
Clothing	1986	2696	4306	5605	7090	12167	11614	12596
Other	1409	1367	1810	2039	2100	4404	4490	4606
Total Trade	7664	9085	13029	15357	17500	27730	28043	29334
Fibre Equivalent	8831	10469	15014	17696	20166	31955	32133	33803
Trade Share %	29.55	31.99	40.58	46.74	48.71	57.00	56.99	58.03
Fibre Consumption	29887	32723	36996	37861	41400	56059	56380	58254

Note:
(1) * is estimated in TOI study (without modifications).
(2) Alternative I is basically derived using the trend growth similar to the one assumed in TOI analysis. However, modification in data has been done on the basis of ICAC and data from other sources.
(3) Alternative II is based on the assumption that slow down in developed countries consumption will not take place.
(4) Item-wise weights are actual weights rather than fibre/filament equivalent.
(5) The above trade statistics do not include data on filament yarn export.

Source: Derived from Textile outlook international, March 1997, FAO (1992), ICACA, and data from various export promotion councils.

Table 5.29
India's Trade during 2005-06 (Alternative II)

(Mn.Kgs)

	Net Trade	*Gross Trade*	*India Share in World Trade*	*World Gross Trade*
Yarn	798	997	22.30	4471
Fabrics	488	636	8.30	7661
Others	519	555	12.05	4606
Clothing	510	550	4.37	12596
Total	2315	2738	9.33	29334
Fibre Equivalent	2656	3145	9.30	33803

Note: (1) Item-wise weights are actual weights, rather than fibre equivalents.
(2) The above trade statistics do not include data on filament yarn export. The export of filament yarn is estimated at 105 million kilograms in case of India during 2005-06.

Source: Estimates are derived on the basis of TOI analysis and data from ICAC, FAO and Association of Synthetic Fibre Industry, Mumbai.

After analysing, India's export potential in quantity terms, an attempt is made to find India's export potential in value terms in the following section.

Total Trade in Terms of Value

India has high share in International trades in quantity terms, despite that its share is low in value terms. As per WTO data, India accounted for 3.34 per cent (including silk and wool) of textiles and clothing world trade in value terms during 1999-2000. The share was 3.15 per cent in case the silk and wool items are excluded from India's textiles and clothing exports, but not from World trade. This is estimated as this study deals with item-wise cotton and synthetic products exports and the world trade data is exclusive of wool and silk trade is difficult to estimate. In quantity terms India's share was as high as 7.52 per cent in case silk and wool items are excluded from India's textiles and clothing exports, but not from World trade. This means India's export share in quantity terms is more than twice the share in value terms.

Table 5.30
India's Gross Export of Cotton Products : 1999-2000 to 2005-06 (Alternative II)

	1999-2000 Mn. Kgs.	*1999-2000 Share in World Trade*	*2005-06 Mn. Kgs*	*Growth Rate 1999-2000 to 2005-06 (% p.a.)*		*Trend Gr. Rate (% pa) 1990-91 to 1999-2000*
				Alternative II	*Alternative I*	
Yarn	555	24.65	703	4.02	-1.24	21.52
Fabrics	278	9.42	436	7.79	6.73	9.69
Other	306	23.54	474	7.57	7.26	13.75
Clothing	212	4.59	436	12.77	12.73	9.85
Total	1350	12.08	2049	7.20	5.16	14.52

Note: (1) India's export data is without silk and wool products.
(2) Item-wise weights are actual weights, rather than fibre equivalents.
(3) The above trade statistics do not include data on filament yarn export.
(4) Trend Gr. Rate are based on semi-log trend.

Source: Estimates are derived on the basis of TOI analysis and data from ICAC, FAO and Association of Synthetic Fibre Industry, Mumbai.

Table 5.31
India's Gross Export of Synthetic Products : 1999-2000 to 2005-06 (Alternative II)

	1999-2000 Mn.Kgs.	*1999-2000 Share in World Trade*	*2005-06 Alt II Mn.Kgs*	*Growth Rate 1999-2000 to 2005-06 (% p.a.)*		*Trend Gr. Rate (% p.a.) 1990-91 to 1999-2000*
				Alternative II	*Alternative I*	
Yarn	120	7.71	294	16.11	16.06	26.07
Fabrics	76	2.35	200	17.50	15.25	12.52
Other	20	1.23	81	26.25	23.74	14.08
Clothing	36	0.95	114	21.18	18.93	9.32
Total	252	2.47	688	18.22	16.93	16.48

Note: (1) India's export is without silk & wool products when world trade includes all fibre.
(2) Item-wise weights are actual weights, rather than fibre equivalents.
(3) The above trade statistics do not include data on filament yarn export.
(4) Trend Gr. Rate are based on semi-log trend.

Source: Estimates are derived on the basis of TOI analysis and data from ICAC, FAO and Association of Synthetic Fibre Industry, Mumbai.

Table 5.32
Fibre-wise Net Trade India's (IInd Alternative)

(Mn. Kgs)

	2005 Total	*2005 Cotton*	*2005 Synthetic*	*2005 Gross Over Net TradeRatio*		
				Total	*Cotton*	*Synthetic Items*
Yarn	798	538	260	1.25	1.31	1.13
Fabrics	488	373	115	1.30	1.17	1.74
Other	519	454	65	1.07	1.04	1.25
Clothing	510	426	84	1.08	1.02	1.36
Total Trade	2315	1791	584	1.18	1.14	1.18

Note: 1. Item-wise weights are actual weights, rather than fibre equivalents.
2. The above trade statistics do not include data on filament yarn export. The export of filament yarn is estimated at 105 million kilograms in case of India during 2005-06.

Source: Estimates are derived on the basis of TOI analysis and data from ICAC, FAO and Association of Synthetic Fibre Industry, Mumbai.

India's low share in value terms seems to be mainly due low per unit value realisation due to dominance of low end and low quality products. The low share of synthetic products in Indian exports is also one of the reasons for it. Another possible explanation for low share in value terms seem to be the inclusion of value of filament yarn export in world value trade figures unlike in case of world quantity trade. India's share in filament yarn trade is very small.

To project India's share in world value trade, it is important to estimates per unit value realisation. The item-wise world trade data in value and quantity terms during 1994 is available from UN, commodity trade statistics report. The item-wise per unit value worked out for year 1994 from WTO data are adjusted to arrive at per unit value for the year 1999-2000, by using data from other sources. These are then applied on the item-wise world trade in quantity terms to arrive at anticipated total world trade in value terms during 1999-2000. The per unit values are adjusted with the help of latest per unit world prices available for few items from Japan Textile News (JTN). The future trade values for 2005-06 are worked out by projecting the per unit value realisation and multiplying it with the item-wise trade in quantity terms projected earlier in two alternatives.

The projections for per unit item-wise value of exports ($/Unit) for Indian products could not be worked out on the basis of past trend, as the trend growth rates worked out for the period 1990-91 to 1999-2000 are not statistically significant. The trend show decline across the board or at the maximum stagnation for most of items. In this situation, the two alternatives are taken for per unit item-wise export value. In Alternative I for India, the per unit realisation during 2005-06 are expected to be somewhat higher than the prices during 1999-2000 for products in which there is possibility of quality improvement. The quality changes include the change in composition of a given item such as rise in share of dyed fabrics in fabrics export etc. In Alternative II for India, the prices for year 2005-06 are taken as same as that of year 1997-98 prices. The prices for year 1997-98 are taken as there is not much difference between the per unit value realisation during 1997-98 and 1999-2000 and data for year 1999-2000 is provisional. This is based on the assumption that due to excessive competition, it is possible that despite improvement in quality, the prices may remain at the level of 1997-98.

In case of world trade, item-wise per unit value realisations are taken at level anticipated during 1999-2000 in both the Alternatives. This is because international prices of textiles and clothing items have also not shown any significant consistent growth in the recent past as per the available information from JTN.

The item-wise prices per unit anticipated in case of India's and world trade are given in Table 5.33.

By applying the per unit price realisation on quantity-wise exports, India's exports in value terms are worked out in the Tables 5.34 and 5.35.

Table 5.33
India's per Unit Export Realisation

($/Kg)

	Cotton India 2005-06		*Synthetic India 2005-06*		*India 1997-98*	*World 1999-2000 2005-06*
	Alt. I	*Alt. II*	*Alt. I*	*Alt. II*		
Yarn	3.33	3.25	2.68	2.61	3.18	4.74
Fabrics	7.22	6.88	7.68	7.31	6.98	10.06
Other	5.39	5.13	11.05	10.52	5.69	12.10
Clothing	18.67	17.78	43.08	41.03	20.91	22.15
Total		6.51		10.74	7.14	14.15
Filament Yarn					1.91	9.00
Grand Total		6.51		8.95	6.95	

Note: (1) Price per unit for India in Alternative II are taken same as during 1997-98.
(2) Estimates are derived on the basis of per unit value analysis and trade analysis derived earlier.

Source: Derived by using approximation from various Journals such as UN publications JTN, TOI etc. and various Indian export promotion councils.

Table 5.34
India's Anticipated Export in Value Terms during 2005-06
(Alternative I)

(Mn. US $)

	Cotton India	*Synthetic INdia*	*India*	*World*	*Share in World Trade(%)*
Yarn	1715	788	2503	20984	11.93
Fabrics	2967	1375	4342	75561	5.75
Other	2512	774	3286	54329	6.05
Clothing	4807	4351	9158	257250	3.56
Total	12001	7288	19289	408124	4.73
Filament Yarn		184	184	33901	0.54
Grand Total		7472	19473	442025	4.41

Note: (1) Silk and wool products export are excluded.
(2) Estimates are derived on the basis of per unit value analysis and trade analysis derived earlier.

Source: Derived by using approximation from various Journals such as UN publications JTN, TOI etc. and various Indian export promotion councils.

Table 5.35
India's Anticipated Export in Value Terms during 2005-06
Alternative II

(Mn. US $)

	Cotton India	*Synthetic India*	*India*	*World*	*Share in World Trade (%)*
Yarn	2285	766	3052	21193	14.40
Fabrics	3148	1462	4610	77070	5.98
Other	2255	852	3107	55733	5.57
Clothing	8140	4677	12817	279001	4.59
Total	15828	7758	23586	432996	5.45
Filament Yarn		200	200	33901	0.59
Grand Total		7958	23786	466897	5.09

Note: (1) Silk and wool trade not included in case of India.
(2) Estimates are derived on the basis of per unit value analysis and trade analysis derived earlier.

Source: Derived by using approximation from various Journals such as UN publications JTN, TOI etc. and various Indian export promotion councils.

Thus, India's gross exports are expected to increase from US$ 10.71 billion in 1999-2000 to in the range of US$ 19.47 billion to US$ 23.79 billion by 2005-06, thereby growing in the range of 10.47 per cent per annum to 14.23 per cent per annum. The rise in share of synthetic and value added exports are expected to cause high growth in value terms. India's textiles and clothing export from 1990-91 to 1999-2000 for all fibres grew at 9.56 per cent per annum. On the other hand world export is expected to grow in the range of 4.78 per cent per annum to 5.75 per cent per annum during 1999 to 2005. The world export may vary between US$ 442 billion to US$ 467 billion by 2005 depending upon competition. The world export during 1991 to 1999 increased at a rate of 4.97 per cent per annum. India's share in World trade by 2005 is expected to be in the range of 4.41 to 5.09 per cent. However, silk and wool export is excluded in the case of India, while it is covered in the case of world trade. Thus India's share may be slightly higher in case silk and wool export is also included in exports from India, as in the case of word trade.

Domestic Final Consumption in India by the Year 2005-06

TOI study estimated the per capita domestic demand for economies of South Asia at 3.3 kg by 2005—a rise of 1.66 per cent per annum on the 1995 level of 2.8 kg. The consumption level in South Asia has grown at approximately 2.92 per cent per annum during the period 1985 to 1995. In our study, we have estimated the per capita domestic demand to be in the range of 3.3 to 3.5 kg for South Asia by the year 2005 (Table 5.36)—a rise in the range of 1.66 to 2.26 per cent per annum during 1995 to 2005. The estimates given in Table 5.11 are for the entire South Asia region, with wide disparities among various countries growth rates and per capita level and hence the same growth rate cannot be assumed for India.

The country-wise data is available from FAO for the year 1992. South Asia accounts for 19.83 per cent of the total world population, while the fibre consumption was only 7.73 per cent of the total world fibre consumption. Within the region, Pakistan has the highest per capita consumption of fibre, Sri Lanka and India are among the middle range, while Bangladesh and Nepal could be considered as having low per capita consumption. The degrees of variation could be judged from the fact that India's per capita fibre consumption is almost half that of Pakistan's, while Nepal's per capita consumption is less than one-sixth of Pakistan's.

In this kind of scenario, it is better to analyse India's per capita consumption independently. Analysis in Chapter 4 for the past pattern of India's fibre-wise per capita consumption has been undertaken separately for Cotton and synthetic products. The per capita availability of cotton fibre declined from 1.79 kg in 1983 to 1.57 kg in 1991-92 to 1.56 kg in 1997-98 and then steeply to 1.19 kg during 1999-2000. The cotton and synthetic fibre consumption, on the other hand, declined from 2.24 kg in 1983 to 2.23 kg in 1991-92 before rising to 2.76 kg in 1997-98. There was however decline after 1997-98 to 2.41 kg in 1999-2000. This shows that India's per capita consumption which started picking up after 1991-92 shows signs of reversal during 1998-99 and 1999-2000. It is better to study this pattern in the light of other changes to quantify the alternative scenarios till year 2005-06.

Methodology Adopted in this Study to Derive Domestic Demand

We tried to fit an equation, which have taken into account certain basic facts such as demand for particular type of textiles depends on own price, substitute products and real income. The objective is to predict the domestic demand by 2005. This kind of equation seems good enough, as food prices and durability are not very significant variables as analysed in the Goswami's (1985) results. The regressions are fitted for the period 1975 to 1998 in our study.

We have not applied the equation for only household sector but also included the non-household sector. Hence, we have worked out income and price elasticises for overall domestic demand and not only for household sector. This is important as demand in household and non-household sectors are interlinked to a large extent and separate elasticities could be misleading. The previous studies were unable to study the combine pattern of household and non-household segment demand due to lack of data for non-household sector. In the absence of unreliable data for the non-household sector consumption, the availability of fabrics for domestic use of cotton and synthetic fabrics is used as substitute for consumption. The total fabrics, yarn and fibre available for domestic use is worked for the year 1983 and for the period 1988-89 to 1999-2000 in Chapter 4.

For earlier years data, we have built estimates using several sources including ATỊRA study. ATIRA study on technological and structural options for the future of Indian textile sector, June 1987, sponsored by Ministry of Textiles has analysed the Indian fibre consumption. In this study an attempt was made to examine domestic consumption in terms of raw fibre equivalents for the period 1975 to 1985. For this purpose, mill consumption of cotton formed the starting point. The raw fibre equivalent of exports in the form of yarn, cloth, made ups and garments was estimated using appropriate conversion factors and it was subtracted from the mill consumption of fibre to arrive at domestic availability of cotton fibre. Since exports of man-made fibre were small, domestic availability was worked out by including imports into domestic production. In this analysis one major problem was that conversion rate was taken arbitrarily and was not scientifically drawn. However, as per capita availability of fibre, yarn and fabrics for year 1983 is worked out in our study as well in Chapter 4, the data for year 1983 thus overlaps in ATIRA and our study. We were able to make adjustment in ATIRA analysis about per capita availability of fabrics by making adjustment for difference in conversion rates in our study and ATIRA analysis. The per capita availability of fabrics in square metres is worked out on the basis of estimated mid year population for the period 1975 to 1985.

Thus the data on per capita cotton and synthetic fibre consumption for the period 1975 to 1999-2000 is worked out except for the years 1986 and 1987. The data for year 1986 and 1987 is worked out by using the available data on per capita availability of fabrics for the periods 1985 and 1988-89 and applied on it the growth rates of household sector consumption available from Textile Committee data after adjustments. Thus the per capita availability of fabrics cotton and synthetic fabrics for the entire period 1975 to 1999-2000 is worked out, which is used as substitute for domestic final consumption.

This study however have not worked out elasticises for various income segments separately. Several studies in the past have tried to work out income and price elasticises for different income classes. In the absence of data on various income groups share, these kinds of segregations cannot be used for predictions.

The price and income elasticises in this study are worked out by fitting regression equations using cotton and synthetic quantity as dependent variables and wholesale price index of commodity, the wholesale price index of its substitute, quality of product and substitute products and per capita GDP as independent variables. However, we go on dropping those variables, which turned out to be insignificant. Ultimately we ended up using following two equations for prediction purposes.

First Equation

In the first equation, we have taken per capita cotton quantity consumption as a function of per capita GDP, as well as wholesale prices ratio of man made and cotton products. The equation is fitted in double log form.

Log (per capita cotton fabrics in square metre for domestic final consumption) = A0 + A1 log (per capita GDP) + A2 log (WPI of manmade fabrics prices/WPI of cotton fabrics prices)+ A3 Auto-regressor.

Log (Per Capita Cotton Quantity) = —4.716791(—2.63) + 1.115860 (2.67) Log (Per capita GDP) + 1.4333805 (4.20) Log (WPI Man Made fabrics prices/WPI cotton fabrics prices) + 0.33 (1.31) (AR)

Note: Figures in brackets are t-Statistics

$R2 = 0.84$

Adjusted $R2 = 0.82$

Durbin-Watson Stat = 1.88

N= 24

This means the relative change in quantity of cotton fabrics is positively related to relative prices of synthetic and cotton fabrics and per capita GDP and the equation is corrected for auto-correlation.

Second Equation

In the second equation we have taken per capita synthetic fabrics consumption as function of per capita GDP, wholesale prices Index (WPI) of synthetic products deflated by WPI of all commodities and manmade and cotton fabrics relative quality. The equations are fitted in the double log form.

Manmade fabrics quality is worked out by deflating manmade fabrics average price with wholesale price index of manmade fabrics. Similarly, cotton fabrics quality is worked out.

Log (per capita synthetic/cotton fabric in square metre) = A0 + A1 Log (per capita GDP) + A2 Log (WPI of manmade prices/WPI of Cotton Prices) + A3 Log (Manmade and Cotton Quality ratio)

Log (Per Capita Man-made/Cotton Quantity) = 8.220606(5.63) -0.682829(-1.99) Log (Per Capita GDP)-2.547410(-9.59) Log (WPI Manmade/WPI All commodities) + 0.634014(2.91) Log (Man-made and Cotton Quality ratio)

Note: Figures in brackets are t-Statistics
$R^2 = 0.98$
Adjusted $R^2 = 0.98$
Durbin-Watson Stat = 1.93
N = 24

This means the relative change in quantity of synthetic and cotton products are negative related to relative prices of synthetic and cotton fabrics and per capita GDP and positively related to relative quality of synthetic and cotton products. This means as GDP increases the cotton consumption goes up at relatively higher rate than synthetic and so the ratio declines. Similarly, the relative increase in synthetic fabrics prices compared to cotton affects negatively the relative consumption of synthetic and cotton fabrics.

By using these equations we have derived the future per capita demand for fabrics on the basis of following assumptions.

The GDP would grow by 6 to 8 per cent per annum during 1999-2000 to 2005-06. Population is assumed to grow at 1.84 per cent per annum, cotton products prices would rise by 5 per cent point higher compared to WPI of all commodities over the period 1999 to 2005 as higher demand for cotton products and other policy changes are likely to push prices to international level. The synthetic prices on the other hand are expected to rise by 5 per cent point lower than the rise in WPI of all commodities during the period 1999 to 2005 due to expected lowering down of excise and custom duties. The prices are expected to decline steeply as these changes are likely to increase the competitiveness of Indian synthetic industry by increasing as size of operation at higher lead of demand.

The quality of cotton fabrics in the past has deteriorated and of synthetic products was improving. It is expected that the quality of both cotton and synthetic products would improve at same rate in future with the de-reservation of products for SSI sector and other policy changes. So the two scenarios are worked out on the basis of above assumptions and GDP growth rate in the range of 6 to 8 per cent per annum in Tables 5.36 and 5.37.

Alternative I

This shows that per capita domestic consumption is expected to grow by 3.56 per cent per annum in fabrics equivalent square metres and 3.25 per cent per annum in fibre equivalent kilograms. The lower growth in fibre terms is because of relatively lower weight of synthetic fabrics, the growth for which is expected to be high. The per capita consumption of cotton fibre is worked out higher despite low per capita cotton fabrics consumption as it is going to be partially replaced by rise in cotton blended share.

Alternative II

This shows that per capita domestic consumption is expected to grow by 4.76 per cent per annum in square metre and 4.62 per cent per annum in kilograms (due to rise in share of synthetic fibre). By applying the conversion rates, one could work out the yarn required to satisfy the domestic demand of the household and non-household sectors.

In these two scenarios, the share of cotton in domestic consumption by 2005-06 is expected to be in the range of 46.5 to 48.5 per cent, which is likely to be slightly higher than world average share. The estimates given in Tables 5.36 and 5.37 do not include silk and wool fibres. In case these fibres are taken into account, the share of cotton fibre in total fibre consumption in India including silk and wool may fall in the range of 45 to 47 per cent by year 2005-06. The share of cotton fibre in international demand is around 44 per cent during 1995, which is further expected to decline to 41 per cent by the year 2005.

Table 5.36

Per Capita Final Domestic Consumption (at 6% p.a. GDP growth) : Alt. 1

	Per Capita Domestic Availability						*Total Domestic Availability*		*Cotton Fibre*
	Cotton Fabrics Sq.Mts	*Synthetic Fabrics Sq.Mts*	*Total Fabrics Sq.Mts*	*Cotton Fibre Kgs*	*Synthetic Fibre Kgs*	*Total Fibre Kgs.*	*Fabrics Sq.Mts*	*Fibre Mn. Kgs*	*Share %*
1999-2000	6.75	17.63	24.38	1.19	1.22	2.41	24049	2377	49.19
2005-06	7.65	22.43	30.08	1.36	1.55	2.92	33109	3214	46.58
CGR % p.a. 1999-00 to 2005-06			3.56			3.25	5.47	5.16	
2010-11	8.48	27.74	35.33	1.53	1.86	3.39	42597	3919	45.13
CGR % p.a. 1999-00 to 2010-11			3.43			3.15	5.33	4.65	

Note: (1) Domestic availability is inclusive of imports.
(2) Fibre and yarn requirements are worked out by using conversion rate for cotton and synthetic products.

Source: Derived by applying income & price elasticities.

The further economic reforms could ensure high growth in per capita consumption and shift in consumption pattern from cotton to synthetic products. In fact, considerable shift in favour of synthetic products has already taken place during nineties after the introduction of new economic reforms.

Total Domestic and Export Demand by 2005-06

Two alternatives have been worked out both for domestic and export scenarios by 2005-06. It is possible that scenario in one market would affect the growth prospects in the other market. The ultimate equilibrium would depend upon demand and supply conditions in domestic and export markets. The four alternatives of demand are possible by applying two alternative scenarios in both exports and domestic demand. The two extreme cases are summed up in the following section. The actual level of growth is expected to fall in between these two extreme alternatives depending upon various demand and supply conditions.

Before we sum up the two extreme cases of overall demand by the year 2005-06, it is important to sum up the similar findings for the base year 1999-2000. The results show the requirements of fibre, yarn and fabrics for the base year 1999-2000 after taking into consideration the imports in textiles and clothing products at several stages of production.

Total Demand During 1999-2000

In terms of fabrics, yarn and fibre equivalent, the total demand in terms of square metre and kilograms during 1999-2000 is given in Table 5.38. This is the requirement to be met from the domestic industry after taking into account the import content at several stages of production. The fabrics equivalent demand is distributed among garments, made-ups and piece-length garments (tailor made-garments) in Table 5.39.

The two extreme alternatives worked out for year 2005-06 are given in following sections.

Alternative I (Alt. I)

The combination chosen in this alternative is of low export

Table 5.37
Per Capita Final Domestic Consumption (at 8% p.a. GDP Growth) : Alt II

	Per Capita Domestic Availability						*Total Domestic Availability*		*Cotton Fibre*
	Cotton Fabrics Sq.Mts	*Synthetic Fabrics Sq.Mts*	*Total Fabrics Sq.Mts*	*Cotton Fibre Kgs*	*Synthetic Fibre Kgs*	*Total Fibre Kgs.*	*Fabrics Sq.Mts*	*Fibre Mn. Kgs*	*Share %*
1999-2000	6.75	17.63	24.38	1.19	1.22	2.41	24049	2377	49.19
2005-06	8.66	23.55	32.22	1.53	1.63	3.16	35465	3478	48.42
CGR % p.a. 1999-00 to 2005-06			4.76			4.62	6.69	6.55	
2010-11	10.67	29.35	40.02	1.89	2.03	3.92	48252	4726	48.21
CGR % p.a. 1999-00 to 2010-11			4.61			4.52	6.54	6.45	

Note: (1) Domestic availability is inclusive of imports.
(2) Fibre and yarn requirements are worked out by using conversion rate for cotton and synthetic products.

Source: Derived by applying income & price elasticities.

Table 5.38
Fabrics, Yarn and Fibre Equivalent Total Demand during 1999-2000

	Fabrics Equivalent			*Yarn Equivalent*			*Fibre Equivalent*		
	Cotton	*Synthetic*	*Total*	*Cotton*	*Synthetic*	*Total*	*Cotton*	*Synthetic*	*Total*
	Mn. Sq. Mts			*Mn. Kgs.*			*Mn. Kgs.*		
Export	6618	1292	7910	1350	321*	1671*	1644	297*	1941*
Filament Yarn Exports					69	69		69	69
Imports	49	783	832	5	61	66	10	60	70
Net Exports	6569	509	7078	1345	329	1674	1634	306	1940
Domestic $	6660	17389	24049	857	1262	2119	1174	1207	2381
Total	13229	17898	31127	2202	1591	3793	2808	1513	4321

$ inclusive of imports.

* Means excluding filament yarn exports requirement, which is estimated at 69 million kilograms during 1999-2000.

Source: As derived by the author.

Table 5.39
Fabrics Equivalent Demand in Various forms during 1999-2000

(Mn.Sq. Mt)

	Fabrics			*Made-ups*	*Garments*	*Hosiery*	*Total*
	Fabrics	*Garments in piece length*	*Total*				
Domestic Consumption	5100	10409	15509	1407	3822	3311	24049
Gross Exports	2804		2804	2758	2347	*	
	(101)		(101)	(22)	(1255)	*	7910
Imports	175		175	478	34	145	832
Total	7729	10409	18138	3687	6135	3166	31127
Share	24.83	33.44	58.27	11.85	19.71	10.17	100.00

Note: *Gross exports, figures for each category are inclusive of respective hosiery products for each category. The figures in bracket indicate the quantum of knitted or hosiery products. Hosiery exports are equivalent to 2699 Mn.Sq.Mt.

Source: As derived by the Author.

and low domestic demand. The fabrics, yarn and fibre equivalent requirements are given in Table 5.40.

The demand of fabrics is expected to grow at the rate of 6.59 per cent per annum, yarn at 5.16 per cent per annum and fibre at rate of 4.89 per cent per annum. The total requirement of cotton by 2005-06 is expected to be 20.24 million bales to meet the textiles, clothing and other requirements except the net export of raw cotton. This is against the similar requirement of cotton of 16.52 million bales during 1999-2000. This means cotton requirement is expected to grow at a rate of 3.44 per cent per annum. The overall demand of cotton was 17.25 million including export of raw cotton. It is expected that export of raw cotton would decline in future. The production of cotton was only 15.6 million bales during 1999-2000 and production has in fact declined after 1996-97.

The fabrics equivalent projections are further distributed among garments, made-ups and piece-length garments (tailor made-garments) as given in Table 5.41. The projections till year 2005-06 for various segments is worked out by using the growth rate for each segment during the period 1990-91 to 1999-2000 and adjusting the values thus arrived at proportionately to arrive at the projected overall demand for fabrics derived in Table 5.40.

Alternative II (Alt. II)

The combination chosen is of high domestic and export demand. The fabrics, yarn and fibre equivalent requirements are given in Table 5.42. The fabrics, yarn and fibre are expected to grow at 6.59, 5.16 and 4.89 per cent respectively.

In this alternative, it is assumed that GDP is expected to grow by 8 per cent per annum and exports are expected to grow at high rate. In terms of fabrics yarn equivalent, the total demand during 2005-06 to be met from the domestic industry is worked out in Table 5.42.

The cotton requirement by 2005-06 is expected to be 22.6 million bales to meet the textiles and clothing requirements. This is against the similar requirement of cotton of 16.52

Table 5.40

Fabrics, Yarn and Fibre Equivalent Total Demand during 2005-06 (Alt. I)

	Fabrics Equivalent			*Yarn Equivalent*			*Fibre Equivalent*		
	Cotton	*Synthetic*	*Total*	*Cotton*	*Synthetic*	*Total*	*Cotton*	*Synthetic*	*Total*
	Mn. Sq. Mts.			*Mn. Kgs.*			*Mn. Kgs.*		
Export	10922	3441	14362	1826	644*	2470*	2240	625*	2865*
Fil. Yarn Exp.					105	105		105	105
Imports	698	1116	1814	213	128	340	297	122	419
Net Exports	10224	2325	12548	1613	621	2234	1943	608	2551
Domestic $	8420	24689	33109	1097	1798	2895	1497	1706	3203
Total	18644	27014	45657	2710	2419	5129	3440	2314	5754
CGR	5.89	7.10	6.59	3.52	7.23	5.16	3.44	7.34	4.89

CGR : Compound Growth Rate % p.a. in Total Demand during the period 1999-2000 to 2005-06.

Fil. Yarn Exp. : Filament Yarn Exports.

$ inclusive of imports.

* Means excluding filament yarn exports requirement, which is estimated at 105 million kilograms during 2005-06.

Source: As derived by the author.

Table 5.41
Fabrics Equivalent Demand in Various Forms during 2005-2006 (Alt. I)

(Mn. Sq. Mt.)

	Fabrics			*Made-ups*	*Garments*	*Hosiery*	*Total*
	Fabrics	*Garment in Piece Length*	*Total*				
Domestic consumption	5618	13081	18699	2066	6758	5586	33109
Gross Exports	5101		5101	4626	4635	*	14362
	(184)		(184)	(37)	(2478)		
Imports	848		848	255	282	429	1814
Total	9871	13081	22952	6437	11111	5157	45657
CGR	4.16	3.88	4.00	9.73	10.41	8.47	6.59
Share	21.62	28.65	50.27	14.10	24.34	11.30	100.00

CGR : Compound Growth Rate % p.a. during 1999-2000 to 2005-06.

* Gross Exports, figures for each category are inclusive of respective hosiery products. Hosiery exports are equivalent to 2699 Mn.Sq.Mt. The product-wise estimates for hosiery products is given in brackets.

Source : As derived by the author.

Table 5.42
Fabrics, Yarn and Fibre Equivalent Total Demand during 2005-06 (Alt. II)

	Fabrics Equivalent			*Yarn Equivalent*			*Fibre Equivalent*		
	Cotton	*Synthetic*	*Total*	*Cotton*	*Synthetic*	*Total*	*Cotton*	*Synthetic*	*Total*
	Mn. Sq. Mts.			*Mn. Kgs.*			*Mn. Kgs.*		
Export	11205	3883	15088	2049	688*	2737*	2515	630*	3145*
Yarn Exports					105	105		105	105
Imports	773	1282	2055	258	165	423	349	140	489
Net Exports	10432	2601	13033	1791	628	2419	2166	595	2761
Domestic $	9532	25921	35453	1232	1901	3133	1684	1794	3478
Total	19964	28522	48486	3023	2529	5552	3850	2389	6239
CGR	7.10	8.08	7.66	5.42	8.03	6.56	5.40	7.91	6.31

CGR : Compound Growth Rate % p.a. during the period 1999-2000 to 2005-06.
Fil. Yarn Exp. : Filament Yarn Exports.
$ inclusive of imports.
* Means excluding filament yarn exports requirement, which is estimated at 105 million kilograms during 2005-2006.
Source: As derived by the author.

million bales during 1999-2000. This means cotton requirement is expected to grow at a rate of .36 per cent per annum.

The fabrics equivalent projections are further distributed among garments, made-ups and piece-length garments (tailor made-garments) by using the same method as explained in Alternative I and results are given in Table 5.43.

The above two scenarios show the range of textile and clothing demand by 2005-06. The second alternative seems more optimistic. Looking at the past trend, the above predictions do not seem very much off the mark.

Prospects till 2010-11

The overall demand for the year 2005-06 is likely to be somewhere between these two extremes. An assessment is made for assessing the likely scenario by year 2005-06 and then later for year 2010-11, on the basis of performance of textiles and clothing industry in the recent past.

Review of Industry Performance since 1996-97

The performance of the textile industry during the last five years is not very encouraging. A major reason is the decline in cotton production in the country, from a peak level of 17.8 million bales in 1996-97 to 15.6 million bales in 1999-2000. Cotton products were displaced by blended products, which in turn, after 1997-98, gave way to products made from 100 per cent non-cotton yarn (both spun and filament). As a result, the spinning industry was able to maintain moderate growth till year 1997-98, but was affected thereafter. The rapid growth of the filament yarn industry was stimulated by a sharp cut in excise duties during the four-year period from 1994-95 to 1997-98. The capacity utilisation of spinning industry was affected as growth of spun yarn slowed down. On the other hand, expansion and modernisation in spinning industry was continuously taking place at fast rate without any proper exit for that obsolete spindles, while the exit of obsolete machinery was difficult.

The growth was relatively better in weaving segment due to high rise in production of filament fabrics. One could

Table 5.43
Fabrics Equivalent Demand in Various Forms during 2005-2006 (Alt. II)

(Mn. Sq. Mt.)

	Fabrics			Made-ups	Garments	Hosiery	Total
	Fabrics	Garment in Fiece length	Total				
Domestic consumption	6018	14012	20030	2213	7238	5962	35443
Gross Exports	5512		5512	4810	4766	*	15088
	(199)		(199)	(38)	(2548)		
Imports	961		961	289	319	486	2055
Total	10569	14012	24581	6734	11685	5476	48476
CGR	5.35	5.08	5.20	10.56	11.34	9.56	7.66
Share	21.80	28.91	50.71	13.89	24.10	11.30	100.00

CGR : Compound Growth Rate % p.a. during 1999-2000 to 2005-06.
* Gross Exports, figures for each category are inclusive of respective hosiery products. Hosiery exports are equivalent to 2785 Mn.Sq.Mt. The product-wise estimates for hosiery products is given in brackets.
Source: As derived by the author.

consider the growth in production of overall fabrics as moderate. The sector-wise analysis shows the share for the powerloom sector is rising, while the performance of mill sector continued to be dismissal. Thus, there continued to be shortage of good quality fabrics for the garment industry.

In terms of exports, the Indian textile industry has grown at reasonable rates over the last few Years. The relative shares of the various components in value terms appear to have remained quite stable over the period, indicating uniform growth across segments. In none of the segments, whichever way they are defined, do the country's exports show signs of moving up the value chain.

Considering the recent dismissed performance and no signs of reversal in nearly future, one could consider Alternative I as likely scenario till year 2005-06. While, Alternative II projections are considered as optimistic scenario for the year 2005-06. The projections for the year 2010-11 are thus made keeping in mind the likely scenario till year 2005-06.

India's Exports by year 2010-11

For the exports segment, there are chances of deceleration after India achieved a share of more than 8 per cent in world trade in quantity terms. In fact, the growth in world trade is also expected to slow down after achieving high share in world fibre consumption. One could expect 60 per cent share of trade in world fibre consumption as high. The world fibre consumption is expected to be 63975 million kilogram by year 2010-11. Thus both India's export and world trade growth are expected to slow down after achieving high share in world trade and world fibre consumption respectively. The item-wise expected exports during 2010-11 is given in Table 5.44.

India's share in world trade is expected to increase from 7.5 per cent during 1999-2000 to 9.7 per cent during 2010-11 in quantity terms (fibre-equivalent) and from 3.15 per cent to 5.9 per cent in value terms during the same period. India's exports are expected to triple from US$ 10.71 billion in 1999-2000 to US$ 31.21 billion during 2010-11. The world exports are expected US$ 557 billion during 2010-11. Thus India's exports share in world trade in value terms is expected to rise to 5.6 per cent.

Table 5.44
India's Trade

(Mn.Kgs)

	2010-11 Net Trade Mn. Kgs	*2010-11 Gross Trade Mn. Kgs*	*2010-11 India share in World Trade Mn. Kgs*	*2010-11 India's Trade US$ Million*
Yarn	618	893	19.17	2840
Fabrics	628	803	10.05	5603
Others	753	805	14.27	4582
Clothing	795	870	5.71	18182
Total	2794	3371	10.06	31206
Fibre Equivalent	3073	3708	9.66	

Note: (1) Item-wise weights are actual weights, rather than fibre equivalents.
(2) The above trade statistics do not include data on filament yarn export. The export of filament yarn is estimated at 105 million kilograms in case of India during 2005-06.

Source: Estimates are derived on the basis of TOI analysis and data from ICAC, FAO and Association of Synthetic Fibre Industry, Mumbai.

India's Domestic Demand by year 2010-11

The likely scenario till 2010-11 (Table 5.36) is based on GDP growth rate of 6 per cent per annum and under similar assumption as Alt. I till year 2005-06.

Item-wise Total Demand by year 2010-11

Combining the expected item-wise exports data with the domestic demand, the item-wise likely demands till year 2010-11 are worked out in Tables 5.45 and 5.46. The fibre demand is expected to grow by 4.84 per cent per annum, yarn by 5.01 per cent and fabrics by 6.38 per cent per annum during the period 1999-2000 to 2010-11. The fabrics demand in various categories is given in Table 5.46.

Table 5.45
Fabrics, Yarn and Fibre Equivalent Total Demand during 2010-11

	Fabrics Equivalent			*Yarn Equivalent*			*Fibre Equivalent*		
	Cotton	*Synthetic*	*Total*	*Cotton*	*Synthetic*	*Total*	*Cotton*	*Synthetic*	*Total*
		Mn. Sq. Mts.			*Mn. Kgs.*			*Mn. Kgs.*	
Export	13487	7983	21470	2263	1108*	3371*	2793	1075*	3868*
Fil. Yarn Exp.					149	149		149	149
Imports	984	1633	2617	352	225	577	476	191	667
Net Exports	12503	6350	18853	1911	1032	2943	2317	1033	3350
Domestic $	9973	32624	42597	1348	2205	3553	1753	2166	3919
Total	22476	38974	61450	3259	3237	6496	4070	3199	7269
CGR	4.94	7.33	6.38	3.63	6.67	5.01	3.43	7.04	4.84

* Means excluding filament yarn export, which is estimated to be 149 million kilogram during 2010-11.
$ inclusive of imports.
Fil. Yarn Exp. : Filament Yarn Exports.
CGR : Compound Growth Rate % p.a. during 1999-2000 to 2010-11.
Source: As derived by the author.

Table 5.46
Fabrics Equivalent Demand in Various Forms during 2010-2011

(Mn. Sq. Mt.)

	Fabrics			*Made-ups*	*Garments*	*Hosiery*	*Total*
	Fabrics	*Garment in Piece Length*	*Total*				
Domestic consumption	6908	17950	24858	3228	12323	9799	50208
Gross Exports	6956		6956	6978	7576		21510
	(251)		(251)	(56)	(4051)		
Imports	2394		2394	153	1786		4333
Total	11470	17950	29420	10053	18113	9799	67385
CGR	3.65	5.08	4.50	9.55	10.34	10.82	7.27
Share	17.02	26.64	43.66	14.92	26.88	14.54	100.00

Gross exports figures for each category are inclusive of respective hosiery products. The figures in bracket indicate the quantum of knitted or hosiery products for each category. Hosiery exports are equivalent to 4609 Mn.Sq.Mt.
Gross exports figures in bracket are of hosiery products, which are included in the non-bracketed figure of respective items.
CGR : Compound Growth Rate % p.a. during 1999-2000 to 2010-11.
Source: As derived by the author.

Fibre/Filaments Requirements by years 2005-06 and 2010-11

We have worked out India's fibres/filaments requirements on the basis of expected scenario by 2005-06 (Two Alternatives) and 2010-11. India's requirement of various fibres/filaments along with its share in world demand of fibre/filaments by 2005-06 and 2010-11 are given in Table 5.47.

India's share in world fibre consumption is likely to be in the range of 10.36 to 10.86 per cent. The further segregation of fibre/filament wise composition is given in Table 5.48.

The share of 100 per cent cotton fibre in domestic consumption of cotton and synthetic products is expected to decline from 49.19 per cent in 1999-2000 to 45.13 per cent in 2005-06 and further to 44.73 per cent in 2010-11.

In case silk and wool fibre is also included the share of cotton fibre in India's fibre consumption is expected to decline to around 43 per cent during 2010-11 fum 47.5 per cent estimated during 1999-2000. On the other hand, India's cotton fibre share in mill consumption is expected to be around 55 per cent during 2010-11 as compared to 64 per cent during 1999-2000. The decline in share of cotton fibre in mill consumption is expected to be caused by change in domestic pattern of household and non-household consumption and increase in India's competitiveness of synthetic products for exports.

Additional Spun Yarn Requirements by 2005-2006 and 2010-11

2005-06

To work out the spindle requirement by 2005-06, it is important to work out the filament yarn(which is not spun) content in it. The filament content is around 51 per cent of the total man-made fibre/filament consumed in the country and 48 per cent in the total man-made spun/filament yarn during 1999-2000. It is expected that filament content may rise in the man-made spun/filament yarn, as growth rate of filament is much higher in the country. We assume that filament share in manmade spun fibre/filament yarn may go up to 51.5 to 52

Table 5.47
Mill, SSI and Ex-factory Requirements of Fibre/Filament Blends in India and World by 2005-06 and 2010-11

	India's Mill and Other Fibre Consumption 2005-06 (Million Kgs.)	*World Fibre Consumption 2005-06 (Million Kgs.)*	*India's Share in World during 2005-06*	*India's Share in World during 1994-95*	*India's Mill and Other Fibre Consumption 2010-11 (Million Kgs.)*
Cotton	3440-3850	23100-23724	14.89-16.23	10.54	4070
PSF	765-801	9000-9223	8.50-8.68	4.14	1095
VSF	244	1900-2000	12.84-1220	11.20	250
ASF	104	2800	3.71	2.34	142
Others	10		—		15
Total MMF	**1123-1159**	**13700-14023**	**8.20-8.26**	4.95	**5572**
PFY	1051.5-1090	11510-11900	9.14-9.16	5.76	1505
NFY	55	4100-4300	1.34-1.28	1.50	95
CFY	67	670-700	10.00-9.57	8.76	72
Polypropylene	17.5-18	—	—		25
Total Filament	**1191-1230**	**16280-16900**	**7.32-7.28**	4.81	**1697**
Others not specified	—	1500-1672	—	—	—
Total Above	**5754-6239**	**54580-56319**	**10.54-11.08**	7.59	**7269**
Silk & Wool	86.5	1800-1935	4.81-4.47	4.11	105
Grand Total	**5840.5-6325.5**	**56380-58254**	**10.36-10.86**	**7.57**	**7374**

Source: As derived by the author from TOI and ITMF analysis.

Table 5.48
Requirement of Various Fibre/Filaments in India's and World by 2005-06

	India's Mill and other Fibre Consumption 2005-06 (Million Kgs.)	*World Fibre Consumption 2005-06 (Million Kgs.)*	*India's Share in World by 2005-06*	*India's Share in World by 94-95*	*India's share in Total Fibre-wise Mill Consumption by 2005-06*	*Share of various fibre in World fibre-Consumption by 2005-06*	*India's Mill and other Fibre Consumption 2010-11 (Million Kgs.)*
Cotton	3440-3850	23100-23724	14.89-16.23	10.54	58.90-60.86	40.73-40.97	4070
Polyester	1816.5-1891	20510-21123	8.86-8.95	4.99	31.10-29.89	36.26-36.38	2600
Cellulosic	311	2570-2700	11.52-12.10	10.47	5.26-4.88	4.56-4.63	322
Nylon	55	4100-4300	1.28-1.34	1.50	0.93-0.86	7.27-7.38	95
ASF	104	2800	3.71	2.34	1.76-1.63	4.81-4.97	142
Wool/Silk	86.5	1800-1962	4.41-4.47	4.11	1.46-1.36	3.19-3.32	105
Others	27.5-28	1500-1672	1.67-1.83	3.08	0.47-0.44	2.66-2.87	40
Total	5840-6325.5	56380-58254	10.36-10.86	7.57	100.00	100-100	7374

Source: As derived by the author from TOI and ITMF analysis.

per cent by year 2005-06. This means spun yarn requirement will be in the range of 3883 to 4237 million kilograms, out of which expected production by the SSI spinning units may be 210 million kilograms. The production of spun yarn was 3046 million kilograms during 1999-2000, out of which 155 million kilograms was produced in the SSI spinning units. Thus the additional spun yarn production requirement in the organised units is expected to be in the range of 782 (3883-3046-(210-155)) to 1136 (4237-3046-(210-155)) million kilograms.

2010-11

To work out the spindle requirement by 2010-11, it is expected that filament content may rise to 57 per cent by year 2010-11. This means spun yarn requirement will be in the range of 4651 million kilograms, out of which expected production by the SSI spinning units may be 285 million kilograms. The production of spun yarn was 3046 million kilograms during 1999-2000, out of which 155 million kilograms was produced in the SSI spinning units. Thus the additional spun yarn production requirement in the organised units is expected to be in the range of 1475 (4651-3046-(280-155)) million kilograms during the period 1999-2000 to 2010-11.

Expected Count-Composition of Spun Yarn by year 2005-06 and 2010-11

To work out the spindles requirements, it is important to know the count composition of spun yarn produced. The count composition will depend upon the demand and supply scenario by the year 2005-06 and 2010-11. The major cotton yarn exporting countries in world are India and Pakistan. Pakistan's relative count composition of cotton yarn production and exports is of coarser varieties compared with India. Similarly, Europe and Japan are one of the majors importing countries of cotton yarn and India's export composition of cotton yarn is of finer varieties compared with overall import demand of these countries. This indicates that demand in world is of coarser varieties compared to the products exported from India. Thus it is a possible that India's count composition of yarn may become coarser in future.

As one of India's competitive advantage lies in its ability to provide diverse kind of products, which could be produced from wide composition of count ranges of cotton yarn. This kind of diverse composition of production is not available in other exporting countries. The count compositions of other spun yarn (specially of cotton blend) are also affected by varieties of cotton. Considering these factors along with the already low count composition achieved in the past, the further chances of decline in count composition seems remote in the medium to long run.

Moreover, the demand and supply availability is going to play an important role in determining the count composition of yarn in India. The shortage of cotton could push the production of cotton yarn towards finer composition, while the International demand is expected to be of dominantly coarser count composition. The high pressure on demand of cotton thus would not allow the count composition of Indian products to become too much coarser. Thus, the count composition of Indian products by year 2005-06 and 2010-11 is not expected to be much different from count composition of spun yarn during 1996-97.

Excess Capacity and Expected Replacement of Spindles

As derived in Chapter 2, 0.86 million additional spindles of 1996-97 technology are required during 1999-2000 to produce the spun yarn with spindles installed later than year 1981-82.

Optimal Achievable Productivity of Installed Spindles during 1999-2000 to 2005-06

The optimal achievable productivity of modern spindles was calculated by us in Chapter 2 and was worked out 139.77 gms/spindle/shift at 1996-97 technology. The productivity was almost the same for cotton and other spun yarns at the count composition of yarn produced during 1996-97. Considering the impact of technology progress on modern spindles, there may be some increase in optimal achievable productivity. As worked out in Chapter 2, the impact of technological progress causes the increase in optimal productivity at a rate of 1 per cent per annum. The average productivity of spindles is expected to be 144 kgs/spindle/shift during 1999-2000. As the investment of new spindles are expected to be spread over 6 years period during 1999-2000 to 2005-06, the average productivity of additional spindles should be 148.36 kgs/spindle/shift ($144 \times (1.01)^6 = 148.36$ (or 133.53 kgs/spindle/year at 90 per cent utilisation.

As the spindles are expected to be installed at accelerated rate over time due to rise in demand over time, the weighted productivity should be more than 133.53 kgs/spindles/year. However, this should be sufficient to take care of depreciation of total installed spindles after 1999-2000.

Additional Spindles Required to Produce Spun Yarn during 1999-2000 to 2005-06 with Spindles Installed after 1980-81

The additional spun yarn production requirement in the organised units worked out during the period 1999-2000 to 2005-06 is expected to be in the range of 782 to 1136 million kilograms. These require 5.86 to 8.51 million (782/133.53 to 1136/133.53) additional spindles during 1999-2000 to 2005-06.

In addition 0.86 million additional spindles of 1996-97 technology (or 0.81 million at technology of spindles installed during 1999-2000 to 2005-06) are required during 1999-2000 to produce the spun yarn with spindles installed later than year 1981-82. This is quite valid assumption as it is worked out in Chapter 2, that most of spun yarn produced during 1999-2000 was already produced with spindles installed later than year 1981-82. Thus total requirement of spindles ranges between 6.67 (5.86 + 0.81) to 9.32 (8.51+ 0.81) million.

It is expected that around 40,000 additional rotors would be invested. This means around 2.0 million equivalent spindles. Therefore, there is need of 4.67 (6.67-2.00) to 7.32 (9.32-2.00) million spindles by 2005-06 to meet the additional demand. This comes to around 0.78 to 1.22 million spindles on an average per year.

It is possible that the additional requirement of spindles

may be caused by faster replacement of spindles than expected in this scenario. However, the possibility is that the excess demand and replacement may try to balance each other. Thus in case of low demand replacement rate may rise and vice versa.

Optimal Achievable Productivity of Installed Spindles during 1999-2000 to 2010-11

As the investment of new spindles are expected to be spread over 11 years period during 1999-2000 to 2010-11, the average productivity of additional spindles should be 148.37 kgms/ spindle/shift ($139.77 \times (1.01)^6 = 148.37$) or 133.5 kgs/spindle/ year at 90 per cent utilisation.

As the spindles are expected to be installed at accelerated rate over time due to rise in demand over time, the weighted productivity should be more than 133.5 kgs/spindles/year. However, this is expected to take care of depreciation of total installed spindles.

Additional Spindles Required during 1999-2000 to 2010-11 to produce spun yarn with spindles installed after year 1991-92

The additional spun yarn requirement in the organised units is expected to be in the range of 1475 million kilograms during the period 1999-2000 to 2010-11. These require 11.05 million (1475/133.5) spindles during 1999-2000 to 2010-11.

In addition, it is likely that spindles older than 1991-92 may go out of operation by year 2010-11 due to rise in replacement rate over the period of time. This means 6.79 (0.86+3.14+2.79) million (Table 2.30) additional spindles of 1996-97 technology are required to produce the spun yarn with spindles installed after 1991-92. This is quite valid assumption as it is worked out in Chapter 2, that most of spun yarn produced during 1999-2000 was produced with technology not older than 24 years. The 6.79 million equivalent spindles of 1996-97 technology are equivalent to 6.21 (6.79/ 139.73/152.82) at technology of spindles installed during the period 1999-2000 to 2010-11.

Thus total requirement of spindles ranges between 17.17 (11.05+6.21) million during the period 1999-2000 to 2010-11. It is expected that around additional 80,000 rotors would be invested, which are equivalent to 4.0 million spindles. Therefore, there is need of spindles in the range of 13.17 million during 1999-2000 to 2010-11 to meet the additional demand and replacement requirement. This is estimated to be on an average around 1.20 million spindles per year during the period 1999-2000 to 2010-11. In case replacement rate will be lower, the additional demand for spindles may be around 1 million per year.

Evaluation of Recent Developments in Textile Policy to Achieve the Targets

The projections made in this study are feasible but certain policy measures are required to be introduced to materialise it. The process seems to have already begun with the introduction of New Textile Policy (2000) and the Finance Bill 2001.

The New Textile Policy (NTP 2000) was announced on November 2, 2000. The most significant feature of the policy is that garments have been dereserved from the small-scale sector. The policy changes introduced during the 1980s and 1990s and ninties include flexibility in fibre-mix use, allowing expansion of weaving capacity, reduction of custom and excise duties on the import of machinery and synthetic fibres and liberalising trade reforms for cotton and cotton yarn. The persistence of reservation of garments for the small-scale sector was one of the main reasons for the failure of a generally favourable policy environment to induce modernisation in not just the garment segment, but also in weaving.

In the domestic market, fabric is mainly demanded in smaller lots by small garment units spread all over the country. The production of fabric in smaller lots is not very efficient for the mill sector, especially for units operating with modern technology such as air jet or shuttle less looms, both of which operate at very high speeds. Thus, modernisation could not take place in weaving units except a few producing fabrics such as denim, mainly for exports. The dereservation of the garment industry will, over time, induce restructuring in the entire textile and clothing industry after the spinning stage. As was expected as a follow-up step after dereservation, the Finance Bill 2001 introduced MODVAT from the fibre to the garment stage with a 16 per cent excise duty. However, certain exemptions in the form of excise concession for hank yarn meant to be consumed in the handloom sector and for manual dyeing break the chain in MODVAT process. Similarly, the duty at the processing stage by independent processing houses for the small units is shifted away from ad valorem to specific duties. Thus the purpose of introducing MODVAT has been diluted. Moreover, excise duty avoidance at the fabrics stage by various units mainly in the decentralised sector could contribute to the slow growth of the organised garment industry. As most of yarn is consumed for production of fabrics, a possible solution is to impose excise duty at yarn stage both for value addition at yarn and fabrics stage with some possible options including the reimbursement of excise paid at later stage.

The garment industry also has several options by which it can avoid excise duty. Job work is exempted from any excise duty and hence a unit can evade taxes by reporting in-house production as job work done. Similarly, the garment exporters need not pay any excise duty if their domestic sales are less than Rs. 1 Crore. These exemptions increase the oevasion and hence weaken the impact of MODVAT.

NTP 2000 promised to review the entire tax structure, but the issues were not addressed in the Finance Bill 2001. Grey fabric is taxed at 8 per cent ad valorem, while dyed fabrics at 16 per cent. In fact duty on dyed fabrics was always at higher rate compared to grey fabrics. Under these rates, the escalating duty on additional value added discourage investment in large dyeing units. These go on splitting into smaller units and quality was compromised to get advantage of excise benefits meant for smaller units. The high price of better quality dyed fabrics is putting a constraint on the demand for them. The export of better-dyed products was also suffering, as exports alone are generally not attractive. Exports of grey fabrics constitute around 50 per cent of country's total fabric exports.

Another problem area, which was not addressed in the finance bill, is the relatively high excise and custom duty on synthetic yarn compared to cotton yarn. On the other hand, the excise duty on synthetic and cotton fabrics is currently at same rate. This causes a tax escalation on the cotton products at the value added stages. The new policy may not be adequately able to induce the desired modernisation at the weaving and dying stages unless a uniform rate of excise duty is imposed on cotton and synthetic yarn. India is presently a major exporter of cotton yarn and cotton fabrics but not of cotton made-ups or synthetic products. A rational policy would be the equalisation of duty rates across cotton and synthetics at all stages of production.

To meet the total demand requirements estimated by NTP 2000, cotton availability would need to grow in the range of 3 to 4 per cent per annum over the next ten years. This study has estimated the required growth at rate of 3.95 per cent per annum during 1999-2000 to met the demand of 23.9 million bales for textiles and clothing products. The fact is that cotton production has not grown at the desired rate during last four years. This has affected the growth of the industry. In such a situation, it is tempting to retain curbs on exports of raw cotton. Curbs may well serve the short-run interests of downstream processors, but it is entirely questionable whether they serve the long-term objective of increases in cotton production. However, given the changing international trade environment, the country may move naturally to a more rational management of cotton availability, allowing imports to substitute for domestic shortfalls.

On the issue of dealing with sick units and surplus manpower, NTP 2000 says that employment protection in terminally sick units is neither conducive to efficient allocation nor incremental employment generation. The extent of sickness can be gauged by the large number of old spindles lying idle, despite large-scale modernisation in the spinning segment. In NTP 2000 emphasis is placed on a pragmatic and rational exit policy with adequate protection of workers' interest. However, the anticipated squeeze in employment is a serious socio-economic matter, especially because the existence of a vast army of workers is at stake. Thus, the government may need to take other measures. One possible alternative is the government has to facilitate the provision of training infrastructure for the workers employed in the small garment and handloom units to help them find an alternative employment.

The industry is set to face a dramatically new environment when domestic markets are opened up to imports. While this was expected to happen this year with the elimination of the final set of quantitative restrictions, the government has postponed the lifting of these restrictions citing the possibility of substantial damage to the livelihood of workers employed in this industry. However, this is only a postponement and at best buys time for the industry to push through a very quick process of restructuring for improved efficiency.

Prospects for 2010-11

The projections till year 2010-11 are based on 6 per cent per annum growth and achieving a level of slightly more than 10 per cent equivalent fibre exports in world textiles and clothing trade. This is based on the consideration that even if the exports growth for a few years is likely to be high, there is limit to which India's share could be achieved in world trade. Similarly, the current scenario of Indian economy is quite pessimistic and it may take a while before it could recover. So achieving a 8 per cent overall growth during 1999-2000 to 2010-11 may be difficult even if the GDP growth rate may pick up at later stage. Thus the Alternative I is considered as more realistic.

The prospects for textiles and clothing industry are expected to be different for the cotton and synthetic products and at various stages of production as discussed in the following section.

Cotton

The growth in this segment of industry will primarily depend upon the availability of raw material constraint. We are presently running short of cotton fibre. A minimum growth in cotton production of 3 per cent per annum during the period 1999-2000 to 2010-11 is required, which will have a gap of 10 per cent in demand and supply. This gap of 2.3 million bales could be met by net import of cotton. Thus it is important that the growth in production of cotton should be assigned priority. The cotton requirement is expected to be 23.9 million bales (excluding raw cotton exports) by year 2010-11, even after considering the import of cotton textiles and clothing products to the extent of 2.8 million bales. The domestic demand of cotton fibre is expected to grow by 3.71 per cent per annum and demand for gross exports by 4.94 per cent per annum during the period 1999-2000 to 2010-11 (Tables 5.38 and 5.45). The share of cotton fibre in total textiles and clothing demand (cotton and synthetic) is expected to decline from 65 per cent to 56 per cent. The decline in share of cotton is expected to take place both in exports and domestic segment. The share of cotton in export segment is expected to decline from 84.7 per cent in 1999-2000 to 72.2 per cent by 2010-11. The share of cotton in domestic segment is expected to decline from 49.3 per cent in 1999-2000 to 44.7 per cent in 2010-11. This means India's domestic consumption is fast approaching to the world average of cotton share in total fibre consumption. However, India's per capita consumption is quite low at 2.41 kgs during 1999-2000 and expected to reach at 3.39 kgs during 2010-11. The per capita consumption of cotton in it is 1.19 kgs during 1999-2000 and is likely to be 1.53 kgs during 2010-11 (Table 5.36).

Synthetics

There are good prospects for the growth of synthetic products, the demand for which is growing both in the domestic and exports market. The expected growth in demand for synthetic fibre/filaments is 7.04 per cent per annum during the period 1999-2000 to 2010-11. The demand for exports are expected to grow by 12.41 per cent per annum and that of domestic demand by 5.46 per cent per annum. The imports of synthetic products are expected to grow at higher rate of 11.10 per cent per annum (Tables 5.38 and 5.45).

The production stages in cotton and synthetic products are similar; we therefore analyse the prospectus at various stages of production one by one.

Yarn

The main changes in this stage include changes in the composition of cotton and other spun yarn. The further increase in share of other spun yarn is expected in future. India with the largest share in wool cotton yarn export accounts for around one-fourth of the world's export. The further rise in India's share in world cotton yarn export is not likely in medium to long run. In fact, there is a possibility that the rise in demand of value added products might force the decline in direct export of cotton yarn over the period of time. The main growth in cotton yarn demand is likely to take place from the high demand prospects for value added products in cotton segment.

The demand for yarn is expected to grow by 5.01 per cent per annum during the period 1999-2000 to 2010-11. The growth of cotton yarn is expected to be 3.63 per cent and that of synthetic yarn by 6.67 per cent per annum (Tables 5.38 and 5.45)

The growth of spun yarn however is expected to be at lower rate of 3.92 per cent per annum as considerable growth of filament yarn is expected to take place. The growth of spun yarn is the organised sector is estimated to be 3.83 per cent per annum. To meet this demand and replacement of old spindles, the additional total spindles are expected to grow on an average in the range of 1 to 1.20 million spindles per year during the period 1999-2000 to 2010-11. The 1.20 million spindles per year are expected to be installed each year in case the spindles in operation are not older than 1991-92.

In case of optimistic scenario, the replacement of old spindles may not be that high.

Fabrics

This stage of production could undergo a considerable change in sectoral composition depending upon whether tax avoidance at several stages of production is addressed properly and MODVAT is being properly implemented. The finance bill addressed several issues, which were important for this segment of the industry such as extending the MODVAT till garment stage of production. However, it appears to have fallen short of requirements by providing several ways to avoid tax. Moreover, excise duty on grey and dyed fabrics is not rationalised.

India is competitive upto the fabric stage of production. India export of cotton fabrics is estimated to be around 10 per cent of world export of cotton fabrics during 2010-11. The demand in this segment is expected to grow both in cotton and synthetic products. In the cotton segment the rise in demand is expected to mainly take place through rise in export of quality fabrics, especially of dyed products, at fabrics and made-ups stage. In the synthetics segment, good growth is expected at each stage of production.

The expected growth of fabrics is 6.38 per cent per annum during the period 1999-2000 to 2010-11. The demand for cotton fabrics is expected to grow by 4.94 per cent per annum and that of synthetic fabrics by 7.33 per cent per annum during the same period (Tables 5.38 and 5.45). The total demand for fabrics is expected to be 61450 million sq.mt. during 2010-11. This growth in demand for fabrics is expected to be caused by demand from various segments.

Fabrics in piece length

The share of this segment in total demand of fabrics is expected to decline from 25 to 17 per cent during 1999-2000 to 2010-11 due to rise in consumer preferences for ready-made products and its easy availability (Tables 5.39 and 5.46). The growth in this segment is expected to take place at only 3.65 per cent per annum during the period 1999-2000 to 2010-11. The demand for fabrics in piece length is expected to be 11470 million sq.mt.

during 2010-11, out of which 60 per cent will be in the domestic segment, which would require stitching by tailors.

Garments in piece length

The share of this segment in total demand of fabrics is expected to decline from 33.5 to 26.5 per cent during 1999-2000 to 2010-11 due to shift in consumer preferences for ready-made products and its easy availability (Tables 5.39 and 5.46). The growth in this segment is expected to take place at only 5.08 per cent per annum during the period 1999-2000 to 2010-11. The demand for fabrics in piece length is expected to be 17950 million sq.mt. during 2010-11.

Hosiery Products

The share of this segment in total demand of fabrics is expected to increase from 10 to 14.5 per cent during 1999-2000 to 2010-11 due to shift in consumer preferences in favour of hosiery products (Tables 5.39 and 5.46). The growth in this segment is expected to be highest at 10.82 per cent per annum during the period 1999-2000 to 2010-11. The demand for hosiery fabrics is expected to be 9799 million sq.mt during 2010-11, most of it is consumed in the form of garments. In addition to this demand of hosiery fabrics, the exports of 4358 million square metre in the form of fabrics, made-ups and garments is expected to take place as given in Table 5.46.

Made-ups

The share of this segment in total demand of fabrics is expected to increase from 12 to 15 per cent during 1999-2000 to 2010-11 due to shift in consumer preferences in favour of ready-made products and its easy availability (Tables 5.39 and 5.46). The growth in this segment is expected to be 9.55 per cent per annum during the period 1999-2000 to 2010-11. The expected demand of made-ups is 10053 million sq.mt during 2010-11.

Ready-made Garments

As mentioned earlier, important steps have been taken, such as dereservation of the garment industry and the beginning to extend MODVAT till the garment stage. However, tax avoidance problems need to be addressed properly to provide a level playing field to all segments of the industry and allow the modernisation. In case the proper policies are formulated, the share of this segment in total demand of fabrics is expected to increase from 20 to 27 per cent during 1999-2000 to 2010-11 due to shift in consumer preferences in favour of ready-made products and its easy availability in new economic environment (Tables 5.39 and 5.46). The growth in this segment is expected to be 10.34 per cent per annum during the period 1999-2000 to 2010-11. The demand of ready-made garments is expected to be 18113 million sq.mt during 2010-11.

In addition, the demand for hosiery fabrics is expected to be 9799 million sq.mt during 2010-11, most of it is going to be consumed in the form of garments. Moreover, the demand for fabrics in piece length is expected to be 11470 million sq.mt. during 2010-11, out of which 60 per cent will be in the domestic segment, which would require stitching by tailors (Table 5.46). Thus the stitched products demand in ready-made and tailor made garments is expected to be 39382 million sq.mt, which is 58 per cent of the total demand of fabrics in the form of fabrics, made-ups and garments during 2010-11. This is the major contribution of this study as the estimates of production of garment were very vague till now.

Optimistic Scenario till year 2010-11

As discussed earlier, the most likely alternative is Alternative I till year 2010-11. However, the most optimistic scenario could be the one with around 11 to 11.5 per cent higher growth than the Alternative I, predicted in this study till year 2010-11. The major change of around 13 per cent higher domestic demand is expected compared to Alternative I, while exports are likely to be only 6 to 8 per cent higher than Alternative I by the year 2010-11. Thus, on these possibilities, one could make the item-wise estimate in optimistic scenario by year 2010-11.

Summing Up

- ➡ The three major countries identified as major importers of textiles and clothing goods are EU, US, and Japan. These three countries import account for 67.85 per cent of the total world textiles and clothing exports during

1996. India's share in the imports of these three countries was 3.26 per cent as compared with 3.15 per cent share in world trade. Thus India has a balanced presence in most of the countries in the world, whether quota or non-quota. The main net importers of textiles and clothing goods were US, EU, Japan, United Arab Emirates, Canada and Switzerland. The main net exporters are China, Taiwan, South Korea, India, Turkey, Pakistan, Hong Kong, Indonesia and Thailand.

- The major importers also have the highest import restrictions on textiles and clothing as is clear from intra-regional preferential treatment and trade for these countries. In textiles intra European trade is to the extent of 68.59 per cent of total imports and in clothing it accounted for 44.53 per cent, which added up to 54.35 per cent for combined textiles and clothing imports. The analysis of top ten suppliers of MFA Textiles to EU reveals that India ranked no 1 both in terms of quantum and value of MFA imports during 1995.

- The restrictions seem to have affected the level and direction of world trade. The high level of customs duties and other barriers lower the level of trade. In addition, the preferential treatment given to various countries changes the direction of trade flows. Once the MFA would be phased out and restrictions on other countries would be lowered, the impact of preferential treatment will be reduced and it would have an impact on the future growth and direction of trade. This will also affect the composition of trade as trade of intermediary products is expected to be lower.

- The analysis for world demand and trade of fibre is based on TOI analysis on region-wise mill consumption of fibre, domestic demand and gap between mill consumption and domestic demand. The growth is projected on the analysis of shipment of various machinery, fibre availability etc. and expected pattern in income and consumption.

- The growth of exports from India to two major quota countries, namely, EU and USA, was only 8.11 per cent during 1990 to 1997 despite high potential, as compared to 16.43 per cent growth in overall exports of textile and clothing items. The quota levels have affected India's exports potential adversely. In future also, the growth due to quota acceleration is expected to be only 5.96 per cent during the period 1996-97 to 2005-06, which is likely to affect the potential growth in exports till MFA phase out.

- Quotas seem to have mainly affected India's export performance in those products for which the level and growth rates are kept low despite high potential. The quota limit depends upon the past performance and it is a major constraint in fashion goods for which demand changes frequently.

- India enjoys a major advantage in that it has competitive position in wide and diversified products due to its capability to produce a large range of counts. Moreover, India has a competitive advantage in cost of production at yarn, fabrics and garments stages and cheap availability of cotton is one sector in it. India's share to potential importers is expected to increase as the preferential treatment is going to be reduced with lowering of barriers. Moreover, India's export to non-quota countries is also expected to increase as the prices are going to be lowered with the lowering of customs duties. However, it may be partially offset by some decline in export to non-quota countries as indirect route used for export to developed countries may no more be relevant after MFA phase out.

- Despite various advantages, India's exports are expected to grow at a relatively lower rate compared with very high growth rate achieved in the past, as the base level has become high. But it will be higher than the expected growth rate based on quota acceleration. India's share in world trade is expected to increase from 7.5 per cent during 1999-2000 to 9.7 per cent during 2010-11 in quantity terms (fibre-equivalent) and from 3.15 per cent to 5.9 per cent in value terms during the same period. India's exports are expected to triple from US$ 10.71 billion in 1999-2000 to US$ 31.21 billion during 2010-11. The share of cotton in export segment is expected to decline from 84.7 per cent in 1999-2000 to 72.2 per cent in 2010-11.

- India's domestic demand is worked out by analysing price and income elasticities and synchronising it with the overall world and South Asia's analysis regarding mill consumption and domestic demand. The share of cotton in domestic segment is expected to decline from 49.3 per cent in 1999-2000 to 44.7 per cent in 2010-11. This means India's domestic consumption is fast approaching to the world average of cotton share in total fibre consumption. However, India's per capita consumption is quite low at 2.41 kgs during 1999-2000 and expected to reach at 3.39 kgs during 2010-11. The per capita consumption of cotton in it is 1.19 kgs during 1999-2000 and is likely to be 1.53 kgs during 2010-11.
- The fibre demand is expected to grow by 4.84 per cent pr annum, yarn by 5.01 per cent and fabrics by 6.38 per cent per annum during the period 1999-2000 to 2010-11. The various segments of fabrics are expected to grow at different rates. The growth in fabrics in piece length is expected to take place at only 3.65 per cent, garment in piece length by 5.08 per cent, hosiery by 10.82 per cent, made-ups by 9.55 per cent, and ready-made garments by 10.34 per cent per annum during the period 1999-2000 to 2010-11
- A minimum growth in cotton production of 3 per cent per annum during the period 1999-2000 to 2010-11 is

required, which will have a gap of 10 per cent in demand and supply. This gap of 2.3 million bales could be met by net import of cotton. Thus it is important that the growth in production of cotton should be assigned priority. The cotton requirement is expected to be 23.9 million bales (excluding raw cotton exports) by year 2010-11, even after considering the import of cotton textiles and clothing products to the extent of 2.8 million bales.

- The additional total spindles are expected to grow on an average in the range of 1 to 1.20 million spindles per year during the period 1999-2000 to 2010-11 depending upon the growth and replacement level. The 1.20 million spindles per year are expected to be installed each year in case the spindles in operation are not older than 1991-92.
- The demand of ready-made garments is expected to be 18113 million sq.mt. during year 2010-11. In addition, the demand for hosiery fabrics is expected to be 9799 million sq.mt during 2010-11, most of it is going to be consumed in the form of garments. Moreover, the demand for fabrics in piece length is expected to be 11470 million sq.mt. during 2010-11, out of which 60 per cent will be in the domestic segment, which would require stitching by tailors. Thus the stitched products demand in ready-made and tailor made goods is expected to be 39382 million sq.mt., which is 58 per cent of the total demand of fabrics during 2010-11 in the form of fabrics, made-ups and garments. The estimates of production of garment were very vague till now.
- In an optimistic scenario, the growth is expected to be approximately 11 to 11.5 per cent higher than projected in the likely scenario for the period 1999-2000 to 2010-11.

APPENDIX 5.1

Quota and Other Restrictions Used for Textile and Clothing Imports under the EU "Textiles Policy", 1996

	Tariffs (%)	*Quotas*	*Certificate of Origin*
Preferential Countries			
Tunisia[a]	0	No	EUR1
Morocco[a]	0	No	EUR1
Lome Countries			
Mauritius[a]	0	No	EUR1
Least developed countries			
Bangladesh[a]	0	No	GSP form A
Efta (European Free Trade Area)			
Switzerland[a], Norway[a], Liechtenstein[a], Iceland[a]	0	No	EUR1
OECD Countries			
USA, Japan, Canada, Australia, Mexico, New Zealand	0-25	No	Yes
Turkey[b]	0	No	No
Autonomous regime countries			
North Korea, Bosnia-Hercegovina, UAE Croatia, Former Yugoslav Republic of Macedonia	0-25	Yes	Yes
Central and Eadtern Europe[c]			
Poland, Romania, Czech Republic, Hungary, Russia, Slovak Republic	0-25	Yes	Yes
WTO/GATT registered countries under the MFA	0-25	Yes	Yes

Note: [a] 0% duty is payable provided the EU's preferential rules of origin are met; other wise, duty is payable at a rate of up to 25%.

[b] Turkey was accorded customs union status with effect from January 1, 1996.

[c] Following a mid-term review of the agreements with the CEE countries it is likely that a small number of categories will be liberlised and outward processing traffic (OPT) quotas increased.

Source: Compiled from *Official Journal of the European Communities*, various issues.

APPENDIX 5.2

Impact of Quota Growth on Quantitative Restrictions Under Article 2 of the Agreement on Textiles and Clothing

Country	*Canada 1994 '000 S.MT*	*Canada 1994 Tonnes*	*Canada 2004 '000 S.MT*	*Canada 2004 Tonnes*	*Canada % p.a. Growth Rate*	*E.U. 1994 Tonnes*	*E.U. 2004 Tonnes*	*E.U. % p.a. Growth Rate*	*Norway way 1994 Kgs.*	*Norway way 2004 Kgs.*	*Norway way % p.a. Growth Rate*
Bangladesh	34029	4730	91201	12677	10.36						
Fiji											
Hong Kong	120353	16729	189759	26377	4.66	169048	205201	1.96	1487833	1789475	1.86
India	26086	3626	61028	8483	8.87	213044	356756	5.29	383667	518581	3.06
Indonesia	24441	3397	57179	7948	8.87	118937	232058	6.91	215800	383431	5.92
Korea	167294	23254	377120	52420	8.47	135269	207333	4.36	144000	255858	5.92
Macau	3583	498	9022	1254	9.67	25754	32053	2.21	165833	256018	4.44
Malaysia	21853	3038	47049	6540	7.97	38232	67740	5.89	105000	162102	4.44
Myanmar	2182	303	4077	567	6.45						
Pakistan	31235	4342	77244	10737	9.48	188450	367457	6.91	188333	279517	4.03
Phillipines	22302	3100	56006	7785	9.65	25974	55051	7.80	105833	188044	5.92
Singapore	13563	1885	27935	3883	7.49	19907	35137	5.85	83104	128299	4.44
Sri Lanka	14036	1951	32839	4565	8.87	9733	29618	11.77	105333	162617	4.44
Thailand	26735	3716	56357	7834	7.74	85208	153671	6.07	246167	384803	4.57
Total Above	**507692**	**70569**	**1086816**	**151067**	**7.91**	**1029556**	**1742075**	**5.40**	**3230903**	**4508745**	**3.39**

(Contd.....)

(Contd......)

Country	USA 1994 '000 S.MT	USA 1994 Tonnes	USA 2004 '000 S.MT	USA 2004 Tonnes	USA % p.a. Growth Rate	Total Quota Items Tonnes 1994	Share of Various Countries 1994	Total Quota Items Tonnes 2004	Share of Various Countries 2004	Total Quota % p.a. Growth Rate
Bangladesh	341747	47503	914815	127159	10.35	52233	2.72	139836	4.04	10.35
Fiji	9540	1326	23687	3292	9.52	1326	0.07	3292	0.10	9.52
Hong Kong	1115975	155121	1345803	187067	1.89	342385	17.86	420434	12.14	2.07
India	364474	50662	805072	111905	8.25	267716	13.97	477662	13.79	5.96
Indonesia	454593	63188	1057950	147055	8.81	185739	9.69	387444	11.18	7.63
Korea	943129	131095	1137334	158089	1.89	289762	15.12	418098	12.07	3.73
Macau	110858	15409	329946	45862	11.52	41827	2.18	79426	2.29	6.62
Malaysia	491382	68302	1147532	159507	8.85	109677	5.72	233949	6.75	7.87
Myanmar						303	0.02	567	0.02	6.45
Pakistan	536188	74530	1311684	182324	9.36	267510	13.95	560798	16.19	7.68
Phillipines	452251	62863	995138	138324	8.21	92043	4.80	201348	5.81	8.14
Singapore	184823	25690	292792	40698	4.71	47566	2.48	79846	2.31	5.32
Sri Lanka	240756	33465	533236	74120	8.28	45254	2.36	108465	3.13	9.13
Thailand	607471	84438	1373551	190924	8.50	173609	9.06	352813	10.19	7.35
Total Above	**5853187**	**813593**	**11268540**	**1566327**	**6.77**	**1916949**	**100.00**	**3463978**	**100.00**	**6.10**

Note: S.Mts. are converted into Kilograms by using Secretariat of the International Cotton Advisory Committee criteria of 7194.24 Square Metres per Ton.

Source: ITCB estimates based on notification to the WTO. Reproduced in Agrreement on Textiles and Clothing : Progress, Problems and Prospectus for Developing Countries of the ESCAP Region.

6

Summary and Conclusions

The textile and clothing sectors have undergone several structural changes during the 80's and the 90's as a result of the new economic environment. These liberalisation policies could be mainly divided into two phases. On the basis of these structural changes, the prospects of textiles and clothing industry during 2005-06 and 2010-11 are worked out. Thus this study is broadly sub-divided into following periods.

- First Phase of Liberalisation 1983 to 1990-91, to capture the impact of New Textile Policy (NTP, 1985) introduced during 1985.
- Second Phase of Liberalisation 1990-91 to 1999-2000, to capture the impact of Economic Reforms introduced during 1991.
- To project the alternative possible future scenarios of the Textiles and Clothing industry by the year 2005-06 and 2010-11 (after the MFA phase out).

The impact of liberalisation policies was not homogeneous throughout the various production stages in textiles and clothing sectors, because of specific reasons. These reasons primarily related to protection and lack of competition and economies of scale. These were causing lack of modernisation in weawing and dyeing segment, while rapid technology change took place in the spinning sector.

Production, Productivity and Technological Change in the Spinning Sector

In the spinning sector, economic liberalisation policies in the two phases brought wide opportunities for investment as capital became cheaper and export were freed from various restrictions of earlier policy regime. During these liberalisation phases investment in modern spindles and rotors got accelerated. The number of spindles less than 10 years old are estimated at 13.21 million equivalent new spindles during 1999-2000 compared with 11.59 million equivalent during 1996-97. This constitutes 37.2 per cent of the installed spindles during 1999-2000 compared with 32.7 per cent in 1996-97, 25.7 per cent in 1990-91 and 21.6 per cent in 1983. In 1976, the per cent of new spindles (less than 10 year old) was only 14.1 per cent. Although the investment grew at high rate even during pre-liberalisation phase of 1976 to 1985-86, it got accelerated after the introduction of NTP and especially after the second phase of liberalisation policies.

The major acceleration in spinning capacity took place after the launch of the second phase of liberalisation. During the seven-year period from 1983-84 to 1990-91, covering the impact of NTP, the investment in new spindles was only 0.74 million spindle equivalent per year compared with an average of 1.32 million spindles equivalent investment during the six year period from 1990-91 to 1996-97. It further increased to 1.40 million spindles equivalent during the four years period from 1996-97 to 1999-2000. The acceleration in the investment process during the second phase of liberalisation was mainly on account of exchange rate policies and trade liberalisation including opening up of exports. This has improved yarn exports and lowered the production cost and hence ultimately helped the growth of exports of fabrics in various forms.

The impact of technological progress in spinning sector on productivity, through the use of production frontier as worked out from SITRA norms in this study brings out interesting results. The production frontier represents alternative combinations of yarn counts, which could be produced with the given number of spindles of latest available technology during 1996-97. The minimum spindles required of the latest available technology during 1996-97 are then compared with the actual spindles installed. This analysis for spinning sector is restricted till year 1996-97, as the data structure after year 1996-97 provided by Textile Commissioner changed. Textile Commissioner's data on count composition yarn is not separately available for the mill and SSI spinning units. It has been combined for both the sectors. As the data regarding capacity utilisation, age composition is not available for the SSI sector, the detailed analysis undertaken till year 1996-97 could not be extended for the latter period. Thus the analysis for the spinning sector for the period 1996-97 to 1999-2000 is based on certain assumptions to arrive at some results and is not the detailed one.

During 1996, we were operating 46.64 per cent below the production frontier and hence were producing only 53.36 per cent of the optimal production, which could be produced with the installed number of spindles at the latest available technology. It was worked out that 28.48 per cent of production below the frontier was explained by idle spindles, 10.10 percentages by low capacity utilisation and 8.06 percentage by age composition of machinery. This, however, does not mean that we would have moved 28.48 percentage points closer to the frontier in case idle spindles would have been working or 10.10 percentage points closer to the frontier in case working spindles would have been fully utilised. This would have caused only partial upward movement because of gap between age composition of these installed spindles and latest available technology during 1996-97.

The liberalisation policies have affected the working environment in spinning industry in several ways. The total excess spindle over minimum required at the latest available technology at 100 per cent capacity utilisation were 57.89 per cent during 1983, which declined to 51.95 per cent in 1991 and further to 46.64 per cent in 1996. The various factors, which have brought these overall changes, include change in idle capacity and age composition of machinery.

The total number of idle spindles as a percentage of installed spindles declined from 28.68 per cent to 19.99 per cent during the first phase of liberalisation (1985 to 1990). However, they increased during 1990 to 1996, the second phase of liberalisation, from 19.99 per cent to 28.48 per cent. The number of idle spindles declined as increase in demand, caused by lifting of export barriers, was not sufficiently met by increase in spinning capacity, during the first phase. On the other hand, as machinery became cheaper, during the second phase of liberalisation, utilisation of outdated spindles declined.

The capacity utilisation of working spindles improved during the second phase of liberalisation policies. The increase in capacity utilisation for working spindles could not take place during the first phase as in addition to increase in the number of newly installed spindles, idle spindles also become active with a view to meeting increasing export demand.

During the second phase, additional new capacity was installed at an accelerated rate. However, capacity utilisation of working spindles also improved as old spindles were moved out of operation due to obsolete technology. The loss of working hours for working spindles as a percentage of installed spindles declined marginally from 14.51 per cent in 1983 to 14.09 in 1991 and further to 10.11 per cent in 1996.

As the old spindles were pressed into operation during the first phase of liberalisation (1985 to 1990) the productivity gap increased compared to what could be optimally produced with the latest available technology. It comes out that the extra spindle used due to technology gap increased from 14.72 per cent in 1983 to 17.87 per cent of the total installed spindles in 1991. However, old spindles become obsolete during the second phase of liberalisation and rise in investment in modern spindles led to a rise in productivity of working spindles. The extra spindles required as a percentage of installed spindles due to technology gap came down from 17.87 per cent in 1991 to 8.06 percentage in 1996.

The number of excess spindles being used can be determined by the difference between the working spindles and the minimum number of spindles required of latest technology (1996-97). This excess, expressed as a proportion of the minimum number required, may be a better measure of the technology gap. The excess spindles required due to technology gap declined from 35.06 in 1983 to 32.75 in 1990 and further to 15.40 per cent in 1996.

The productivity of working spindles increased very nominally during the first phase of liberalisation and increased at around 2.85 per cent per annum during the second phase. The productivity index improved from 75.33 in 1990 to 86.66 in 1996. This is worked out by assuming productivity index of spindles of latest available technology during 1996-97 as 100.

The increase in investment in new spindles during the last two decades should become clear from the fact that to produce the total spun yarn production in the organised sector with spindles less than 15 year old during 1996-97, a total of 5.18 million spindles were required. Hence, the technology gap between working spindles and latest available technology during 1996-97 does not seem to be too wide. From the past pattern, it could be expected that by year 2010-11, the spindles older than 1981-82 may not be very active in reality. This would mean that around 17.92 million spindles of relatively old technology presently installed in the organised sector may go out of operation by the year 2010-11 either due to closure or would remain out of operation for most part of the year or may wind up. The number of closures may go up further in case age composition of working spindles would further decline.

We have analysed the productivity trends in Indian spinning industry, the efficiency at which an average spindle works, and the age composition of spindles installed. For the purpose of working out spindle requirement in future from the available demand of spun yarn, it is important to standardise the production per spindle.

Production per spindle depends on four factors, namely, (1) type of fibre; (2) count of the yarn-spun; (3) carded vs. combed; and (4) hosiery vs. woven. There is need to standarise the expected weighted average productivity in future depending upon the expected combination of the above four parameters in future. The exact estimates of the above four parameters in future along with total spun yarn production are very difficult to derive, but some approximation has to be made to predict the spindle requirements on the basis of fibre, yarn, and fabrics demand by year 2005-06 and 2010-11. After studying the changes in the spinning sector, an attempt has been made to find the overall structure of the textile industry at other production stages such as fabrics, made-ups and garments, which in turn are used to derive the backward requirements till the fibre stage.

Comparison of Estimates of Production of Fabrics

The conversion rate of yarn into fabrics is the parameter used to estimate the production of fabrics in the absence of observed estimates. The actual estimates of production of fabrics are difficult to be observed as it is dominantly produced in the decentralised sector. There is considerable controversy regarding the official statistics on the production of fabrics and the share of various sectors in the total production of fabrics. The per capita domestic availability of fabrics by official statistics is much higher than the per capita household purchases estimated by the Consumer Household Survey, Textile Committee. The difference is too large to be explained by the purchases of the non-household sector.

The whole controversy has been generated because the official estimates of production of fabrics for the decentralised sectors are based on arbitrary conversion rates of yarn into fabrics. In fact, the comparisons of officially assumed weight of fabrics with the weights of fabrics produced and exported internationally, points to the fact that the conversion rates assumed by the official statistics are way off the mark and are overestimated. We tried to find out the conversion rates based on the count range-wise analysis in each sector. As shares of various count-ranges change, the conversion rates are bound to change over a period of time.

In our analysis, count range-wise conversion rate for mill sector was derived with the help of SITRA statistics. ATLRA data for the year 1983 are available for count-wise various varieties produced including their reed, picks, count and ply. From these construction parameters, the conversion rate or weight of fabrics has been derived for each variety and count of yarn by using the formula for fabrics weight.

By giving count-wise weight according to the composition of fabrics produced in the mill sector, the conversion rate for each count-range in the mill sector has been worked out. The count range-wise conversion rate of fabrics derived above are very close to the count range-wise conversion rates derived from the available data on consumption of yarn and production of fabrics by the mill sector for the year 1983. Thus the estimates derived by the above method seem quite realistic.

On the basis of estimates of conversion rates derived for the mill sector, the conversion rates for various count ranges were derived for the powerloom and the handloom sectors. These are derived on the basis of the assumption that the weights of fabrics from the powerloom and the handloom sectors are slightly lighter than the weight of fabrics in mill sector due to loose reeds and picks in the construction of fabrics.

The conversion rates derived by us in this manner are applied on the fabrics equivalent exports in square metre to get estimates of exports of fabric in kilograms. The fabrics exports in kilograms thus obtained tally with the available data from ICAC and thus it seems that the estimates of conversion rates derived in this study are reliable. The estimates of production of fabrics derived on the basis of these conversion rates and delivery of fibre-wise yarn to various sectors are much lower than the official estimates of production of fabrics. The estimate of production of fabrics derived in this study is 31127 million square metres compared with 38627 million square metres as per official statistics during 1999-2000. The main difference is in estimates of production of cotton fabrics. The production of cotton fabrics as per our estimates is 14236 million square metres as against official estimates of 18989 million square metres.

The results derived in the study shows that the share of cotton fabrics production in total production of fabrics in the country declined from 66.67 per cent in 1983 to 60.71 per cent in 1990-91 to 42.50 per cent in 1999-2000. On the other hand, production of blended fabrics declined from 12.03 per cent in 1983 to 11.32 per cent in 1990-91 and then increased to 20.20 per cent in 1999-2000. Among the blended fabrics, the share of cotton-blended fabrics declined from 61.85 per cent in 1983 to 45.89 per cent in 1990-91 and then further to 37.36 per cent in 1999-2000. The production of 100 per cent spun fabrics also showed a similar trend and its share in production of total fabrics declined from 5.07 per cent in 1983 to 4.94 per cent in 1990-91 and then rose to 10.16 per cent in 1999-2000. The share of filament fabrics has shown maximum growth. The share of production of filament fabrics increased from 16.20 per cent in 1983 to 23.52 per cent in 1990-91 and further to 39.80 per cent in 1999-2000. These results show that the production of filament fabrics has grown at a high rate during both the phases of liberalisation, while the production of non-cotton spun fabrics has shown high growth rate during the second phase of liberalisation.

Fabric Equivalent Exports

The fabric equivalent exports in various forms have also been worked out. The total exports of cotton fabrics in the form of fabrics, made-ups and garments grew from 862 million square metres in 1983 to 2566 million square metres in 1990-91 and further to 6618 million square metres in 1999-2000. The share of cotton fabrics in the total cotton fabrics equivalent exports has declined from 45 per cent to 34 per cent during 1983 to 1999-2000, of cotton made-ups and cotton garments from 28 to 37 and 27 to 29 per cent respectively during the same period. The exports of synthetic fabrics in the form of fabrics, made-ups and garments grew from 104 million square metres in 1983 to 532 million square metres in 1990-91 and further to 1292 million square metres in 1999-2000. The share of synthetic fabrics in the total synthetic fabrics equivalent exports accounts for 34 per cent, of synthetic made-ups and synthetic garments

37 and 29 per cent respectively during 1999-2000. The total fabrics equivalents exports of cotton and synthetic products thus increased from 966 million square metres in 1983 to 7910 million square metres in 1999-2000.

The main purpose of the numerous exercises undertaken was to estimate the demand for textiles and clothing products in order to determine the growth rate of the textile industry, and to estimate production broken down into fabrics, made ups and garments from the mill, powerloom, handloom and hosiery sectors. The total production is also broken down into the export and domestic segments. While production data for yarn is taken from official sources, that for fabric was derived using numerous conversion rates, which were calculated on the basis of variety-wise data of fabric from SITRA.

The share of fabrics produced from various fibres in total production of fabrics is obviously much different than the share given in the official statistics. There is also difference in the fabrics equivalent exports in various forms due to difference in conversion rates. The analysis in this study is based on various other conversion rates as well, which include conversion of pieces and rupees value worth of exports into square metre equivalent. These conversion rates are derived from the analysis of item-wise export and domestic data and are not based on arbitrary assumptions. Similarly, an attempt has been made to calculate yarn equivalent exports in the form of yarn, fabrics, made-ups and garments. This was used to work out the fibre equivalent exports of textiles and clothing production and then to find the domestic availability of yarn and fibre. The domestic availability of fibre match with similar data from the Food and Agriculture Organisation of the United Nations (FAO).

Per Capita Domestic Availability and Consumption

The per capita availability of fabrics as derived in this study increased from 18.12 square metres during 1983 to 20.80 square metre during 1990-91 and further to 24.38 square metres during 1999-2000. The official estimates were lower during

1983 compared to estimates made in this study, but the difference in conversion rates has made considerable difference in growth rates. During 1999-2000, the official estimates were not only high compared to estimates derived in this study, but the margin widen considerably. The per capita availability in terms of kilograms however has increased at a very slow rate from 2.24 kilogram during 1983 to 2.43 kilograms during 1990-91, before declining to 2.34 kilogram during 1999-2000. The dissimilarities in per capita consumption in square metres and kilograms are primarily caused by change in composition of cotton and synthetic fibre for which conversion rate of yarn to fabrics are much different. The share of cotton fibre declined from 80 per cent in 1983 to 73 per cent during 1990-91 and further to 49 per cent in 1999-2000.

The availability of fabrics for domestic consumption derived in this study is compared with the domestic consumption of fabrics. The domestic availability of fabrics has been worked out by subtracting fabrics equivalent exports in various forms such as fabrics, made-ups and garments from the production of fabrics. The per capita availability of fabrics for domestic consumption is close to similar estimates of the Textile Committee on household and non-household sector consumption. The Consumer Household Survey estimates have certain inherent problems due to wrong identification of fibre and sector of the fabrics. Thus the sector-wise and fibre-wise estimates of household consumption cannot be fully relied upon. However, as the fabrics produced in the handloom sector are easily distinguishable from others, an attempt is made to work out the total consumption (domestic plus exports) of handloom fabrics. The consumption estimates of handloom fabrics differ widely from the estimates of its production derived earlier in this study. The difference in these estimates is due to the diversion of hank yarn to the powerloom sector for the production of fabrics. The diversion of hank yarn to the powerloom sector is worked out over the period of time by applying conversion rates on the above difference in estimates of handloom fabrics.

Hank Yarn Diversion to the Powerloom Sector

The cotton hank yarn requirement in the handloom sector on the basis of these estimates was 415 million kilograms during 1983, which was 129 million kilograms higher than the delivery of hank yarn to the decentralised sector. During 1990-91, the hank yarn requirement in the handloom sector was reduced to 323 million kilograms, which means 19 million kilograms lower than the hank yarn delivery to the decentralised sector of 342 million kilograms. In 1999-2000, the demand for cotton hank yarn in the handloom sector is estimated at 304 million kilograms compared with the delivery of cotton hank yarn of 514 million kilograms. This means that around 210 million kilograms of cotton hank yarn was diverted to the powerloom sector during 1999-2000, which accounted for 41 per cent of the cotton hank yarn delivery to the decentralised sector. This means that the diversion of cotton hank yarn to the powerloom sector has increased at a very rapid rate during the second phase of liberalisation. In fact, till 1989-90 and for the year 1991-92, the delivery of hank yarn was not enough to meet the requirements of production in the handloom sector. The production of cotton hank yarn grew at a much faster rate than its consumption in the handloom sector. This facilitated the diversion of hank yarn to the powerloom sector. The powerloom sector thus enjoyed the benefit of excise relief on the hank yarn.

Assuming that same percentage of synthetic spun hank yarn of the total synthetic spun hank yarn delivery to decentralised sector is being diverted to powerloom sector as in case of cotton hank yarn. The total amount of cotton and synthetic hank yarn being diverted to powerloom sector is thus estimated to be 235 million kilograms during the year 1999-2000.

Employment Growth in Textiles and Clothing Sector

Based on the estimates of hank yarn diversion to the powerloom sector, the sector-wise estimates of production of fabrics are further revised. From the revised estimates of production of fabrics, an attempt is made to find the total employment in textiles sector on the basis of technical parameters. The estimates derived this way differ widely from the Ministry of Textiles estimates of employment. The estimates of main employment in textiles and ready-made garments sector as derived in our study are 8.15 million as compared to 7.30 million during 1993 (NIC 23, 247, 248, 260, 263, 265, 266, 267 and 268). The estimates of textiles and clothing including tailoring were 10.17 million (main) and 13.14 million (main and casual) respectively during 1999-2000, which are much lower compared to textile ministry estimates of 21.75 million.

The estimates of main employment in textiles and clothing sector derived in this study grew by only 2.93 per cent per annum and main and casual by 1.47 per cent during 1990-91 to 1999-2000. This is against the high growth of value added in textiles and clothing sector. The GDP in textiles and clothing sector grew by 6.1 per cent per annum during 1990-91 to 1999-2000 as against the overall GDP growth of 6 per cent per annum during the same period. Thus the share of textiles and clothing in total GDP grew marginally to 2.52 per cent during 1999-2000 from 2.44 per cent during 1990-91. The production of fabrics in quantity terms also grew by 5.59 per cent per annum during the same period. Thus the employment per unit of output has come down and thus the labour productivity has increased due to shift in production from handloom to powerloom sector during ninties. However, considering the fact that the growth in registered manufacturing sector was jobless during nineties despite 7 to 8 per cent growth in its value added, the performance of textile and clothing sector seems not bad. This cannot be considered good either as the industry is highly labour intensive especially garment sector, which has high potential for growth. Moreover, the analysis undertaken in this study do not take into account increase in labour productivity due to technology progress, it only takes into account the change in labour productivity due to shift in production from one sector to another. The modernisation did take place after mid eighties and hence might have improved labour productivity. But the modernisation could not be sustained at rapid rate, which is obstructed by fear of loosing incentives of SSI sector, once unit graduate itself from SSI to large-scale sector. However, some growth in modernisation and hence labour productivity did take place and thus the actual growth in employment might have been lower than projected in the above analysis. Even on the basis of no growth in labour productivity within the sector, the entire period 1983 to 1999-2000 reflected the very nominal growth of 0.15 per cent in employment in textiles and clothing industry (it is 1.48 per cent per annum during 1990-91 to 1999-2000).

In the handloom sector, the policies failed not only to generate employment growth in the sector, but infact declined by (-) 3.27 per cent per annum during ninties. The growth in employment has mainly taken place in powerloom and ready-made garment segment. Thus the policy to protect the handloom sector by imposing obligations on the production of hank yarn did not work. The employment per unit value added is 12.5 to 16 times higher in case of handloom sector compared to powerloom sector. But it should also be kept in mind that despite decline in employment in the handloom sector, it still accounts for 2.38 million equivalent main employees during 1999-2000 and 4.76 million casual and main workers. Thus although it is important to take decision on the removal of hank yarn obligations and excise concessions on hank yarn as significant part of it is diverted to the powerloom sector, there is need for some caution. One possible way is to subsidise the handloom fabrics or provide concessions to handloom weavers directly. The other option is to provide training to handloom weavers to help them find an alternative employment.

Relative Performance of Various Sectors in Exports and Domestic Market Segments

The sector-wise availability of fabrics for total domestic use (including household and non-household) is worked out by subtracting exports from production. The relative performance of various sectors is worked out by deriving growth rates and relative share of exports and domestic production. Because of higher growth of output in powerloom sector, its share in total production of cotton and synthetic fabrics increased from 35.94 per cent in 1983 to 61.88 per cent in 1990-91 and further to 72.57 per cent in 1999-2000. Also, the share of the hosiery sector increased, from 7.16 per cent in 1983 to 10.52 per cent in 1990-91 and further to 15.07 per cent in 1999-2000. On the other hand, share of both mill and handloom sectors show a consistent decline since 1983. The share of the mill sector in total production declined from 25.76 per cent in 1983 to 12.68 per cent in 1990-91 and further to 4.68 per cent in 1999-2000. Thus the introduction of various liberalisation policies has not improved the performance of the mill sector and diversion of production from mill and handloom sector to powerloom sector has continued. The main reason for the mill sector not to grow is its inability to provide fabrics in smaller lots to the garment sector. The restrictions imposed on the entry of the large-scale sector into garment production for the domestic segment is the major cause for it. Although these restrictions do not apply to garments produced for exports, this is not sufficient for the mill sector to become competitive and to utilise economies of scale. The share of the handloom sector also declined during these two phases from 31.14 per cent in 1983 to 14.91 per cent in 1990-91 and further to 7.68 per cent in 1999-2000.

The performance of the handloom sector in the exports segment was relatively good till 1994-95. Exports of cotton fabrics from the handloom sector in various forms grew at the rate of 3.51 per cent during 1990-91 to 1999-2000 compared with a negative growth from the mill sector. There is some controversy about the powerloom sector's exports being sent as handloom exports to get advantage of handloom quota. From the analysis of data from Handloom Export Promotion Council, it appears that it is mainly a part of propaganda to put pressure on the government to remove all kinds of restrictions including lowering of hank yarn obligations. If duplication is taking place on a large-scale, how can one explain the decline in the share of the handloom exports in total cotton fabrics equivalent export after 1994-95, including in the made-ups exports, where the quota was high? In absolute terms, the exports of cotton equivalent fabrics from the handloom sector declined from 782 million square metres in 1994-95 to 664 million square metres in 1996-97, and were 704 million square metres in 1999-2000. Had the powerloom sector been significantly using the export quota of the handloom sector by way of duplication, it would have done the same after 1994-95 as well. It is more relevant in the context that fabrics equivalent exports from powerloom sector grew from 2198 million square metre during 1994-95 to 3378 million square metre during 1999-2000. The growth in powerloom made-ups exports was in fact highest, where despite high quota of handloom sector, its share declined. The exports of powerloom made-ups grew from 696 million square metre during 1994-95 to 1337 million square metre during 1999-2000. Thus there is no compelling reason to believe that after 1994-95, the powerloom sector could not use the export quota meant for the handloom sector, if it was able to do the same on a significant scale earlier.

The analysis brings out the fact that the handloom sector is unable to compete in the new economic environment as institutional and other market supports are being gradually phased out. The first area of casualty was, of-course, the domestic market as a result of the gradual phasing out of the various marketing schemes. In case of the export market, it was able to survive for some time on account of the existence of the quota system and through improvement in the quality of fabrics. But the handloom sector has become more and more vulnerable without institutional support during the liberalisation phase. The decline in market for handloom products in the domestic market added to its vulnerability and reduced its profitability. This affected the performance of the sector in the export segment as well. Thus, in the new economic environment, the handloom sector is finding it difficult to survive in both the domestic and the export segments.

The obligation placed on the mill sector to produce a certain minimum percentage of their total spun yarn in hank form and the inability of the handloom sector to absorb it, causes the diversion of hank yarn to the powerloom sector. Thus the powerloom sector enjoys the benefit of excise relief meant to be consumed by the handloom sector and raises its competitiveness vis-a-vis the mill sector. However, one should take into consideration the fact that the yarn consumption in the form of hank yarn do not constitute a large share (19.88 per cent only) of the total yarn consumed in the powerlooom sector during 1999-2000. Thus excise duty evasion cannot be justified for the better performance of the powerloom sector. Moreover, it is difficult to explain the low growth of mill sector in grey fabrics on which no excise duty was imposed till recently. Thus the rise in the share of the powerloom sector in this segment cannot be explained by biased policies. In fact, the mill sector seem to be the real beneficiary of policy regime in terms of availing finance at cheap rate and acquiring premium quota.

The general argument put forward for the poor performance of mill sector in grey fabrics is that the fabrics produced in mill sector is generally of better variety, which require better processing facility. The escalating high duty on dyed fabrics till finance bill 2001-02 discourage this and hence affects demand for grey fabrics in domestic market. The high excise duty on dyed fabrics affects mills' domestic demand and ultimately exports by not allowing the use of scale economies. This in a way amounts to admission that the mill sector is competitive only in a few products of better quality for which only better dying facility is suitable. Thus the mill sector operates in niche markets.

It seems from the discussion that the powerloom sector is competitive in the production of fabrics on the basis of cost considerations. This is mainly because due to various rigidities in policy, the textiles and clothing sector has developed a structure that precludes the achievement of economies of scale. The reservation for the small scale sector to produce fabrics for the domestic segment leads to demand of fabrics in smaller lots by the garment producer spread all over the country.

The production of fabrics in smaller lots is not very conducive for the mill sector. Consequently, the mill sector is not investing in technological up-gradation. On the other hand, the powerloom sector is not investing much for technological progress as wages are quite low compared to other sectors and any investment decision is weighed against the cost of capital to replace cheap labour. The other reason for low quality improvement is that policy regime discourages the graduation of small into medium or large firms. Thus the problems in the weaving sector are much more complex compared to spinning sector. This is the area of worry. In addition, technological progress is hindered by an irrational excise duty structure. The high excise duty on dyed fabrics compared to grey fabrics restricts the growth of better processing or integrated plants.

Having discussed the relative performance of the various sectors in the domestic and exports segments an attempt is made to determine the extent of change in quality in consumption pattern for the domestic and export segments.

Variety-wise Domestic and Export Demand of Fabrics

Woven fabrics can be consumed in the form of garments in piece length, piece length, readymade garments and made-ups. The ratio of various products in the household sector for the years 1983, 1992 and 1998 as given by the Textile Committee are used to work out the item-wise availability of fabrics for domestic consumption for the household and the non-household sectors. This is worked out on the assumption that the share of various items in the household and the non-household sectors is the same. For the intervening years, the values are interpolated assuming constant growth rate and latter adjusted proportionately to arrive at figures of domestic availability of fabrics for each year.

From the item-wise analysis of domestic consumption, it appears that the share of household variety (made-ups), garments in piece length and readymade garments and piece length have not changed much over the period of time. However, the change took place mainly within the composition of readymade garments and piece length. The share of piece length declined from 33.70 per cent in 1983 to 24.59 per cent in 1999-2000 and that of readymade garments increased from 7.69 per cent to 18.43 per cent during the same period. Hence, it seems that consumer preference has shifted in favour of readymade garments over time. The trend for cotton and synthetic products is different, as the consumer prefers to use piece length made of synthetic rather than of cotton.

The variety-wise export of fabrics has already been worked out. Thus, by adding the variety-wise domestic and export demand, one could work out the total variety-wise production or demand.

Estimates of Value of Textiles and Clothing Production and Consumption

To work out the value of total textiles and clothing production in the country, the average ex-factory prices of various sectors and segments are used. As the data for ex-factory prices of fabrics produced. The ex-factory price for the mill sector is available, while it is not available for the powerloom, handloom and hosiery sectors. Approximations have been made based on available data on mill sector ex-factory price and retail prices, market prices or export prices for various sectors. The limitations in such cases are that the transport and trade margins are different in different cases.

Werner International data is used to determine the all India average cost of tailoring per square metre for shirts. To derive tailoring costs for other products, the ratio of export prices of these products vis-a-vis shirts is used and applied on shirt tailoring charges. The proportion of these products in the total domestic consumption is worked out from the Textile Committee data and is used to work out the average cost of tailoring per square metre, which in turn is used to work out the total stitching charges.

The changes in per unit export prices of relevant sectors/ items are used as Index to work out ex-factory prices over time from the available data.

The share of value added in production is worked out by using International Textile Manufacturing Federation (ITMF) data on cost of production and tailoring ratio from CSO records. The share of textiles and clothing value added (cotton and synthetic products) in GDP worked out this way is 2.52 per cent during 1999-2000. These estimates are very close to the revised estimates of CSO (NAS). The share of mill sector worked out in this study as percentage of total textiles and clothing value added is 42.29 during 1999-2000.

Although, the revised estimates of CSO presently tally with the overall estimates made in this study. This may not hold in the long run. This is because the CSO estimates over a period of time are derived from the base year's estimates by applying an index of industrial production. The index of industrial production for textile items is based on the production estimates derived from data in *Compendium of Textile Statistics,* Textile Commissioner. CSO has infact stopped using Textile Commissioner's data as it was felt that their estimates of production of fabrics are not scientifically drawn. The difference in growth rate derived from the production data of the Textile Commissioner will depend on the difference between actual and assumed conversion rates for various sectors and the extent of diversion of hank yarn to the powerloom sector. The actual conversion rates themselves vary over time depending upon the share of various sectors, count composition, and construction parameters of fabrics.

The total expenditure by consumers on textiles and garments (cotton and synthetic items) is worked out by multiplying the total fabric available for domestic consumption with its market price. The total expenditure incurred by consumers has been worked out by using two sets of prices provided by the Textile Committee and the Textile Commissioner. The two market prices adopted in this study give wide differences in the estimates of total expenditure on textiles and clothing goods in the country. The share of textile and clothing (government and non-profit institutions is not taken out) in private final consumption expenditure worked out by the two methods is approximately 5.6 per cent and 10.1 per cent, respectively. This difference due to prices needs to be looked into by the CSO and the Ministry of Textiles.

India's Exports Potential by the Year 2010-11

An attempt has been made to discuss India's textiles and clothing potential both for exports and the domestic sector by 2005-06 and 2010-11. The global trade environment is likely to change significantly with the implementation of GATT accord. It is expected that various restrictions imposed by developed countries will gradually be lifted on the exports from developing countries. The restrictions seem to have affected the level and direction of world trade. The high level of customs duties and other barriers lower the level of trade. In addition, the preferential treatment given to various countries change the direction of trade flows. Once the MFA is phased out and restrictions on other countries are lowered, the impact of preferential treatment will be reduced and it would have an impact on the future direction of trade. This will also affect the composition of trade as trade of intermediary products is expected to be lower. Developing countries' share in exports to developed countries is expected to rise significantly after the MFA phase out, as developing countries are expected to absorb a significant share of those countries to which the preferential treatment is given by the developed countries. This is going to be relevant for India as well. On the other hand, the impact of lowering of restrictions on the rise in demand of India's export to non-quota countries is going to offset the loss of exports to these countries caused by irrelevance of indirect routes. India's export to quota countries indirectly routed through non-quota countries on which barriers were comparatively lower is bound to affect due to overall lowering in restrictions including for India.

India's performance in the past was adversely affected mainly in those products for which the level and growth rates are kept low despite high potential. The major constraint was felt in fashion goods items in which demand exists for a short period as quota limits depend upon the past performance.

The future growth of India's export cannot be predicted from the extrapolation of past trend. This is because India's exports during the nineties have grown at a very fast rate and India has already achieved a high base level. Perhaps, it would not be possible to sustain the growth rate achieved recently. India's export potential and its ability to increase its share in exports after MFA phase out will essentially depend on the level of restrictions in the past, country's share in world trade, relative cost competitiveness of the country at various stages of production, quality of the products, etc. This necessitate the importance of continuous improvement for modernisation to remain competitive.

Using ITMF data, it is found that India's per unit cost of production is lower than that of Brazil, Italy, Indonesia, Korea, USA and Turkey, both for yarn and fabrics. The data from Werner International shows that India has cost competitiveness in the production of garments compared with USA, Mexico and Thailand. In addition to other advantages, India has easy availability of raw cotton and labour and large base of exports.

India enjoys a major advantage as it is capable of producing wide range of products based on the availability of cotton of various staple lengths. This is one of the major strengths of the Indian textiles and clothing industry, which should be maintained and exploited.

The EU, United States and Japan, the major importers of textile and clothing items accounted for 68 per cent of the global imports of textiles and clothing items during 1996. These are the countries imposing the highest restrictions on textiles and clothing imports and hence India's share in imports of these countries is likely to increase with the MFA phase out. However, India has a balanced presence presently in most of the countries in the world, whether quota or non-quota. The only exceptions are a few countries like Japan, where India does not have a significant presence, but its share is rising in these markets as well. India's share in EU, USA, Canada and Japan's import was 3.75 per cent as compared with its share of 3.36 per cent in world trade.

However, it comes out that the export growth from India to quota countries was at a lower rate than growth in exports to other countries. India's export to EEC and USA of quota items grew at 7.58 per cent per annum, of total restricted items at 8.11 per cent per annum and of total items to EEC and USA at 8.83 per cent per annum during 1983 to 1997. It was much lower than the overall growth of exports of 16.43 per cent from India during the same period.

Despite various advantages, India's exports are expected to grow at a relatively lower rate compared with the very high growth rate achieved in the past, as the base level has become high. But it will be higher than the growth rate of 5.96 per cent per annum worked by ESCAP on the basis of available information on quota acceleration of till year 2005-06. However, the actual growth rate would depend upon various factors such as world and South Asia's growth of textiles and clothing trade.

For this, an excise has been undertaken to estimate the item-wise total world trade by the year 2005. This has been worked out by using estimate given by John Coker (1997) in Textile Outlook International (TOI). The TOI model is based on income and fabric consumption pattern for various countries. Considering all the aspects in this study, item-wise estimate of global and regional trade given in TOI have been used with some modifications including changes in the share of various items in trade.

Textile Outlook International estimates are based on the assumption that growth in per capita consumption of some of the developed countries would decelerate as they have already attained the peak level. The model based on these assumptions with some modifications is considered as Alternative I. However, in Alternative II, we have assumed that deceleration in demand by developed countries may not actually take place since prices are likely to rise at lower rate due to reduction in trade barriers. This means in Alternative II, it is assumed that developed countries per capita consumption may continue to grow at a rate achieved during 1980 to 1995. This is in addition to higher increase in per capita consumption in Eastern Europe and the former USSR on the lines as projected in Alt. I. However, some other changes in per capita consumption of other countries regions is expected in the revised scenario.

India's export potential for the year 2005-06 is derived on the basis of the two alternatives of world and South Asia's trade. India's exports are expected to be somewhere between these two alternatives. There is also a possibility that the overall world trade may not grow as rapidly as assumed in Alternative II, but India's share in it may increase and vice versa. However, the present scenario in the country do not reflect the possibility of high growth. Thus, the likely scenario by 2005-06 is Alternative I. Alternative II projections are considered as optimistic scenario for year 2005-06. The projections for the year 2010-11 are thus based on Alternative I.

Based on above analysis, India's export of yarn is expected to increase from 675 million kilograms in 1999-2000 to 893 million kilograms during 2010-11, showing a rise of 2.58 per cent per annum as against a rise of 21.73 per cent per annum during 1990-91 to 1999-2000. The export of cotton yarn may rise in the short run, but is likely to come down to the present level of exports as it gradually gives place to value added exports. The yarn equivalent fabrics exports is expected to rise from 354 million kilograms in 1999-2000 to 803 million kilograms in 2010-11, showing a rise of 7.73 per cent per annum as against the rise of 10.23 per cent during 1990-91 to 1999-2000. The yarn equivalent made-ups export is expected to increase from 325 million kilograms during 1999-2000 to 805 million kilograms during 2010-11, showing a rise of 8.60 per cent per annum as against the rise of 13.77 per cent during 1990-91 to 1999-2000. In the case of garments, the yarn equivalent export is expected to increase from 248 million kilogram from 1999-2000 to 870 million kilograms to 2010-11, showing a rise of 12.09 per cent per annum as against the rise of 9.75 per cent during 1990-91 to 1999-2000.

The total yarn equivalent exports in textiles and clothing products is expected to grow by 7.95 per cent per annum and fibre equivalent by 7.35 per cent during 1999-2000 to 2010-11 as against 14.68 per cent and 14.87 per cent per annum respectively during 1990-91 to 1999-2000.

India may also be an importer of various intermediary and final products. This is because higher exports would also lead to increase in import of intermediate products to overcome the shortage of raw material and quality products. The imports of textiles and clothing products are estimated to be in the range of 577 million kilograms equivalent yarn by 2010-11 as against 66 million kilograms during 1999-2000.

The cotton content share in net fibre equivalent export is expected to be in the range of 72.21 percent during 2010-11 as against 84.70 during 1999-2000. This means synthetic product exports are expected to rise at a faster rate than exports of cotton products.

The projections for exports are worked out in dollar equivalent terms as well. The per unit value for exports for various items are taken only marginally higher than 1997-98 prices to account for qualitative changes. In the second alternative, per unit price is taken at the same level as in 1997-98, as higher growth is only possible at low prices. The prices are taken at 1997-98 level as data for latest years is not find and growth in per unit export price for various items is very low and insignificance based on 1990-91 to 1999-2000 data.

India's exports of cotton and synthetic products are expected to increase from US$ 10.71 billion in 1999-2000 to US$ 31.21 billion by 2010-11, showing a rise of 10.21 per cent per annum. In the past, India's total textiles and clothing exports grew by 9.56 per cent per annum. The projections therefore seem consistent with the past trend rate. Future growth may be higher in case per unit prices show higher increases. World total textiles and clothing trade is expected to grow to US$ 557 billion in 2010-11. This means India's share in world trade is expected to grow from 3.15 per cent in 1999-2000 to 5.6 per cent by 2010-11.[1]

Potential Domestic Demand by 2005-06 and 2010-11

After analysing the exports demand equivalent of fabrics, yarn and fibre, an attempt is made to find similar estimates for domestic demand. The estimates have been worked out on the basis of income and price elasticities. Future projections in this study are based on the assumption that GDP is expected to grow in the range of 6 to 8 per cent per annum, population by 1.84 per cent per annum, cotton products prices at 5 per cent higher than the WPI for all commodities and synthetic prices at 5 per cent lower than WPI of all commodities over the 6-year period from 1999-2000 to 2005-06 and trend pattern continued after that as well. This means that cotton prices will continue to grow by 0.82 per cent per annum higher than WPI and synthetic prices lower by same margin during the period 2005-2010-11.

Total demand for fabrics for domestic consumption is expected to increase by 5.33 per cent per annum during the period 1999-2000 to 2010-11. The total demand for fibre in domestic consumption is expected to increase by 4.65 per cent per annum. India's per capita fibre consumption is estimated to be 3.39 kgs during 2010-11. The share of 100 per cent cotton fibre in domestic demand of cotton and synthetic products was 49.19 per cent during 1999-2000. This may decline to 45.13 per cent by 2005-06 and further to 44.73 per cent by 2010-11.

In case silk and wool fibre is also included, the share of cotton fibre is expected to decline to around 43.5 per cent during 2010-11 of compared to 47.5 per cent estimated during 1999-2000.

The share of cotton fibre in world total fibre consumption is 44 per cent (including wool and silk) during 1995. The

[1] India's exports in this study accounts for only cotton and synthetic products, while world expected trade include all fibres.

international share of cotton fibre is expected to decline to 40.5 per cent in total fibre consumption by year 2010-11.

Total Demand and Supply Conditions by the Year 2010-11

The projections for year 2010-11 are based on Alternative I, which is not too optimistic considering certain demand and supply constraints and are based on the assumption of 6 per cent per annum GDP growth. The total demand for fabrics is expected to be 61450 million sq.mt. during 2010-11, out of which 69 per cent share is expected to be for domestic segment. The share of synthetic fabrics in total demand is expected to be 63 per cent. The expected growth of fabrics is 6.38 per cent per annum during the period 1999-2000 to 2010-11. The demand for cotton fabrics is expected to grow by 4.94 per cent per annum and that of synthetic fabrics by 7.33 per cent per annum during the same period. The growth in fabrics in piece length is expected to take place at only 3.65 per cent, garment in piece length by 5.08 per cent, hosiery by 10.82 per cent, made-ups by 9.55 per cent, and ready-made garments by 10.34 per cent per annum during the period 1999-2000 to 2010-11.

The demand of ready-made garments is expected to be 18113 million sq.mt. during year 2010-11. The growth in this segment is expected to be high with the speeding up of economic reforms. In addition, the demand for hosiery fabrics is expected to be 9799 million sq.mt. during 2010-11, most of it is going to be consumed in the form of garments. Moreover, the demand for fabrics in piece length is expected to be 11470 million sq.mt. during 2010-11, out of which 60 per cent will be in the domestic segment, which would require stitching by tailors. Thus the ultimate demand of ready-made and tailor made goods is expected to be 39382 million sq. mt., which is 58 per cent of the total demand of fabrics in the form of fabrics, made-ups and garments.

The fibre demand is expected to grow by 4.84 per cent per annum, yarn by 5.01 per cent and fabrics by 6.38 per cent per annum during the period 1999-2000 to 2010-11. The various segments of fabrics are expected to grow at different rates.

The growth in industry will primarily depend upon the availability of raw material specially cotton. We are presently running short of cotton fibre. A minimum growth in cotton production of 3 per cent per annum during the period 1999-2000 to 2010-11 is required, which will leave a gap of 10 per cent in demand and supply. This gap of 2.3 million bales could be met by net import of cotton. Thus it is important that the growth in production of cotton should be assigned priority. The cotton requirement is expected to be 23.9 million bales (excluding raw cotton exports) by year 2010-11, even after considering the import of cotton textiles and clothing products to the extent of 2.8 million bales.

The additional total spindles are expected to grow on an average in the range of 1 to 1.20 million spindles per year during the period 1999-2000 to 2010-11. The 1.20 million spindles per year are expected to be installed each year in case the spindles in operation are not older than 1991-92.

The additional looms required to produce the additional fabrics requirement may be difficult to work out, as it would all depend upon choice of techniques and sectoral growth pattern. Moreover, the data regarding the age composition of existing weaving capacity is not available.

The total fibre/filament requirement was 4321 million kilograms during 1999-2000. It is expected to grow in the range of 4.84 per cent per annum to 7269 million kilograms by 2010-11. The cotton fibre share in it was 65 per cent during 1999-2000. It is expected to decline in the range of 56 per cent.

India's mill fibre consumption share in total world fibre consumption is expected to increase from 9.25 per cent during 1999-2000 to 11.05 per cent during 2010-11. India's share of cotton fibre for mill consumption in world is expected to increase to 15.19 per cent during 2010-11 depending upon various demand and supply situations prevailing in the country and abroad.

Some Policy Suggestions

Several policy changes are required in order to enable the

textiles and clothing industry to meet the challenges in the new world economic environment after the MFA phase out. Possible constraints, which may hinder the growth potential of industry, include non-availability of cotton and lack of technological development in weaving, dyeing and garment units. Further, there is a possibility that developed countries may adopt restrictive safeguards in the form of product of origin clause, labour and patent laws, most favoured nation status as well as environmental issues on synthetic products including use of dyes. Thus the path to growth may not be very smooth unless the government takes appropriate steps to tackle the issues.

The biggest challenge in achieving the growth targets projected in this study seems to be in ensuring raw cotton availability in the range of 23.9 million bales. Assuring farmers international prices of cotton could raise the production of raw cotton. The government must take proper steps to increase the productivity of cotton in the country as India's productivity is amongst the lowest in the world. At the same time, steps should be taken to improve the quality of cotton. Further, the shortage of cotton could be met by allowing free trade of cotton at international prices. During 1999-2000, the production of cotton was estimated at 15.60, export 0.1, and imports 1.9 million bales. The mill and ex-factory consumption was 17.15 million bales (consumption was 15.18 million bales in mills, 0.88 million bales in SSI spinning units and 1.1 million bales in ex-factory).

The projection regarding cotton requirement of 23.9 million bales is based on the assumption that the domestic demand of textiles and clothing products for the household and non-household sector would shift rapidly towards synthetic products. It is expected that the share of cotton fibre in total cotton and synthetic fibre consumption would be reduced to approximately 43.5 per cent by the year 2010-11. This is possible in case government takes proper steps and lowers the excise burden on synthetic products. The lowering of prices would raise the demand for synthetic products domestically and may help in utilising scale economies. The utilisation of scale economies in synthetic products may also help in raising exports of synthetic products.

As mentioned above, availability of raw cotton would be one of the important factors to decide the future growth rate in textiles and clothing industry. In case of raw cotton shortage, there is a possibility that India may witness lower production of yarn and fabrics than predicted in the above alternatives. India is presently exporting a large quantity of cotton yarn to countries of East Asia and South Asia. In fact, we may have to start importing considerable amount of cotton yarn. The situation in India resembles that in China. China was once the largest exporter of cotton yarn, but is presently a net importer.

The analysis of the share of cotton handloom fabrics in total production of woven cotton fabrics points to the fact that the economic reforms have adversely affected the performance of the handloom sector. The handloom sector's share in total production of woven cotton fabrics was as high as 34.99 per cent in 1983, which declined to 17.37 per cent in 1990-91 and further to 9.04 per cent in 1999-2000. The handloom sector's share declined at even faster rate in total production of fabrics from as high as 32.49 per cent in 1983, which declined to 15.54 per cent in 1990-91 and further to 7.68 per cent in 1999-2000. The decline in the share of handloom in total production of woven fabrics has been caused by changes in various policies and the increase in competitiveness of the powerloom sector in the new regime. The share of the powerloom sector has increased at the cost of both handloom and mill sectors.

The estimates of main employment in textiles and clothing sector grew by only 2.93 per cent per annum and main and casual by 1.47 per cent during 1990-91 to 1999-2000. The production of fabrics in quantity terms grew by 5.59 per cent per annum during 1990-91 to 1999-2000. Thus the employment per unit of output has come down though the labour productivity has increased due to shift in production from handloom to powerloom sector during nineties. However, considering the fact that the growth in registered manufacturing sector was jobless during nineties despite 7 to 8 per cent growth in its GDP, the performance of textile and clothing sector seems not bad. However, looking at the entire period 1983 to 1999-2000, the growth in employment has taken place at a very marginal rate. The growth in employment in textiles and clothing sector including tailor made products is estimated to grow by 0.15 per cent during 1983 to 1999-2000 as against 1.48 per cent per annum during 1990-91 to 1999-2000. These estimates are based on the assumption that additional outputs in a sector generate same amount of employment. However, the labour productivity must have increased in the sector due to capital deepening and technology progress. The technology progress has taken place in the powerloom sector after mid eighties to take benefit of the export opportunities, while it could not persist for long at the same rate due to fear of losing incentives of SSI sector. Considering the growth in labour productivity in each sector, the actual growth in employment generation would have taken place at a lower rate especially during eighties. Thus the policies pursued till now failed to bring the desired technology progress in textiles and clothing sector and the growth in employment in this labour intensive sector were also not to the expected level.

The economic reforms so far have not succeeded in bringing the much-required technological progress in the weaving sector due to lack of competition among the various sectors. In fact, technological progress has also not taken place in dyeing and garments units. This can be partially attributed to irrational excise duty structure prevailing at present. The best way to rationalise excise duty structure is by imposing excise duty at the yarn stage even for fabrics (including on hank yarn) so that the decentralised powerloom sector could not escape from it. It is better to impose excise duty on yarn considering the value of grey fabrics, and considering the average conversion rate in specific count ranges. For dyed products, the excise duty should be imposed on the value of output after providing MODVAT at grey fabrics stages. The excise duty impact should same on additional value aided at grey and dyed stage. This will create a competitive environment for the mill and powerloom sectors and improve technological development at fabrics and dyeing stage. However, manual dyeing should be given some concession and may be considered for low rates of excise duty.

One could argue that the increase in duty on yarn (including hank yarn) would affect the growth of the handloom sector. In this study, it has become clear that a large proportion of hank yarn is being diverted to the powerloom sector. Thus although it is important to take decision on the removal of hank yarn obligations and excise concessions on hank yarn as most part of it is diverted to powerloom sector, there need to be some caution. The government should subsidise the handloom sector to meet the social objectives by way of subsidising the handloom fabrics or providing concessions to handloom weavers directly. The hank yarn obligations and excise concessions on hank yarn should be removed.

The most crucial policy decision taken in NTP 2000 in promoting competition among the various sectors was to allow free entry of large units in the garment sector for the domestic market. This would allow, economies of scale to be fully exploited even at the fabrics stage and encourage competition among the various sectors. The main cause for the competitiveness of powerloom sector was lack of demand by small garment units spread all over the country in smaller lots, which was not conducive for production in the mill sector.

As was expected as a follow-up step after dereservation, the finance bill 2001 introduced MODVAT from the fibre to the garment stage with a 16 per cent excise duty. However, certain exemptions in the form of excise concession for hank yarn meant to be consumed in the handloom sector and for manual dyeing break the chain in MODVAT process. Similarly, the duty at the processing stage by independent processing houses for the small units is shifted away from ad valorem to specific duties. Thus the purpose of introducing MODVAT has been diluted. Moreover, excise duty avoidance at the fabrics stage by various units mainly in the decentralised sector could contribute to the slow growth of the organised garment industry.

The garment industry also has several options by which it can avoid excise duty. Job work is exempted from any excise duty and hence a unit can evade taxes by reporting in-house production as job work done. Similarly, the garment exporters need not pay any excise duty if their domestic sales are less than Rs. 10 million. These exemptions increase the evasion and hence weaken the impact of MODVAT.

However, one problem area which was not addressed in the finance bill is the relatively high excise and custom duty on synthetic yarn compared to cotton yarn. On the other hand, the excise duty on synthetic and cotton fabrics is currently at same rate. This causes a tax escalation on the cotton products at the value added stages. The new policy may not be adequately able to induce the desired modernisation at the weaving and dying stages unless a uniform rate of excise duty is imposed on cotton and synthetic products. India is presently a major exporter of cotton yarn and cotton fabrics but not of cotton made-ups or synthetic products.

Thus it is important to modify these policies to stimulate competition among the various sectors. The quality of products did not improve in the past. This was partially due to a rise in demand for coarser products and partially due to relatively inferior product combinations. The improvement in quality is important as India is going to face new challenges from the relatively new entrants such as Sri Lanka, Bangladesh and Nepal at lower end products in the international market. The free flow of yarn and relatively cheap labour costs in these countries would make these countries comparatively more competitive at fabric and garment stages of production. Pakistan and China are already the major competitors of India in low quality products. In addition, China is maintaining its comparative advantage in quality products. The newly industrialised countries are posing a major competition among higher quality products. However, the competitiveness of these countries is getting reduced over a period of time, as wage cost is already very high in these countries. There is a strong case, therefore, for India to promote its quality products in the coming year. The well-known areas of weakness are ginning, dyeing and quality fabrics, where it is important for India to improve its quality. India's future growth would depend very much on how it could project itself as a quality producer. This will give India a higher growth potential in value terms. In case the quality of fabrics and dyeing would not improve, the garment producers may have to resort to high imports in order to meet the demand for quality fabrics. This is very likely in a free trade environment. The increase in imports of fabrics, in turn, would affect the yarn as well as fibre requirements. So, future growth in textile industry would depend quite a lot on the technological as well as qualitative improvements in the textiles and clothing sectors.

As weaving capacity is expected to increase at a very fast rate, the dyeing demand is going to rise proportionately if not more than proportionately. It is important to ensure that funds are available for large-scale investment both in large- and small-scale sectors. However, India should identify the potential growth sectors in the textiles and clothing industry, as priority areas and government should facilitate cheaper credit on a priority basis even for small-scale dyeing and weaving units for specific periods. Textile Upgradation Fund has already been created that provides funds for upgradation to the tune of Rs. 250,000 million during the next five years at the rate of 5 per cent per annum (much lower than the market rate). However, this is mainly meant for the large-scale sector. The amount to be disbursed out of this to small-scale sector by SIDBI is fixed at Rs. 80,000 million, despite the fact that the small-scale sector contributes a major share of production of fabrics in the country. Small-scale sector also contributes a large share in dyeing and garment segments. It is infact, these sectors which require urgent attention regarding modernisation.

There is need to bring down interest rates for working capital as well. This is possible by bringing more efficiency in bank operations. In addition to the finance, the electricity cost as well as infrastructure development such as transport and communications are the other areas where government attention is immediately required. Otherwise, the targets expected may go awry. Thus the problems of infrastructure constraints for SSI sector should be addressed properly.

India's spinning and weaving industry needs complete restructuring. Modernisation in spinning has taken place at very fast rate but still old spindles are not wound up despite the existence of sufficient number of new spindles to produce the required spun yarn. This has caused excess capacity and led to under-utilisation of new spindles. This erodes the profitability of investment and acts as disincentive for new investment. Modernisation could be stepped up by imposing a uniform tax on per unit spindles installed. This may also prevent the SSI sector from installing very old/scrapped spindles.

The government should no longer be spending money on revival packages. There is no point in reviving old machinery and spending more on it than on new machinery. Instead, workers should be given proper compensation packages for rehabilitation.

On the issue of dealing with sick units and surplus manpower, NTP 2000 says that employment protection in terminally sick units is neither conducive to efficient allocation nor incremental employment generation. The extent of sickness can be gauged by the large number of old spindles lying idle, despite large-scale modernisation in the spinning segment. In NTP 2000 emphasis is placed on a pragmatic and rational exit policy with adequate protection of workers' interest. However, the anticipated squeeze in employment is a serious socio-economic matter, especially because the existence of a vast army of workers is at stake. Thus, the government may need to take other measures. One possible alternative is the government has to facilitate the provision of training infrastructure for the workers employed in the small garment and handloom units to help them find an alternative employment. It seems that government has an important role to play in the development of the textiles and clothing industry. The various possible constraints in the form of cotton availability, dyeing and lack of quality improvements could hinder the growth prospects of the industry, unless properly tackled. Thus in addition to above measures, all efforts have to be made to remove the supply bottlenecks, which could come in the way of meeting the potential demand.

The industry is set to face a dramatically new environment when domestic markets are opened up to imports. While this was expected to happen this year with the elimination of the final set of quantitative restrictions, the government has postponed the lifting of these restrictions citing the possibility of substantial damage to the livelihood of workers employed in this industry. However, this is only a postponement and at best buys time for the industry to push through a very quick process of restructuring for improved efficiency.

Bibliography

Abid. Hussain Committee (1990), To Review the Progress of Implementation of theTextile Policy, announced on 6th June 1985, New Delhi.

Ahmedabad Textile Industry Research Association (ATIRA) (1984) and AIMA (Ahmedabad Institute of Management Association), Inter-firm Comparison of Costs, Productivity and Damage (Composite Mills), July to September 1983, Ahemdabad, 1984.

Ahmedabad Textile Industry Research Association (ATIRA), (1985), mimeo.

Ahmedabad Textile Industry's Research Association (ATIRA) (1987), Technological and Structural Options for the Future of Indian Textile Sectors, sponsored by The Ministry of Textiles, Government of India.

All Pakistan Textile Mills Association (APTMA), Chairman's Review 1995-96.

Apparel Export Promotion Council, Hand Book of Export Statistics, various issues, New Delhi.

Association of Synthetic Fibre Industry Handbook of Statistics on Man-Made Synthetic Fibre/Yarn Industry: Part One, Various Issues, Bombay.

ATIRA, BTRA, NITRA, SITRA, (1991) Norms for the Textile Industry, Northern India Textile Research Association, Ghaziabad.

Bedi, Jatinder S., Economic Liberalisation and Changes in the Structure of the Indian Textile Industry' Thesis submitted to Jawaharlal Nehru University, Center for Economic Studies and Planning, 2000.

Barthwal, R.R. (1977) "The Determinants of Profitability in Indian Textile Industry", The Indian Journal of Economics, April, 1977.

Bhalla, A.S. (1964), "Investment Allocation and Technological Choice—A Case of Cotton Spinning Techniques", Economic Journal, September, 1964.

Bhattacharya, N. (1964), A Survey of Work Done on Demand Projections at the Indian Statistical Institute, 1964 (mimeo).

Bhide Sheela Thakar (1996), India's Textile and Clothing and Exports to the U.S.A. and the E.E.C: The Multifibre Arrangement and Beyond, doctoral thesis, University of Geneve.

Central Statistical Organisation (CSO), (1989) Source and Method, Central Statistical Organisation, Ministry of Planning and Programme Implementation.

Central Statistical Organisation (CSO), (1998-99), Quick Estimates of National Income, Consumption Expenditure, Saving and Capital Formation.

Central Statistical Organisation (CSO), Various issues on National Accounts Statistics, Central Statistical Organisation, Ministry of Planning and Programme Implementation.

Centre for Monitoring Indian Economy Pvt. Ltd. (CMIE), Economic Intelligence Service, Various Issues.

Chandra Pankaj and P.R. Shukla (1994), Manufacturing Excellence and Global Competitiveness: Challenges and Opportunities for Indian Industries, Economic and Political Weekly, Vol. XXIX(2), February.

Chandra Pankaj (1999), Strategy for Global Competitiveness of Indian Textile Industry,

Chandrasekhar, C.P. (1981), Growth and Technical Change in the Indian Cotton Mill Industry: 1947-77, doctoral thesis, Jawaharlal Nehru University, New Delhi.

Cline, W. (1987), The Future of World Trade in Textile and Apparel, Institute for International Economics, Washington.

Coelli, Tim (1999) *et al.,* An introduction to Efficiency and productivity analysis, Amsterdam, Kulwer Academic Publishers.

Coker John (1997), "World Textile and Clothing Consumption: Forecasts to 2005", Textile Outlook International (TOI), The Economist Intelligence Unit, January.

Desai Ashok V. (1983), "Technology and Market Structure under Government," Economic and Political Weekly.

Directorate General of Commercial Intelligence & Statistics (DGCIS), Foreign Trade Statistics, Various Issues, Ministry of Commerce.

Economic and Social Commission for Asia and the Pacific (ESCAP) (1996b), Protection in the Textile and Clothing Sector, Prospects for Textile and Clothing Sector of the ESCAP Region in the Post-Uruguay Round Context, prepared under the ESCAP/UNDP Regional trade Programme (RAS/92/035), Studies in Trade and Investment 17 United Nation, New York.

Economic and Social Commission for Asia and the Pacific (ESCAP), (1996a), Agreement on Textiles and Clothing: Progress, Problems and Prospects for Developing Countries of the ESCAP Region", document prepared by the ESCAP/UNCTAD/UNDP to Assist in preparation for the First WTO Ministerial Conference, Bangkok.

Erzan R., J. Goto and P. Holmes (1990), "Effects of the Multi-Fibre Arrangement on Developing Country Exporters: An Empirical Invstigation", in C. Hamilton, ed. *Op. cit.*

Erzan R., K. Krishna and L. Hui Tan (1991), "Rent Sharing in the Multi-Fibre Arrangement. Theory and Evidence form U.S. Apparel Imports from Hong Kong", PRE Working Papers No. 597, World Bank, Washington.

Faini Riccardo (1995), "Demand and Supply Factors in Textile Trade", Beyond the Multifibre Arrangement: Third World Competition and Restructuring Europe's Textile Industry, edited by Navaretti Giorgio Barba, Riccardo Faini and Aubrey Silberston, Organisation for Economic Co-operation and Development, Paris.

Faini, R. and A. Heimler (1994), "The Quality of Production of Textiles and Clothing and the Completion of the Internal Market", in T. Venables and A. Winters, eds., The Impact of Europe 1992 on European Trade and Industry, Cambridge University Press, Cambridge.

Faini, R., J. DE Melo and W. Takacs (1992), "The Effects of EC-92 on the Multi-Fibre Arrangement", European Economic Review, No. 36.

Falvey, R. (1979), "The Composition of Trade Within Import-Restricted Product Categories", Journal of Political Economy, Vol. 87, No. 5, pp. 1105-1114.

Food and Agriculture Organization of the United Nations, World Apparel Fibre Consumption Survey, Various Issues, Rome.

Gadgil, D.R. (1971), Industrial Evolution of India in Recent Times: 1860-1939, Oxford University Press, Bombay.

Goldar, Bishwanath (2000), Productivity Growth in Indian Manufacturing in the 1980s and 1990s, Institute of Economic Growth.

Goswami Omkar (1985), "Indian Textile Industry, 1970-1984: An Analysis of Demand and Supply, Economic and Political Weekly, Vol. XX(38), September.

Goto, J. (1990), "A Formal Estimation of the Effect of the MFA on Clothing Exports from LDCs", PRE Working Papers No. 455, World Bank, Washington.

Government of India (1985), "Statement on Textile Policy: June 1985", Ministry of Supply and Textiles, Department of Textiles.

Government of India (2000), "Statement on Textile Policy", Ministry of Supply and Textiles, Department of Textiles.

Government of India (1989), Report of the Working Group on Textile Industry for the Eighth Five Year Plan, Ministry of Textile.

Government of India (1990), "The Textile Industry in the 1990s: Restructuring with a Human Face," Report of the Committee to Review the Progress of Implementation of Textile Policy of June 1985, New Delhi.

Government of India (1995), Annual Report 1994-95, Ministry of Textiles, New Delhi.

Government of India (1996), Report of the Sub-Group on Organised Sector, Powerlooms and Cooperatives for the IXth Five Year Plan (1997-98 to 2001-02), Ministry of Textiles.

Government of India (1999), Economic Survey 1998-99, various issues, Ministry of Finance, Economic Division.

Government of India (1985), Report of the Expert Committee on the Textile Industry, Ministry of Supply & Textiles.

Government of India (1999), Report of the Expert Committee on the Textile Policy, Ministry of Textiles, Report Submitted in Parliament in 2000.

Government of India (1999), Annual Report, various issues, Ministry of Textiles.

Hamilton, C. (1991), "European Community External Protection and 1992: Voluntary Export Restraints Applied to Pacific Asia", European Economic Review, Vol. 35.

Hertel, T.W. and M.E. Tsigas 1996, "Structure of GTAP" Global Trade Analysis, Modeling and Applications New York: Cambridge University Press.

India (1979), "Choice of Technology in Textile Industry", Planning Commission, Delhi.

International Cotton Advisory Committee (ICAC), Cotton: World Statistics, Various Issues, Washington D.C., USA.

International Cotton Advisory Committee (ICAC), The Cotton Market Situation, Washington D.C., not dated.

International Cotton Advisory Committee (ICAC), World Textiles Demand, Various issues, Washington D.C., USA

International Textiles Manufacturing Federation (ITMF), (1987), From Low-Cost to High-Tech Competition, by Herwig M. Strolz, New Delhi.

International Textiles Manufacturing Federation (ITMF), Zurich

Investment Information and Credit Rating Agency of India Limited, (ICRA), 1996, Draft Report on Cotton Sector, New Delhi.

Investment Information and Credit Rating Agency of India Limited, (ICRA), 1994, Cotton Yarn Spinning in India, by Sumitra Chaudhuri, New Delhi.

Iyengar, N.S. and L.R. Jain (1974), "Changes in the Pattern of Consumption in India", Artha Vijnana, September, 1974.

Jain, L.C. (1983), "Handlooms Face Liquidation—Powerlooms Mock at Yojana Bhavan", Economic and Political WeeklyI, 27th August.

JTN (Various Issues), Osaka Senken, Tokyo, Japan.

Karve, D.G. (1955), Chairman, Report of the Village and Small Scale Industries Committee, Planning Commission, October, 1955.

Khanna Sri Ram (1991), International Trade in Textiles: MFA Quotas and a Developing Exporting Country, Sage Publications, New Delhi.

Khanna Sri Ram and IBC Research Team (1997), "Trends in US Textile and Clothing Imports", Textile Outlook International (TOI), The Economist Intelligence Unit, January.

Kothare, N.R. and K.A. Menon (1977), "Trends in the Finances of Cotton Textile Industry", Reserve Bank of India Bulletin, January, 1977.

Krishnamurthy K. and D.U. Sastry (1970), Inventories in Indian Manufacturing, Academic Books, Delhi.

Krishnamurthy K. and D.U. Sastry (1975), Investment and Financing in the Corporate Sector in India, Tata McGraw-Hill, Delhi.

Krishnan, T.N. (1964a), "Demand for Mill Cloth in India", Artha Vijnana.

Krishnan, T.N. (1964b), The Role of Agriculture in Economic Development, un-published doctoral thesis, Massachussets Institute of Technology.

Kumar Dharma, S.P, Nag and L.S. Venkataraman (1965), Resource Allocation in the Indian Cotton Textile Industry, Asia Publishing House, New Delhi.

Kumarasundram, S. (1962), "The Balance of Payments Implications of Industrial Production: The Textile Industry", Reserve Bank of India Bulletin, March 1962.

Lokanathan, P.S. (1935), Industrial Organisation in India, Allen and Unwin, London.

Majumdar Madhavi (1996), "The MFA Phase-Out and EU Clothing Sourcing: Forecasts to 2005", Textile Outlook International (TOI), The Economist Intelligence Unit, March.

Mazumdar Dipak (1991), "Import-Substituting Industrialisation and Protection of the Small-Scale: The Indian Experience in the Textile Industry", World Development, Vol. 19, No. 9, Great Britain.

Mazumdar, D. (1984), "The Issue of Small Versus Large in the Indian Textile Industry", World Bank Staff Working Paper No. 645, Washington, D.C.

Mehta Ashok (1964), Chairman, Report of the Powerloom Enquiry Committee, Government of India.

Mehta Rajesh (1996), "Textile and Apparel Trade: Impact of `New Regionalism'", Economic and Political Weekly, Vol. XXXI(23), June.

Mehta S.D. (1953), The Indian Cotton Textile Industry, The Textile Association of India, Bombay.

Mehta, M.M. (1949), Structure of Cotton Mill Industry of India, Central Book Depot, Allahabad.

Mehta, S.D. (1954), Cotton Mills of India,1854 to 1954, The Textile Association of India, Bombay, 1954.

Mehta, S.S. and V. Shanbhag (1989), Indian Textile Futures: Towards and Intersectoral Perspective, Gandhi Labour Institute, Ahmedabad Textile Industry's Research Association, Friedrich Ebert Stiftung, Ahmedabad.

Misra Sanjiv (1993), India's Textile Sector: A Policy Analysis, Sage Publications, Delhi.

Mitra Arup (1999), "Total Factor Productivity Growth and Technical Efficiency in Indian Industries", Economicand Political Weekly, Vol. XXXIV(31), July.

Morris Cavid Morris (1965), The Emergence of an Industrial Labour Force in India (A Study of the Bombay Cotton Mills in India, 1854-1947), Oxford University Press, Bombay.

Murthy Sukumari (1983), "An Approach to Estimate Demand Models for Clothing in India", Anvesak, Sardar Patel Institute, June, 1983.

Murty, G.V.S.N. (1977), On Differential Effects of Price Movements, Indian Economic Review, Vol. XII (New Series), No. 2.

Naik, Gopal (1998), Sudhir Kumar Jain, Santosh Kumar Singh, Econometric Modelling of the Indian Cotton Industry, Indian Institute of Management, Ahmedabad, August, 1998.

Navaretti Giorgio Barba (1995), Trade Policy and Foreign Investments: An Analytical Framework, Beyond the Multifibre Arrangement: Third World Competition andRestructuring Europe's Textile Industry, edited by Navaretti Giorgio Barba, Riccardo Faini and Aubrey Siiberston, Organisation for Economic Co-operation and Devlopment, Paris.

Nayyer Deepak (1973), "An Analysis of the Stagnation in India's Cotton Textile Exports during the Sixties", Bulletin of the Oxford Institute of Economics and Statistics, February, 1973.

Office of the Development Commissioner for Handlooms (1998), All India Handloom Minister's Conference, Agenda, Ministry of Textiles.

Office of the Textile Commissioner, Basic Facts on Textile Industry, Various Issues, Mumbai.

Office of the Textile Commissioner, Basic Textile Statistics for 1995-96, various issues, Mumbai.

Office of the Textile Commissioner, Compendium of Textile Statistics 1996, various issues, Mumbai.

Office of the Textile Commissioner, Indian Textile Bulletin, Various Issues, Mumbai.

Pankaj Chandra (1999), "Competing Through Capabilities: Strategies for Global Competitiveness of Indian Textile Industry", Economic and Political Weekly, Vol. XXXIV(9), February.

Papola, T.S. (1968), "Wage Determination in the Indian Cotton Textile Industry", International Labour Review, January, 1968.

Paul Sammuel and Vasant L. Mote (1970), "Competitiveness of Exports: A Micro-level Approach", Economic Journal, December 1970.

Porter Michel E. (1990), The Competitive Advantage of Nations, Macmillan, London.

Purananda J and K.S. Hanumantha Rao (1966), "Corporate Dividends and Target Payout Ratios in the Indian cotton Textile Industry, 1946-63", The Journal of Industrial Economics, November, 1966.

Radhakrishna, R. and Atul Sarma (1975), "Distributional Effects of the Current Inflation", Social Scientist.

Raj, K.N. (1956), "Small Scale Industries: Problems of Technological Change", The Economic Weekly, 7 & 14 April, 1956.

Rao V.G., K.S. Hanumantha Rao and A.S. Rama Sastry (1970), "Saving Behaviour of Small Cotton Textile Firms in India: 1961-64", Indian Journal of Economics, July, 1970.

Rao, V.L. (1980), India's Export Determinants, Doctoral thesis, Delhi University, 1980.

Ratnam, T.V., Indra Doraiswamy, S. Seshadri and R. Rajamanickam (1996), Productivity in Spinning, The South India Textile Research Association, Combatore.

Ratnam, T.V., Indra Doraiswamy, S. Seshadri, R. Rajamanickam and K.P. Chellamani (1995), Norms for Spinning Mills, The South India Textile Research Association, Combatore.

Regulation: A Case Study of the Indian Textile Industry", Economic and Political Weekly, 20 January, 1983.

Rosen George (1959), Industrial Change in India, Asia Publishing House, Bombay.

Roy Tirthankar (1998a), "Development or Distortion?: 'Powerlooms' in India, 1950-1997", Economic and Political Weekly, Vol. XXXIII(16), April.

Roy Tirthankar (1998b), "Economic Reforms and Textile Industry in India" Economic and Political Weekly, Vol. XXXIII (32), August.

Roy Tirthankar (1998c), "A New Textile Policy: Do We Need One?", Economic and Political Weekly, Vol. XXXIII(40), October.

Roy Tirthankar (1996), "Market-Resurgence, Deregulation and Industrial Response: Indian Cotton Textiles in the 1990s", Economic and Political Weekly, XXXI(21), Review of Industry, May.

Sastry V.K. (1966), Dividends, Investment and External Finance Behavior of the Corporate Sector in India, doctoral thesis, University of Pennsylyvania.

Sastry, D.U. (1984), The Cotton Mill Industry in India, Oxford University Press, Delhi.

Sastry, N.S.R. (1943), A Statistical Study of India's Industrial Development, Thacker & Co., Bombay.

Sen, A.K. (1960), Choice of Techniques, Oxford, Basil Blackwell.

Singh Jatinder (1989), Production Conditions and Total Factor Productivity in the Cotton Textile Mills' Sector: An Inter-State Analysis: 1974-75 to 1981-82, M.Phil. dissertation submitted to the Jawaharlal Nehru University, New Delhi.

Singh Man Mohan (1964), India's Export Trade and the Prospects for Self-Sustained Growth, Clarendon Press, Oxford.

Small Industries Development Bank of India (SIDBI) (1999), Readymade Garment Industry: A Sectoral Study, Lucknow.

Sreenivasan Kasthuri (1984), India's Textile Industry: A Socio-Economic Analysis, The South India Textile Research Association, Coimbatore.

Srivastava, Vivek and Ananya Sengupta (2000), Biases In The Estimation Of Total Factor Productivity: Some Evidence From Indian Data, NCAER Discussion Paper No. 13, June, 2000.

TEXPROCIL, Facts on the Indian Cotton Textile Industry, Bombay, note dated.

Textile Committee (1977), Report on Income and Price Elasticities for Textiles, 1977.

Textile Committee, Consumer Purchase of Textiles, Household Sectors, Various Issues.

Textile Committee, Consumer Purchase of Textiles, Non-household Sectors, Various Issues.

Textile Outlook International, Various Issues, Business and Market Analysis for the Textile & Apparel Industries, The Economist Intelligent Unit, U.K.

Textile Policy Statement tabled before Parliament on 7th August, 1978.

Textile Policy Statement tabled before Parliament on 9th March, 1981.

The Cotton Textile Export Promotion Council (1995), 41st Annual Report, various issues, Bombay.

The Cotton Textile Export Promotion Council, Handbook of Export Statistics various issues, Bombay.

The Indian Cotton Mills' Federation, Annual Report, various issues, Mumbai.

The Indian Cotton Mills' Federation, Handbook of Statistics on Cotton Textile Industry, various issues, Twenty-seventh edition, New Delhi.

The South India Textile Research Association (SITRA) Focus, Various Issues.

The South India Textile Research Association (SITRA), How to Assess Your Productivity, Coimbatore.

The South India Textile Research Association (SITRA), Norms for Spinning Mills, Coimbatore.

The South India Textile Research Association (SITRA), Productivity in Spinning, Coimbatore.

The Synthetic and Rayon Textile Exports Promotion Council (SRTEPC), Man-Made Textiles Statistics, Various Issues.

Trela I. and J. Whalley (1988), "Do Developing Countries Lose from the MFA?", NBER Working Paper No. 2618.

Trela I. and J. Whalley (1990), "Unraveling the Threads of the MFA", in C. Hamilton (ed.), *op. cit.*

Uchikawa Shuji (1999), "Economic Reforms and Foreign Trade Policies: Case Study of Apparel and Machine Tools Industries", Economic and Political Weekly, Vol. XXXIV(48), November.

Uchikawa Shuji (1998), Indian Textile Industry: State Policy, Liberalisation and Growth, Manohar, New Delhi.

United Nations Conference on Trade and Development (UNCTAD) (1995), Preliminary Analysis of Opportunities and Challenges Resulting from the Uruguay Round Agreement on Textile and Clothing.

United Nations, (Various issues), Commodity Trade Statistics, Statistical Papers, ST/ESA/STAT/SER.D/Various numbers.

Werner International Inc. Management Consultants (1996), Competitiveness the International Challenge, by Raoul Verrer at the IIMF Annual Conference, September 25th, Washington D.C.

Werner International Inc. Management Consultants, Various Issues, Brussels, Belgium.

World Bank (1999), Cotton and Textile Industries: Reforming to Compete.

World Development Report (Various Issues), Selected World Development Indicators, World Bank, Oxford University Press.

World Trade Organisation, WTO (Various Issues), The State of World Trade, Trade Policy and World Trade Organisation, Annual Report, Geneva.

WTO document, G/TMB/N Series.

Index

A

Abid Hussain Committee, 22-23
Age Composition of Spindles Installed, 104-08
Agreement of Textile Clothing, 344
Ahmedabad Institute of Management Association, 139
Ahmedabad Textile Industry Research Association, 12, 14,139, 412-13
All India Annual Survey of Textile Committee, 297
All India Federation of Cooperative Spinning Mills, 51, 68, 139-40, 142
Apparel Export Promotion Council, 187
Ashok Mehta Committee, 7
ATIRA technical data, 26-27

B

Barthwall, R.R., 12
Bedi, Jatinder S., 20
Bhalla, A.S., 11
Bhattacharya, N., 12
Bhide, Sheela Thakur, 275
Bowreah Cotton Mills, 5

C

Capacity expansion, 10
Capacity utilisation in weaving segments, 124-26
Central statistical organisation, 213, 297-304, 473
  Comparison of coverage adopted to, 299-300
  Cotton Textiles, 300-02
  Methodology, 297-98
  Synthetic textiles, 302-04
Chandrasekhar, C.P., 12
Cline, W., 19
Cobb-Douglas Production Function, 38, 41, 97-99
Coker, John, 335, 348, 356
Compendium of Textile Commission, 48
Competitiveness of powerloom sector, 16-19
Conversion rates between yarn and cloth, 130-31
Conversion rate of fabrics from yarn, 138-47
Conversion rate of fabrics produced from synthetic yarn, 155-56
Conversion rate of fibre to yarn, 123
Cost compression, 377-91
Cost of cotton fabrics production, 382
Cost of cotton yarn production, 378-82
Cost of garments, 385-91
Cost of synthetic products, 382-85
Cotton fabrics production, 147-55

Compression of different sector's Producing, 149-55
Count range wise, 148-49
Mill share in production, 147
Cotton fibre, 120-21
Cotton mills industry, 7
Cotton textiles and clothing products, 188-90
Cotton Textiles Export Promotion Councils, 187, 198
Cotton vs synthetic products, 285-86
Cotton yarn, 51
Cotton yarn production, 62-68
Carded and combed share in production of, 64-66
Count-range wise data on total production, 62-64
Production per modern spindles of 1996-97 technology at full capacity utilisation, 66-68
Cross-section analysis, 98
Customs duties on synthetic, 24

D

Decentralised sector, 126
Demand and supply pattern in Indian textiles and clothing products, 186-333
Contral statistical organisation, 297-304
Changes in domestic consumption patterns of fabrics, 286-90
Garment in piece length, 287
Hosiery garments, 288
Household varieties, 287-88
Piece length, 287
Readymade garments, 287
Share of varieties of fabrics, 288-90
Cotton and synthetic products in various forms during 1995-96, 221-24
Cotton products, 290
Cotton textiles and clothing products, 188-90
Cotton vs synthetic products, 285-86
Diversion of cotton hank yarn to powerloom sector, 251
Domestic segment, 271-72
Employment in, 316-17, 465-67
Garment sector, 319
Handloom sector, 317, 467
Mill sector, 318
Output and, 319
Powerloom and hosiery sector, 318
Total estimates of, 320-24
Expenditive on textiles and clothing final consumption, 314-15
Export and consumption of fabrics data, 187
Exports of cotton and synthetic textiles and clothing products during 1995-96, 220-21
Exports of cotton garments, 202-05

Exports of cotton made-ups, 198-202
Exports of cotton women and hosiery fabrics, 197-98
Exports of cotton woven fabrics in kg., 195
Exports of hosiery fabrics, 196
Export segment, 268-71
Fibre/Filament equivalent exports and domestic availability, 243-46
Fibre/Filament-wise production of synthetic fabrics, 213
Fibre/Filament-wise synthetic made-ups exports during 1995-96, 217-18
Handloom sector, 281-85, 470-71
Hosiery sector, 272
Import content, 247-50
Overall comparison of products and total consumption, 188
Powerloom sector, 281-85, 470-71
Sector level discrepencies, 250-51
Sector-wise revised estimates of cotton fabrics production, 259-61
Synthetic Fabrics equivalent exports during 1995-96, 213-17
Synthetic products, 290
Synthetic textiles and clothing products exports, 213, 228-32
Total cotton fabrics equivalent exports, 205-08
Total cotton fibre equivalent exports, 211-13
Total cotton yarn equivalent exports, 208-10
Total exports and domestic availability of cotton and synthetic textiles and clothing products, 232-36
Total export of fabrics, 187-88
Total production of fabrics based on revised estimates of hank yarn diversion, 262-68
Total value added in textiles and clothing sector for cotton and synthetic products, 311-14, 472-74
Total value of cotton and synthetic products, 293-96
Total value of stitching for readymade garments, 305-11
Value added estimates in cotton and synthetic textiles sector, 305
Variety-wise fabrics production, 293, 471-72
Yarn equivalent exports and domestic availability in various forms, 243

D

de Melo, J., 342
Desai, Ashok V., 12
Development Commissioner for Handloom, 137

Dharma Kumar, 12
Director General of
Commercial Intelligence and Statistics, 191, 194-95, 203
Diversion of Cotton Hank Yarn to powerloom sector, 252-59
Domestic demand methodology, 412-18
Domestic segments, 271

E

Economic reforms 1991, 2, 23-25
Economic survey 1999, 1
Employment, 316, 465
Employment coefficients, 316
Erzan, R., 340
ESCAP, 341, 345-46
EU imports and restrictions, 337-39, 345
Excise duty on grey and dyed fabrics, 30-31
Export Promotion Council, 202
Exports of cotton fabrics, 9, 190-95
Exports of cotton garments, 202
Export segment, 268-71
Exports of cotton made-ups, 198-202
Exports of cotton woven and hosiery fabrics, 197-98
Exports of cotton woven fabrics in kg., 195
Exports of hosiery fabrics, 196
Exports Oriented Unit, 60

F

Fabrics,
Availability of spun yarn for production in decentralised sector, 134-38
Per capita availability of, 128-34
Production in decentralised sector, 128-34
Sector-wise total production of, 161-64
Total production of, 161
Fabrics consumption and production estimates, 28-29, 460-62
Fabrics equivalent exports, 462-63
Faini, Ricardo, 19, 340-42
Falvey, R., 342
Federation of Indian Textiles Engineering Industry, 104-05
Fibre/Filaments consumption, 119
Fibre/Filaments equivalent exports and domestic availability, 243-46
Fibre/Filament wise total exports of synthetic products during 1995-96, 218-20
Fibre/Filament-wise synthetic made-ups exports during 1995-96, 217-18
Fibre level availability of fabrics for domestic consumption, 236-42
Fibre to fabrics production, 113-15
Filament fabrics production, 158-60
Filament yarn, 118-20
Fibre/Filaments consumption, 119-20
Spun yarn and, 118-19

Finance Bill 2001, 30, 439
Five yarn plans
 9th, 127
Food and Agriculture organization, 31-32, 191, 232, 348, 356, 360, 411

G

Gandhi, 11
Gandhian philosophy, 7
Garment Export Entitlement Policy, 196, 203
GATT, 344
Ginning and pressing, 121-22
Global Trade Analysis Project Model, 347
Goswami, Omkar, 13, 412
Goto, J., 19, 340

H

Hamilton, C., 340
Handloom Export Promotion Council, 16, 187, 194, 275, 277, 468
Handloom (Reservation of Articles for Production) Act 1985, 259
Handloom Sector, 272-80, 317
Hank yarn, 60-62
 Count Range production per spindle, 62
 Count range wise delivery of, 60-62
Hank yarn diversion to powerloom sector, 29-30, 465
Hank yarn to powerloom sector literature, 15-16
Hanumantha Rao, R.S., 12
Heimler, Alberto, 19, 341
Hertal, T.W., 19, 341
Hicks non-neutral technological progress, 100-03
Hosiery sector, 272
Hosiery sector production, 18
Hosiery yarn, 51-55
 Productivity norms for, 54-55
Hourly labour cost, 377
Houthakkar-Taylor, 13

I

ICAC, 31, 191, 195, 232, 346, 348
ICRA, 14, 131
Idle spindless status, 72-77
 Mills not reported closed, 76-77
 Yarn-wise status of closed spindles, 73-76
Import content, 247-50
Import substitution policy, 6
Indian Cotton Mills Federation, 48, 137, 146
Indian spinning sector, 37-111, 455-60
 Changes in structure of industry during 1996-97 to 1999-2000, 90-92
 Comparison of spindles with spindles installed, 71-72
 Count-wise constant return to scale over time but allows for changes in count comparison, 99-100
 Data sources and approach, 48-51
 Economics of Scale in Case Time Variable, 13
  Replaced with modernisation variable, 95

Economics of Scale in Gross-section analysis, 98-99
Economic of scale in time series analysis, 97-98
Hank yarn, 60-62
Hicks non-neutral technological progress, 100-03
Hosiery yarn, 51-55
Productivity norms for, 54-55
Idle spindless status, 72-77, 457-58
Investment in, 459
Methodology used, 42-48
Other cotton yarn production, 62-66
Polyester cotton yarn, 68-71
Production per modern spindles, of 1996-97, 66
Productivity of new spindles, 96-97, 456
Review of literature, 37-42
Spun yarn productivity, 68
SSI spinning units, 89-90
Technological impact in, 456-57
Working spindles status, 77-89, 457-59
Woven cotton yarn, 55-60
Exports and consumption in Mill Sector of, 55
India's export to quote and non-quote countries, 377-76
India's position in world textile industry, 376-77
India's textiles and clothing exports to major importers in world, 367-73
Additional spindles required during 1998-2000 to 2010-11 to produce spun yarn, 438-39
Additional spindles required to produce spun yarn during 1999-2000 to 2001-06, 437-38, 451
Additional spun yarn requirements by 2005-06 and 2010-11, 432-35
Competitive advantage of a nation, 376-77
Cost comparison, 377-91
Cost of cotton yarn production, 378-82
Cost of fabrics production, 382
Cost of garments, 385-91
Cost of synthetic products, 382-85
Hourly labour cost, 377-78
Domestic demand methoditity, 412-18, 450
Domestic final consumption in India by yarn 2005-06, 411-12
Estimates for India, 393-98
Excess capacity and expected replacement of spindles, 436
Expected count-composition of spun yarn by year 2005-06 and 2010-11, 435-36
Fibre/Filaments requirements by year 2005-06 and 2010-11, 432
India's domestic demand by year 2010-11, 480-81

India's exports by year 2010-11, 428-29, 474-79
India's export to quota and non-quota countries, 373-76
India's performance since 1996-97, 426-28
India's textiles and clothing exports to major importers in world, 367-73, 449
International textiles and clothing scenario by 2005, 348-53
Item-wise total demand by year 2010-11, 429-31
Key concerns for India, 391-93
Major trading countries in world, 336-40, 447-48
EU imports and restructions, 337-39
Major exporters, 331
Major importers, 336, 448
Protectionist policies among major importers, 337
USA imports and restrictions, 339-40, 448
Methodology used, 334-36
New Textile Policy of 2000, 439-42
Optimal achievable productivity of installed spindes during 1999-2000 and 2005-06, 436-37
Optimal achievable productivity of installed spindles during 1999-2000 to 2010, 438
Overall demand for year 2005-06, 426, 479-80
Policy suggestions, 481-89
Prospects for 2010-11, 442-47, 451
Cotton, 443
Fabrics, 445
Fabrics in piece length, 445
Garments in piece length, 446
Hosiery products, 446
Made-ups, 446
Optimistic scenario, 447
Ready made garments, 446-47
Synthetics, 443-44
Yarn, 444
Protectionist-policies impact on world trade, 340-42
Protection on quality of output, 342-44
Quota acceleration due to MFA phase out on, 449
TOI model-modifications, 353-67
Total demand during 1999-2000, 418-26
Total domestic and export demand by 2005-06, 418
Total trade in terms of value, 404-10
Industrial Finance Corporation of India, 18
International Textile and Clothing Scenario by 2005, 348, 404
Alternative I, 350-98
Alternative II, 398-404
International Textile Manufacturing Federation, 48, 71, 104-06, 351-52, 381, 473

Investment Information and Credit Rating Agency of India Ltd., 13-14
Isequant, 45, 101
Iyengar, N.S., 12

J

Jain, L.C., 131
Jain, L.R., 12
Janta Cloth Scheme, 259

K

Kanungo Committee, 7
Karve Committee, 7
Khadi, 2
Krishnamurthy, K., 12
Kumarasundram, S., 12

L

Lancashire, 5
Linear Expenditure system, 129
Loknathan, P.S., 11
Looms, 9

M

Malinguist-Approach Codli, 45
Man-made fibre, 114
Man-made filament yarn, 131
Mazumdar, D., 17, 281-82
Mehta, M.M. 11
Mehta, S.D., 5, 11
Mill cloth production, 8
Mill Sector, 124-26, 280-81
Ministry of Textiles-Reports, 48
Mitra, Sanjiv, 13-14, 17, 130-33, 281-82
Mitra Arup, 41, 97
MODVAT, 30, 284-85, 440, 484-86
Mote, Vasant L., 12
Multi Fibre Arrangement, 4, 11, 19-20, 247, 335, 337-43, 345

N

National Textile Corporation, 76, 126, 142, 202
Nehru, 5
New Textile Policy, 2, 11, 20-23, 37, 72
New Textile Policy 2000, 30, 282, 284, 439-42, 485-86, 488
Non-cotton Fabrics Total Production, 160-61
Non-cotton Spun Fabrics Production, 158
Non-SSI weaving units, 201

O

Ownership wise distribution of looms installed, 126

P

Pankaj, Chandra, 392
Papola, T.S., 12
Paul, Sammuel, 12
Polyester cotton yarn, 68-71
  Count-range wise combined productions, 68-69
  Count-range wise production per spindle, 69-71
Powerloom, 1-2, 11
Powerloom Sector, 281-85
Prabhu Spinning Mills, 75
Production of fabrics literature, 13
Production Possibility Frontier, 45, 301
Protectionist policies impact on world trade, 340
Protection on quality of output, 342-44
Purananda, J., 12

R

Raj, K.N., 11
Rao, V.L., 12
Readymade garments
Total value of stitching for, 305-11
Renew of literature, 110-20
Rosen, George, 11
Roy, T., 18, 205
Rute looms, 22

S

Sastry, D.U., 12-13
Sastry, N.S.R., 11
Sastry, V.K., 12
Satyam Committee on Report of Export Committee on Textile Policy, 133
Sector-wise revised estimates of cotton fabrics production, 259-61
Sen, A.K., 11
Short staple spinning, 116-18
Shukla, P.R., 392
Siek units, 488
SIMA, 48, 51, 54-55, 61, 139
Singh, Jatinder, 8-9
Singh, Man Mohan, 12
Small Industries Development Bank of India, 69
South Asia, 364-67
South India Textile Research Association, 14, 27, 42, 48, 50-51, 54-55
Spindle capacity, 8
Spinning sector, 25-26, 455
Spun production, 8
Spun yarn,
Production of, 115-16
Weighted average productivity, 68
Spun yarn availability for production of fabrics, 134
Sreenivasan, Kesthuri, 5-6
SSI spinning units, 89-90, 117
State Textile Corporation, 126
Structural changes in Indian textile industry, 112-85
Comparison of different sectors producing cotton fabrics, 149-55
Conversion rates of fabrics from various synthetic yarn, 155-56
Conversion rates of fabrics from yarn, 123, 138-47, 164
Cotton fibre, 120-21
Cotton fabrics-count-range-wise production, 148-49
Cotton fabrics production, 147-48, 168
Decentralised sector, 126-27
Filament fabrics production, 158-60
Filament yarn, 118-20
Ginning and pressing, 121-22
Hosiery sector, 148
Mill sector, 124-26
Non-cottton spun fabric production, 158
Per capita availability of fabrics, 128-34
Ratio of blends taken to workout conversion rates for yarn and fabrics, 185
Sector-wise total production of fabrics, 161-64, 185
Short staple spinning, 116-18
Spun yarn production, 115-16
Stages of production from fibre to fabrics, 113-15

Synthetic yarn production, 156-58
Total production of fabrics, 161
Weaving process, 123
Sub-group on overview of textile industry, 127
Sukumari Murthy, 12
Swadeshi movement, 7
Synthetic and rayon textile exports promotion council, 187, 213
Synthetic Febrics equivalent exports during 1995-96, 213-17
Synthetic fibres, 9-10
Synthetic Textiles and Clothing Products exports, 213, 228-32
Synthetic yarn, 156
Count range-wise production of, 156

T

Takacs, W., 342
Technological upgradation Fund, 18
TEXDROCIL, 1, 27, 68, 139-40, 242
Textile Commissionor, 1, 29, 75-76, 133, 457
Textile Committee, 1, 12, 14, 16, 27
Textile Export Entitlement Policy, 196
Textile industry, 1-36
Background of, 4-6
Capital availability, 3
Conversion rates of fabrics to yarn, 1-2
Defect in textile policy, 9-10
During 1950-85 period, 6-13
Dying process of, 2-3
Fabrics consumption and production estimates, 28
Hank yarn diversion to powerloom sector, 29-30
India's share in world textiles, 10
Liberalisation, 3-4, 455
New Textile Policy 2000, 300
Objectives of study, 4
Organised mill sector, 2
Profections regarding India's trade, 31-32
Scope of study, 25
Spinning sector, 25-26
Structural canges in, 1-2
Total demand by year 2010-11, 33
Unorganised sector, 2
Value added and employment, 30
Weaning sector, 26-28
Textile Outlook International, 31-32, 334-35, 348-49
Textile Outlook International Model-Modifications, 353-67
Discrepancies in FAO and ICAC data and other adjustment, 360-64
Estimates of Gross World Trade by 2005, 353-56
Extension for fibre-wise analysis from TOI aggregate analysis, 356-60
South Asia estimates, 364-67
Textile Policy 1981, 8
Textile Policy 1985, 9-10
Total Cotton Fabrics equivalent exports, 205-08, 211-13

Total cotton yarn equivalent exports, 208-10
Total Domestic and export demand by 2005-06, 418
Total exports and domestic availability of cotton and synthetic textile and clothing products, 232-36
Total factor productivity, 37, 102
Total factor productivity growth, 37-38
Total production of fabrics based on revised estimates of hank yarn diversion, 262-68
Trans log production function, 38
Trela, I., 340

U

Uchikawa, Shuji, 10
UNCTAD, 341
Up Sahakari Katai Mills, 75
Uruguay round agreement, 345
USA imports and restrictions, 339-40

V

Value added and employment, estimates, 30
Vasanta Mills, 75

W

Weaving Capacity, 8, 487
Weaving process, 123
Weaving sector, 26-28
Werner International data, 472
Whalley, J., 340
Wool, 115
Working spindles status, 77-89
  Age composition of installed spindles and productivity growth, 83-89, 100
  Age of installed spindles, 80-83
  Average working hours of, 77-80
World Bank, 349
World Textile and clothing consumption forecasts, 335, 348
World Trade Organisation, 346, 356
World War II, 5
Woven Cotton Yarn, 55-60
  Count-wise composition of cotton yarn exports, 57-58
  Count-wise delivery of, 55-57
Woven fabrics production in decentralised sector, 147-48

Y

Yarn export, 24
Year-wise exports of synthetic fabrics, 224-25
Year-wise exports of synthetic garments, 225-28
Year-wise exports of synthetic made-up, 225